St Winefride, Her Holy Well

and the

Jesuit Mission
c.650–1930

T. W. Pritchard

T. W. Pritchard

St Winefride, her Holy Well and the Jesuit Mission, c.650–1930
First published in Wales in 2009
πon behalf of the author
by
BRIDGE BOOKS
61 Park Avenue
WREXHAM
LL12 7AW

A CIP catalogue in publication entry for this book
is available from the British Library

ISBN 978-1-84494-060-8

Printed and bound
by
Cromwell Press Group
Trowbridge

Contents

Foreword

by

Right Reverend Edwin Regan, Bishop of Wrexham

I t gives me immense pleasure to write the foreword to this magnificent treatise on the story of St Winefride and Holywell. I congratulate Archdeacon Pritchard on his masterly work and meticulous research into the history of the persons and events that make up the living tradition of this 'Lourdes of Wales'.

This book will appeal at various levels. It is the story of the triumph of the human spirit that kept alive a tradition spanning 1400 years. It will speak to those interested in the story of Wales, for Archdeacon Pritchard has captured in vivid prose the characters that had a part to play in the formation of modern Wales. This is a story that ripples out wider than north-east Wales. At a deeper level, the story of St Winefride is a testimony to the strength of the Catholic Faith that survived against all the odds the savage persecution of penal days and the wearing influence of time. The fact that its author is a minister of the Church in Wales gives us cause to thank God for the growth of love and respect that now exists between our Churches. Let us continue to pray and work for that unity for which the Lord himself prayed.

In this book we meet the great recusant Catholic families whose sterling support for St Winefride shines through the centuries. It is good to pay tribute to the sacrifices they made for their Catholic Faith. However, we also encounter the nameless Catholic people of Holywell whose devotion to St Winefride and her well down through the ages passed on from one generation to the next the wonderful story that speaks to us today.

A new chapter is being written in this beautiful story with the recent and providential coming of the Vocationalist Fathers and the Sisters of St Bridget, in answer to our prayers to St Winefride. The Vocationalist Fathers continue the tradition of the Jesuit, Franciscan and Diocesan priests in the pastoral care of Holywell and in spreading devotion to St Winefride. The loving hospitality given by the Sisters of Charity over many years is now being offered by the Bridgettines as they live out their lovely charism of deep contemplation and generous hospitality. I thank them all most deeply on behalf of the Diocese of Wrexham and all those who love St Winefride.

Holywell is a precious jewel in the glorious crown of the Diocese of Wrexham. We owe a temendous debt of gratitude to Archdeacon Pritchard for helping us to appreciate the multi-layered story that unfolds in the pages of this book.

Read it and be inspired.

SECTION ONE

The Cult of St Winefride

1. Making the Cult

Introduction

The purpose of this chapter is to acquaint the reader with the sources for the recorded lives of St Winefride, explain her association with the holy well named after her and to give some understanding of the background to the cult which developed in her honour in the Middle Ages, and explain the literary form of hagiography to which her lives belong. To these ends her two Latin lives will be compared, of which the first, the *Vita prima*, or 'Anonymous Life', will be quoted in full.

The elements which have had a lasting influence on her cult at Holywell, Gwytherin and Shrewsbury will be singled out as being important in the continuation of the cult through the centuries: such as the holy well, stones, moss, cure tradition and the role of the virgin martyr. Their contribution to the experience of pilgrims to the sacred place will reoccur throughout the book.

St Winefride at Holywell

We are told that St Winefride[1] was born at Holywell, in Tegeingl, formerly a district of what is now Flintshire in north-east Wales, sometime near the beginning of the seventh century AD. Wales at that time was divided into small kingdoms which were often at war amongst themselves. They did, however, have a common enemy, the Saxons, and other marauders such as the Irish, who plundered, killed and in a few places settled along their rugged and vulnerable coastline. What united the Welsh kingdoms were their language, customs, law and religion. This was their strength and enabled them to resist to some extent the cultural influences of their enemies from the east. As western Europe accepted Christianity, Britain experienced some conversions during the 350 years of Roman occupation, which ended at the beginning of the fifth century. Early medieval Wales was essentially Christian, and monastic practice was well established by the early sixth century. The foundation of churches and Christian communities was attributed in Wales, as elsewhere in Europe, to particular individuals who were designated as saints by their contemporaries. From the sixth century onwards the names of notable missionary saints were remembered and associated with particular places such as St Deiniol (d. 584) at Bangor in Gwynedd, St Beuno (d. c.650) at Clynnog Fawr,[2] St Asaph (late sixth century), and others to whom local churches were dedicated. The spread of Christianity in Wales took place independently of the mission of St Augustine of Canterbury, sent by Pope Gregory I to convert the Saxons, who landed in Kent in 597 AD.

Beuno, the most important saint of north Wales, and comparable to David in the south, came from mid-Wales and settled for a time in Holywell. Here he was invited by Tyfid, his brother-in-law, to instruct his niece, Winefride, in the faith. Beuno is the most important figure in the lives of St Winefride and is reputed to have restored her to life after her decapitation by an angry local prince, Caradog ab Alaog, for resisting his sexual advances. Where her severed head fell, a miraculous healing spring burst forth. This gave the name to the settlement now known as Holywell (Welsh, *Treffynnon*). This legend is the foundation for the veneration of St Winefride, virgin and martyr, and the growth of her medieval cult. By the end of the fourteenth century, her feast day was ordered to be observed throughout the province of Canterbury, by which time her cult was well established, with Holywell as one of the leading pilgrimage centres in medieval Britain.

Winefride held a high position amongst Welsh female saints, which is attested by the existence of two lives written in Latin in the twelfth century. Other abridged versions followed in the later Middle Ages, written in the Latin, Welsh, and English languages; a later English one in the fifteenth century was written and published by William Caxton. Because of the strength of her cult and the reputation of her healing spring, Holywell has continued as a pilgrimage centre from medieval times to the present day.

Holywell is unique amongst Welsh Catholic centres in that a continuity of Catholic worship and pilgrimage was maintained throughout the penal times stretching from the death of Mary I (1558) to 1800, when a new Roman Catholic church dedicated to St Winefride was built in the town. This continuity was entirely due to the tenacity and purpose of local Catholic families, who sustained the brave Mission of the Society of Jesus established in Holywell from around 1590 until their departure in 1930. From the mid-seventeenth century onwards, the Jesuit mission in north Wales was known as the Residence of St Winefride in honour of the saint, and the care of pilgrims visiting the spring was the fathers' chief pastoral activity.

Equally fascinating is the sacred place which marked the martyrdom of the virgin St Winefride. The building of the well chamber and chapel above, known as St Winefride's Well, was constructed at the end of the Middle Ages. It epitomised the development of the cult of St Winefride, the scale of her veneration, and the place she held in the hearts of people of all ranks. The building is an architectural jewel, not only one of the wonders of Wales but recognised as a National Heritage site of European significance. It is a splendid example of late-medieval piety, and was completed in time to include the emblem of the Spanish Catholic consort of Henry VIII, Katherine of Aragon. The architects of this beautiful building were possibly those who constructed Henry VII's (d. 1509) magnificent chapel in Westminster Abbey. It was long stated that Henry VII's mother, Margaret Beaufort, a rich and pious patron of renaissance learning, married to Thomas Stanley, earl of Derby, was responsible for the building, although this is not proven. However, there is a profusion of Tudor and Stanley heraldic emblems in both the well crypt and the chapel above it. On the other hand, contemporary Welsh poets praise Abbot Thomas Pennant as the builder and patron. What evidence there is for architect and patron of the magnificent late-Perpendicular building is discussed below.

The medieval splendour of the building especially designed for pilgrims is to be imagined. Part of the ritual was to venerate the image of St Winefride. Pilgrims on entering the well chamber, in their procession and circulation around the basin, would see paintings and stone carvings of scenes from her life and that of her mentor St Beuno. Crutches and other objects left by those who experienced healing testified to the virgin's power.

The proud manager of this great building enterprise was Thomas Pennant (*c*.1481–1522), abbot of Basingwerk. The abbey had protected the interests of St Winefride from at least the middle of the thirteenth century until its dissolution in 1536. These glorious years before the destruction of the Reformation were recorded by the poet Tudur Aled (*c*.1475–1525) who in telling the *The Story of St Winefride and her well* concludes:

> Heaven's chrism is at the source of the stream,
> In Beuno's place, in Pennant's hand.
> For the same abbot we hope
> That God sees his glory and his work.
> May it be in the choir of York, or in Non's city,
> That he finishes the Well's arch [3]

Understanding the medieval cult: the part played by the saints

In the medieval world to which she belonged, St Winefride was regarded as a saint and her life was written to describe the reasons why she was given that title. A saint was a person regarded as set apart for a sacred purpose, dedicated to God's service. The word as used in the New Testament means all the members of the Christian community. Later, the word was applied to special members of the Church, who were recognised for their exceptional devotedness to God, as growing closer to him by means of self-denial, and through the practice of prayer and contemplation. Eventually, the title of saint was given to those who were venerated because they had suffered and died for their faith, the martyrs. The anniversaries of their deaths were honoured and celebrated as feast days by the local community, and their burial places and bodily remains carefully preserved. Because of the manner of their death, it was believed that they continued to live in the presence of God. For this privilege, the martyrs were honoured by the Christian community, which trusted they had access to the divine power which enabled them to act as intermediaries between God and humanity.

Miracle worker

Proud of this link with the heavenly places and the divine power, the local community adopted their saint. They venerated this holy person and committed themselves to his or her power and mediation. They were protectors of the community: it was their territory and must be honoured as such if the saint was to continue to act as their agent of God's power. This protection and power could be extended to other places.

The favour and power of the saint was displayed by miracles. The saint was regarded as the medium for obtaining supernatural power, and the ability to perform miracles was an indispensable test of sanctity. The saint's work was to obtain and dispense from God the supernatural power in order to assist their community with problems of daily living. In such a capacity they were regarded as wonder workers able to prophesy the future, control the weather, provide protection against fire and flood, and perform all manner of tasks believed impossible.[4] There was also a strong belief that they had a part in healing the sick. Christ's power was delegated to the Church with the saint as his representative. The words of Jesus re-echo in the *Lives of the Saints*, and are continually reiterated in the accounts of miracles associated with St Winefride: '… the blind receive their sight, the lame work, the lepers are cleansed, the deaf hear, the dead are raised up, and the poor have the Gospel preached to them'. (Matt. 11, 4f; cf. Luke 7, 22). Miracles of a more personal nature were ascribed to saints as they sought to preserve their honour and protect their property. Giraldus Cambrensis remarked that the Welsh and Irish saints had a reputation for being vindictive. The sacred territory of the saint was protected by his or her supernatural powers from being violated by sacrilege, theft, murder or other offences. The supernatural was brought into the realm of native law. God's honour was invoked as both a witness and judge when the relics of the saint were used in the swearing of oaths. The angry saint punished the perjurer with vengeance.

Power of relics

Saints' relics were most valuable objects and regarded as such by all classes. If they were not in your possession, you had the assurance that they had been placed in a reliquary in your church or in the shrine of a nearby abbey, or wherever was customary at the time. They could be visited and their aid solicited.

The relics *were* the saints, they were perceived as being alive. They afforded immediate contact with supernatural power and were able 'to bring the continual action of divine providence to a local level.'[5] Relics even had legal rights; they received gifts and offerings made specifically to them. They were fundraisers, and attracted countless pilgrims. As such they were the best investment religious communities could make in the Middle Ages, and were obtained by gift, purchase, and sometimes stolen. Their acquisition, by whatever means, was often celebrated by a written account describing the ceremony of their 'translation' or removal to a new and final resting-place. This happened to the remains of St Winefride buried at Gwytherin in the seventh century and removed to their abbey almost five hundred years later by the monks of Shrewsbury.

Wells and sacred places
In some cases pre-Christian sites became associated with the lives of saints. The adoption of wells and springs were later seen as examples of the Christianization of pagan places, with the concept of the spring as a connection with the other world. Water is an important Christian symbol as a means of grace, the transmission of God's power through the sacrament of baptism, a rite of purification, regeneration, and new life.

More certain is a tradition going back to the martyrdom of the Apostle Paul associated the severing of his head and the place where it fell as the source of a sacred spring. Francis Jones observed that 'the emergence of a well is

1. The Martrydom of St Winefride nineteenth century.
Repainting of the 1583 fresco by Circignani ('Pomerancio') in the chapel of the Venerable English College, in Rome.
A. In defence of her chastity, the virgin St Winefride is beheaded by Caradoc, son of the North Welsh King Alâog; where her head falls a well, famous for miracle, springs up in the valley. B. Caradog, is carried off by the devil. C. St Beuno rejoins the virgin's head to her body and she lives for a further fifteen years.

characteristic of the martyrdom of many saints, and locomotion after death and the carrying of a severed head is sometimes present also.'[6] He referred to the pattern of events in the lives of beheaded virgins as being constant: 'the virgin flees from a would-be lover; he catches and beheads her; a well appears where the head fell; the virgin is sometimes restored to life and lives for many years after the experience.'[7]

In a pre-literate environment such as existed in the early Christian centuries in Britain, the power of saints and the growth of their cults was cultivated and disseminated by means of those recognisable characteristics of their presence: miracles, relics, and sacred places. Some of them, such as holy wells and springs,[8] attracted pilgrims and economic benefit to the Christian communities that had been associated with the saint in his or her lifetime. These communities believed that their saints continued to reside in their midst, and that they were natural heirs and guardians of their traditions, jealously preserving their relics and reputations as miracle workers.

Throughout Europe a popular literary form developed whose purpose was to publicise the merits of particular saints. This is called hagiography: stories about the holy ones. It is from this literary tradition that we inherit, for example, the lives of St Beuno and St Winefride.[9]

Writing the lives of the saints. Hagiography
Writing about saints from the early Christian ages was regarded as an important way of communicating the continuing record of the faith of the Church and particular members who were regarded as outstanding examples of holy lives. The lives of the saints were first recorded in the New Testament and Apocryphal Gospels. The *Book of the Acts of the Apostles* is the first of this literary genre. It is a precursor of what followed for the next fifteen-hundred years, with its mixture of events, witness, conversion, martyrdom, sacramental fellowship, miracles, missionary activity, church discipline, etc. Early lives of the saints were written particularly to commemorate martyrs, with accounts of trials, condemnations and executions of those who suffered at the time of persecution. These accounts were written down to be read on the anniversary of the martyrs' death, and formed a cycle of readings for the churches' liturgical calendars.

As Christianity spread throughout the Roman Empire and later became organised into individual provinces and dioceses, with their leaders meeting together in Councils of the Church, the lives of the saints were honoured, and their memories treasured both locally and universally. The fellowship of the Church was seen as the Church militant here on earth and the Church triumphant in heaven. Obviously Church doctrine, teaching, art, music and architecture emphasised the power and glory of Almighty God and the saint's place in the heavenly courts. Whilst all this imagery and beauty appealed to their imaginations, their thoughts and behaviour were directed by what they heard about the personal example of sanctity and triumph of their fellow human beings who had obtained the martyr's crown and were now in a position to help them. They appealed to the saints to intercede and intervene for their benefit through the generosity of their miracles. Such power was respected, reliable, held in honour and veneration, and, when demonstrated, reported and acclaimed.

This acclamation by the common people was remembered and transmitted by word of mouth from generation to generation, respected and accepted as authentic and authoritative. This oral tradition of sanctity became part of the shared treasure of the good news of salvation. Alongside God's revelation, enshrined in the scriptures, there grew up a new set of stories from local church communities. Tales related from memory, oral tradition, community folk-tales, declaring the miraculous powers of their local saint were conjoined with the written word of scripture and became a two-edged sword in the primitive and unending struggle between good and evil.

In more literate parts of the Church the lives of the saints were written down, compiled from oral tradition and modelled on the classical narratives of the ancient world. There was an intermixture between oral and written tradition. In the local Church it became the task of the monasteries and dioceses to commit to writing a variety of records: chronicles to record major events, and charters providing legal documents witnessing property gifts and rights, and often including the lives of the saints associated with the property.[10] This process developed in the monasteries throughout Europe from the early Middle Ages. The lives of the saints became specialised productions and followed a recognised pattern, the chief purpose of which was to demonstrate the sanctity of the particular saint. They related their hero's arrival, founding of a church, deeds, miracles of healing and vengeance, control over nature, personal characteristics of asceticism, influence in the local landscape, manner of death and post-mortem influence. Historical fact was fused with folk legend, and the reaction of the saint in times of crisis given particular attention. The lives emphasised those things we have noted – miracles, relics, territorial rights over churches and cemeteries, and other sacred places, and pilgrimages.

Welsh Christianity, although it was in some ways distinctive, was in the main stream of European practice and considered itself to be within the sphere of influence of papal authority. It was self-sufficient and content with its own household of saints. Its main characteristic was the establishment of monasteries that represented the religious activity of the tribe. These were called mother churches, *clasau*, ruled by an abbot and a group of canons, sharing a common income but living as secular clerks, some married and even transmitting their property and ecclesiastical office to their children. Some of these later evolved into Welsh kingdom bishoprics. Other churches founded by the mother churches were called *llannau*, after their distinctive enclosure, the *llan*.

The impact of the Norman conquest eventually transformed the Welsh Church.

There was no diocesan organisation in the area of Tegeingl and northern Powys until the creation of the diocese of St Asaph in 1143, and it took another hundred years for the beginnings of parochial organisation to emerge. This was not thoroughly achieved until the political settlement in 1284.

One of the earliest effects of this change and assimilation is seen in the composition of the lives of the Welsh saints and the copying of a variety of collections of records made in monasteries. Although many of them were brief, they were to provide invaluable information towards an understanding of the early Welsh Church. They consisted of annals from the fifth to the thirteenth century, charters recording the transfers of property, and genealogies.[11] In the eleventh and twelfth centuries early lives of the Welsh saints, written in Latin, begin to appear. These followed ancient Welsh sources but were meant to influence the new ecclesiastical regime. An example is the *Life of St David* written by Rhigyfarch (1056–99), a member of a distinguished family of Welsh scholars and clerics from the ancient *clas* community at Llanbadarn Fawr. Familiar with the lives of the Welsh saints written centuries earlier, Rhigyfarch, a cleric of St David's, wrote with the intention of convincing the Norman invaders of the ancient roots of the Welsh Church. His motive was to convince the intruders of the metropolitical claims of the western Welsh diocese, the centre of which he portrays as a monastic structure belonging to the late eleventh-century European Church.[12]

The Church along the border of north and eastern Wales in some areas received attention from the Norman conquerors. For example, the Norman earls established Benedictine houses in Shrewsbury (*c.*1083) and Chester (1093). Within a short period of time monks of both these monasteries became involved in the cult of St Winefride.

The twelfth century lives of St Winefride
St Winefride was accorded two Latin lives, probably written independently of each other in the middle of the twelfth century. Both lives reveal to us much about the main characters, Winefride and Beuno, and their legends and traditions. We are given an insight into Welsh ecclesiastical organisation in the early middle ages, the establishment of a church at Holywell and the beginning of the long history of pilgrimage to the well. The lives lead us from seventh-century Wales to the more sophisticated world of Anglo-Norman monasticism. One of them has as its finale the intriguing account of the removal in 1138 of St Winefride's remains from the churchyard at Gwytherin, near the river Conwy in north Wales, to a shrine in the abbey of Shrewsbury in Shropshire.

These two Latin lives have formed the basis of later accounts of the life of St Winefride, either abridged editions, or English translations.[13] Traditionally they have been known by their Latin titles. The *Vita S. Wenefrede*, with its appendix of miracles, the *libellus miraculorum*, was written in the twelfth century, and is

2. *St Winefred's Well. Line engraving by P. Mazell after Moses Griffiths. Published in T. Pennant, A Tour in Wales, 1778.*

generally referred to as *Vita prima*, the 'First Life'. The date, *c*.1135, is often suggested because of its reference to the expulsion of the French from Gwynedd and its omission of mention of the removal of Winefride's relics from Gwytherin. But uncertainty remains surrounding its authorship and date of composition, and for simplicity in the discussion it is designated as the *Anonymous Life*. The facts surrounding the authorship of the other life, the *Vita et translatio S. Wenefredae*, generally referred to as *Vita secunda*, pose no problems, for it was written by Robert, prior of the Benedictine abbey of SS Peter and Paul in Shrewsbury, in *c*.1138–42. As the title suggests, it falls into two parts: the *Life of St Winefride* and the translation of her remains from Gwytherin. In this discussion it is designated as *Robert's Life*.

It has been suggested that these two lives were written independently of each other, but their authors may have used as a common source a Latin life of St Winefride's mentor St Beuno, *Vita Sancti Beunoni*. This was the main source for the vernacular *Buchedd Beuno* in the *Book of the Anchorite* of Llanddewibrefi of 1346.[14]

It is therefore possible from the *Anonymous Life* and *Robert's Life* to produce an account of the life of St Winefride which sees her against a background of Celtic pre-history, Christianity in Wales in the early Middle Ages and the reforming influences of European monasticism. It is these sources which were the main means for the development and spread of the medieval cult of St Winefride.

The *Anonymous Life* (*Vita prima*), written before 1138, has attached to it a series of miracle tales associated with the well, but which was originally separate from the life. The contents of the *Anonymous Life* give no indications either of author or source; but, as almost all the life is concentrated on Winefride's life in Holywell, with the complicated events of her subsequent life compressed into a

3. St Winefride and her Well; detail of a window in Shrewsbury R C. Cathedral.

small final section, it can be held as certain that it was based upon an earlier, lost, life.

This concentration on Holywell means that the present life was composed in, or at least for use in, Holywell; but there is no clue as to by whom, it is too early to have any connection with Basingwerk; and the absence of any reference in the life or, for that matter, in the *Miracula*, to St Werburgh's Abbey, Chester, must also mean that it is not connected with that house either.

In contrast *Robert's Life* (*Vita Secunda*), is very much longer.[15]

Extracts from the the lives of St Winefride
The quotation of extracts from the lives of St Winefride is designed to present the reader with the events in both lives and enable them to be acquainted with the traditional account of the life of St Winefride. The scheme employed is to quote the whole of the *Anonymous Life*, with a comparison with *Robert's Life* given in the accompanying notes to the text. These extracts are followed by the relevant chapter of the Welsh life of Beuno, the *Buchedd Beuno*. The part of *Robert's Life* which is not covered by the *Anonymous Life*, which includes the major part of the account of Winefride at Gwytherin and her 'translation' to Shrewsbury, are summarised.

The Anonymous Life of St Winefride[16]

HERE BEGINS THE LIFE OF ST WINEFRIDE, VIRGIN AND MARTYR. If it is good to hide the secret of a king, no less is it irksome to refrain from publishing the great deeds of God. I have accordingly undertaken, by the help and favour of God, to write down what the tradition of older times has handed down to us regarding the Blessed Winefride, to the praise of God, and the exhibition of exalted merit – for they are things well worthy to be left on record.

There lived, in the days when Cadfan[17] was King of North Wales, a famous chief named Tyfid, son of Eiludd, who was the possessor of three manors in Tegeingl [Flintshire]. His three manors were respectively named Abeluyc, Maengwen, and Gwenffyyn. Tyfid had no son, and one only daughter, whose name was Winefride; and who, from her earliest years, fixed her whole affection upon the Heavenly Bridegroom, and dedicated her virginity to Him alone, rejecting in anticipation all mortal aspirants to her affections or her hand. Her

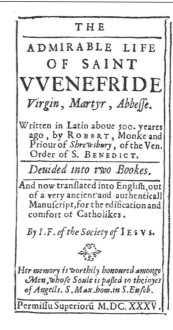

4. John Falconer, SJ, The Admirable Life of Saint Wenefride, *St Omer, 1635:*
frontispiece and title page

father, being made aware of this resolution, could not but, feel some regret that his daughter's renunciation of marriage, as she was his only child, made it impossible to preserve his inheritance in his own line. On the other hand, he could not but rejoice to think that his child had given herself to God, and the chief accordingly determined to secure her such an education as should fit her for the life on which she proposed to enter.

While he was under the influence of this resolution, the blessed prelate Beuno, having been driven forth from his own dwelling by the pressure of the numerous branches of the house of Selyf ap Cynan ap Brochfael[18] took refuge at the house of Tyfid and continued to reside there. The chief, finding him to be a learned and religious man, consulted him about his daughter, and asked his opinion as to how she should be educated. Beuno listened to his account with great attention, and said to him: 'If you will make over your estate to God, in trust to me, I will live here with you, and instruct your daughter in the law of God.' To this Tyfid replied: 'My lord, there is no one who would more willingly do this, if it were in my power. And, if the time were not too long, I would ask you to remain here while I go to the King and obtain his consent to the arrangement you propose.' He answered: 'Go, my dear son, and God go before you to give you good success.' Tyfid accordingly proceeded to the residence of the King, his lord, and earnestly entreated his assent to the disposition of his patrimony which he proposed to make.[19] The King's reply was in these words: 'Reverend man, it stands neither within my right nor yours to alienate your patrimony from the

5. *Cadfan (died c.AD 625) Stone, The wise and most renowned of all Kings, Llangadwaladr, Anglesey.*

public service of the State and of the community. But I give you permission to dedicate any one you like of your three manors to the service of God, provided you will leave me the other two.'

Tyfid hastened home with this favourable reply, which he reported to Beuno, and added: 'If, therefore, you wish to remain with me, you are now at liberty to choose out any part of my inheritance the spot which pleases you best.' The blessed Beuno then said: 'I should prefer to dwell in the solitude of Beluyc.' And so it was done. Beuno, with Tyfid his patron, built a cabin in the valley called in the language of the Britons, Sychnant; erected there a little church, in which he said Mass daily, and daily gave instruction to the maiden Winefride in the Sacred Scriptures.[20] Tyfid and his household assisted every day at the office of the Mass, and Beuno always followed it with a catechetical address.

One Sunday,[21] it happened that Tyfid and his wife had gone early to Mass, while Winefride still remained at home, in order to bring with her the fire, water, salt, and other things required for the Holy Sacrifice. Just then Caradog, son of Alaog, a prince of royal birth, who had been out hunting wild beasts, came weary with the chase, and very thirsty, to ask for drink. Reaching the house, he inquired who was its owner; but he had, also, another purpose which was beginning to form itself in his mind. The girl, being alone in the house, went at once to greet him, and answer his enquiries respecting her father, and gracefully saluting him informed him that her parents were gone to hear the preaching of Beuno at Mass. Caradog gazed at the fair and rosy complexion of the maiden, and admired her beauty of face and figure, which was very great. His heart began to burn with desire for her, and leading her into the house, where they were alone, he forgot his thirst in the vehemence of his love. 'Dearest maid,' he said, 'listen to my entreaty, and allow me to become a recognized suitor for your hand. I love you most earnestly.' To this the maiden replied: 'My lord, such words of commendation should not be addressed by a man of your rank and lineage to a humble maiden such as I am. Indeed, I cannot do what you request. I am betrothed to another, whom I am just about to wed.' This reply filled Caradog with fury. 'Away with such trifling and folly,' he exclaimed, 'and consent to my wishes. I will make you my wife.' The girl was now seriously alarmed at his violence, and set her wits to work to devise a means of escape. 'Allow me,' she said, 'to retire for a few minutes to my chamber and change my dress, that I may be fitter to enjoy your society. I will leave undone the task entrusted to me, and place myself at your disposal.' Caradog answered: 'If you will promise not to be long, I will wait a little while.'

Thankful for the reprieve, the girl passed quickly through the chamber and ran down into the valley, anxious only to conceal herself and get out of his sight, Caradog soon discovered that she had deceived him, and furiously angry, mounted, set spurs to his horse, and went off in pursuit.[22] The girl had all but reached the door of the monastery, where she hoped to obtain protection from God and from Beuno, and was just about to step across the threshold, when he reached her with his sword and cut off her head.

Her parents saw it, and were for some time in a stupor of astonishment and grief. When they recovered from this, their tears and sorrows were pitiable to witness. Beuno also witnessed the tragedy, and, overwhelmed with grief, left the altar and came to see who had done this murderous deed.[23] Raising his eyes he saw Caradog, standing with his bloody sword in his hand; and perceiving him to be the murderer, he cursed him as he stood. The miserable man melted away before their eyes, like wax before the fire. Beuno went to the corpse of the dead girl, carrying her head, which had rolled inside the door, and earnestly beseeching God to restore her to life, lest his enemy should triumph over him, he fitted the head to the body. His prayer was heard. The body returned at once to life and animation, only showing a slender scar running all round the neck. And on the spot where her blood had flowed there was an earthquake, with a loud noise, and a great stream of water burst forth, and has continued to flow from that day to this. The stones in the stream have been ever since, and are still, the colour of blood; the moss has the scent of incense, and is a remedy for various diseases.

Beuno, understanding that God had wrought this miracle on her account, said to her, in the hearing of her parents:

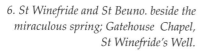

6. St Winefride and St Beuno. beside the miraculous spring; Gatehouse Chapel, St Winefride's Well.

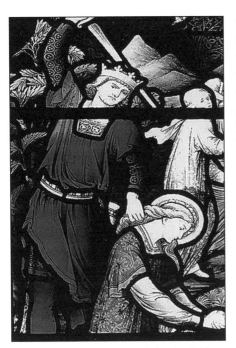

7. *The beheading of St Winefride: detail of a window in Shrewsbury R C Cathedral.*

'My sister, God intends this spot to belong to you. I must go elsewhere, to the place where God has appointed that I am to end my days.[24] I have a request to make to you, which is, that you will send me every year a cloak made by your own hands.' 'My lord she said, 'I will very gladly do so, but I am afraid I shall have very great difficulty in sending it, especially as I do not know where you are going to live.' To whom the holy man answered: 'Have no anxiety on that point. There is a stone in the middle of the river on which I have been accustomed to meditate and pray. Put the cloak upon this stone when the day comes round, and if it comes to me, let it come.' Thus, with mutual benedictions, they parted.

The blessed Winefride lived for many years[25] in that solitude, as Beuno had advised her. Once every year on the vigil of St John Baptist, she sent a cloak to Beuno, in the manner he had indicated, laying it out upon the stone, and the stone carried it down the stream, dry outside and in, out into the sea, and by sea to the harbour of Sachlen, and to the hands of Beuno. Thus Beuno every year received the maiden's gift. And the merits of the virgin imparted to the cloak this virtue, that wherever Beuno wore it the rain never wetted him, nor the wind moved his hair. Hence he went by the name of Beuno of the Dry Cloak.

About this period, as it is related, Winefride went to Rome[26] to visit the sacred resting-places of the Apostles, and devoutly offer herself wholly to God in presence of their relics. This done, she returned to her desert. In those days the holy men of all Britain assembled in the Synod of Winefride, and Winefride, with other saints, also repaired thither. By this Synod all the institutions of religion were fixed and settled, that is to say, the saints who had previously lived singly and dispersed, with no Rule but that which their own will imposed, were collected in suitable dwellings, with a view to the improvement of their mode of life, under experienced Superiors placed at the head of each house. Thus it happened that blessed Winefride was appointed to preside over eleven virgins, who received from her the pattern of holy conversation. The bearing and eloquence which she displayed surpass our powers of description; her language, and the thoughts she expressed are said to have been sweeter than honey and purer than milk, to the apprehension of those who listened to her. Hence she was always called White Winefride; for she spoke with the whiteness of wisdom, and lived in faithful and constant observance of her vows. The spot where she dwelt with her maidens is called Gwytherin. And there, when her course was ended, she fell asleep, and was buried on the eighth day before the Calends of July, and with the virgins her companions rests in Christ, to Whom is honour and glory for ever and ever, Amen.

Here ends the Life of St Winefride, Virgin and Martyr.

The section from Buchedd Beuno which gives
an account of Beuno and Winefride[27]

ST BEUNO'S LIFE AND MIRACLES, translated from the British MS …

Then Beuno left that place, and walked on the side of the river Dee, to get a place to pray to God in. And he found none till he came to Tyfid, the son of Eiludd ; and this Tyfid gave Beuno a town to inherit for ever; and there Beuno built a church, and dedicated it to God. Within a short time Tyfid left this solitary place to Beuno. And on a workday Tyfid and his wife went to church to hear mass and sermon from Beuno, and left his daughter at home to keep house. And behold she saw the king of that place coming to the house whose name was Caradog. She immediately met him, and was civil to him. He asked where her father was; she answered, 'At church: if you have any business with him, stay for him, and he will come presently.' 'I will not stay, except you promise to be my concubine.' The maid answered, 'I will not be thy concubine, for you are a king, and descended from kings, and I am too mean to be your concubine. But,' says she, 'if you stay till I return from my chamber, I will do what you please': and under pretence of going to her chamber she fled to the church where her father and mother were. The king, perceiving her to fly, pursued her, and overtook her as she was entering the church door, and with his sword struck off her head into the church, and the body fell without. Beuno and the father and mother saw this: and Beuno looked in the king's face, and told him, 'I will beg of God that he spare not thee any more than thou has spared this good maid.' And in that instant the king melted into a pool, and he was no more seen in this world. Then Beuno took the maid's head, and put it on her body, and spread his own mantle over the body , and bid the father and mother that lamented over her be quiet a little while, and leave her as she was till mass was over. Then Beuno offered to God; and as soon as mass was over the maid was

*8. St Beuno replaces St Winefride's head: detail of a
window in Shrewsbury R C Cathedral.*

alive, and she wiped the sweat off her face: so God and Beuno made her full well. Where the blood fell on the ground a fountain arose, which to this day cures men and cattle of their distempers, and the fountain was called from the maid's name Wenefrede's Well. And many saw this and believed in Christ: but the greatest man that believed was Cadfan, king of North-Wales, who gave Beuno a great deal of land.

Abstracts from Robert's Life

These brief summaries are given here because space forbids a full quotation of *Robert's Life*. However, some extracts from this life, translated by Thomas Swift, SJ, appear in the discussion on cultic centres, below.

One: Winefride at Gwytherin

After the death of Beuno Winefride no longer sent her gift of a cloak. With his death and those of some of her fellow nuns she became distracted and was restless in spirit while she remained at Holywell. Beuno had told her that, after seven years, she would be called elsewhere. This had come to pass, and she prayed that God would direct her to a place where she could please herself and profit others, and that He would continue unchanged His blessings at Holywell.

Thus Winefride was directed to go with a companion to Bodfari, eight miles away, to seek guidance from Diheufyr, the holy man who dwelt there. The sacredness of this place was demonstrated by the performance of many miracles on sick persons, and the spring Diheufyr had caused to burst forth. The maiden consulted with Diheufyr, who told her that it had been revealed to him that she should journey further to Henllan, where the holy man Sadwrn would give her definite instructions as to where she would dwell for the rest of her life. On reaching this place Sadwrn, after much prayer, revealed to her that this was Gwytherin, where the devout and holy Eleri was abbot and there were virgins dedicated to the service of Christ, a place 'honoured by the relics and the memory of many saints.' Here, Winefride was told, she would remain until her death, as an instructor and example to the community of virgins there.

At Gwytherin she was kindly received by Eleri, who introduced her to the nuns, commending her martyrdom suffered in the defence of her virginity. Here, Eleri entrusted Winefride to the care of his mother Tenoi. Many came to Gwytherin, to see the maiden who bore the scar on her neck of the decapitation she had suffered for the love of Christ, and been restored to life again. When Tenoi died, Winefride succeeded her in charge of the community of virgins. Her reputation was such that she was revered, loved and deferred to by Eleri and great men who lived in Wales and her power was seen through countless miracles and cures that took place there.

When the time came for her departure from this world, Winefride bade the virgins to keep their vows of chastity and guard their faith. Receiving the last rites from Eleri, she died at the beginning of November and was buried in the churchyard at Gwytherin next to Tenoi and with the confessors Senanus and

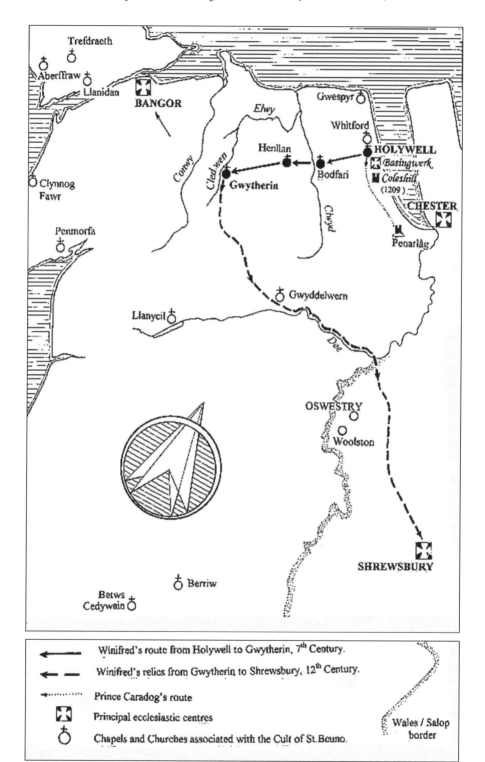

9. The Journey of St Winefride to Gwytherin and her translation to Shrewsbury.

Chebius and other holy men and women. After her death many came to Gwytherin to be cured of their infirmities.

Abstract from *Robert's Life*.
The 'Translation' of St Winefride's
remains from Gwytherin to Shrewsbury in 1138

In the reign of the first Norman king William, Roger, Earl of Shrewsbury, founded a Benedictine Abbey in Shrewsbury, dedicated to the Apostles Peter and Paul. After a while, the monks and abbots desired to increase the prestige of their monastery, and, as the custom was to enhance its reputation by the patronage and relics of a saint. This they set out to do, and looked to Wales, the country nearby, to begin their search for suitable relics. Not having decided where to begin their search they received unexpected help from their fellow Benedictines at St Werburgh's, Chester. Through the sickness of one of their brethren the monks at Shrewsbury were directed to the spring of St Winefride, to intercede for him. His recovery took place at the same hour that they were saying Mass for him at the Holy Well. This made them determined to obtain the relics of St Winefride, and eventually the necessary permission and promise of protection from the bishop of Bangor was obtained for them to exhume her remains from Gwytherin and translate them to Shrewsbury.

In the year 1138 a group of seven, including the priors of the abbeys of Shrewsbury and Chester made the journey to Gwytherin to obtain the relics. On reaching their destination the monks met with some hostility from the people of Gwytherin who showed a strong desire to keep the remains of St Winefride in the place where they had rested for five hundred years. Eventually divine intervention persuaded the people of Gwytherin, to co-operate with them.

When the time came for the exhumation of the relics of the saint, Prior Robert was inspired without human direction to go straight to the place where Winefride was buried. At the head of her grave, was a little wooden church, accessible to the great numbers of people who wished to pray there and ask for cures. So sacred was this place that, if any animal strayed on the grass covering the saints' bodies, they died on the spot, and people who profaned the enclosure were punished. Robert described the exhumation as a ritual act, undertaken to the accompaniment of prayers and solemn chanting. It was experienced as a nativity, a rebirth, as the bones of Winefride were reverently taken from the dark womb of the earth, brought into the sunlight and wrapped in swaddling clothes.

On their journey home the relics of Winefride demonstrated her power. At one place where they halted, a sick man was cured by drinking water mixed with the dust found in the blessed maiden's skull. After seven days they arrived in Shrewsbury, to be met with great rejoicing. The holy relics rested in the church of St Giles, awaiting the bishop's permission for their permanent removal to the abbey in fulfilment of their mission to Wales. This was the last act in *Robert's Life of S. Winefride and her Translation*, and it is not surprising that it became the chief literary source for the development and growth of the cult of St Winefride, which contributed to its popularity and inspired the devotion of pilgrims. To record his successful quest for the relics of St Winefride, Robert wrote a magnificent drama which he divided into three acts, set in Holywell, Gwytherin, and Shrewsbury. Each act played out the events of her life in these places and was written to show their sacredness. The full restoration of Winefride after beheading was emphasised as Robert developed her multi-powerful role of virgin, martyr, healer, into that of an abbess and exemplar of monastic virtues. His finely tailored narrative showed that, at each of these places, Winefride retained her presence and power which was vouchsafed by relics and a continuous flow of miracles.

The Translation of the relics of St Winefride was the triumphant climax of Robert's story. The sequence of Winefride's life, her death and resurrection at Holywell, earthly burial, and rebirth at Gwytherin, reaches greater heights at Shrewsbury. In recounting the placing of Winefride's relics upon the altar which had been built in honour of the holy apostles Peter and Paul, Robert shows that Winefride's exultation was accomplished at Shrewsbury. Here she entered into fellowship with the chief of the apostles, and was placed with them in full view of the people. In her new home she was incorporated with them and the people of God in the body of Christ, and joined with them in His continuing presence in the Eucharist. The relics of St Winefride established, as the monks had set out to do, the abbey of Shrewsbury as a cultic centre, of which Robert's account was a celebration.

A description of miracles in the Anonymous Life *and* Robert's Life

Attached to the *Anonymous Life* is a section which is twice the length of the life. It is described as 'part two; the miracles, which occurred at St Winefride's Well.' *Robert's Life* also contains chapters arranged together describing a group of miracles at St Winefride's Well. The account comes in a section that marks a transition between the death of the saint at Gwytherin and the translation of her relics. Robert's account of the translation also contains a small number of miraculous events which occurred on their return to Shrewsbury. Obviously miracles were the stock in trade of the hagiographer, and were major items in the propaganda and publicity campaign to promote both saint and cultic centre. In both lives miracles are divided into the two categories of punishment and healing. The lives do not share the same miracle events, but hold the same view of their origin: 'God who alone works wonders, does not cease to work these miracles here for his virgin and martyr Winefride, either to help the kindly or punish the impious. God in perfect Trinity lives and reigns, one for all ages.'

Anonymous Life.

The healing miracles

Both lives describe healing miracles in biblical terms. They are mighty works, wonders, and signs of the operation of the power of God: 'the blind receive their sight, the lame walk, the lepers are cleansed, the dead are raised up and the poor have the Gospel preached to them.'[28] Following on from the age of the Gospel is the belief in the continuation of miracles. The apostolic and universal Church is shown as sharing in Christ's power. It is delegated through Christ to those who believe in Him. Especially close to God are those who, like, St Winefride, have sacrificed their lives for him. 'The noble army of martyrs,' have the privilege of being the channels of his grace. The martyrs are present in the church through their relics. And this is why both lives of St Winefride describe her relics and their involvement in the ritual of healing at her sacred places.

As an agent of God's grace the virgin martyr Winefride is portrayed as being compassionate and generous and the miracles associated with her in both lives are many and varied. For example the mentally sick and disturbed, including some led to the Well in chains, find peace of mind. There are examples of healing through exorcism. The corpse of a dead girl brought to lie in church overnight is found to be alive next morning. The virgin provides cures for physical infirmity, paralysis, fever, chest and stomach illnesses, menstruation problems, and other ills. The water in the well is said to express Winefride's approval when it flows for three days as a milky liquid with special healing powers, to celebrate the expulsion of the French (the Normans) from the whole of Gwynedd. The place of the miracle at Holywell is usually described as the spring, with some preparation made through vigil and prayer in church. The disposition of the petitioner is important: faith, generosity of spirit, penitence, and thanksgiving are mentioned in the healing events. *Robert's Life* deliberately reports a group of miracles at Holywell with the purpose of showing that through Winefride 'divine power works wondrously' in both places: at Shrewsbury in the newly created shrine, and at Holywell at the spring with its relics of water, spattered stones, and moss.

Punitive miracles
In both lives a group of miracle events are punitive: for violation of the churchyard, and stealing the equipment of the mill on the stream. They act as a warning for evil doers. The virgin is able to track down thieves and, as such, these miracle events are cautionary tales to show that she exercises social control and discipline in her sacred space. Although both lives divide their groups of miracles into the two groups of punishment and healing, neither of them repeat the same stories.

There is another difference, however. Robert's approach to the violation of sacred precincts and protection of sacred places is Norman and Continental in cultural context whereas the editor of the collection of miracles in part two of the *Anonymous Life* is expressing ideas which belong to Wales. His 'keep out' warning is written in Welsh not Norman-French!

The punitive miracles in the *Anonymous Life* are similar to those in other Welsh lives of the saints and have a background in the native Welsh law of the early Middle Ages. This was administered until the thirteenth century through the co-

10. St Giles's Church (Shrewsbury) 1778 engraving from The History and Antiquities of Shrewsbury, *Charles Hulbert, 1837.*

11. The Abbey Church 1778 (Shrewsbury) 1778 engraving from Hulbert's edt. of Phillip's History of Shrewsbury.

12 & 13. Shrewsbury RC Cathedral: windows depicting (left) St Winefride's shrine carried into Shrewsbury Abbey; (right) the healing of the crippled man.

operation of God, the saints and the Church in the daily administration of secular law.[29] Three categories are mentioned in these miracle events. Perjury was a serious crime and penance for the most heinous offence could last years, with a heavy fine. To swear an oath was to invoke God as both witness and judge in the proceedings. In Wales the oath was sworn in church on relics, not necessarily bones, but other objects associated with the saint. If the court was held in the churchyard, the holy ground was adjudged sufficient authority. A breach of the oath affronted the saint's *braint* or honour.[30] this is made quite clear in the second miracle in the *Anonymous Life*:

> Another time it happened that a man, accused of theft, committed perjury on the spring and the sacred precincts of the martyr's' church. In due time it became known how the blessed virgin felt about those who presumed to do a forbidden act. A goat which the man had eaten uttered a horrible bleating from inside the stomach of the thief, and so it was clear that he was guilty. This is a horrible event: what was denied by the oath of a rational animal was disclosed by a brute animal and, what is more astounding, by one that was already eaten. It leaves no doubt the Lord works wonders for his saints, for he is utterly wonderful in all his saints (Ps. 67, v.36)[31]

The church territory, which extended sometimes beyond the cemetery was regarded as *nawdd*, 'sanctuary, place of refuge,' which enjoyed the protection of the saint.[32] Sacrilege[33] was punishable by a fine, *dirwy*, 'honour-price,' exacted for injuries committed against churches. The fine was due to the saint and paid on his behalf to the clergy. If a person committed an offence while under the protection of relics he lost this immunity. Sacrilege occurs most frequently in the *Anonymous Life*. The property of the virgin was violated when someone attempted to interfere with the stones in the stream. Men sent to despoil Winefride's territory stole animals tethered to the church wall, and as a consequence suffered a horrible death. A church deacon was robbed while collecting tithes and suffered further injury. His assailants were caught by the power of the virgin and punished. An attempt was made to remove *Maen Beuno* (Beuno's Stone) from the stream, and the culprit's wife was also punished for unlawfully bathing in the well and polluting Winefride's sanctuary reserved especially for the sick. Two clerics were punished for sacrilege for stealing from the church. The one who stole a portable book was whipped, the other hanged for stealing a missal.

The influence of the lives of St Winefride on the cultic centres
The lives of St Winefride established cultic centres at the three sacred places associated with the saint at Holywell, Gwytherin and Shrewsbury. Her martyrdom, its effect on Winefride, together with other objects such as miracles and relics linked these places. Also each place had its own significance, with its own distinctive elements of cult. Although St Winefride's Well at Holywell eventually emerged as the primary cultic centre, Robert in his *Life of St Winefride* integrates the three places and nowhere suggests rivalry between them. Instead, he sets out to demonstrate that each sacred place enriches the cult of St Winefride. His narrative is designed to make each place a cultic centre in its own right, with their collective purpose to extend the influence and enhance the worthiness of the virgin, martyr and abbess, Winefride.

Holywell as a cultic centre
The martyrdom event
The lives of St Winefride make her martyrdom vivid, dramatic and unforgettable. The story is meant to capture the imagination and devotion of the pilgrim. Winefride, who had already renounced the idea of marriage, and in her own words was 'betrothed to the Son of the Eternal King,' had the misfortune to be visited by a lustful prince by the name of Caradog. The virgin rejected his sexual advances, and was pursued by her frustrated assailant who decapitated her with a blow from his sword. 'The licentious Prince heard that he was despised … his passion overmastered him … he drew his sword from the scabbard, and cut off her head.'[34]

In testimony of the severing of Winefride's head from her body, her martyrdom, and its re-attachment by St Beuno, she bore a permanent neck scar. 'A slender scar like a white thread was visible all round her neck, marking the place where the head had been severed, and remained visible throughout the rest of her life in testimony of the wonderful miracle of which she had been the subject.' 'It is also related that the white thread on the neck was plainly visible to all those to whom she was permitted to appear after her death.'[35] The martyrdom of Winefride at Holywell established a feast day celebrated on 22 June, in honour of the virgin martyr on the anniversary of her decollation

Incorporated in the narrative of the martyrdom event at Holywell are a number of motifs common in early Christian religion which are meant to appeal to the senses, in order to fix in the imagination of believers the sacredness of the place, and to stimulate their spiritual experience. The proof of the power of St Winefride at her sacred place at Holywell, her presence there to intercede on their behalf, was seen in the tangible features to be found there. Here at Holywell were common objects, those of nature: water, stones, and moss, in abundance, self-renewing, inexpensive, transportable, and most importantly having healing properties. The lives establish these simple objects as the relics of St Winefride.

Ffynnon Gwenfrewi *(St Winefride's Well)*
The immediate happening, simultaneous with the martyrdom of Winefride is the miraculous appearance of the spring, which becomes her holy well. The importance of the spring is repeated in *Robert's Life*.

'And the moment the head fell to the ground, and on the spot it touched, a copious spring of the purest water gushed forth, and continues to flow to this day, giving healing to multitudes through the merit of this blessed maiden.'[36] In order to leave the reader in no doubt, Robert repeats the association of the place where Winefride's head touched the ground with the place where the spring appears.

'The place where her blood was spilt was originally called the Dry Valley; but from the time the fountain sprang up on the spot where her head in falling touched the ground, and which has continued to flow to this day, healing all diseases both in men and cattle, the place has been called by her name.'[37]

It is this story of the appearance of the spring which gave the town its name. The name 'holy well' or 'village of the well,' first occurs as *Haliwel* in 1093, and in its Welsh form, *Treffynnon*, 'the town of the well,' in 1329.[38] Such was the reputation of the power of the spring that by the end of the Middle Ages it was described as one of the wonders of Wales.

In Flynteshyer at Hallywell there ys a wonderful ffayr Well Called St Winefrides Spring: The water therof even at the very spring gusheth forth wth such force, that it yt carryeth away downe Streame any thing that ys receaved therein, and that before yt touche the grounde.

The sheer power of the spring was a tremendous influence on pilgrims; the exhilaration of bathing in the pure, cooling waters an invigorating experience for penitent and suffering pilgrims. These sentiments were well expressed in the nineteenth century by the Jesuit poet Gerard Manley Hopkins.

> Water, which keeps thy name, (for not in rock written,
> But in pale water, frail water, wild rash and reeling water,
> That will not wear a print, that will not stain a pen,
> Thy venerable record, virgin, is recorded)
> Here to this holy well shall pilgrimages be.[39]

The sacramental importance of the water of St Winefrides Well associated with the rites of the Church in baptism and the eucharist became important themes in later medieval Welsh poetry, as we shall see later.

Stones spattered by the blood of Winefride
Stones spattered and everlastingly stained with the blood of Winefride to be found in the spring and stream were regarded as relics to her martyrdom and represented as such in Robert's *Life of St Winefride*.[40]

From the blood that streamed from her body, and flowed down the hill, the stones, both in the source of the stream and on its banks, were coloured crimson; and wonderful to relate, they still retain their crimson colour, as will be seen by all that look at them. They appear as if covered with clotted blood, which, however, no industry or perseverance can wash away.[41]

14. St Beuno replaces St Winefride's head: detail of window in St Beuno's College, Tremeirchion.

The evidence of the stones as relics of Winefride's suffering is repeated in *Robert's Life* in a statement made by Beuno to Winefride on his departure from Holywell: 'Behold the traces of your passion. These stones, sprinkled with your blood, prove that you suffered martyrdom for God, for they are still reddened with your blood, to your honour, and for a memorial of you to many that shall come.'

Beuno informs Winefride that the stones are one of three gifts given to her by God. These, he tells her 'shall be the title of your praise and imprint in the minds of posterity the love and reverence of your devotion. These stones, red with your blood, shall never cease to be spotted with that blood, but in memory of your passion will retain the hue of gore for ever, by the power of God, and in memory of the triumph of your chastity.'[42]

The poet Michael Drayton (1536–1631) viewed the stones according to the legend:

> And, that for her alone the water should not mourne,
> The pure vermillion bloud, that issu'd from her vaines,
> Unto this very day the pearly Gravell staines:
> As erst the white and red were mixed in her cheeke.[43]

At the end of the sixteenth century, the Jesuit Father Edward Oldcorne received a remarkable cure from a cancer in the mouth by sucking one of these stones. Whilst visiting a Catholic household he spied a stone spotted with drops of blood taken out of the fountain which 'a priest had put on the altar with other relics. And when Father Oldcorne saw it, he took it and kissed it with great reverence and retreating to a private place on his knees he began to lick the stone and put part of it in his mouth, praying quietly. And behold, after half an hour he was cured of all his melancholy and infirmity.'[44]

Beuno informs Winefride that the second gift God has given her relates to the prayers of sufferers.

> Whoever shall at any time, in whatever sorrow and suffering, implore your aid for deliverance from sickness or misfortune, shall at the first, or second, or certainly the third petition, obtain his wish, and rejoice in the attainment of what he asked for. And if at the third petition he fail to obtain it, he will know that he is shortly to terminate this mortal life, and for this reason, by the secret judgement of God, is denied his request, but for his soul's sake should persevere in his invocation of your assistance to obtain what is far better than anything he may have asked.[45]

Maen Beuno (St Beuno's Stone)
The pattern of making three petitions to Winefride became a ritual of invocation,

and involved three passages through the water of the well. This ritual was also associated with another object to be found at the well. The place where Beuno prayed often, and where he addressed Winefrede on the occasion of his depart-ure, was on a large stone in the stream.[46] This Robert referred to as *Maen Beuno* (Beuno's Stone). It is still used by pilgrims in their devotions and it is customary for them to descend into the water and kneel in prayer on the stone. The *Maen Beuno* is in the outside pool at the base of the steps leading into the water. The stone was protected and those who attempted to remove it were punished.[47]

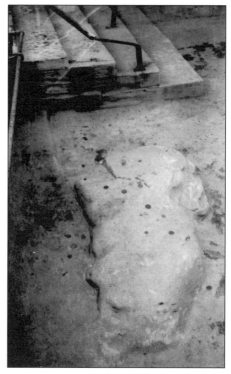

15. Maen Beuno, *St Beuno's Stone.*

Maen Beuno was thus an essential link between Beuno and Winefride after his departure from Holywell. It was on this stone that God gave his third gift to Winefride. It was by means of the stone that she sent annually a cloak to Beuno which, despite its journey through the sea, arrived 'dry inside and out and gave Beuno the epithet *casul-sych* 'of the dry cloak.' It was legends in their lives which united Beuno and Winefride as figures of devotion at the cultic centres to which they were attached.

Mosses

'Its rocks still seem as bloody today, as they did on that first day. The moss smells like incense and it cures various illnesses.' *Anonymous Life* (section 6).

Although neither the taking away of moss from the well, nor its manufacture into garlands is mentioned in the two lives they were regarded for centuries as a consolation to those who could not make a pilgrimage being carried to them made up in garlands. There were two kinds of moss formerly growing at the well: *Byssus jolithus,* the moss which produced bright red stains on stones in the well and *Jungermannia asplenioides*, which clung to the sides of the well, which had the smell of violets or incense. Known as St Winefride's hair[48] it could be dried and later moistened with water from the well and used as a poultice.

> her mosse most sweet and rare
> Against infectious damp for Pomander to weare.[49]

16. *Moss from the well, from* Tour in Wales, *T. Pennant, 1778 (illustrator Moses Griffith).*

It was this moss that was reported to have effected a cure in August 1809 of Sister Mary Ann Wood, a lay sister of the Franciscan nunnery at Taunton. Her arm, injured three months earlier and pronounced damaged beyond hope of recovery, was healed by the application of a piece of moss sent from Holywell.[50]

Holywell Church

The centre of the cult at Holywell was the church and well. The church was used by the pilgrims for religious exercises such as vigil, penitence, and exorcism, which they observed before entering the water and for thanksgiving, afterwards. A few yards above the well is the church described in *Robert's Life* as built by Beuno on land given to him by Winefride's father Tyfid.[51] When Beuno left Holywell he gave the church to Winefride. He 'conducted her to the church, and there said to her: I leave to you this temple and buildings round it, constructed partly by my own labour, and partly at the expense of your parents, that when I am gone away, you, and the virgins whom you gather round you, may serve God as you propose, always keeping before you the example I have set you.'[52]

Gwytherin as a cultic centre

The *Anonymous Life* has little to say about Gwytherin, merely stating that sometime in the period after the departure of Beuno: 'Winefride went to Rome to visit the sacred resting-places of the Apostles, and devoutly offer herself wholly to God in presence of their relics. This done she returned to her desert.' *Swift* (section 11).

What is most significant is what the life has to say about the way in which Winefride was chosen to be an abbess after her attendance at the Synod of Winefride. At this Synod: 'all the institutions of religion were fixed and settled,' through which, as the author explains, the holy men and women instead of living by themselves, 'were collected together in suitable dwellings, with a view to the improvement of their mode of life, under experienced Superiors placed at the head of each house. Thus it happened that blessed Winefride was appointed to preside over eleven virgins, who received from her the pattern of holy conversation;' and 'the spot where she dwelt with her maidens is called Gwytherin. And there, when her course was ended, she fell asleep, and was buried on the eighth day before the Calends of July and with her companions rests in Christ …'[53]

St Winefride as abbess

Robert had no knowledge of the *Anonymous Life* and in writing his account of *The Life of and translation of Winefride* he had to rely on other sources. In his life he provides a different account, to which he adds two sections of new material: the account of the expedition to Gwytherin to exhume the bones of St Winefride, and their translation to Shrewsbury. Robert's intention in writing his life was not only to make this event in the life of Winefride appear as a smooth transition from one cultic centre to another, but also to show that her worthiness and reputation increased in this progress. At Holywell, in the seventh century, she was merely a local saint performing miracles there. At Gwytherin she became a saint of the Welsh church. Here her miracles continued, pilgrims increased and St Eleri declared 'that God had appointed her for the illumination of their country.'[54]

When her remains were finally translated to Shrewsbury in the twelfth century her reputation and cult was in the hands of the Benedictines, who advanced her honour and gave her a more universal recognition which eventually led to her inclusion in the Calendar of Canterbury Province.[55]

One device Robert employs in advancing the cult of Winefride from local to international status is by portraying her as an abbess chosen by God and instructed and commissioned by Beuno:

He received her vows and clothed her with the sacred veil. She continued to advance in perfection and delighted her teacher and director in the ardour and love of God. He declared that by God's command she is to succeed him and that He has chosen her to bear the palm of conspicuous merit in His presence by the double example of her martyrdom and holy life.

17. Holywell Parish Church before restoration in 1769.

18. *St Winefride with palm (martyrdom) and book (abbess); alabaster and mosaic, formerly part of St Winefride's altar, Shrewsbury R.C. Cathedral.*

Robert anticipates the removal of the abbess Winifrede to Gwytherin by Beuno informing her that after seven years' service to God she will, under divine direction, seek another abode. 'God will direct your course, and through you will illuminate the darkness of the hearts of many.'[56]

At Gwytherin, abbot Eleri introduces Winefride to the community of women as an example. By witnessing her life the maidens may become more devout in God's service, by copying her they might lay up their merits besides hers in Heaven, and Gwytherin become celebrated on her account as long as the world shall last. She is, says the abbot, 'the virgin Winefride,' 'who to preserve her chastity inviolate, gladly suffered death and for which she will obtain from the hand of God, the palm of a martyr and an illustrious confessor.'[57] The maidens are exhorted to: 'Reverence her, imitate her, follow her as a guiding star, cast upon her all your cares, not doubting that she will be in all things your helper with God.'[58]

At Gwytherin Winefride died a natural death on 2 November and was buried in the churchyard next to Tenoi and the confessors Seanus and Chebius and other holy men and women. *Robert's Life* publicised Gwytherin not only as the resting place of saints, but also as a place to which pilgrims resorted to receive healing and venerate sacred objects associated with Winefride.

The churchyard and sacred objects belonging to Winefride at Gwytherin
The Gwytherin episode in *Robert's Life* was written not only to enhance Winefride's reputation but also to give a credible provenance to her relics, and to prove that there was an historical tradition surrounding the site going back at least five hundred years. Considered as a piece of twelfth-century hagiographic writing, Robert of Shrewsbury's account is remarkable in showing a sympathetic understanding of the Welsh Church and a grasp of the circumstances prevailing in a remote religious settlement in upland Wales in the seventh and twelfth centuries.

The significance of Gwytherin
Gwytherin lies about five miles due east of the river Conwy in an upland area at the head of the narrow valley of the river Cledwen. The *llan* was of a large oval

shape, part of an ancient compact village settlement, the site of which may be within an Iron Age promontory fort. The occupation of the site for a church or monastery goes back at least to the fifth or sixth centuries AD, the 'age of the saints'.[59] Winefride died there in the middle of the seventh century *c.*635 AD. In Roman times it was in the Welsh tribal area of the Decangli, and in the early Middle Ages bordered on the Welsh kingdom of Gwynedd. It was a land fought over by the native Welsh and successive Saxon and Norman invaders from the east, part of the disputed territory, the *Perfeddwlad* (middle country), between the rivers Conwy and Dee. In 1143, it became a parish in the newly-created diocese of St Asaph.

In searching for knowledge of the seventh-century Winefride, five hundred years after her death, Robert informed his friend Guarin, prior of Worcester, that he had based his *Life of Winefride* on documents 'preserved in the churches of the district where she lived' and the reports of trustworthy priests. In addition he made every effort to avoid any difficulties in obtaining Winefride's remains from Gwytherin by obtaining safe conduct to carry out his mission from the local Welsh chieftains and permission from David the Scot, bishop of Bangor, to translate her relics. In preparation for his expedition to Wales he was assisted by the Benedictines from Chester and accompanied by their prior, who arranged friendly guides and interpreters of the Welsh language. Robert's account of the topography of the place and the details he gave of the ancient churchyard at Gwytherin could still be recognised at the end of the seventeenth century. We know this from the eighteenth-century reports of rural deans to the bishop of St Asaph and evidence of the antiquary Edward Lhuyd (1660–1709).

Thomas Wynn the rural dean noted in his report to the bishop of St Asaph in 1729 that:

> There are within this Churchyard the Ruins of Winifred's Chapel. The supposed Gravestone of Winefride's lies flat upon the Ground within the Ruins of the Chapel which has been supported by decent Pillars in the memory of Man: At which time, as an unwarrantable tradition relates, several sick persons were cured of their maladies by being put to lie under this Stone.[60]

The rural dean was referring to the ancient Christian practice of sacred incubation, through which, by lying on the tomb of the saint, the sick hoped to facilitate a cure.

The important feature in the churchyard was *Kappel Gwenfrewi*, the centre of Winefride's cult at Gwytherin until it fell into disrepair in the seventeenth century, and was scandalously used as a quarry by the rector Richard Evans to build a house for himself well after the Reformation.

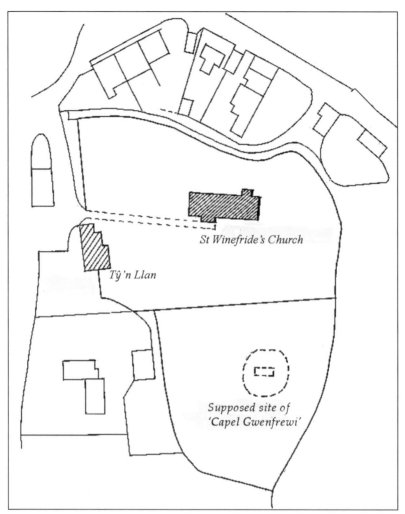

19. Gwytherin, Denbighshire

The Gwytherin reliquary

A drawing of this object was made by or for Edward Lhuyd in *c*.1696, and known as *Arch Gwenfrewi yn eglwys Gwrtheryn*. This was a wooden reliquary, a receptacle designed to preserve and exhibit, possibly corporeal relics (teeth, hair, nails), but, more probably, other non-corporeal objects associated with Winefride that remained after her burial and were treasured and venerated as relics.

This exciting link with the historical Winefride should remove any doubts of her existence as a female Welsh saint who flourished in the first part of the seventh century. In 1776, Thomas Pennant, on his visit, related that 'in the church is shewn the box in which her reliques were kept, before their removal to Shrewsbury.' J. O. Westwood made the last definite reference to the reliquary in 1858 when he wrote that 'within the church are preserved two old rude, wooden chests, in one of which a piece of wood is shown as being a portion of the coffin of St Winefride.' Although the reliquary has been broken up, the other wooden chest survives at the Well Museum, Holywell.

A Jesuit priest, Father J. G. Wynne, visited Gwytherin in 1844, and acquired a fragment of the reliquary which he later presented to St Winefride's Church, Holywell. The parish clerk at Gwytherin told Wynne that 'the greater part had been carried off by people who occasionally came there and often gave him a shilling to let them cut off a piece of the chest by way of remembrance of their visit.'

An examination of Wynne's fragment and Lhuyd's drawing *c.*1699 has enabled scholars to reach some positive conclusions about the reliquary.[61]

It was shaped like a house or temple, a design common throughout Europe. The Gwytherin example was made of oak and portable. Its size has been estimated to have been about fifteen-inches long and decorated with metal mounts. The experts have disagreed on its provenance. But because of its location near both the Irish seaboard and the Saxon invasion route it incorporates features of both Irish and Anglo-Saxon design. It could have been made in Wales in the eighth or ninth centuries. Other portable shrines are known to have existed in Wales. The shrine of St David was pillaged in 1088 and that of St Cybi disappeared much later.

Contrary to what Thomas Pennant might have been told in the eighteenth century, the reliquary would have been too small to hold Winefride's bones. It was the usual custom of the Welsh to allow their saints to rest where buried and not to disinter them. Robert was convinced that he brought back to Shrewsbury what he had heard about from his enquiries in Wales: the bones of Winefride.

20. Arch Gwenfrewy, or Reliquary of St Winefride, from Gwytherin; drawing based upon those of Edward Lhuyd and Moses Griffiths).

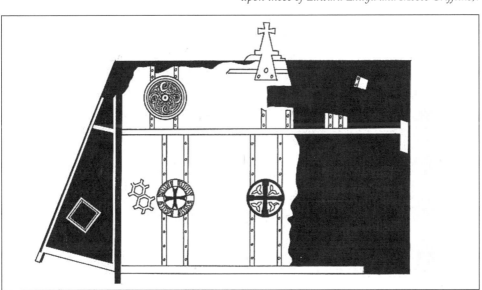

21. 'St Winefride's Coffin' medieval chest, formerly in Gwytherin, now in the museum at St Winefride's Well.

In the seventeenth century, Gwilym Pugh (c.1618–c.1689), who served as a captain in the army of Charles I and eventually became a Benedictine, kept alive the devotion to the cultic centre at Gwytherin. He was from the old Catholic stronghold of Penrhyn Creuddyn, not far from Gwytherin, and his familiarity with the place was reflected in his *Carol Buchedd Gwenfrewi* (lines 181–92)

> Mewn ysgrin hi a roddwyd, mewn gweryd gosodwyd
> Yn barchus llei claddwyd Gwenfrewi;
> Yn y ddaearen bu yn gorfedd y seren
> Wrth feddau Saint Sennen a Chbyi.
>
> Pedwarcant blwyddyn y cadwodd Gwytherin
> Esgyrn ac ysgrin Gwenfrewi,
> Nes i Rupert yn unig, oedd brior Beneddig,
> Gan ei symud i'r 'Mwythig ei chyrchu.
>
> Mewn ysgrin o arian rhoed creiriau y lleian
> I'r 'Mwythig pan symudan' Gwenfrewi;
> Gadawan' yr hen ysgrin yn eglwys Gwytherin
> Fal y gallo'r pererin ei pharchu.

[She was placed in a coffin, she was placed/ respectfully in the earth where Gwenfrewi was buried/ in the soil lay the star/ by the graves of saints Sennen and Cybi./For four hundred years did Gwtherin keep/ the bones and coffin of Gwenfrewi/ and Rupert [i.e. Robert] on his own, who was a Benedictine prior/ fetched it, moving it to Shrewsbury./ In a coffin of silver were the relics of the nun placed/ when they move Gwenfrewi to Shrewsbury/ they leave the old coffin in the church of Gwytherin/ so that the pilgrim may respect it.][62]

Shrewsbury as a cultic centre

The description given above of the translation of St Winefride's relics to Shrewsbury has shown that the main purpose of Robert's *Life of St Winefride* and her translation was to promote Shrewsbury Abbey, as the custodian of her relics, into her chief cultic centre. The way in which this was done is discussed in the next chapter.

22. Reliquary of St Winefride at Shrewsbury R C Cathedral.

NOTES

1. The form of the name of Winefride and its spelling varies. The variations include Gwenfrewi, Winefrith, and Winifred. The form used throughout this study is Winefride, which is the spelling commonly used in Holywell today.

2. For this date see Patrick Sims-Williams under Beuno DNB.

3. T. M. Charles-Edwards, tr., *Two Mediaeval Welsh Poems*. (Llandysul; Gwasg Gomer, 1971) Tudur Aled's text, with notes., pp. 10–7; quotation p. 17.

4. K. Thomas, *Religion and the Decline of Magic* (Penguin 1970), pp. 27, 28, 36.

5. P. J. Geary, *Furta Sacra. Thefts of Relics in the Central Middle Ages* (Princeton, New Jersey, 1990) p. 34.

6. F. Jones, *The Holy Wells of Wales* (Cardiff, 1992), p. 36.

7. Ibid, p. 39.

8. For example St Seriol's Well at Penmom; St Winefride's Holywell; the well at Llangybi, Caerns – see W. Davies, *Wales in the Early Middle Ages* (Leicester University Press, 1982), p. 179. Other examples: St Beuno's Well, Clynnog; St Non's, St David's; Our Lady's, Penrhys, &c.

9. For a recent discussion see J. Cartwright (ed), *Celtic Hagiography and Saints' Cults* (UWP, Cardiff, 2003) and O. Davies, *Celtic Christianity in Early Medieval Wales* (UWP, Cardiff, 1996).

10. For example *The Book of Llandaff* and fn 7.

11. See W. Davies, op cit p. 198f.

12. See O. Davies op cit pp. 20–4.

13. Both the *Anonymous Life* and *Robert's Life* have been translated into English. Amongst these are :

Caxton *c.*1485; I. F. John Falconer, SJ, *Robert's Life* 1635 with the title *The Admirable Life of Saint Wenefride, Virgin Martyr, Abbesse*, republished in English Recusant Literature 1558–1640, vol. 319 (Ilkley and London, 1976). This was reprinted with a long preface and comment by William Fleetwood, bishop of St Asaph, in 1713 as an attack on Philip Metcalfe S. J.'s republication in 1712 of a translation of *The Life of Saint Winefride*. English translations of the two *Lives* of St Winefride in 1888 by Thomas Swift is referred to below as are recent translations in 2000 by Ronald Pepin and Hugh Feiss *Two Mediaeval Lives of Saint Winefride*, for these see footnote 31 and footnote 16.

14. 'A Latin *Vita sancti Beuoni* alluded to by Robert of Shrewsbury, in his *Vita sanctae Wenefredae*, chap. 20, is not extant, but was probably used *c.*1135 in the anonymous *Vita Sanctae Wenefredae*, and was the main source for the vernacular *Buchedd Beuno* in the *Book of the Anchorite of Llanddewibrefi* of 1346 although the latter also draws on Robert's *Vita* for its account of St Beuno and St Gewenfrewi.' (Winefride): see Patrick Sims-Williams under Beuno in DNB, p. 565.

15. *Robert's Life* is discussed below in much detail. His sources would have been derived from Holywell – most probably via St Werburgh's Chester, and Gwytherin. Both the *Anonymous Life* and *Robert's Life* lack genealogical information. Neither *Vita* knows the name of Winefride's mother (Gwenlo); neither knows that Beuno (both *Vitae*), and Eleri and Tenoi (in Robert's *Vita* only) are related to Winefride via her mother's family. The later Welsh, fourteenth century, *Life of Beuno*, *Buchedd Beuno*, similarly does not know that Winefride and Beuno were related. The Winefride account in the Buchedd appears not to depend upon either of the two *Vitae Wenefredae*, but upon a third, unknown source possibly the putative *Vita sanctae Beunoni*; and thus provides an independent witness to the tradition. I am grateful to T. Gray Hulse for this information.

16. Translation quoted from *The Life of Saint Winefride, Virgin and Martyr*, ed. Thomas Swift, SJ, (Holywell, 1888), pp. 6–12. Father Swift based his *Life* upon Carolus de Smedt, SJ, *Acta Sanctarum Novembris I* (Parisiis, 1887), pp. 691–759. Swift's name-forms, which follow the medieval Latin text, have been brought into line with modern Welsh orthography.

17. Cadfan (d. *c.*625), early king of Gwynedd. His gravestone is in Llangadwaladr church, Anglesey. The translation of the inscription from Latin reads: King Catamanus (Cadfan in Welsh) wisest (and) most renowned of all kings (lies here).

18. *Robert's Life* does not mention 'the sons of Selyf', and his knowledge of Beuno apart from the Holywell episode is limited.

19. *Robert's Life* shows no knowledge of Tyfid's three 'manors' or his obligations in Welsh Law on the alienation of land to the Church.

20. In *Robert's Life* Tyfid's donation of land to Beuno is given on condition that Beuno instructs his daughter Winefride, and her vocation is due to his influence. In the *Anonymous Life* Winefride has decided before the arrival of Beuno to become a nun.

21. In *Robert's Life* Winefride remains at home because she is ill, and Caradog (son of Alaog) is a prince and a king's son. In the *Anonymous Life* Caradog is 'a prince of royal birth.'

22. In the *Anon Life* Caradog pursues Winefride on horseback. She reaches the threshold of the church before the prince strikes her. In *Robert's Life* Caradog catches Winefride near the Church, on a slope ,which causes her decapitated head to roll into Church while the body remains outside where it fell. Robert omits mention of the horse,

23. In *Robert's Life* Beuno witnesses Caradog cleaning his sword on the grass, and when he curses him the Prince 'melted and disappeared,' 'many' affirming that the earth had opened and swallowed the body into hell. Beuno finishes saying Mass before restoring Winefrede to life, after which she bears a scar at the place of the fatal blow which is white "like a thread" round her neck. In the *Anonymous Life* it is merely a 'slender scar.'

24. In the *Anonymous Life* Beuno leaves Holywell immediately after his request that Winefride send him a cloak. In *Robert's Life* Beuno continues to give her instruction and veils her as a nun, and specifically names 'St Beuno's Stone,' although he omits the fact that he was accustomed to pray on it.

25. Robert gives seven years as the time Winefride spent in Holywell after the departure of Beuno. He relates the story of the cloak being sent annually as arranged, but does not mention it being transported by *Maen Beuno* to the landing place of Sachlen.

26. *Robert's Life* rejects the tale of Winefride's pilgrimage to Rome. He doesn't mention 'the Synod of Winefride'. The *Anonymous Life* places Winefride's second death at Gwytherin on the same date as her martyrdom, 22 June (this must have been a specifically Holywell tradition); for Robert, the second death occurs on 2 November (clearly, the Gwytherin tradition). After Winefride's departure from Holywell, Robert is (excepting the tradition of the Roman pilgrimage and the Synod) our only source for the life of Winefride, as known to Welsh tradition. Details of *Robert's Life* are given below in the text.

27. This quotation from *Buchedd Beuno* is from Bishop Fleetwood's translation in *The Works of William Fleetwood* (Oxford, 1854), 3 vols, vol. 3, pp. 322–3.

28. New Testament: St Matthew, ch 11, v, 4f and St Luke, ch 7, v. 2

29. H. Pryce, *Native Laws and the Church in Medieaval Wales* (Clarendon, Oxford, 1993) p. 70.

30. Ibid, pp. 39–40.

31. R. Pepin and H. Feiss, Two Mediaeval *Lives* of Saint Winefride (Wipf and Stock Publishers, Eugene, Oregon, 2004) (previously published by Peregrina 2000), H. Feiss, *Anonymous Life*, pp. 103–4.

32. Pryce, op cit, p. 165f.

33. Ibid, p. 177.

34. Swift, p. 25 the following quotations from Swift are from *Robert's Life.*

35. ibid, p. 28.

36. ibid, p. 25.

37. ibid, p. 28.

38. H. W. Owen and R. Morgan, *Dictionary of Place-Names of Wales* (Gomer, 2007), p. 197.

39. From Hopkin's unfinished verse-drama, *St Winefrid's Well*. W. H. Gardner (ed), *Poems and Prose of Gerard Manley Hopkins* (Harmondsworth, 1953 & 1974), p. 72–7 at p. 77.

40. S. Baring Gould and J. Fisher, *Lives of the British Saints,* vol. 3, p.191 'The red ferruginous veins in the stone of the well, and the crimson Muscus subrubeus or (Lin) Byssus iolithus found growing on them in the water, was easily supposed to be the blood of the martyr miraculously reproduced in testimony to the truth of the story.'

41. Swift, op cit, pp. 28/9.

42. ibid, p 32.

43. M. Drayton, *Polyolbion Song X*, 1612, J. W. Hebel (ed), (Blackwell, Oxford, 1933), pp. 204–5.

44. *Analecta Bollandinana 6,* 1887, pp. 313, 315.

45. Swift, op cit, p. 33.

46. *Anonymous Life*, s.7.

47. *Anonymous Life*, miracle, 15.

48. It may still be seen in Ffynnon Fair, Cefn Meiriadog, near St Asaph.

49. Drayton, op cit.

50. Catholic Record Society (abbrev. CRS), vol. 24, 1922, pp. 110–11. Neither of the mosses at Holywell have survived the chemical treatment of the water.

51. Swift, op cit, p. 19.

52. Swift, ibid, p. 33.

53. Swift, ibid, pp. 11/12.

54. Swift, p. 49.

55. 1398, Winefride's feast was made obligatory throughout the Canterbury Province (south England and Wales); that is from this time, the observance of her feast on 3 November was obligatory in every church throughout the Province.

56. Swift, paraphrase, pp. 31/2.

57. Swift, ibid, pp. 44/5.

58 Swift, p. 48.

59. N. Edwards and A. Lane, *The Early Church in Wales and the West* (Oxbow 16, 1992), p. 9.

60. NLW, St Asaph Rural Deans Reports 1729, NLW MS SA/RD/18

61 N. Edwards and T. Gray Hulse, 'A Fragment of a Reliquary Casket from Gwytherin, North Wales,'

The Antiquaries Journal, 72 (1992), 91–101. All the writers quoted here are referenced in this article. 62. Critical edition and translation of the carol in Maredudd ap Huw, 'A critical examination of Welsh Poetry relating to the native saints of North Wales (c.1350-1670)', unpublished PhD thesis, University of Oxford, 2001: text and translation, pp. 204–22; notes, 395–7.

2. The development of the Cult

The powerful portrayal of St Winefride in her two twelfth-century lives provided a physical focus for her veneration. The devout could visit the sacred places associated with her. Prior Robert of Shrewsbury had provided the kind of publicity that was designed to attract pilgrims. The Holywell spring, the Shrewsbury shrine and, to a lesser extent, Winefride's chapel and reliquary at Gwytherin, became part of the pilgrim's itinerary throughout the Middle Ages and beyond.

Control of these sacred places became the concern and responsibility of the Church. The most powerful and widespread religious institutions in post-conquest Norman period were the monasteries which were in a unique position to fulfil the role of institutional guardian of the cult of a saint. They could provide what was necessary for the welfare of all. The honour of the saint was promoted and protected through worship and a liturgical framework was established in the monastery itself and in the places associated with the cult. At Holywell the church above St Winefride's well was ideally situated for essential devotions such as veneration, litany, procession, vigil, mass, exorcism and thanksgiving.

23. Holywell church.

Eventually, copies of the lives of the saints began to circulate amongst learned clerics and between monasteries to be read in public worship. There was the possibility of a European dissemination of information through the chapters of the various monastic orders and the interest of the Norman magnates. The monastery possessed the resources and manpower to provide hospitality and almsgiving to pilgrims. The founders of these religious houses were the most powerful men in the land: superstitious, pious and wealthy Norman magnates, usually with the support of bishops and the king himself. In north and mid Wales the princes of Gwynedd and Powys were equally protective and concerned about the holy places that came to them by turn of conquest. The possession by a monastery of a church, tithes and monetary offerings associated with a sacred place became a valuable part of their economy and were jealously safeguarded throughout their existence until dissolved in the late 1530s.

As we have seen from the lives, St Winefride's 'territory', in Tegeingl, in north-east Wales, was subject to political unrest for six or seven hundred years until the Edwardian settlement in 1284. In 1170, after the conquest, the Norman earl Hugh succeeded the Saxon earl Edwin of Mercia, as the dominant political force in Tegeingl. Hugh Lupus, earl of Chester, with the advice of Anselm, re-founded the former Saxon monastery as the Benedictine abbey of St Werburgh in Chester and in 1093 Countess Adeliza was granted Holywell church with St Winefride's well attached. As long as successive Norman earls retained their hold over Tegeingl, St Winefride's 'territory' was under their influence and they could give the well and church above it to whom they pleased and so could the princes of Gwynedd when in turn the well fell into their hands. In this way, control over St Winefride's well changed hands throughout the period from *c.*1093 to 1240. St Winefride's well, together with Holywell church, passed to the Benedictine monastery of St Werburgh and, when they lost it to Basingwerk Abbey, the newly established religious house in Flintshire founded in *c.*1131 on the bank of the river Dee below Holywell. The site of this first foundation is uncertain although Hen Blas, at Coleshill, a little further to the east of Basingwerk, has been suggested.[1]

It is obvious from Robert's *Life of Winefride* written in 1138 that it had its origins in the newly-created cultic site at Shrewsbury. Furthermore, that the monks from there were aided by their fellow Benedictines at Chester to whom the cultic sites at St Winifred's well and Holywell church then belonged. What is not clear is where the *Anonymous Life* was written, why and when it was composed and if there are any textual relations between the two lives. These questions have been discussed at length by Fiona Winward[2] who in the course of her study mentions the possibility of the rival cultic centres at Basingwerk or St Werburgh's monasteries as possible places for authorship at various times in the twelfth century. The common source deriving from the lost Latin *Life of Beuno* mentioned above is also discussed as well as Welsh and English influences in the composition of the *Anonymous Life*.

Summary of main political events affecting the possession of Holywell Church and St Winefride's Well, 1093–1240

1093 Hugh Lupus Earl of Chester (d. 1101) gave Holywell Church with St Winefrides Well to his wife Adeliza who gave it to the monks of St Werburgh's, Chester.[3]

1119 Charter of Earl Richard (1101–20) confirmed the grant of Burel to the monks of St Werburgh's of 'the church of Holywell with the tithes of his mill and all his substance.'[4]

1115 and 1119 pilgrimages of Earl Richard to St Winefride's Well.[5]

1131 Earl Ranulph II (1128/9–53) founded a house of Savignac monks at Basingwerk.[6] to whom in 1135 Robert de Pierrepoint granted the town and Church of Holywell.[7]

1135 the Normans were expelled from Gwynedd. Holywell Church and St Winefride's Well belonged to Basingwerk until c.1153.[8]
King Stephen (1135–54)
Owain Gwynedd Prince of Gwynedd (1137–70).

1138 Prior Robert translated St Winefride's relics from Gwytherin to Shrewsbury.
Earl Hugh 11 (1153–81)
King Henry II (1154–89).

1157 Holywell Church and St Winefride's Well granted by Henry II to St Werburgh's Abbey.[9]

1147 Savignac order absorbed by Cistercian's, a daughter house of Combermere 1154., assigned to Buildwas 1156.[10]

1157 The 1131 monastery said to have been refounded on a new site at Basingwerk by Henry II.[11]
King Henry II rebuilt the Castle at Basingwerk said to have been destroyed there in the reign of Stephen.[12] It was razed to the ground in 1167 by Owain Gwynedd.[13]
Earl Hugh II (1153–81) Henry II (1154–89).

1159 Henry II is said to have established a house of Knight's Templar at Basingwerk. This is discounted by David Knowles.[14]

1188 Visitation of Archbishop Baldwin of Canterbury to Wales accompanied by Giraldus Cambrensis. They stay at Basingwerk. There is no mention of St Winefride's Well by them.[15]
Pilgrimage by King Richard 1 (1189–99) sometime during his brief visit to his English Kingdom when he was attacked by the Welsh.[16]

*c.*1196 Llywelyn ap Iorwerth 'the Great' (1197–1240) Holywell Church and St Winefride's Well granted to Basingwerk.[17] 'In the wars with the princes of Wales the monks of St Werburgh's have lost their church at Hallewell which was £100 value.'[18]

1209 Earl Ranulph 111 (1181–1232) built a castle on the hill above Holywell.[19]

1240 Confirmation by Dafydd ap Llywelyn (d.1246) of his grants to Basingwerk Abbey including the Church of Holywell.[20]

1253 a request was made to the General Chapter of the Cistercian Order for the Feast of St Winefride to be a major feast of twelve lessons at both Buildwas and Basingwerk. Abbeys.[21]

The complexities of the political situation and strife between Welsh princes in their opposition to English kings and earls of Chester and the effect it had on the major cultic centres at Holywell, Basingwerk and St Werburgh's from 1093–1240 is shown on the table of events on page 47.

As far as the fortunes of St Winefride were concerned the decade of the 1130s was the most significant of the twelfth century. The strong Norman king, Henry I, died in 1135, to be succeeded by the weak King Stephen (1135–54). The strong and able military leader Owain Gwynedd gained power in 1137 in the neighbouring Welsh kingdom. Henry II, during his long reign from 1154–89, reasserted Norman power in Tegeingle and is said to have refounded Basingwerk Abbey in 1157. This political uncertainty was to last until 1284 with frequent changes of fortune in Tegeingle. The monastery of Basingwerk was in a crucial and vulnerable position trying to maintain allegiance to, and favour of, whichever power was in the ascendancy during this long period of strife. The small monastery was at the crossroads of power, a valuable place for truce and negotiation. St Winefride's well continued as a place of pilgrimage for those willing to face the trials of travelling in an area too often the scene of conflict.

The church by the well

A church is still sited on this spot,[22] very close to the well and just above it to the south-east, within a few yards of the stream that flows to the estuary of the Dee at Greenfield. If the traditions upon which the early lives are based are correct, it was Beuno who was the founder and builder of the first church when he came there at the beginning of the seventh century. In the *Anonymous Life* he is said to have 'built a small church in the ravine called 'Sechnant' (*Sychnant*, 'dry valley'), in which he celebrated Mass'. In *Robert's Life*, Winefride's father, Tyfid, 'handed over to the blessed man that manor on which to build a church and construct dwellings for the servants of God to stay therein'. Robert's account seems to say a great deal about the church property belonging to Beuno and of Winefride's sending him an annual gift to Clynnog Fawr.

There are the odd references, which suggest an ancient foundation. For example, in *Valor Ecclesiasticus*, the official valuation of the wealth of Basingwerk made to the Crown in 1535, it is stated under 'Temporalities': 'Rent paid to St Bewnon [Beuno], per annum, without the domain of Holywell … 2 shillings.'[23] Beuno's name occurs on the hill to the west of the church in *Ffynnon Beuno* and *Gerddi Beuno*, an early settlement area of quillets or lynchets. There is another reference in a charter by Llywelyn the Great, granted sometime between 1196 and 1202, which suggests that Holywell church was portionary, that is, it was made up of a body of inherited canons, who shared 'portions' of the revenue from the land attached to the church. If this is proved, there will be no doubt that Holywell was an early Welsh, rather than a Norman, foundation.

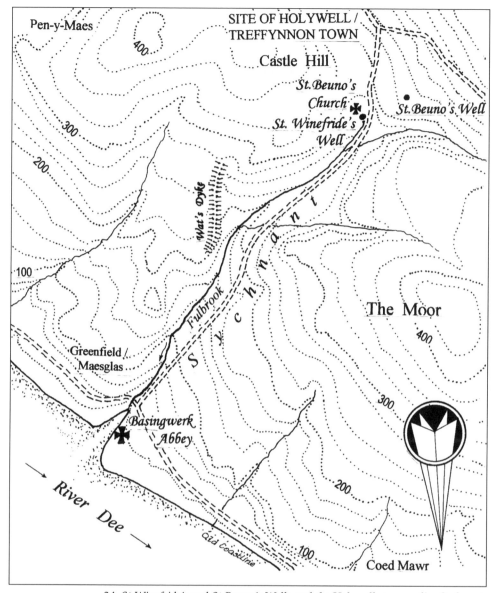

24. *St Winefride's and St Beuno's Wells and the Holywell stream, alias Sychnant.*

Grant in pure and perpetual alms for the relief of the poverty of the monks and for the souls of himself and of his father, mother and ancestors, of the church of Holywell with all its appurtenances, saving the rights which the clerks Absolom, Ivo and Adam have therein as long as they live, so that once vacant each prebend shall revert fully to the monks.[24]

There is significant place-name and archaeological evidence for Saxon settlement in the valley of the stream which runs from St Winefride's well down to the estuary at Basingwerk. The name Halliwel – Holywell; Angles' field; –

Englefield; Basingwerk, deriving from Basing (Basa's people) and werk (*weorc* earthwork fortification), an obvious reference to Wat's Dyke that was constructed before Offa's Dyke which dates from the late eighth century.[25] In 821, Cenwulf king of Mercia, died at the 'fort' of Bassa.

It is a little disconcerting not to find St Winefride's well nor the church above it, mentioned in Domesday Book in 1086, nor is a priest recorded, although there were four in Flintshire. However, the authors failed to record churches and other manorial property which are known to have existed. But there are townships listed such as Fulbrook and Wellstone. However, we have the first written record of the church at Holywell in 1093 seven years after Domesday. In this first Norman recording of the church the pattern is established of it being granted to a monastic foundation. The sequence of the possession of the church was to alternate between the monks of St Werburgh's in Chester and Basingwerk Abbey.

Holywell church in the possession of St Werburgh's abbey in Chester

The summary given above shows that St Werburgh's held Holywell church in the early part of the twelfth century, until 1135 when it was lost in the reign of King Stephen and returned to them twenty years later, in the reign of Henry II, by Earl Hugh II (1153–81) who 'gave the church of Holywell with all its appurtenances for the use of the monks, and one dwelling plot of the said town, sixty feet in length.'[26] Towards the end of the twelfth century 'in the wars with the princes of Wales they lost their church' and *c*.1196 it was granted by Llwelyn ap Iorwerth to Basingwerk Abbey.

The foundation of Basingwerk Abbey

In 1131–2, Ranulf II, earl of Chester (1129–53), invited monks from the abbey of Savigny in south-west Normandy to settle in Tegeingl, probably somewhere between the present towns of Holywell and Flint, but not where the present abbey ruins stand.[27] Ranulf was generous to the monks giving them the manor of Fulbrook and a silver mine there.

In 1147, the monasteries of the order of Savigny were incorporated into those of the Cistercian order. Ten years later, the newly constituted monastic community at Basingwerk received a charter of confirmation from King Henry II and was placed under the supervision of Buildwas Abbey in Shropshire.

Henry II's charter of 1157 restored the abbey's fortunes. From him they received the manor of Glossop in Derbyshire, which was to become their most valuable asset and what they valued more, his political protection during these most troublesome times. The monks at Chester recorded: '1157 In this year (the abbey of) Basingwerk is founded. A battle royal fought at Coleshill, in which Eustace the constable perished with many of his comrades; and King Henry fortified Rhuddlan and Basingwerk, and conquered the Welsh.'[28] Henry II had won back Tegeingl which had been lost in 1149. He was determined to hold it and to this

25. Basingwerk Abbey 'North West View'. Engraving by S. and N. Buck 1742.

end he rebuilt the earth and timber castle of Basingwerk which had been destroyed during Stephen's reign. It is said that in 1159 Henry provided further protection for the monks and the pilgrims visiting St Winefride's well by establishing a house of Knights Templar there.[29] They were a religious brotherhood, founded in Jerusalem some forty years previously, to protect Christian pilgrims in the Holy Land, and to fight to safeguard the territory conquered by the Crusaders. A strange and chivalric guardianship of warrior-monks to protect the territory of the Welsh virgin martyr from her countrymen. An uneasy peace was maintained until 1165 when Prince Owain Gwynedd hit back. After his death, his son Dafydd swore fealty to the English king. He was removed in 1197 and was succeeded by his nephew Llywelyn ab Iorwerth, 'the Great' (1173–1240), who until his death in 1240 was to hold most of the Perfeddwlad. But the earl of Chester, Ranulf III (d.1232), was not going to give up without a fight and in 1210 raised a castle at Holywell to fortify what was now a frontier zone and protect the pilgrims.[30]

The princes of Gwynedd, Llywellyn the Great and his son Dafydd (1240–46), were now in a position to show their favour to the Cistercians. Llywellyn gave them the church of Holywell, St Winefride's well, Gelli grange, pasture land and confirmed old gifts and made new ones, as did his son when he succeeded him.[31] For the gift of land in Penllyn and Llyn Tegid at Bala, the princes expected some recompense in the form of customary Welsh gifts of food, *gwestfa*, provisions of bread, butter, fish and cheese for a hunting party of 300 of their men once a year. Dafydd's successor, Llywelyn ap Gruffudd (1246–82), increased this requirement to supply 500 men with two foals and money in lieu if they did not hunt.[32]

Soon after they had received their charter from Dafydd ap Llewellyn in 1240 the monks of Basingwerk were faced with an uncertain political situation. This

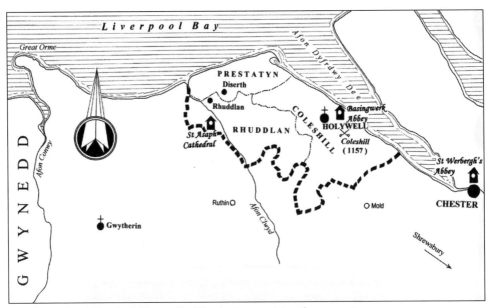

26. *The Medieval Hundred* (Cantref) *of Tegeingl, comprising the commotes* (cymedau) *of Coleshill, Prestatyn and Rhuddlan.*

continued throughout the rule of Llywelyn ap Gruffydd, (d.1282) who prospered at first because of the weakness of the English king, Henry III, and opposed him by supporting his enemy Simon de Montfort (d.1265). Relations with the English Crown deteriorated further on the accession of Edward I in 1272. Llywelyn persistently refused to do homage to him and the king decided to break him. There was no lasting peace until this happened. The monastery at Basingwerk was in a buffer zone which frequently turned into a battlefield. At this time the bishop of St Asaph 'was forced owing to the ruin of the diocese by fire and slaughter, to beg and live on borrowed money'.[33]

The final crisis was reached after 1277. The monastery was on the invasion route to Llywelyn's heartland west of the Conwy and, to make the passage safer, the English king ordered the monks to cut down their wood at Gelli. Basingwerk was thus clearly identified with the invading English host. Although they were given letters of protection from the king, their property suffered since the invaders lived off the land. It was reported after the death of

27. *Arms of Owain Gwynedd (died 1170), Prince of North Wales, to be seen on the chapter stalls in Bangor Cathedral*

Llewellyn 1282 and the final Welsh defeat in 1283 that:

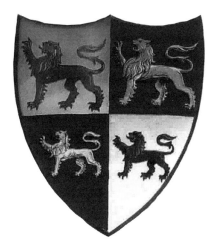

Sailors of the Cinque Ports, who were in the King's expedition in Wales, and their servants entered the granges of the abbot of Basingwerk at Caldey in Wirral and took away goods to the value of £9. Other granges in Englefield suffered when certain persons of the King's expedition stole corn, other goods, drove away animals, and did damage to the value of £40. Members of the household of William le Botiler entered 'a town of the abbey called Haliwelle, burned it and drove away animals of the abbot and his villeins to the value of £8.' The King' soldiers took colts and mares to the value of £10 from the abbot's stud, and corn of the tithes of the church at Haliwell worth £20. Further injury was committed when Prince Llewellyn, and his brother Dafydd entered the abbey and took £10 sterling and two horses valued at £10.[34]

28. Arms of Llywelyn ap Iorwerth (Llywelyn the Great), Prince of North Wales 1196-1240, to be seen on the chapter stalls in Bangor Cathedral.

This claim for damages gives some indication of the prosperity of the abbey and some of its possessions in Holywell, other parts of Tegeingl and on the Wirral. There were other properties outside Wales which remained unmolested, for example, Glossop in Derbyshire.

Compensation in north Wales, amounting to about £1,700 for war damaged churches was paid out on 3 November (Feast of St Winefride) 1284, at Chester. Basingwerk Abbey received £100 in damages, Philip, the vicar of Holywell, sixty shillings compensation, John, monk of Basingwerk, one mark (13s. 4p. – 66 n p), as the abbot's agent. He was described as 'procurator of Holywell church' and amongst his duties was the collection of tithes and pilgrims' offerings. The other cleric who received compensation of one mark was Madog 'chaplain of Holywell'.[35]

From such payments we may speculate on the relationship between the abbey and the local church at Holywell. Three clerics were mentioned as holding some office in the town of Holywell as surrogates or assistants to the abbot. There may have been more. In the claim by the abbey authorities relating to the extensive damage caused in the town of Holywell there is no mention of any particular premise relating to or designated as 'St Winefride's Well'. But compensation was paid to the vicar for damage to the church. The church building was probably the only substantial structure associated with the well at this time for the use of pilgrims. We have seen that *Robert's Life* of Winefride, written about 150 years previously, is fairly accurate about topographical details and the miracles in both lives are detailed in their mention of the church, mill and stream. Whatever arrangements were in place they must have seemed satisfactory to both the monks and the pilgrims. The thirteenth century drew to a close with a political settlement enforced on the Welsh, which was to bring peace until the destructive uprising of Owain Glyndŵr a hundred years later. The cult of St Winefride had taken hold and her guardians at Basingwerk remained firm in their devotion to her cause.

The development of the cult; pilgrimage

Pilgrimage throughout the Middle Ages was one of the universal features of the Christian Church. It spilled out beyond Europe to Jerusalem in the Holy Land. It was more than a journey to the places associated with Jesus and his Apostles. It became a series of military crusades to recapture the holy city from Islam undertaken by European kings at the direction of the Pope. The prize was more than territorial conquest, it was the salvation of the immortal soul and the welfare of the body.

On the *Mappa Mundi* in Hereford Cathedral, Jerusalem is placed at the centre of the world. This was the most important place for pilgrims to visit and other journeys took them to Rome to view the relics and holy places of the chief apostles Peter and Paul and the tombs of martyrs. The popes issued pilgrims there with plenary indulgences,[36] granting them full remission from purgatorial punishment in jubilee years. Equally popular after the ninth century was Santiago de Compostela in Spain where the corpse of the apostle St James the Greater, martyred by King Herod, was discovered. St James is represented in art as the archetypal pilgrim and Sir Walter Raleigh even after the Reformation took him as his model.

> Give me my scallop-shell of Quiet
> My staff of Faith to walk upon;
> My scrip of Joy, immortal diet;
> My bottle of Salvation;
> My gown of Glory, hope's true gage;
> And thus I'll take my pilgrimage.[37]

Pilgrimages undertaken overseas today might be seen as international, but in the Middle Ages, they were regarded as merely travelling from one part of Christendom to another; the Church was universal. Christian Europe was then a cultural unity, with its peoples sharing common values of charity, belief in miracles, veneration of saints and their power to aid the penitent sinner and those afflicted by sickness with no other remedy but a visit to a shrine or healing well.

Each nation had its own special saints, and sacred places: St Albans, Canterbury

(Thomas à Becket), St Davids, Durham (Cuthbert), Bury St Edmunds, Hereford (Thomas Cantilupe), Lincoln (Hugh), Lichfield (Chad), the shrines of Our Lady and many others. These saints were biblical, martyrs of the early church, Saxon, Norman, Welsh, Scots, Irish, Cornish, and were remembered daily in rotation in Church calendars and the liturgy. Other saints became the patrons of local guilds or were relied upon to perform particular favours. As the Middle Ages drew to a close, the images of saints were magnificent, prolific, omnipresent, and they were the chief ornament of rood screens, wall paintings, and stained glass. The cult of the saint was also a private matter reserved to the individual in their domestic devotions by the ownership, design and use of their own prayer diary, the book of hours.

Why did pilgrims come to St Winefride's Well? One answer is that the cult of St Winefride became popular through her twelfth century lives and other versions, which

29. St Winefride.

circulated in the late Middle Ages. She had her own feast day and lessons in the Sarum Calendar used in the Province of Canterbury. Most effective, however, in drawing pilgrims to Holywell was the reputation of her well gained as a curative shrine where people could find healing, spiritual comfort and make their devotions and offerings to their spiritual protector. The path to the well became a familiar part of the pilgrims' route.

An anonymous medieval poem, *Cywydd Gwenfrewi a'i Ffynon* [A *cywydd* to Gwenfrewi and her well][38] (lines 35–64), describes the reputation of the healing well and the cures received at Holywell.

> *Gwenfrewi loywgu lwys,*
> *Bur odiaeth, o baradwys,*
> *Hon a gafas gan Iesu*
> *Ystôr, fawr ei hystori fu.*
> *Y deillion o dywyllwg*
> *I oleuni, di a'u dwg;*
> *Os byddar fydd gwâr gwirion,*
> *Fe glyw fry'r galw o'r fron;*
> *Y mudion a gai ymadrodd*

Gloyw bur, a'i gael o'i bodd.
Os crupul trachul heb droed,
Fe ddaw adre' ar ddeudroed
A bwrw'r ffon gron gryno
I ffordd a myned ar ffo!
Fe gâi ynfadwyr ynfydion
Synnwyr deg, os yno don'
Gan y ferch y sy'berchen
Ar iechyd y byd o'i ben.
Os cleifion efryddion fydd,
Hi a'u lleinw mewn llawenydd.
O bob gwlad yn ffynadwy
I'r ffynnon a ddôn' bob ddwy;
Pob dwyfil dieiddil y dôn'
Ar ffyniant, bawb i'r ffynnon
I brofi muragl purwin
A'i flas ymhell na'r gwin.
Iachâ'r byd, gloywbryd glwys,
A tho' eneeidie' 'mharadwys;
Dyro inni oleuni'r wledd
A bodd Duw ni bydd diwedd.

[35] Bright and dear [and] beautiful Genfrewi,/ exceptionally pure, of paradise/ obtained from Jesus/ a treasure whose renown was great./ [39] The blind from darkness/ to light you bring;/ if a gentle innocent be deaf,/ he hears above the call from the hill;/ the dumb would obtain/ bright and pure speech obtaining it by her favour./ [45] If it be an emaciated cripple without a foot,/ he will return home on two feet,/ and cast away the stout [and] useful stick/ and flee!/ [49] Foolish madmen would obtain/ the sense of ten men, if they come there,/ from the girl who is owner/ of the health of the world throughout it./ If there be disabled [and] sick,/ she will fill them with joy.[55]/ From every country in twos [i.e. the countries]/ they come happily to the well;/ every two thousand [people] come vigorously [and] happily./ All to the well/ to experience the miracle of pure wine/ whose taste is far better than wine./ [61] Heal the world, one of beautiful fair appearance,/ and place souls in paradise;/ give unto us the light of the feast/ to which, God willing there will be no end.

Who could resist such an invitation to receive the power and favour of St Winefride and the blessing of healing at her well? Pilgrims who had experienced such a miraculous cure would not leave it unrecorded. Many of the sick pilgrims had nowhere else to turn. They came desperate men and women, as a last resort believing that St Winefride would grant them that most precious gift, restoration of health. Their journey was invariably made through the help of their local community and at their bidding as a modern pilgrimage is to Lourdes. Many of the medieval poems in Welsh to St Winefride mention the part played by the eucharist in healing and as restoration to the community in the body of Christ. Their neighbours would suggest that a particular saint might be able to help them and they would join in an act of corporate intercession to the saint.

In the Middle Ages when scientific knowledge of healing was practically non-existent, people were more ready to believe that healing was most likely to have taken place through the intervention of God and the favour of his saint rather than in some instances naturally. Later in the story of healing at St Winefride's Well in the sixteenth and seventeenth centuries more detailed narrative accounts of cures will be considered. Local newspapers contain detailed narrative accounts of cures at the well from the end of the nineteenth century onwards and in the twentieth century many accounts of cures have been kept.

The reason why pilgrimages have been undertaken to St Winefride's Well down the centuries has remained the same. It is primarily a journey in faith to a holy place involving sacrifice and self-discipline. The experience is meant to be self-illuminating, a journey in union with God, a true 'pilgrim's progress' in the sense in which John Bunyan described it. A series of trials and tests bringing the believer closer to God with a fuller realisation of his own spiritual needs. As that great fourteenth century mystic Margery Kempe put it: 'I asked the Lord if I should go on a journey; he said, "Go in my name. I will go with you and bring you back in safety."' Pilgrims have a goal to come to St Winefride's Well to say their prayers in the saint's company. There is always spiritual benefit, a cure of the soul, if not a miracle of bodily healing. The scene has always been as Celia Fiennes described it 1698 'an abundance of the devout on their knees … all round the Well'.

In the Middle Ages the preparation for a pilgrimage was organised and blessed by the participant's community. If the pilgrimage was far distant and across the seas extra precautionary arrangements were made. All debts were settled, permission received from the overlord, and letters of commendation issued recognising the bearer as a pilgrim as distinct from a wanderer, to enable him or her to receive privileges of alms and lodgings. The local church ceremoniously equipped him in pilgrim's garb; scrip, staff and hat which were sprinkled with holy water. To emphasise that they were being sent on a religious mission, the pilgrims made their confession and before parting joined with their community in the eucharist. Finally their guild or fraternity escorted them to the city gate and the great adventure began.

Pilgrims were not alone on the road. Following one of the established pilgrimage routes which crossed Britain and Europe, they would meet en route a variety of others making the same journey, in the hostels situated within a day's walk, or at other shrines. By the fourteenth century St Winefride's Well was one of the major shrines to be visited and one of the places contained within in the vast triangle of pilgrim centres as far away as the holy well of Jesmond Dene in Northumberland and Walsingham in Norfolk.[39] Some pilgrims travelled in organised groups like those Chaucer immortalised as they journeyed from the Tabor Inn to Canterbury intent on enjoying themselves: well-seasoned travellers, no stranger to such an enterprises, like the experienced Wife of Bath who had been everywhere and savoured every adventure. Other pilgrims, under safe-conduct, were compelled to make their journeys by a magistrate or ecclesiastical court as a penance to purge themselves of the crimes they had committed. They were easily recognised by their garments, and if they had committed a capital crime by chains about their necks, arms and waists. Minstrels would accompany some groups, tales would be exchanged and useful information obtained. One thing all pilgrims were keen to learn was the benefit they could obtain from visiting certain shrines or holy places.

Many pilgrimages were embarked upon to obtain an indulgence for the pilgrims and those they represented. Their families and neighbours who benefited from such an investment financed the pilgrims for this purpose. It was of immense spiritual value mitigating their punishment after death, for an indulgence gave them some reduction from their time in Purgatory, the place where the soul went after death to be purged of sin before entering into eternal salvation. This 'temporal punishment' could be lessened by the granting of an indulgence. The specific time granted in an indulgence referred to the amount of punishment that would have been remitted by the same length of time in undertaking canonical penance. Only the Pope could grant a full release or plenary indulgence, but generally shorter periods of remission were granted. No indulgence ever gave the power to release pilgrims from guilt as well as penance. confession was therefore an essential preparation to every pilgrimage. Indulgences could be obtained to aid the repairs of damaged churches and shrines if visited by the pilgrim.[40] In 1427, the abbot of Basingwerk was licensed to dispense Pope Martin V's indulgence for a period of ten years. It specified a period of remission 'of a year and forty days penance to penitents who visited the well on the principal feasts of the year and dedication, the octaves of six of them, and the six days of Whitsun week, and of a hundred days to those who during the said octaves and days, visit and give alms for the repair of the Chapel of Saint Winefride the Virgin, called Holliwell whose buildings are collapsed'.[41] The buildings under the shadow of the nearby Castle Hill had suffered destruction during the rebellion of Owain Glyndŵr (1400–06), together with the tower of the existing church which probably dates from this period.

The pilgrims may have approached Holywell from Chester and, whilst there, visited the relics of St Werburgh and the Rood. Leaving the city they could take the route to St Davids or turn along the north-Wales coast to other centres such as Clynnog and the two ancient pilgrim paths of Llŷn.

One may imagine what the experience of the pilgrim on reaching Holywell was.[42] In the Greenfield valley, on the road to the well, the pilgrims found prayer stations.[43] Some of them would have spent the night at the abbey, in the accommodation provided for them, where they would, if necessary, receive alms or medical attention before the final mile to the Well. The Benedictine Rule prescribed that all guests should be received, both rich and poor. As late as the end of the fifteenth and the beginning of the sixteenth centuries, Abbot Thomas Pennant had built substantial accommodation for pilgrims. Tudur Aled reported that the guests there were so numerous that they had to be accommodated for meals at two sittings. In all probability local inns and alehouses also provided hospitality. King Richard II is said to have visited St Winefride's shrine at Holywell in 1398[44] and on 16 August Benedict, vicar of Holywell, received a

30. *Pope Martin V who, in 1427, granted an Indulgence to pilgrims visiting the Well the proceeds of which were devoted to the repair of the buildings at the Well or Church at Holywell*

grant from the king 'of sixpence a day, being about to erect a house at Holywell where poor pilgrims visiting St Winefrides might be received and entertained'.[45] No doubt King Richard was so beleaguered by his enemies at this time that he directed Archbishop Walden to further the cult of St Winefride by ordering the celebration of her festival with nine lessons along with those of David and Chad. At the opposite end of the pilgrim's route at St Davids the bishops had, in 1287 and 1385, made special provisions in the cathedral statutes for pilgrims, taking them into their protection and building 'a hospital in which wearied travellers may be entertained'.[46] This obligation was common to monastic orders and no doubt observed at Basingwerk and in the town of Holywell being under the abbot's jurisdiction.

Having reached Basingwerk the pilgrims were on the last lap of their journey, the climax of which would take place the next day after a short night's rest. Their arrival was on the eve of the Feast of St Winefride's Martyrdom, her decollation on June 22, a long summer's day to savour the delights of celebrating not only Winefride's Day but whatever favour she could bestow on them. If accommodation was scarce, the weather was probably favourable for sleeping out in makeshift shelters in the abbey grounds. The abbey's bells and the birdsong from the nearby woods would rouse them at dawn and after washing in the stream they were ready to start for the shrine following the stream a mile or so up hill. The monks provided a simple breakfast of milk and bread and fish from the river or nearby seashore. Their meal finished, led by a Cistercian brother to guide them, excitedly they set off to the shrine. After three hundred yards the guide halted the procession at a prayer station to point to the pathway leading to the site where Winefride kept her convent before she left for Gwytherin. After simple devotions, the monk would point out to sea to the north-west and traced for them the route Beuno's cloak escorted by the curlew was borne on his rock to Clynnog. Then they continued climbing the hill clutching tight their pilgrim's staffs and singing a psalm. The sick were tenderly carried St Christopher-like by the strongest, with their guide reassuring them that they would soon be in the presence of St Winefride.

The earth was wearing its rich garment of trinity green and the trees flowered in white blossom for the festival. Ahead southwards the sun was beginning its course up the hill before them. They did not follow the cold clear winter star as the wisemen did at mid-winter but the warm brilliant sun at the summer solstice. They looked for their own physical and spiritual rebirth in the water of Winefride's Well. And they had a foretaste of what awaited them as they caught the reflection of the myriad dazzle and dance of the sun in the clear water of the spring stream as it tumbled joyfully down to the sea. It was as the priest poet described it centuries later 'pale water, frail water, wild and reeling water in this leafy lean over...moist and musical'.[47] After another stop they made the final ascent.

On turning the next corner they were met by the familiar sight of a shrine in festive mood. It seemed as if the whole world were present. Rather like the day of Pentecost with people speaking in tongues, mostly, it must be admitted, in the language of the native Welsh excitedly, melodiously, and demonstratively selling their wares and directing strangers to their stalls. Beggars there were in abundance lying on both banks of the stream, blocking the way to the church and the healing water. People jostled each other, desperate, anxious, and determined not to be deprived of any contact with the power of St Winefride.

But the patient monks of Basingwerk and the parish clergy of Holywell were as skilful as the temple keepers at Jerusalem in the time of the old dispensation. Everything to them was orderly. For every purpose there was a place, for the pilgrim to obtain his desires a ritual, for St Winefride to dispense her bounties an inexhaustible jewel chest, and an offering for the shrine. No one was sent empty away.

The monk who had brought them from the monastery took charge and led them further up the hill from where they could look down at the place where Winefride's decapitated head touched the ground and the spring burst forth. They turned to the left and were led into the church, Beuno's church, his legacy to Winefride, where some of their fellow-pilgrims had kept vigil through the short summer night. They moved out of brilliant sunlight away from the noise of the market place and the thunder of the spring into the hushed reverence of the church. Here was an image of St Winefride inviting them to her presence. Now the pilgrims were at peace and in this familiar ritual of flickering candles, and the smell of incense, they joined their earnest intercessions throwing themselves upon her compassion before the altar and adding their candles and requests to the many offered that day. As if in a trance they moved slowly in this holy place until they went out by another door.

Following another path they stumbled down to the edge of the wonderful, powerful, miraculous well. The water erupted, tumbled, boiled, roared and rushed forth not as an evil force but 'as clear as glass, greenish like beryl or aquamarine, trembling at the surface with force of the springs.' Tinted blood red were the stones to remind the pilgrims of the virgin's martyrdom.[48] They were stunned by the thought that such healing power was at the disposal of Winefride; any doubts which previously lingered in their minds, were completely removed. She had the power to work miracles and the marvelling multitude shared the same conviction. 'They were on their knees in abundance round the well in prayer.' The weak were gently carried to the healing water by their fellow pilgrims and immersed by the assistants at the well. Those who could walk followed the ritual and bathed three times. Others turned aside to use the eye well. Some when the opportunity presented itself knelt, arms uplifted, on Beuno's Stone in the water to say their prayers. All were preoccupied by their own necessity. Many cried out as the shock of the water sent excruciating waves of pain through their bodies as a sign of healing. There were times when the lame walked, the deaf heard, the dumb spoke, and all manner of signs and wonders took place with few of them which passed unnoticed by the vigilant priests.

There was a booth set up at which the pilgrims could transact the most important business of obtaining the indulgences they had come for and those for other members of their community. An offering was made towards the repair of the buildings and the pilgrim was handed his indulgence. He peered eagerly at the scraps of paper, which promised precious days of remission from Purgatory and carefully put them in his scrip or bag, which he wore around his neck across his body. This was filling up with blood-tinted pebbles, and dried sweet smelling moss to be wetted and used as a poultice, green and

31. A sick pilgrim carried through the waters: stone corbel overlooking the holy well.

stringy, known as Winefride's hair, and *ampullae* containing holy water from the well. Another official pinned to his hat the lead pilgrim's badge of St Winefride's Well to add to his collection.

The most moving objects to be seen were a variety of non-monetary votive offerings left by pilgrims as a symbol of their miraculous cures: crutches, candles, coins, jewels, clothing, wax or silver images of human limbs, eyes, breasts, teeth, ears, etc.[49] Earlier in their progress they had passed one of the shrine's richest offerings: a gown of russet velvet adorning the image of St Winefride with which it was decked out on feast days. Isabella, countess of Warwick, had bequeathed it to the shrine in 1439.[50] Her husband, Earl Richard, had been more generous four years earlier when he commissioned a golden statuette of himself weighing twenty pounds for dedication to St Winefride's shrine in Shrewsbury.[51] After the ritual of the progress round the church and the well, and the completion of their transactions, the pilgrims walked down the stream and back into the clamour of the world outside. The street in front of the little houses stretching up to the town cross was one big bazaar with booths of vendors of religious souvenirs. It was time to go home.

The flowering of the cult: *c.*1430–1540

The final century before the Reformation saw the flowering of the cult of St Winefride in Britain. The centres at Holywell and Shrewsbury benefited most and here we may trace evidence of artefacts of royal and noble patronage. St Winefride was taken up by the monarchs of the competing dynasties of Lancaster and York, and received the devotion of the new house of Tudor. The Welsh bards, the poets of her homeland, devotedly sang her praises in their own language. Naturally the saint was highly popular in her homeland, north-east Wales, and at the end of the fifteenth- and beginning of the sixteenth-centuries the crypt and chapel of St Winefride's over the well was built as the most lasting of her medieval monuments. The shrine at Shrewsbury was destroyed at the Reformation and the reliquary and chapel at Gwytherin gradually decayed and disappeared through neglect. There are few artefacts which survived the iconoclasm of the 1550s, and the seventeenth-century civil wars. These are mainly fifteenth- and sixteenth-century stained-glass windows, a few pieces of sculpture, and portrayals of the saint in illuminated manuscripts. But there is enough to imagine the extent of the spread of her cult and the high regard in which she was held.

Royal connections

Edward (d.1376) the Black Prince was connected with Flintshire as earl of Chester and recruited archers from the area; in 1398 his son Richard II came on pilgrimage and established a royal chantry at Holywell and subscribed towards a pilgrim's hostel near the well.[52] Henry V continued this patronage and in preparation for his military campaign in France came to the well to ask the saint's blessing. He returned after the victory at Agincourt to express his gratitude. As the chronicler recorded: 'going with great reverence on foot from Shrewsbury to St Winefride's Well in North Wales.'[53] It has been suggested that this was part of Henry's policy of 'wooing Celtic sensibilities,' demonstrated by his gruelling pilgrimage and direction to Henry Chichele, archbishop of Canterbury, to raise the status of four saints' days: those of George, David, Chad and Winefride. The king was grateful to the Welsh archers for their part in the victory over the French and relieved that Glyndŵr was dead.[54]

Henry intended to found a chantry at Shrewsbury 'to the praise of Almighty God and St Winefride' but died before it was realised. This desire was later fulfilled by his son Henry VI who, in 1449, conferred on the abbey ten pounds a year of the revenues of the parish of Nesse to fund a chantry in the conventual church of St Peter, Shrewsbury.[55] Henry VI's tutor, Richard Beauchamp, earl of Warwick,[56] patronised Winefride's shrine at Shrewsbury, and left money to build a chantry chapel in St Mary's, Warwick. It is one of the most splendid examples of its kind in England. The stained glass for the east window was made by John Prudde (c.1447), King Henry VI's glazier and included Beauchamp's four favourite saints: St Thomas of Canterbury, St Alban, St John of Bridlington and St Winefride. The Welsh saint is robed as a prioress in deep purple, wears a crown and carries an elaborate pastoral staff and an open book.[57]

A royal chantry chapel at Holywell

For nearly 140 years (1398–1536/7) the English monarchy had an almost continuous link with the cult of St Winefrede through the foundation of a chantry at Holywell. It was a place established for daily prayers and masses to be said for themselves and the souls of their ancestors. For this purpose they kept a priest whom they supported by an annuity or small pension. The chantry at Holywell was most certainly a small altar chapel in the parish church, or part of the well shrine. Only a small minority of chapels in churches had specially endowed priests of this kind. In *Valor Eccclesiasticus*, completed in September 1535, the chapel of St Winefride had two ecclesiastical values. One was the value of the offerings at the shrine, the other in respect of the royal chantry which was returned as an ecclesiastical benefice in the hands of the Crown.

The information relating to the establishment of a chantry dates from an unspecified year in the reign of Richard II (1377–99) is given in letters patent issued by Edward IV on 29 March 1465. The chantry was supported by an income from rent from the king's mills in the county of Flint with the chaplain appointed and paid by the Crown to perform specific duties. The document stated:

Know ye that we have granted to Geoffrey Lewys, chaplain, an annual pension of 12 marks during his life, to celebrate masses in the chapel over the well (*supra fontem*) of Holliwell in our county of Flint, in honour of the Blessed Virgin and Martyr Winefrede, as was done from the time of our noble progenitor Richard II until a short time since, to be received out of the issue of our mills of Disserth and Pentre, to the intent that divine services may be lawfully kept up (*custodiri*) there in honour of God and the said Saint. And we have granted him that for his life he shall be our chaplain, which is of our foundation, to celebrate there for us and the souls of our progenitors.[58]

Sometime during his reign Edward (*fl.*1461–83) came on pilgrimage to Holywell, an event referred to by the poet Tudur Aled (*c.*1465–1525): 'Edward came to his land to her, And the moss upon his crown.' It seems feasible that the pilgrimage coincided with the re-establishment of the chantry. The sight of the splendid figure of the young Yorkist king with Winefride's moss adorning his crown was a gesture treasured at Basingwerk and told by the monks there to the poet.

The royal chantry was continued by Edward's successors in various forms. On 7 April 1484, Richard III, 'out of devotion for St Winefride and her well where she was martyred,' granted the abbot of Basingwerk an annuity of ten marks from the exchequer of Chester 'for the maintenance of a chantry priest continually to celebrate in the chapel over (*de super*) the said well.'[59] Following Richard's defeat at Bosworth in 1485 his victor, Henry VII, renewed this provision and appointed 'Howell ap Day chaplain with an annual pension of £10 for life, to celebrate divine service daily in the chapel of St Winefride in Holiwell.'[60] Henry VIII maintained a succession of chaplains: 4 June 1515 – Edward Pennant, clerk, annual pension ten pounds,[61] succeeded in 1525 by Owen Hensheman and, on 8 May 1531, by Peter Fowler – both on the same terms.

Iconography of St Winefride at Shrewsbury

All we know about the medieval iconography to St Winefride at Holywell is what remains in the carvings of the chapel and crypt erected within less than forty years of the Reformation. The rich decoration in the church above the well: images, wall paintings, and stained glass, did not survive these years of change, and what little might have survived disappeared when the church, apart from the tower, was rebuilt in 1770. But a parallel to what may have been found at Holywell may be discovered through an examination of the representation of St Winefride in medieval carving and other artefacts in the old abbey building at Shrewsbury now Holy Cross Church.[62] This link has been revived in the twentieth and twenty-first centuries at Shrewsbury Abbey, and in Shrewsbury R.C. Cathedral of which St Winefride is secondary patron.

Abbot Nicholas Stevens (abbot 1361–99) rebuilt the shrine of the saint and probably placed it in a chantry chapel constructed to the saint's honour and for the benefit of the many pilgrims. A small fragment may survive,[63] part of the

32. Guest accommodation at Basingwerk Abbey.

reredos, which is now placed under the St Winefride window in Holy Cross Church, the old abbey church. This remnant has been described

> as a sculptured stone three feet by two feet, within foliated tabernacles, three figures each twenty-two inches high. In the centre is a female bearing a clasped book, on her right hand is St John the Baptist, with his symbol of the lamb, and on her left, a mitred abbot, his hand elevated in the act of benediction. Perhaps two of these figures have been meant for Saint Wenefrede and St Beuno.[64]

This shrine may have been built by Abbot Stevens to house the newly acquired bones of St Beuno. They were ill-gotten having been stolen from Rhewl, near Llangollen in Denbighshire, by monks and servants of the abbey who were fined for the felony but kept the relics.[65] Whether for all their troubles they got the right relics is a matter for conjecture. On his death St Beuno's body was coveted by three communities: Clynnog Fawr, Nefyn and Bardsey and legend has it that as his body was being carried to burial, the procession halted and a dispute took place about its final resting place. Before it was settled the bearers fell asleep and when they awoke found three coffins resembling each other in every respect. It is said that Clynnog secured the true one.[66]

Another interesting artefact is the common seal of the fraternity of the blessed Winefride the Virgin. On 9 February 1487, Abbot Thomas Mynde was granted permission by royal patent to establish a confraternity within the premises of the

33. *St Winefride flanked by St Beuno and St John the Baptist: suggested fragment of her former shrine in Shrewsbury Abbey, illustration from* A History of Shrewsbury, *Owen & Blakeway.*

monastery. The statutes he proposed were similar to those of confraternities throughout England. There may have been a similar body in Holywell linked with Basingwerk, established by whatever body of merchants or lead cartel was powerful enough to do so. The rules or statutes show how the cult of St Winefride was likely to be observed by a group of laity in the late Middle Ages. Membership was open to both sexes, all were to assemble on St Winefride's Day, 3 November for Mass. Abbey funds of £10 per annum were to be used to endow two chaplains who would offer daily prayers at St Winefride's altar for the well-being of the king and queen, and of the abbot and his confraternity. 'When a member died, a requiem was to be sung for his soul: but when the founder himself died, he was to be honoured with a requiem every Wednesday and Friday, and with nine full lessons read before the monks and the confraternity on the anniversary of his death.'[67] To celebrate the foundation of the confraternity at Shrewsbury in 1487 Lowry argues that William Caxton printed a brief folio text entitled *The lyf of the holy and blessid vyrgyn saynt Wenefryde* commissioned by Abbot Mynde. The seal of the Shrewsbury Guild shows the martyrdom of St Winefride, an image that may also have been used formerly as a pilgrim's badge. In the same year (1487), to celebrate the prosperity and peace brought by the accession of Henry VII, the rich wool merchants of the Draper's Company probably made a generous donation to the purchase of the large bell weighing 35 cwt. inscribed in Latin. 'Remember, holy Wenefrede, to God us recommend, / That by His pity He may us from bloody foes defend,' and about the middle 'Mary, pure and pious maid! / Those whom I call together aid.'[68]

The iconography of St Winefride in north-east Wales and elsewhere
There are a limited number of pre-Reformation representations of Winefride remaining in north-east Wales. A statue of her was included in the sculpture

saints in King Henry VII's Lady Chapel in Westminster Abbey. Almost all the artefacts honouring Winefride perished in the 'Great Spoliation' and the small number which remain cannot possibly convey the richness and variety of objects of devotion which once existed. But what is lacking in evidence we must attempt to reconstruct in the imagination. Objects commemorating saints were mass-produced at the end of the Middle Ages, chief of which were images in stone, wood, stained glass, illuminated manuscripts and, later, printed books. These were the work of master craftsmen, masons, carvers, metal-workers, etc., employed on building and furnishing cathedrals, churches, royal palaces and chapels and other of the king's works as well as aristocratic patronage. At the end of the fifteenth century St Winefride's crypt and chapel fell within the orbit of such an enterprise and enough clues survive to appreciate its scope and splendour.

34. Seal of the Confraternity of St Winefride, established at Shrewsbury, c.1487. Tours in Wales, 1778, T. Pennant (illustrator, Moses Griffith).

The ecclesiastical seal of the Dean and Chapter of St Asaph Cathedral

We will begin our survey of such artefacts by looking at a small bronze matrix of an ecclesiastical seal outside the list of devotional items given above. It is a functional, utilitarian object having a decorative device common to the Middle Ages; an example of the sacred spilling over into the mundane when the honour of the saint was proudly invoked and exhibited for devotional and authoritarian purposes. This is the official seal used from the mid-fifteenth century onwards by the dean and chapter of St Asaph Cathedral. The chapter was the body of secular clergy, 'the canons', with the dean at their head, responsible for administering the cathedral. When they made important decisions their seal was attached to documents. The seal expressed the corporate nature of the governing body, which exercised its jurisdiction over the mother church of the diocese and is shown as a symbol of one communion in the body of Christ. There are three figures on the seal. None of them are named: two are bishops – in the centre St Asaph standing in eucharistic vestments, pastoral staff in his left hand, his right hand upraised in blessing; dexter (right), the diocesan bishop kneeling in veneration; – with sinister (left), St Winefride as a holy abbess, standing, holding her crook with her left hand and possibly in her right hand a book. Below, centre; in a round-arched niche is the dean to front in prayer, to either side of him some seven canons facing inwards and also kneeling in devotion. The mundane stamp or seal becomes a symbol which expresses the corporate nature of the church and its worship down the ages and its veneration of the founding saint of the diocese Asaph with whom is closely linked Winefride. Her reliquary is the sign that she is a special saint of the diocese venerated for her martyrdom and miraculous works.[69] This assumption that Asaph is on the seal as principal patron of the diocese, and Winefride as the recipient of the most prominent saints' cult, is confirmed by the fact that this dual status, as it might be, is recognised in the post-Reformation, tridentine, *Martrologium Romanum*, drawn up, in the late sixteenth century, under Cardinal Baronius where Asaph and Winefride are the only Welsh saints included.[70] The seal may also reflect a degree of pride on the work of restoration of the cathedral completed by Bishop Richard Redman (1471–95) which included the fine canopied stalls.

Woodcarving
Nothing survives from the Middle Ages of the many images carved in wood representing St Winefride, which must have existed. Many of them would have dated from the mid-fifteenth century onwards as part of the furnishings of the churches enriched in the late fifteenth century rebuilding particularly those in the vale of Clwyd. They would have provided companion images of saints on the rood screen with those in the stained glass. In many of these churches there was an architectural division between nave and chancel, and they had therefore to rely upon an imposing loft and screen for the ritual division of the church.[71] The western front of the loft which faced the people in the nave of the church was utilized for the illustration of legend and story and commemorated the more important doctrines and saints of the church. An example, which still survives, is the legend of St Melangell and the hare carved on the rood screen at Pennant Melangell in north Powys; one may visualize the legend of St Winefride receiving similar treatment in Holywell.

Stained glass
The narration of the story of St Beuno and St Winefride and some of their miracles based on the twelfth-century lives was to be seen in the east window of Capel Beuno attached to Clynnog Fawr church but has long disappeared.[72] Representations of St Winefride in stained glass have survived in two places in north-east Wales: at Llandyrnog in Denbighshire and Llanasa in Flintshire. Both of them date from *c.*1500 and are examples of 'York type' glass.

At Llandyrnog, glass of the same date includes a seven-sacrament window and in other windows displays a common medieval feature, that of a number of saints side by side.

35. Seal of the Dean and Chapter of St Asaph Cathedral.

We see this in the east window in the north aisle with the corporate grouping teaching the doctrine of the communion of saints. Four female saints arranged in the same window make this more interesting: Winefride; Frideswide, abbess (patron saint of Oxford University); Catherine of Alexandra, martyr (patron saint of scholars and learning); and Marcella, a local anchoress.[73] In other lights are St David (possibly St Deiniol).[74] It is interesting to speculate on the choice of subjects for the glass at Llandyrnog. The date of *c.*1500 coincided with that of Ffoulk Salusbury, dean of St Asaph and rector of Llanrhaeadr and Llandyrnog. He was the eldest son of Thomas Salisbury of Lleweni, the leading family in the vale of Clwyd, Lancastrian supporters, patrons of the bards and themselves poets. Ffoulk Salusbury was the patron of Sion ap Hywel who wrote an *awdl* to Gwenfrewi and to her well, in 1512. The learned dean was in 'the thick' of the literary renaissance in the vale of Clwyd. Remembering his Oxford days, he introduced with pride the virgin abbess Frideswide, and brought Catherine in as Winefride's *alter ego*. The presence of Marcella (Marchell) a local anchoress, takes us back once again to *Robert's Life* of Winefride, for she was sister to Diefer, patron of Bodfari, and Teyrnog, the founder of Llandyrnog. This choice of stained glass gives a homely insight into the way country parishioners and their eminent rectors demonstrated their belief in the household of faith. Most communities in the area probably shared the high regard held for St Winefride at Llandyrnog.

The window light of St Winefride at Llanasa was brought, it is said, from Basingwerk Abbey, after the dissolution of the monasteries. The account of its journey to the position it presently enjoys at Llanasa is complicated by questions of provenance, removal, restoration, and correct attribution.[75] Most of the furnishing from Basingwerk Abbey were dispersed and lost. The most substantial objects rescued were the stalls, which went to St Mary's on the Hill, Chester. It appears however that the first lay owner of the abbey, Harry ap Harry, the first of the family of Mostyn of Talacre, had some of the stained glass removed to Llanasa parish church. This transfer was first noticed in 1825 when an account appeared in the *Gentleman's Magazine*.[76] These stained-glass panels were removed from the east of the south aisle and reordered to the east of the north aisle and altered in 1877. The figures involved are an unnamed bishop, St James the Greater, St Laurence (martyr) and the window now attributed to St Catherine. The latter is, however, almost certainly Winefride and shows her

36. St Gwenfrewi: fifteenth-century glass, Llandyrnog church.

with a neck scar. Archdeacon Thomas suggested that it dated from the time of Katherine of Aragon, wife to Henry VIII, because of its inclusion of saints associated with Spain (Laurence and James).[77] It does, however, indicate the rejection of St Winefride by the Anglican Church in the diocese. Perhaps they thought she was too near to St Asaph after the Reformation and she lost the position she enjoyed in the fifteenth century as illustrated by the cathedral seal.

Henry VII and St Winefride

Henry VII's victory at Bosworth was, against great odds, owed in no small measure to the Stanley brothers: Thomas, Lord Stanley, married to the king's mother, Lady Margaret Beaufort; and Sir William Stanley, who was reputed to be one of the wealthiest men in the kingdom. The new king was descended from the Tudors in Anglesey; the Stanley brothers owned great lordships in north-east Wales. The new king needed as much support as he could muster and the least of his gestures was to embrace Winefride in the panoply of saints from whom he sought help.[78] This is why Winefride is among the saints depicted in Henry VII's Lady Chapel in Westminster Abbey. Here Winefride has remained untouched by iconoclasts from the beginning of the sixteenth century. Peter Lord[79] states that 'The sculpture was probably the work of a Flemish artisan, who had an unusual distinctive style, and her image is far from the conventional ideal of a female saint. She is presented as an individual plucked from life.'

The poets and Winefride

Sir Glanmor Williams captured the great surge of creative power and energy which occurred in Wales at the end of the Middle Ages when he said 'there began to unfold the dazzling efflorescence of what was appropriately categorized by the late Saunders Lewis as *Y Ganrif Fawr, 1435–1535* (The Great Century). These were years of an unsurpassed renaissance in Welsh verse and prose.' Part of this great outburst of poetry and religious devotion are poems in the Welsh language sung to the praise and wonder of St Winefride and her well.

The vale of Clwyd was the scene in north-east Wales for a literary renaissance[80] and, along with Basingwerk Abbey, was a major centres for the cult of Winefride. Literary learning was in the hands of the bards; they were the guardians of Welsh scholarship. Dafydd ab Edmund (*fl.*1450–97) of Hanmer, and his nephew Tudur Aled (*fl.*1465–*c.*1525) and Gruffudd Hiraethog (d.1564) were amongst the major exponents of this tradition. The area was rich in county families, great and small, who entertained the bards in their homes and, in return, received eulogies and elegies to their hosts and families.

The two Cistercian abbeys in north Wales, Vale Crucis and Basingwerk, were both liberal in their hospitality to the bards. It was customary for the poets to spend the three great Christian festivals, Christmas, Easter and Whitsun, at the home of one of their patrons where they would experience 'a great feast of praise to God'. The abbeys were also a source of knowledge where precious manuscripts could be read and transcribed. The hall of the abbot's house was a meeting place for distinguished travellers and clerics from Europe and Ireland. It was an outpost of learning and a contact point for scholars. The abbots provided not only intellectual conversation but also good accommodation and the best food and wine, and the guests in return composed eulogies to praise their host and immortalise his abilities and good deeds.

In the time of Abbot Thomas Pennant (*c*.1480–*c*.1515/22) scholarship, patronage, hospitality, eulogy, and devotion combined together in a remarkable, creative way in producing buildings. manuscripts, and fine examples of Welsh poetry which praised both Winefride and the monks. His more famous namesake the antiquarian described him as 'the hospitable, the useful, the valiant Thomas Pennant.'[81] Dr Enid Pierce Roberts has paid tribute to the scholarship of the Pennants at Basingwerk.

37. King Henry VII.

38. St Winefride: stone statue in Henry VII's Lady Chapel, Westminster Abbey. Note the decapitated head lying on the holy well.

> The abbot was author of Latin grammar while his brother the poet-cleric Huw Pennant, compiled and copied manuscripts of pedigrees, history, *Vitae*, religious, astrological and herbal essays and translated the Legenda Aurea into Welsh.[82]

Gutun Owain (*fl*.1450–98) the bard spent considerable time there copying chronicles, genealogies, Welsh versions of the lives of the saints and other material.

Three poets of Abbot Pennant's generation composed memorable works in honour of Winefride. All of them expressed in a vivid way the religious themes of their day. In their poetry they reflect the popular religious ideas of late medieval Catholicism and relate them specifically to Winefride and her well. Like all the poets of their generation their verse was composed as an adoration of the saints and the locations

associated with them. The background to their poetry is the rich cultural flowering in stained glass of the legends of the saints, the expression of the suffering Saviour in carved and painted rood screens and the devotion of the faithful to the sacraments of baptism, the eucharist, and the wounds of Christ. In the life and martyrdom of Winefride they were presented with an ideal subject.

The event of her martyrdom, the severing of her head by Caradog, brought forth blood, and from that place issued a healing spring. They praised her martyrdom as a resurrection event. They compared the mingling of her blood with the water of the spring to the water and wine of the eucharist, the celebration of the passion of Christ. The well was not only the scene of her death it was a place of baptism and new life and miracles of restoration and healing.

The holy well was a sacred place and was revered as such by the poets who evoked a multitude of images to remind them of this. The hill above the well they likened to Calvary and the suffering of Winefride to that of her Saviour. Particularly poignant of suffering were the blood stained stones which were reverenced as relics of Winefride and her martyrdom. The well was likened to a huge baptismal font which received the faithful pilgrim's as the river Jordan did at the time of Christ and John Baptist. The blood-red stones gave the well water a tincture and quality which brought forth comparison to the changing of water into wine at Cana in Galilee. There was no end to the ingenuity of the poets in their imagery and description of St Winefride's Well and which often included a eulogy to the abbot of Basingwerk

Ieuan Brydydd Hir Hynaf (fl.1450–85)

Ieuan was a poet from the district of Ardudwy in Merionethshire who wrote on a variety of themes. Over half of his surviving poems treat religious subjects, as, for example, his celebration of the famous rood at Chester. His praise poem to Winefride was written at the end of the fifteenth century and was probably composed as a result of a pilgrimage to the well and entertainment by the abbot, Thomas Pennant, at Basingwerk. It is entitled *Cywydd i Wenfrewi a'r ffynnon* [A *cywydd* to Gwenfrewi and the well].[83]

His poem praises Winefride and in a brief recollection of the events of her life at Holywell the poet commemorates her martyrdom by Caradog, her restoration by Beuno, and the stone she 'sent' to him 'over the sea.' All of these episodes are derived by Ieuan from the *Anonymous Life*. He informs us that the motive of his pilgrimage to Holywell is to obtain grace and a cleansed soul, and receive drops of her miracles, and in her presence be healthy. He employs the description 'there is rough water and blood upon stones' to develop themes of grace, purification, and healing. Water and blood become symbols of the eucharist and holy baptism, and, 'this water' is seen as 'the best wine to overcome sickness.'

Extracts from the poem give a description of the well and its surroundings, and the variety of pilgrims who come to be healed there.

> *Mae'n y fron, fal manna fry,*
> *Ferw awen i Wenfrewi.*
> *Tai sydd fal y tes iddi,*
> *Tref o gaer nef i'n gwawr ni;*
> *Ac wrth y dref, gwyrthiau a drig:*
> *Dŵr garw a gwaed ar gerrig* [lines 5 to 10]

[There is on the hill-slope, like the manna above,/a bubbling inspiration to Winefride./To her the houses are like sunshine./A heavenly citadel town for our dawn./And near the town, miracles take place;/[there is] rough water and blood upon stone.]

There is a wonderful description of the pilgrims at the well/spring.

> *Mae yn ei ffons, man o'r ffydd,*
> *Y byd megis maen bedydd:*
> *Ac yno mae, gwen a'i medd,*
> *Urddonen i'r ddwy Wynedd.* [lines 41 to 44]

[Here's in her fount, a place of faith./The world as if [in] a baptismal stone:/And there is possessed by the maiden,/A Jordan for the two Gwynedds].[84]

Ieuan lists the healing miracles of Winefride's as given in the Gospels.

> *Os un a ddaw heb synnwyr,*
> *A'i caiff ond enynnu cwyr,*
> *A d'wedyd os mud ydyw,*
> *Os byddar, claear y clyw;*
> *Un heb gerdded i'r redeg,*
> *Dyn dall i weled yn deg.* (lines 27 to 32)

[If one arrives insane/he will receive it [sanity] on lighting a candle/and can speak if mute/If deaf clear will be his hearing/if crippled to run/a blind man to see well.]

Sion ap Hywel ap Llywelyn Fychan (1485–1530)

Sion ap Hywel was a local poet with lifelong associations with Holywell and district, who enjoyed the patronage of local clergy and abbots of Basingwerk and Glyn Conwy. He was a frequent visitor to Basingwerk with other bards, particularly his teacher Tudor Aled, and with them took part in the first Caerwys eisteddfod in 1523 under the patronage of the Mostyn family.

Sion ap Hywel composed 'An *awdl* to Gwenfrewi and to her well, 1512', of seventy-seven lines in length. The poem declares his intention to venerate Winefride and the place of her martyrdom. In his treatment of his subject an underlying theme is the comparison of the benefits of the 'wounds' of Christ at his death and passion, to the 'injury' 'the severed head' which Winefride suffered at her martyrdom, for from the wounds of both victims issue blood and water. Christ's is the eucharistic sacrifice, the mingling of the blood and water in the chalice, as on the cross it flowed from His 'breast', His sacred heart and wounded side. Winefride's is the mingling of her martyr's blood with the water of the well, which issued from the spot where her decapitated head fell. The use of the word 'breast' may also refer to the medieval image of the 'Pelican in her Piety' which feeds its young with its own blood until the pelican itself dies and is a symbol of Christ's sacrificial death. This symbol is to be seen in churches in the vale of Clwyd at Llangynhafal and Llanrhaeadr Nghinmeirch.

> *Gwenfrewy, Duw fry, gwaed y fron, – mor debyg*
> *'Dyw'r aber i'r ffynnon;*
> *A gwaed rhudd yw godre hon,*
> *Gweryd ar y main geirwon.* [lines 1–4]

[Gwenfrewi, God above, the breast's blood how similar/is its flow to this well;/with its red blood bottom/and moss on rough stones.]

Sion rhapsodises on his view of the well. The 'precious blood from the fair neck of Winefride and the crimson tinctured stones fill a fountain full of red-coloured wine from which comes deliverance'. The well is the 'paradise of all Britain' and with the moon's reflection in the water it becomes a 'silver relic', and contains 'excellent milk-breast'. This is perhaps the milky nature of the water after a storm or refers to the miracle at the well when after the expulsion of the French from Gwynedd the water in the well assumed the same quality, which had special healing properties.

> *Llawnin ffons'n llenwi'n un ffair,– llu'n nofio*
> *'N llyn afon y byddair;*
> *Lloer wingrofft, llawr ariangrair,*
> *Llwyth o fryn nef, llaethfron aur.* [lines 9–12]

[The font in a turbulence filling with wine, a throng of people bathing/in the pool of the river of the deaf;/the vineyard moon a silver relic on the ground,/a family from heaven's hill, excellent milk breast.]

The poet sees the hill above the well as Calvary, from which Christ's victory was won and describes Winefride's presence at the well in mystical terms.

> *Wedi hyn, o'r bryn, wir Brynwr – bydoedd*
> *A Bedydd, yr un Gwr,*

Gorau Brenin, gwir Brynwr
Y gwnâi Ddu y gwin o ddŵr.
Y dŵr a anfoned i Wen – deg Frewy,
Dug friwiad bob gwythen;
Y gwaed, purwaed, am y pen,
Yr holl waed yw'r afrlladen.
Afrlladen yw gwen, a genau'r Drindod,
Ac un Duw'n archollau;
Mae'r ffrwd mor braff ei rhadau,
Mae gwres ac mae mwg o'r grau. [lines 26–37]

[Thereafter [i.e. following the martyrdom of Winefride] from the hill, true redeemer of the worlds/the one God , the best King, true Redeemer/did God make the wine from water./The water that was sent to fair Gwenfrewi [she]/bore the wounding of every sinew. The blood, pure blood, around the head,/All the blood is consecrated wafer./The maiden is a wafer, and the mouth [piece} of the Trinity/and the one God as wounds [the crucified Saviour?];/The stream is so powerful in its blessing./There's warmth and vapour from the blood.]

39. *'The Pelican in her Piety': wooden sculpture in the church of St Dyfnog, Llanrhaeadr-yng-Nghinmeirch.*

In the final lines the theme changes from the blood and wine of the eucharistic sacrifice to the water of holy baptism. The well is the fine and holy Jordan because of Gwenfrewi [Winefride] to which 'a multitude makes its way.'

Cyrchu llu ati, llety – llan cleifion
Llanwan' yr afon yn llan Wenfrewy.
O'r berw boglynwyrdd mawr yw'r boglynnu,
Mae aur ar ei delwau, mor wir y dyly;
Mae'r gwyrthiau mor frau, mawr fry – ' Ewropa,
Mae mwnai'r Afia am Wenfrewy. [lines 68–73]

[A multitude make their way to her, lodging at the church of the sick,/they fill the river at Gwenfrewi's church./From the green bubbles great is the gurgling./There's gold on her effigies, justly deserved./The miracles are so generous, more than [miracles] in Europe,/there is the treasure of Africa because of Gwenfrewi.]

Tudur Aled (c.1465–c.1525)
Tudur Aled was one of the greatest among the poets of the gentry in the late Middle Ages. His roots were at Llansannan, near to Gwytherin where Winefride resided as an abbess at the end of her life and he would have visited her reliquary

and chapel there. Poetry was in his blood, a gift which was nurtured by his uncle Dafydd ab Edmund, the chief of Welsh bards. Tudur wrote for patrons in north-east Wales and one of the most memorable and hospitable was Thomas Pennant, abbot of Basingwerk. The bard was impressed by his host whom he described as a man of dark complexion, noble in bearing and a lion in the field. He sang of the hospitality dispensed by the abbot at whose table was to be had huge dishes of fine food: roast meat and poultry, white bread and sugar, and the sweet wines of Aragon and Brittany.[85] Although both bard and abbot had knowledge of the world they had a common devotion to Winefride and served her with distinction.

Tudur much in evidence during his lifetime as a guest at Welsh religious houses spent his last days donned in the Franciscan habit at the Orders Friary in Carmarthen were he was buried. Like his pupil, Sion ap Hywel, he wrote a beautiful poem to Winefride, *Stori Gwenfrewy a'r Ffynnon* [The Story of St Winefride and her Well].[86] Tudur Aled's poem uses theological themes similar to those developed by Sion ap Hywel, but he develops them, as we might expect, in different ways. Both poets make the comparison between Christ's passion and Winefride's martyrdom, although Tudur adds that her lying under Beuno's cloak recalls Christ's burial in the tomb, while her uncle celebrates Mass, at the end of which 'Gwen was raised, and Jordan's bath sprang up'. Sion ap Hywel had more to say about the eucharistic sacrifice and baptism, although Tudur alludes to both sacraments in a most delicate way. Tudur describes the well in terms of baptism

> *Aber brwd o'r brew briwdan,*
> *Os brwd gwlith yr Ysbryd Glân*
> *Irder byd yw'r dŵr bedydd,*
> *A elwir ffons olew'r ffydd.*

[A fervent stream from the boiling, burning wound, / Fervent is the dew of the Holy Ghost / The water of baptism is the fresh growth of the world, / And is called the fount of the chrism of faith. [lines 55–8)]

He recalls the main themes of Winefride's life and the 'relics' of her martyrdom available to pilgrims. The valley of the stream shows forth these treasures and the odour of sanctity:

> *Aroglau nef i'r glyn yw;*
> *Ager gwin o'i gaid,*
> *Fal gwynt o fêl y gyntaid;*

[The perfumes of heaven belong to the valley, / The vapour of wine came from its gravel bed, / Like the smell of the first swarm's honey. [lines 38–40)]

The passion of Winefride's martyrdom and its powerful blessing is beautifully compared with that of her saviour:

> Man pêr ar bob maen purwyn,
> Main ag ôl gwaed mwnwgl gwyn;
> Beth ydyw'r ôl byth a drig?
> Band ei gwaed bendigedig?
> Dagrau fel cawod egroes,
> Defri Crist, o fannau croes,
> Daioni Crist corff dyn, o caid,-
> Derbyn deigr dŵr bendigaid;
> Dyfriw gwaed, fal dwfr a gwin,
> Dwyn iwel wyrthiau dan chwerthin;

[A sweet mark on each white stone,/Stones with the trace of a white neck's blood./What is the trace, which remains forever ?/Is it not her blessed blood?/Tears like a shower of wild rose berries,/Christ's drops, from the arms of the cross,/The health of a man's body, it were obtained,/Came from receiving a tear of the blessed water,/Drops of blood like water and wine,/Joyfully bringing about miracles.' [lines 43–52)]

Tudur sings of the well bringing healing and salvation as 'ointment' and 'medicine for salvation.' Such is its reputation that he has seen 'a hundred people light candles there' and witnessed cures for all ills that through the presence and intercession of Winefride are 'signs of God's power accomplished.' Here at the well the saint is 'doctor' who helps in the cure of the body and the soul. The leading men of the realm, king, nobility and courtier make their way to the well. King Edward IV made his pilgrimage and, in respect to the sanctity of Winefride, placed 'the moss upon his crown.' It is not surprising that old and young and indeed the 'throng of the world's companies' with dignity come there and make garlands out of the moss.

The poem concludes with lines that recall the special character of the holy well and its continuity stretching back to Bueno in the seventh century, and looks forward to his distinguished patron, Abbot Pennant, completing his work at the well. This discussed in the next section. The building of a new crypt to house the well with a chapel over it is the last act of the medieval Catholic Church to show the high regard in which she was held in Wales and beyond before the Reformation.

The cult blossoms: the perpendicular chapel and well chamber of St Winefride

The evidence for the building of the chapel

It is now becoming clear that there is absolutely no documentary evidence to support the claim that Lady Margaret Beaufort, the mother of King Henry VII, and members of the powerful Stanley family into which she married, were responsible for the building of St Winefride's Well. However, it is worth discussing the claims and counter claims for patronage which resulted in the erection of the magnificent late-perpendicular chapel and well of St Winefride which for 500 years has played such a large part in the history of the cult of St Winefride. But first an observation on the difficulties which surround the establishment of any claims relating to the erection of the building.

The most reliable evidence for dating a building is information which relates to its commission by an owner or patron, design by an architect, contract of works, employment of builder and craftsmen, and payment on completion. The survival of such written evidence from late medieval Britain is rare. It occurs when building works were undertaken in the name of the monarch, and paid for by the treasury, and may occur in ecclesiastical archives, if they were not monastic and lost at the dissolution of the monasteries. If such documentary evidence cannot be found, then it must be sought elsewhere. An obvious place to look for it is in the architecture of the building itself, by identifying the style of the building. In the case of St Winefride's Well it is late perpendicular, with a proposed date of around 1500.[87] Further evidence is provided from the carved heraldry in the stonework. This is a way of dating the building, but the trap of equating patronage to the display of heraldic badges is to be avoided. Another speculative area is that created by antiquarian writers, the 'old gossips of historical writing', who, years after an event, may spread false tales which, if plausible, may turn into a tradition which subsequently becomes sacred and not easily disposed of when firmer evidence turns up.

For nearly 300 years there has been an unwarranted attribution that Lady Margaret Beaufort was the patron of St Winefride's Well. Antiquarians who visited the building within the first hundred years of its existence, such as John Leland (1506–62) and John Speed (c.1610) do not make mention of Beaufort or Stanley patronage, neither did William Camden. The first claim for the patronage of Lady Margaret Beaufort was made by Thomas Hearne 223 years after her death (1509). Hearne (1668–1735) was a scholar and sometime librarian of the Bodleian, Oxford, and corresponded with scholars from all over Britain. He wrote in his notes on 9 January 1732/3:

> It is a tradition that Margaret, Countess of Richmond, erected the building over St Winifred's well at Holywell in Flintshire and that the workmen were the same that built King Henry VII's chappel at Westminster, who also (they tell you) built

Wrexham (Church) Tower. According to Willis's Survey of St Asaph, Wrexham Tower was built in 1507 and according to Hollingshed the first stone of Henry VII's chappell was laid in 1502–3.'[88]

The tradition mentioned by Hearne was repeated and enlarged upon forty years later by Thomas Pennant (1726–98), the distinguished antiquarian of Downing, who was closely involved in the affairs of Holywell. He wrote:

40. *Lady Margaret Beaufort, countess of Richmond and Derby: window in St Winefride's RC Church, Holywell.*

> This building, and the chapel over it, rose from the piety of that great house [i.e. the Stanley family], which left these memorials of its benefactions: there are besides some marks of the illustrious donors; for example the profile of Margaret, mother to Henry VII, and that of her husband the earl of Derby, cut on the same stone.[89]

The architectural evidence from the building

What are these memorials of benefaction Pennant speaks of? They are heraldic badges and sculpture carved in stone throughout the crypt and chapel.[90] The late perpendicular style of the vaulted well-chamber with moulded stone arches and timber roof of the chapel over the well are ideal for a display of heraldic ornament and figure subjects on corbel, boss and spandrel.

The Tudor dynasty is well represented. In the crypt at the base of the central pendant boss are the royal arms of England and Wales: a dragon and a greyhound of Henry VII are carved in spandrels at the entrance to the well on the right. Over the outside door to the gallery is the portcullis he derived from his mother, Margaret Beaufort, whilst inside are the arms of Katherine of Aragon,[91] three pomegranates in a shield surmounted with a crown.

The dominant decorative representation is that of the Stanley family.[92] They were linked to the Tudor dynasty by the marriage of Margaret Beaufort to Thomas Stanley who was created earl of Derby in 1485. It is suggested that the two are seen in profile together high in the ceiling of the crypt and there are other badges of the family – the legs of an eagle, the eagle and child, the three legs of Man. Most interesting however are the decorative emblems belonging to Sir William Stanley (d. 1495), younger brother to Thomas, and his wife Elizabeth

41. Example of carving at St Winefride's Well – the Tudor dragon.

Hopton. The arms of Sir William, a wolf's head enclosed in a garter and those of Elizabeth Hopton, a barrel with a plant issuing from it, are in the crypt ceiling. Sir William Stanley was executed in 1495 for his implication with the pretender Perkin Warbeck. He had received the Order of the Garter from Richard III and displayed the wolf's head as chamberlain of Chester. In spite of his disgrace, there is no attempt to expunge his memory from the building.

Randle Holme, the antiquary, left a description of the well armorial features.

Holywell Armes.
France and England jet over the Springs.'
A stages head copassed in a escochion.
An Eagles foot.Three pomgranats with a crowne Royall on the Shield.'A crosse croslet or else cross regulat and trunked.
A woolfes head Araz.
In the dressing Rome. [the gallery over looking the well].
A Eagle and Child in a shield supported by two Angles. [Angels]
A Lion Rampt.[93]

In spite of this profusion of heraldic badges with the labels of Henry VII, Margaret Beaufort and the Stanleys stamped all over the chapel and well crypt, there is no evidence that any of them made a financial contribution to the building. As Jones and Underwood point out 'There is no record of Margaret's ever making any donation. In the summer of 1502 ... it was Thomas Stanley, not his wife, who sent an offering to Holywell on the feast day of St Winefride.'[94]

It is possible that the superb perpendicular design of the well was that of Robert Vertue who worked at Westminster Abbey from 1475 until his death in 1506, in partnership with other masons, including his brother William who died in 1527. Was Hearne wrong in saying that Margaret Beaufort 'erected the building over St Winefride's Well' and correct in his statement 'that the workmen were the same that built King Henry VII's chappel at Westminster'? It might be argued that the stonework of the chapel and well, with the addition of the traditions of the eighteenth-century antiquaries Hearne and Pennant provide enough circumstantial evidence to make a case for the major initiative's lying with Sir William Stanley and his brother Thomas Stanley, earl of Derby, with the support of their wives Margaret and Elizabeth Hopton, and a grateful Henry VII deputing his skilled craftsmen for the enterprise.

However, no mention, has been made of the possibility of the involvement in the building of the chapel by the monks of Basingwerk or their abbot, Thomas Pennant. The antiquary, his namesake, is silent about any part he played in the building of the well and/or chapel, and if he had had any evidence for such a role he would have been proud to mention it.

In the roof of the gallery is the head of an abbot, possibly that of Thomas Pennant, abbot of Basingwerk when the chapel was built. It makes sense that the abbot of the monastery which had been custodian of the well for nearly 300 years should have played a major role in enhancing the shrine of St Winefride. This was the period in north-east Wales of the rebuilding and

42. *Modern stained-glass window in St Winefride's Chapel depicting the heraldry of the Tudors and Stanleys and scenes from the life of St Winefride.*

enhancement of churches and a literary renaissance of which the abbey of Basingwerk was a centre. Abbot Pennant had the reputation of being a builder and added a new guest accommodation, and other buildings to the abbey. These were described by the poet Gutun Owain (*fl.*1450–98):

> a good house for the corn on the other side,
> there is a malt house-and it has a brick house;
> there is a stone wall by Cilgwri,
> and upon it a gate house.[95]

However, more important to our discussion is the praise that he received as a builder from two poets, writing after Gutun Owain was dead, on the building of St Winefride's well and chapel. The first reference was made by Tudur Aled, who describes the site of the well as being 'In Beuno's place, in Pennant's hand' and continues:

> *Am un Abad, mae'n obaith*
> *Ygwyl Duw ei glod a'I'waith;*

Yng nghor yn Iorc, neu 'Nghaer Non,
Y gorffenno gau'r ffynnon.

For the same abbot we hope/That God sees his glory and his work;/May it be in the choir of York, or in Non's city,/That he finishes the Well's arch.'[96]

More informative is the poet Sion ap Hywel who entitles his praise poem 'An *awdl* to Gwenfrewi and to her Well (1512). [*Awdl i Wenfrewi a'i ffynnon (1512)*]

O law Tomas urddaswin
Yr aeth y gost ar waith gwen:
Diwan adeilad, da iawn y dylud,
Da y darparwyd, iti y darperir,.
Pymthecant (mi a'i gw'rantwn)
A deuddeg oed oedd Duw gwyn
Dwy fodfedd am bunt o'r bont i'r clochdy,
O'r ddaer i frig yr eurdderw fry;
Deg mil deg cant yw gwaith y tŷ'n Sychnant
A deugain rifant i dŷ Gwenfrewy.

From the hand of Thomas of distinguished wine/did the expenditure proceed on the/construction work [at the well of] the fair maid:/A stout building, full well were you entitled [to it],/Fifteen hundred (I would aver it)/and twelve [years] was the age of blessed God/ two inches for a pound from the bridge to the belfry,/from the earth to the top of the fine oak above;/ten thousand [and] ten hundred is the labour of the house in Sychnant/and forty do they account to the house of Gwenfri.

And so the poet's provide the most conclusive evidence we have for the date and person responsible, Abbot Thomas who completed the building in 1512.

The architecture and ritual arrangement of the building
St Winefride's Well and Chapel were designed principally for the use of pilgrims coming to the well ,and were organised as such. It was built near other religious buildings that had been there for centuries. The parish church, first mentioned in 1093, and set above the well, was adjacent to the chapel. Somewhere in the church was an altar for a chantry priest to perform his duties; since he was first heard of in the reign of Richard II (deposed 1399). Where did the local clergy live – the vicar, the chaplain, the procurator, all mentioned in 1284? How close was the hospice for pilgrims begun by Benedict, the vicar in 1398? Unfortunately we do not know.

But we are certain of the site of the old parish church, and the well determined its own location. The new buildings erected at the close of the fifteenth and beginning of the sixteenth centuries are set on a hillside, with a crypt covering and enclosing the sacred well and spring, from which issues the stream rushing to the Dee over a mile away. Built over the crypt is a chapel whose entrance and roof levels match those of the parish church adjacent and separated a few yards away from its solid tower. The church too is perched on the hillside overs-hadowed to the south-west by Castle Hill.

The perpendicular, slim and elegant profile of crypt and chapel nestles and provides shelter, sanctuary and entrance to healing well and stream. The well building is a sacred grotto, a sanctuary for the richly-adorned image of St Winefride. For centuries, until the source of the spring was diverted and replaced, there was the awesome experience of hearing a deafening roar of water and seeing it streaming out of the sanctuary of the crypt into the sunlight. Inside the crypt, candlelight chased a myriad of colours on richly-painted vaulted ceilings, picking out carved legends of Winefride and Beuno on the pendant over the pool. Angels accompany them adding dignity to sculptured faces and to the heraldic badges of patrons and benefactors who join the assembly as if on perpetual pilgrimage. The pilgrims' journey in the crypt was short and memorable as they paused to pray and circulated in procession, filled with wonder and enchantment round the vaulted ambulatory. Reciting the creed, rosary beads in their fingers, the pilgrims concentrated in their devotion, made intercession, and solicitation for the precious gifts of forgiveness and healing. To achieve this they made the ritual passage through the smaller pool nearer the entrance. Having passed through this highly charged theatre of experience they came out into the open.

Outside, the stream glinted in the sunlight. Crimson-tinctured stones and twisted garlands of moss were St Winefride's invitation to them to receive blessings and cures gifts and relics to cherish and share with loved ones at home. The whole world was there: all ages and conditions, many desperate, all hopeful, some surprised by joy. Anything might have happened as it had done for centuries. Above there was a canopy of over-arching trees from the eastward heaven above. It is as Tudur Aled said: 'The state of grace (so great is the procession) is indeed a paradise of the soul. Heaven's chrism is at the source of the stream.'

Above the well crypt is the chapel connected with it, most of it built over, and resting upon the outer walls of the chamber below so that the two form structurally one building. Its entrance from above is in the parish churchyard. The chapel chancel at the east end is a few yards below the church tower. The building comprises a chancel of pentagonal shape, a nave of four bays, and a north aisle of three bays with a wooden roof low pitched, of camber beam construction, with arched braces. The carved corbels, both stone and timber, are of a variety of subjects.

The chapel has had a varied history since the Reformation. Ownership of it, when finally confirmed in the 1930s, was placed in the hands of the Anglican

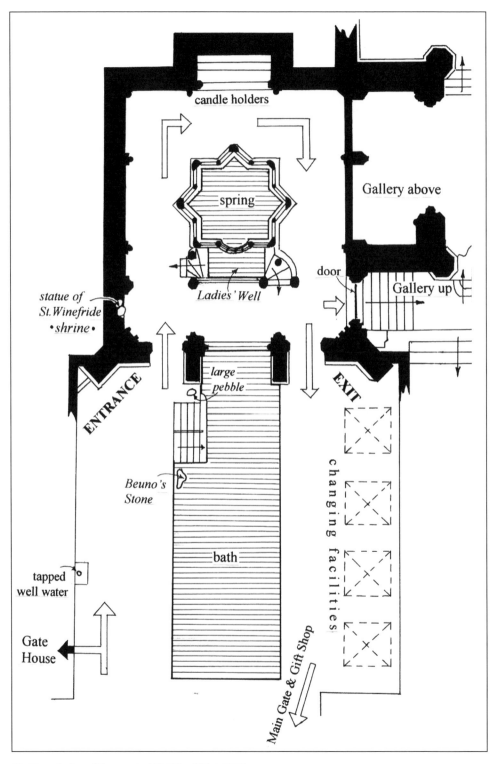

43. *Recent plan of the crypt at St Winefride's Well.*

Church in Wales, whilst that of the well crypt in possession of the local authority. Whereas the well crypt has never ceased to be visited by pilgrims, the chapel has been used for different purposes, some of them secular. A session house in the seventeenth century, for 150 years as a school and for religious purposes used by the parish church. Photographs of the 1940s show it furnished for Anglican worship. It is now empty and unfurnished, but fortunately considerably restored by the Ministry of Works in the 1950s and subsequently Cadw.

There is no documentary description, no record of wooden furnishings, stained glass or other evidence apart from the empty shell of the building, to help us determine its furnishings However another *awdl* by Sion ap Hywel with the title *I'r Grog* [To the rood], which is a meditation on the rood in the chapel 'near St Winefride's Well'. The poet could have been writing about a major furnishing in the newly constructed chapel of the well. The *awdl* opens with the lines: *Duw, 'r wirgrog eurgrair Sydd fab i'r Arglwyddes Fair* [the rood, the golden relic, is God's true cross and as such an object of veneration]. The chapel was used by pilgrims in conjunction with the well when it was first built and from then until it passed into the hands of the church by law established at the Reformation thirty years later. As for its uses: Masses and litanies would be performed, and it would be furnished with at least one altar in the chancel and probably another in the south aisle. There may have been a richly ornate rood screen separating nave from chancel with niches for images of saints. Priests in attendance would hear penitents, record miracles and accept offerings. The building, larger than most well chapels, reflected the popularity of pilgrimages at the end of the Middle Ages.

The number of windows in the chapel provided scope to develop themes close to their patron's heart. Such a suite of stained glass was provided in 1500 by Thomas Stanley, patron of Gresford parish church, who gave the east window there with is Tree of Jesse, figures of the Virgin, St John and Christ displaying His Mother as Queen of the Universe – the theme of the churches dedication to All Saints – and other figures.[97] Maybe the same glazier provided the windows for the Holywell chapel with the Virgin, St Winefride and St Beuno at the top of the list.

As was the custom the craftsmen in stone and wood took a great delight in expressing their faith and humour using the opportunity to poke fun at rich and poor in their sculpture. Their favourite places for display were stone corbels decorating arches or on roof supports and bosses. Many of their traditional figures are to be seen in the chapel although some are difficult to make out because of age and former neglect. When the Commissioners on Ancient Monuments visited in 1910, they reported that the chancel roof was supported by corbels with suggested representations of the seven deadly sins.[98] Christopher David provided illustrations of others;[99] they include bestiary figures, the mantichora (human head on a lion's body), lencrota (a fabulous horse) and griffin (body of a lion, wings and crooked beak of an eagle). Grotesque faces stare and grimace at each other across the nave. There are various figures: the apocalyptic horse and rider, two men in combat and others. There are religious motives: an angel carrying a shield with the five wounds of Christ, a vase of lilies and *fleur de lys* representing the Blessed Virgin, scenes of the months – harvest for September, with wheat and grapes which may also represent the eucharist and acorns for October. Other stone corbels repeat Stanley family badges – the eagle's claw, the barrel with a plant issuing out for Elizabeth Hopton. There are busts of men and women on corbels in the north aisle that may represent Thomas and William Stanley and their spouses. A modern stained-glass window represents St Winefride, the Stanleys and Henry VII. But the empty chapel is rather forlorn, denied its sense of purpose and with its glory departed, a fate which came too soon after its erection.

NOTES

1. D. H. Williams, 'Basingwerk', *Citeaux*, vol. 32 (1981), p. 89.
2. F. Winward, 'The Lives of St Wenefred', *Analecta Bollandiana*, vol. 117 (Brussells, 1999), pp. 81–132.
3. C. David, *St Winefrides Well a history and guide*, 1969, n.p.
4. J. G. Edwards, V. H. Galbraith, E. F. Jacobs (eds), *Historical Essays in Honour of James Tait* (Manchester, 1933); Arthur Jones, *Basingwerk Abbey*, pp. 169–78, pp. 171–2.
5. G. Omerod, *The History of the County Palatine and City of Chester*, (2nd ed, Thomas Helsby, London, 1882), vol. 1, p. 17 and p. 191.
6. D. H. Williams, op cit, p. 89.
7. A. Jones, op cit, p. 171.
8. R. R. Davies, *The Age of Conquest Wales 1063–1415* (Oxford, 1987), p. 46.
9. J. Tait (ed.), 'The Chartulary or Register of the Abbey of St Werburgh, Chester,' *Chetham Society New Series*, vol. 79, p. 236.
10. *The Victoria History of the County of Chester*, (University of London Institute of Historical Research, OUP, 1980), vol. III, p. 151.
11. R. C. Christie (ed), '*Annales Cestrienses* or Chronicle of the Abbey of S. Werburg at Chester', *Lancashire and Cheshire Record Society*, 1887, p. 23.
12. R. R. Davies, op cit, p. 49, and C. R. Williams, *The History of Flintshire*, vol. 1 (Denbigh, 1961), p. 71.
13. See previous fn 12.
14. G. Williams, 'St. Winifred's Well: Ffynnon Wenfrewi', *Flintshire Historical Society Journal*, vol. 36, 2003, p. 36. D. Knowles, *The Monastic Order in England* (Cambridge, 1949), p. 346, fn 2.
15. G. Williams, ibid, p. 36.
16. Ibid, p. 36.
17. H. Pryce (ed), *The Acts of Welsh Rulers 1120–1283* (Cardiff, 2005), p. 346.
18. J. Tait (ref. fn 9), p. 41.
19. G. Williams, op cit, p. 36; see also R. A. Brown and H. M. Colvin, *The History of the King's Works*, vol. 1 (London, HMSO, 1963), p. 67, fn 2.
20. H. Pryce, op cit, p. 460.
21. *Victoria History of the County of Cheshire*, op cit, vol. 3, pp. 151–2 under 'The Abbey of Combermere'.
22. Rebuilt in 1769 and rededicated to St James the Great.
23. *Archaeologia Cambrensis*, vol. 1, 1846, p. 114.
24. Huw Price (ed), op cit, p. 346.

25. B. G. Charles, *Non-Celtic Place Names in Wales* (University College, London, 1938), p. 225.

26. See fn 18.

27. See fn 6.

28. See fn 11.

29. See fn 14.

30. See fn 19, *The History of the King's Works*, vol. 1, p. 67.

31. H. Pryce (ed), op cit, pp. 344–6 and p. 460 and *Archaeologia Cambrensis, vol. I*, 1846, pp. 102–8.

32. D.Williams, op cit, p. 92.

33. D. R. Thomas, *History of the Diocese of St Asaph*, (Oswestry, 1908) vol. 1, p. 49.

34. *Cheshire Sheaf*, vol. X1X, p. 38, 1922, quoting from *Calendar Inquisitions miscellaneous*, vol. 1, p. 302.

35. J. G. Edwards (ed), *Littere Wallie* (Cardiff, 1940), Nos. 135, 144, 150.

36. For first date indulgences issued by Pope see Sumption ref, fn 40, p. 141.

37. Sir Walter Raleigh, *The Passionate Man's Pilgrimage.*

38. *Cywydd Gwenferwi a'i Ffynnon* see Maredudd ap Huw, op cit, pp. 154–9.

39. N. White, *Gerard Manley Hopkins in Wales* (Seren, 1998), p. 47–8.

40. For a discussion on Indulgences see J. Sumption *Pilgrimage* (Faber & Faber, 1975) p. 141–5 and R. W. Southern, *Western Society and the Church in the Middle Ages* (Penguin, 1970), pp. 136–43.

41. *Calendar Papal Registers concerning Great Britain*, vol. 7, p. 504.

42. This is my own speculation.

43 G. H. Jones, *Celtic Britain and the Pilgrim Movement* (Hon. Soc. of Cymmrodorion, London, 1912), p. 406.

44. D. Webb, *Pilgrimage in Medieval England* (Hambledon & London, 2000), p.134.

45. Thirty-sixth annual report of deputy keeper Public Records, 1875, Welsh Records: Recognizance Roll of Chester, p. 214.

46 G. H. Jones, op cit, pp. 450–1.

47. Gerard Manley Hopkins, SJ, see ch. 1, fn 39.

48. R. B. Martin, *Gerard Manley Hopkins a very Private Life* (Harper Collins, 1991), p. 240.

49. R. C. Finucane, *Miracles and Pilgrimages*, (Book Club Associates, 1977), pp. 96–9.

50. A. Walsham, 'Holywell: contesting sacred pace in post-Reformation Wales', p. 213, in W. Coster and A. Spicer (eds) *Sacred Space in Early Modern Europe* (Cambridge).

51. M. J. C. Lowry, 'St Winifred and the Lady Margaret Beaufort', *The Library*, sixth series, vol. 5, No. 2, 1983.

52. See fn 45.

53. C. Given-Wilson (ed), *The Chronicle of Adam Usk* (Oxford, 1997), p. 463.

54. Lowry, op cit, p. 111.

55. Ibid, p. 112–3.

56. See fn 50, his wife Isabella bequeathed her russet coloured gown to deck the image of St Winefride.

57. See E. R. Kibble, *The Stained-Glass Windows in the Collegiate Church of St Mary Warwick* (Leamington Spa, 2005).

58. Chester Recognizance Roll 4–5, Edward IV, M. 8.

59. Chester Recognizance Roll, Richard III, m.Id.

60. Chester Recognizance Roll, Henry VII, m.2.20, May 1486.

61. *Thirty-ninth Annual Report Deputy Keeper*, 1878, PRO, Chester Recognizance Roll.

62. I. Ross, *Shrewsbury Abbey, The Parish Church of the Holy Cross*, R. J. L. Smith Associates, 1999.

63. The evidence from H. Owen and J. B. Blakeway, *A History of Shrewsbury*, 1825, p. 78 is given below. T. Gray Hulse is of the opinion that the figures were part of a tomb chest and if it was a depiction of St Winefride then the accompanying figure is more likely to have been St Eleri rather than St Beuno

64 Owen and Blakeway, ibid, p. 73.

65. A. T. Gaydon, *The Victoria County History of Shropshire* (London, 1973), vol. 2, 1973, p. 33, citing British Museum Hargrave ms 313, ff52 v-53.

66. G. H. Jones, op cit, pp. 34–5.

67. Lowry, op cit, who cites Calendar of Patent Rolls Henry VII and Owen and Blakeway, op cit, p122 f.

68. Owen and Blakeway, op cit, 67–8.

69. For a discussion on the Chapter Seal see D. H. Williams, *A Catalogue of Welsh Ecclesiastical Seals as known down to A.D. 1600: Part III: Capitular Seals,* p. 159 and D. R Thomas, op cit, vol. 1, pp. 376–7.

70. I am grateful to T. Gray Hulse for this observation. He further adds that one of Baronius' helpers was the exiled bishop of St Asaph Thomas Goldwell.

71. F. H. Crossley, 'Screens, Lofts, and Stalls situated in Wales and Monmouthshire, part four: Denbighshire', p. 3, *Archaeologia Cambrensis,* vol. xcix, p. 3.

72. Browne Willis, *Diocese of Bangor* (1721), p. 302–3.

73. M. Gray, *Images of Piety: the Iconography of traditional religion in late medieval Wales* (BAR, British Series, Oxford, 316, 2000).

74. Ibid, p. 34.

75. M. Lewis, *Stained-Glass in north Wales up to 1850* (Altrincham, 1970), pp. 52–3 and plate 53.

76. *Gentleman's Magazine,* November 1825, pp. 401–2 and M. Lewis, ibid, pp. 52–3.

77. Marriage negotiations for the marriage of the Spanish Princess Katheryn to Prince Arthur began in 1489.

78. See M. Gray, 'Welsh Saints in Westminster Abbey', *Trans Hon. Society of Cymmrodorion* (London, 2006), vol. 13, n.s., pp. 9–12.

79. P. Lord, *The Visual Culture of Wales; Medieval Vision* (Cardiff, UWP, 2003), pp. 273–4.

80. For the discussion which follows have relied on: Enid Roberts, 'The Renaissance in the Vale of Clwyd', *Flintshire Historical Society Publications,* vol. 15, 1954–5, pp. 52–63, and Enid Roberts, The impact of the Cistercians on the Welsh Life and Culture in north and mid Wales.' *Transactions of the Denbighshire Historical Society,* vol. 50, 2001, pp. 13–20.

81. T. Pennant, *The History of the Parishes of Whiteford and Holywell* (London, 1796), p. 33.

82. E. Roberts see fn 80 under Denbighshire.

83. In the Middle Ages a *cywydd* was a term for a group of poetic metres consisting of rhyming couplets, each of seven couplets. I am grateful to K. Lloyd Gruffydd for his English translation

84. Medieval [sic] Gwynedd was divided into two parts: *Uwch Conwy* 'above the Conwy, i.e. west of the river, and *Is Conwy* 'below the Conwy' (known as *Perfeddwlad*).

85. C. R. Williams, op cit, p. 132.

86. This *cywydd* has been translated and discussed by T. M. Charles-Edwards, *Two Medieval Welsh Poems – Stori Gwenfrewi a' i ffynnon – The Story of St Winefride and her Well by Tudur Aled (1480–1526)* (Gwasg Gomer, Llandysul, 1971), no pagination.

87. E. Hubbard, *The Buildings of Wales Clwyd* (Denbighshire and Flintshire) (Penguin, 1986), p. 371.

88. W. Salter ed, *Remarks and Collections of Thomas Hearne,* (Oxford Historical Society, 1921), vol. 79, p. 149.

89. T. Pennant, *Tours in Wales,* vol. 1 (London, 1778), pp. 28–31 and repeated in Pennant's *History of the Parishes of Whiteford and Holywell* (London, 1796), pp. 219–25.

90. All are badly weathered. Illustrations of them are to be found in C. David op cit.

91. Arrived England 1501, married first Arthur d.1502 and second Henry 1509.

92. Not as profuse here as in St Mary's Parish Church, Mold, Flintshire.

93. D. Thomas, op cit, p. 31, reference to Harleian MSS 2129, f.175.

94. M. K. Jones and M. G. Underwood, *The King's Mother Lady Margaret Beaufort Countess of Richmond and Derby* (Cambridge, 1992), p. 150.

95. Quoted by D. Williams, op cit, *Caiteaux,* p. 104.

96. T. M. Charles-Edwards, op cit, lines 108–12.

97. Maredudd ap Huw, op cit, pp. 178 & 184.

98. M. Lewis, 'The Glass at Gresford', *Transactions Denbighshire Historical Society,* vol. 7, p. 134.

99. *The Royal Commission on Ancient Monuments in Wales and Monmouthshire II, County of Flint,* 1912, p. 44.

100. C. David, op cit.

SECTION TWO

The Survival of the Cult, 1529 to 1829

Introduction

The ecstatic praise of the Welsh bards for St Winefride, her well and the guardianship of Abbot Thomas Pennant was silent in the face of unimagined changes in religion which occurred when his son Nicholas was the last holder of that office. In the 1530s, the newly built crypt and chapel in honour of St Winefride was threatened with destruction and her cult in dire peril. A situation of uncertainty began which was to last for almost three hundred years. Governmental action was real and, at times, threatening and unpredictable and neither the enemies who attempted destruction nor the faithful who fought for the survival of the cult knew what the outcome would be. Until the middle of the eighteenth century St Winefride's Well was subject to surveillance as a place where an outlawed church and its priests stubbornly and persistently continued a Catholic ministry to pilgrims. All Catholics who refused to attend the services of the Church of England were called recusants (those who refused) and fined. They were legally deprived of full citizenship and subject to severe penal legislation.

The survival of the cult of St Winefride and improbable survival of her well as the scene of regular pilgrimages is the subject of the next three hundred years of its history. The three hundred years divided into distinctive episodes which record the heroic struggle by Roman Catholics to re-establish themselves as a minority Church outside the law of the land and maintain locally some kind of presence and guardianship of the well. The story tells of the faithfulness of the local Catholic community to the continuing medieval practice of pilgrimage, the recording of miracles, and the establishment of new guardians of the cult of St Winefride whose presence and existence was contrary to the law of the land.

The government's attempt to suppress the cult was intermittent. Policy varied from time to time, although no attempt was made to remove penal legislation from the statute book. The effect of legislation depended upon its enforcement. It is the problem of enforcement of the law, which adds an intriguing dimension to the survival of the cult. Many of the local administrators had Catholic sympathies and were reluctant to report or prosecute their relatives or neighbours. The government personnel interested from time to time in the developments at St Winefride's Well were to include Queen Elizabeth I, members of her Privy Council, bishops of St Asaph and Bangor, the Council in the Marches of Wales and   local justices of the peace. The records from government departments of state provide most of the information we have. Their papers are more detailed and regular in times of crisis when the State felt itself threatened from without by invasion from Catholic powers and from within by the presence of seminary priests in obedience to Papal authority.

The Society of Jesus had a Mission in Holywell from *c*.1590 to 1930 and their records provide information for a continuing Catholic presence there and throw light on their determination as new guardians to preserve and reshape the cult of St Winefride. Both Jesuits and Secular priests had a mission in the town of Holywell and the secrecy which surrounded their activities, gives the story a sense of drama and heroic devotion in years of persecution. One of their duties was to safeguard the 'miracle narratives'. For example, there is a collection of these which survive from 1556 to 1674 and give an indication of the variety of cures, the religious background of those who sought the help of St Winefride's Well, and motives of the recorders.[1] The more spontaneous observations of Catholic and Protestant visitors cast an interesting light on the customs and rituals observed at the well and the state of its fabric. In many instances there is evidence of the cult of St Winefride being propagated by the republication and circulation of her *Medieval Lives* and, in some instances, poetic admiration was expressed in honour of St Winefride and her well.

The episodes are arranged chronologically, their substance made up of the themes from the variety of sources referred to above.

3. 1536–1558

King Henry VIII had reigned for twenty years before the first acts of the Reformation Parliament were inaugurated between 1529 and 1536. The monarch, awarded the title 'Defender of the Faith' by Pope Leo X, now turned on his successor Clement VII who had refused to annul his marriage with Katherine of Aragon. Determined to marry Anne Boleyn, and prompted by Thomas Cromwell, he carried through a reformation that was political rather than doctrinal in origin and effected by government and parliament rather than clergy and people. His chief aim was to strengthen the crown at the expense of the church and enrich himself along the way. Led on by advice from a reforming archbishop of Canterbury, Thomas Cranmer, and his ruthless, opportunist and unscrupulous vicar-general, Thomas Cromwell, the King blundered into schism and reformation of the Catholic Church. Unable to obtain a divorce from the Pope, Henry rejected the Pope's supremacy and established himself, through Parliament, as head of the Church in England and demanded an oath of allegiance from all his subjects. The religious landscape in Britain would never be the same again. Further religious reforms were to follow until Henry's death in 1547.

Locally, this first phase of the Reformation set in motion the attack on the cult of St Winefride. The virgin martyr was deprived of her dowry: property and sacred sites accumulated and protected over the centuries by monks of Basingwerk. The early royal injunctions issued in 1536 and 1538 were aimed at the destruction of all that the cult stood for; her standing as a saint, the devotion of the faithful, their pilgrimages and offerings, the images and stained glass set up to honour her. An examination of the enforcement of this legislation up to the time of Henry's death in 1547 will show how effective it was and the impact it had on the religious places in Holywell associated with her.

The dissolution of Basingwerk Abbey 1536

Henry VIII, by his attack on the Church, had alienated himself from the Pope and Catholic powers. The cost of war exhausted his treasury and more money was urgently needed. Desperate to find it Cromwell stumbled on the spoliation of the Church now placed under his master's control as the ideal solution to raise new money independent of parliamentary taxation. His first step was to assess the wealth of the Church in preparation for taxing the clergy. The commissioners' investigations were returned in a document known as *Valor Ecclesiasticus*.[2] Visitors assessed the state of the monasteries concentrating their enquiries upon sexual irregularities and the relics of the saints. With this knowledge and a financial estimate of their capital, the decision was taken in 1536 to suppress monasteries with an income of under £200 and fewer than twelve inmates. All the Welsh religious houses fell within this bracket and suffered the fate of suppression. The greater houses were dissolved (1537–40) mainly by 'voluntary' surrender. The king by appropriating the monastic estates was assured of an income of *c.*£175,000 per annum. However, because of financial difficulties, two thirds of monastic lands were disposed of by the time of his death in 1547.

There appears to have been no open opposition to the suppression of Basingwerk Abbey. The number of inmates was very small and it maybe it was that St Winefride's Well, being a mile away from the abbey, gave some hope of the continuation of pilgrimages. However, the disposal of abbey buildings meant that pilgrims had to find alternative accommodation since the lodgings built in the time of Abbot Thomas were no longer available. When the new occupants replaced the displaced monks they absorbed estate officials and other employees. The abbot, Nicholas Pennant, received a reasonable pension of £17 and his brothers John and David, had been demised abbey tithes and property immediately before the dissolution. This gave the family some kind of influence and interest in the affairs of the locality in spite of difficulties and disputes which arose.

The *Valor Ecclesiasticus* assessed the annual income of Basingwerk Abbey at

44. Basingwerk Abbey: H. Jordan, after H. Gastineau, 1830.

£157 15s. 2d., which was probably undervalued. The exact date of the abbey's dissolution has not survived, but its property was being disposed of by May 1537. It was crucial from the point of view of the Catholic cause and the cult of St Winefride that the abbey property should be in the hands of sympathetic persons.

The abbey property and its disposal

The rectory and tithes of Holywell parish given to the abbey by Robert de Pierrepont in the early twelfth century and the oblations of St Winefride's chapel as part of the rectory were demised by the Crown on 10 May 1537 to Christopher Litcote, a member of the royal household. He farmed them to William Holcoft, who was involved in a dispute with the churchwardens of Holywell. By the time of a second lease to Litcote in 1541, the custom of making oblations to St Winefride had fallen out of use and his rent was reduced by £10 to the sum of £20 9s. 8d. Robert Davies I of Gwysaney, Mold, succeeded Litcote in the lease of this property in February 1547. The Davieses were one of the rising gentry who gained prominence under the Tudors and were rewarded for services at court and in the county of Flintshire. They married into similar upwardly-mobile families and held the rectory, together with its tithes, until the nineteenth century.[3] As such they controlled the use of the chapel over the well and the appointment of the vicar of the parish, the advowson of which they presented to Jesus College, Oxford. Although they were members of the established Church, their views were moderated towards the Catholic community by intermarriage and mutual obligation.

The granges, lands and tenements of Basingwerk[4] were demised by the Crown on 14 May 1537 to Hugh Starkey a court official and sold by the Crown on 28 April 1541 to Henry ap Harry of Llanasa and Peter Mutton of Meliden for the sum of £280 11s. 8d. They soon passed through marriage into the possession of the Mostyn family of Talacre the most prominent Catholic family in Flintshire from Penal times until the estate was sold in 1920. The Mostyns played a significant role in the survival of the cult of St Winefride as leading Catholic gentry with ownership of large estates in the neighbourhood and immediate vicinity of the Well.

The lordship of Fulbrook-Greenfield had been given to the abbey by the charter of Ranulf II in the twelfth century. It was retained by the Crown until the time of James I when it came into the possession of the Egerton family. At this time there was a dispute between one Eldred and Egerton (later Lord Ellesmere) about the ownership of the well. This created a red herring which claimed that the well was part of the manor of Holywell when it clearly belonged to the rectory and for many years it was believed to be in the ownership of the Grosvenor family after they had acquired the lordship in 1809. This continued to cause confusion until the beginning of the twentieth century when it was finally settled.

Other abbey estates were outside the locality of Basingwerk and county of Flint notably on the Wirral peninsula, Penllyn in Merionethshire (which included Llyn Tegid at Bala) and Glossop in Derbyshire.[5]

Although Basingwerk was used as a residence by the Mostyn family of Talacre until at least the end of the seventeenth century parts of the buildings suffered destruction almost immediately after suppression. Crown officials took away liturgical gold, silver, jewels, vestments and some rare books. Other manuscripts were used for their vellum. Lead was stripped from many of the roofs and sent to Holt Castle in 1538 and transported to Ireland in 1546 'for the covering of Dublin castle and for other of the King's Castles and houses'. The only evidence that remains of any of the abbey furnishings are choir stalls taken to the church of St Mary on the Hill in Chester. An entry in the churchwardens' accounts for 1536 reads: 'In there tyme the quere was broght at basenwerke and sette uppe with all costs and chargis belonging to the same.'[6]

The dispersal of abbey property marked the end of a monastic estate generously endowed over the centuries by aristocratic patrons who endowed it in a variety of ways.

Its economy included a silver mine (from Ranulf II), corn, fulling walk and water mills. There was a good acreage of woodland and pastures supporting sheep (a flock of 2000 in 1291). Ranulf II had given them salt interests in Cheshire and local fishing rights made ample provision for fish days. The monks and their agents were regularly busy in fairs and markets at Glossop and Holywell where there was an annual three-day fair at Trinity tide and a weekly market.

The two disputes we have referred to above cast an interesting light on the tensions caused in the locality by religious changes, property ownership, and the tenacity of the old order.

The disputatious abbots
Both abbots of two local Cistercian monasteries had a somewhat seedy reputation by the time of the dissolution. Abbot Robert Salusbury of Valle Crucis near Llangollen, found guilty of highway robbery, was deprived and spent three months in the Tower of London. His contemporary, Abbot Nicholas Pennant, the last abbot of Basingwerk, was calculated in his method of extortion. The Pennant method was designed to be permanent and of future benefit and involved the exploitation of the Basingwerk monastic estates over a period of almost fifty years. The making of long leases to members of their own family, the failure to collect the rents from them, a laxity in using the conventual seal to legalise transactions, and an attempt to possess the tithes of the local townships. This rapacity stretched from the reign of the darling of the Welsh bards, the black-haired, smooth-tongued, generous Abbot Thomas Pennant, to the final years of Basingwerk under his son Nicholas. Abbot Thomas had left the cloisters to marry a wife, Angharad or Mallt, by whom he had a large family.[7] He was determined to create an estate and make it a worthwhile inheritance. We know the names of

his sons by their appearance in litigation concerning former abbey property. The Pennants became a corporation whose business was to siphon off as much gain as possible from the estates under their stewardship. Abbot Thomas trained them in the same rapacious school. They were wolves in sheep's clothing. The astute father used his influence to secure for his sons leading positions in local affairs. His namesake Thomas became vicar of Holywell. Nicholas was abbot and Edward Seneschal of the lordship and a powerful figure in the government of the town of Holywell.

Abbot Nicholas had been summoned to Convocation in 1529 when the crucial Reformation Parliament was in session. This year saw the fall of Cardinal Wolsey and many ambitious courtiers were determined to rise at the expense of the expected reform of the Church. When this happened and church property was shared out, the local Pennants opposed anyone who encroached upon their territory. In the 1530s they were engaged in a programme for the protection of their own interests and property laboriously and patiently built up. They were no different from many gentry in the same position in the upwardly mobile rapidly changing Tudor society. Religious change had thrown every locality into confusion. There was both danger and opportunity. The first incident occurred in the summer of 1532.

The claim of Robert Pigot to be vicar of Holywell

The complaint of Robert Pigot, clerk, was made to the Court of the Star Chamber. He claimed that he had been lawfully inducted as vicar of Holywell in July 1532 and alleged that in the following month, whilst conveying his tithes of oats to the vicarage, he was at the instigation of Abbot Nicholas Pennant violently attacked by a band of twenty-one men. The assailants, led by Robert, prior of Basingwerk, included a monk, Thomas, and the abbot's brothers, David and John. The two clerics armed 'with great quarter-staffs' and the rest with 'bills, bows, clubs, swords and bucklers' chased poor Pigot until he escaped into a friendly refuge, protesting that he would have 'been slain and murdered had not the well-disposed people of the parish aided and rescued him'. Not content with intimidation his attackers robbed Pigot of his oats, forcibly entered and proceeded to occupy the vicarage denying the unfortunate clerk possession of his parsonage. It was reported that Abbot Nicholas publicly stated that he 'would keep the benefice in his own hands until his bastard son was able to possess it'. This incident was linked to a current dispute between Pigot and another clerk, Maurice ap Bell, as to which of them was the rightful vicar of Holywell.

The event divided the populace of Holywell and aroused great animosity. Passions ran so high that the two commissioners at the enquiry held at Holywell in March 1533 sent their findings to the Court without making a local pronouncement. The report shows that the Pennants were not universally popular and that there were witnesses who were not afraid to testify against them.[8]

The dispute at St Winefride's Well between William Holcroft and local church officials

This dispute took place soon after the suppression of Basingwerk Abbey when the rectory of Holywell which included the revenue of St Winefride's Well had been demised by the Crown to William Holcroft a court official. The complaint was heard in 1538/9 in the Court of Augmentation, part of whose business was to administer the lands and revenues of the dissolved monasteries on behalf of the Crown. The experience of William Holcroft provides a rare and early example of discontent in north Wales against the dissolution of the monasteries.[9]

45. *Thomas Cromwell.*

What is not stated in the court record is the culture clash between local Welsh speaking Catholic inhabitants, observing the customs of St Winefride's Well, and the intrusion of an English entrepreneur who was probably allied with the reforming party at court. Holcroft's position was open to attack from the unscrupulous Pennant family no matter what inhibition or reprimand they may have received from civil or ecclesiastical courts for their behaviour in the Pigot affair.[10]

Holcroft accused Nicholas Pennant of theft of tithe corn and forgery by using the conventual seal of the abbey after its dissolution. The late abbot pleaded that his predecessor had leased the tithes of Holywell for sixty years to his brother David, those of Brynford to his brother John, and, of Bagillt to his brother David. But the most interesting part of the record concerns the activities at St Winefride's Well on the eve of the launch of the royal assault on the cult of the saints. Holcroft's case was;

> … that there is and long has been in the parish of Holywell a chapel called St Winefride's Chapel lately belonging to Basingwerk Abbey. In the chapel is an image of St Winefride with a box before it in which people have long put their oblations, and where they offered their oxen, kine, and other things in the worship of that Saint.

The occasion was probably on the feast day of St Winefrede when the place was crowded with pilgrims and locals, some of whom had brought stock with them for the water of the well had long held a reputation for healing of cattle diseases. The basic cause of trouble was that the local people had lost control of the well. They came prepared to protest against the fact that the new financial arrangements were in the hands of a stranger, a situation they judged to be against their own and St Winefride' interests. They resented that their offerings had fallen into lay hands and were being taken away from Holywell. Angry and frustrated, they devised a course of action which deprived Holcroft of his unmerited gain.

Holcroft complained about their strategy. Quite simply, the locals thrust themselves to the fore in the persons of the church reeves Thomas Donald, David ap Henry and Hugh ap Jenkyn. Craftily they diverted the public from putting their offerings in the box placed in front of the statue of St Winefride in the chapel boldly shoving their own two collecting boxes under the noses of the crowd of pilgrims and congregation. Speaking plainly they informed them that 'such money as you offer in to the said stock goes to the King, and shall never be remedy for your souls, for standing here is one of the King's servants ready to take it forth'. The local churchmen implored them to put it instead 'into their own hands for the remedy of their souls'. Holcroft was incensed and condemned their action as 'sinister and crafty enticements.' He reckoned he had lost oblations amounting to £5 13s. 4d. and an ox of the value of £1 3s. 4d.

In resisting change, the locals outfaced their intruder and defended the honour of St Winefride. Theirs was a moral victory over a representative of the new order. Holcroft had his rent reduced by £10 a year a figure which coincided with the annual oblations at the well.

The effect of the dissolution of the monasteries was immediate and nation-wide. The swiftness of their closure was a masterstroke of asset stripping not witnessed before in British history and the whole plan was complete by 1540.

One of the motives for this exercise in pillage had been to rid the religious houses of shrines, relics, and images as a means of removing superstition and abuse. This policy was to be carried further, spurred on by the evangelical bishops at the king's command and orchestrated by Thomas Cromwell vice-regent of the Church in England. All religious buildings were to be purged of cultic features and practices. Pilgrimages were to cease and buildings stripped of the outward trappings of traditional worship and belief. The first command to remove was soon followed by another to destroy all features relating to the saints. Such objects were to be banished from churches, broken up, removed, whitewashed, smashed, sold or burnt as the movement away from Catholic belief progressed. The implementation of change was unpredictable, governmental and diocesan directives liable to go unheeded. They were always, if possible, to be met with passive resistance and stubborn determination to disobey. This was the reaction of countless local communities who wished to continue to observe Catholic rituals which had governed their daily lives for centuries. Its effect was not uniform because the measures, which sought to abolish these 'superstitions', could be evaded by sympathetic bishops, clergy, justices of the peace and local opinion. Some of the orders of central government took years to enforce in remote areas. London and the south of the country succumbed to waves of destruction almost immediately whereas Wales and parts of northern England 'the dark places of the land,' which retained pockets of strong Catholic sympathies, escaped wholesale until as late as the 1630s.

The most important factor which contributed to the uneven progress of the removal of the cult of saints was the part played by the reigning monarch in the progress of religious change from 1529 in the second half of the reign of Henry VIII until over thirty years later, when his last surviving daughter, Elizabeth, was queen and there began a new and final religious settlement. It is not intended to give a detailed account of the progress of the English Reformation but it is necessary to show the influence that successive Tudor sovereigns had on the changes in religion, which influenced the changes in policy effecting the survival of the cult of St Winefride.

The Royal attack on cultic practices
The progress of this unprecedented assault on the affairs of the Catholic Church. recently wrenched from Papal supremacy, was directed over the next thirty years by Henry VIII and his children. Their different attitudes towards the Catholic religion would determine the survival of the cult of St Winefride at Holywell and Shrewsbury. Pilgrimages, images, relics, candles, offerings, stained glass, access to sacred places, and religious buildings were all in jeopardy. The mind of the Tudors on religious affairs may be seen in the changes that they commanded to be made. Their ecclesiastical proposals were called royal injunctions in which were included their attacks on the cult of saints.

Henry VIII (d. 1547)
The decision to break with Rome and Papal authority was a constitutional change rather than a religious movement to adopt the protestant ideas and doctrines of the continental reformers. The reformation in England had not begun. Outwardly Henry always remained a convinced Catholic and still saw himself as 'defender of the faith' and became more conservative in his views towards the end of his life. The reforms he allowed he did not regard as anti-Catholic but for the welfare of his subjects. Such were the publication of the vernacular 'Great' Bible, an encouragement to establish grammar or 'King's' schools and the removal of religious superstition and abuses for which there was much evidence at his time. He sought to improve the economy by encouraging people to work harder and reduce time spent travelling on pilgrimages. He regarded money spent on these as wasteful and likewise on church buildings and offerings to saints and worship of their images and relics. This money should be used to help those in need. It was partly in this spirit, supported by evangelical bishops Cranmer, Ridley and Latimer, and Henry's vice-regent Thomas Cromwell, that directives for reform were issued in 1536 and 1538. Henry had not reckoned with the mixed reactions

46. Henry VIII.

of the majority of Catholics and the destructive fervour of urban Protestants, which greeted these directives. In spite of this wave of destruction the religious life of the country was little changed and went on as normal.

Henry VIII's Injunctions, 1536 and 1538
These royal directives were aimed at religious reform and elimination of superstitious practices and abuses. Specific targets for reform were pilgrimages and customs which had grown round them, particularly those connected with the veneration of saints and relics. Many of these religious practices were seen to be exaggerated and open to abuse from tricksters and charlatans. The government felt that far too much time, energy and money were being devoted to these beliefs and pursuits which could be better spent in the localities in care for pilgrims' families and the poor and needy. St Winefride's Well was affected as an important pilgrimage centre, and like other places throughout the kingdom, open to the same 'superstitions'. In effect the royal Injunctions and future sixteenth century prohibitions were for St Winefride's Well a notice of demolition awaiting to be carried. But when other sacred shrines and places were soon destroyed by the reformers' violent assault, the Well miraculously withstood the attack.

The first reforms were meant to be moderate and aimed at preservation rather than abolition and were drawn up by Thomas Cromwell as an accompaniment to teaching published earlier in 1536, known as the 'Ten Articles' which gave clear instruction on the place of saints in the life of believers. Guidance was given on 'Of honouring of saints' and 'Of praying to saints.' They were to be honoured as 'elect persons of Christ' who 'reign in glory' with Him and subject to 'laud and praise for their excellent virtues' and as examples of those who did 'not fear to die for Christ and his cause.' Saints were to be honoured as 'advancers of prayers and demands of the faithful unto Christ.' The people were to be taught that 'grace, remission of sin and salvation cannot be obtained but of God only, by the mediation of our Saviour Christ.' And they were not to think 'that any saint is more merciful, or will hear us sooner than Christ, or that any saint served for one thing, more than another, or is patron of the same.' It was suggested that the 'keeping of the celebration of Saints' days could 'be mitigated and moderated' by the king as supreme head of the Church.

This advice was followed by Injunctions published later in 1536. They reminded the clergy and their parishioners of the recent decision to abrogate (do away with) a large number of saints days which included that of St Winefride and others particularly during the months of harvest and law terms. Although aimed primarily at reducing the number of saints' days because of their effect on the economy and attempting to increase the number of working days, the eradication of abuse and superstition were the main reasons. Going on pilgrimages, and the extolling of images, relics and miracles were censured in 1536 and more strongly attacked two years later in 1538.

Clergy were required to devote one sermon every quarter year to exhorting their people to works of charity, mercy and faith as commanded in scripture and that they would 'please God more by the true exercise of their bodily labour and providing for their families, than as in wandering to pilgrimages, offering of money, candles, tapers to images or relics, or kissing or licking the same, saying over a number of beads, not understood … or in suchlike superstition. It would profit more their soul's health, if they bestow that on the poor and needy, which they would have bestowed upon images and relics.'

To remove the abuses surrounding pilgrimages and eliminate the practice clergy were ordered forthwith to 'take down and delay'[11] such feigned images abused with pilgrimages or offerings in order to avoid that most detestable offence of idolatry. No longer were candles, tapers or images of wax to be allowed to burn before any image or picture. It appears that concessions were made. Other images which were not 'abused' were allowed to remain, such as those that richly adorned the rood and some lights permitted: at the rood loft, before the sacrament of the altar and above the Easter sepulchre for adorning the church and divine service.

St Winefride's Well appears to have escaped this first wave of attack. Other places of pilgrimage with shrines and images were not so fortunate as we shall see when we have considered the set of injunctions published in the next reign. These came in 1547 on the death of Henry VIII and the accession of the nine-year-old Edward VI.

The reign of Edward VI (1547–53)

Henry VIII had no desire to take the Church further in an evangelical direction but the new boy-king, although head-strong, was under control of the ruling Privy Council led by his uncle, Somerset, and Archbishop Cranmer. The six years of the short reign of Edward VI marked a considerable change in religion and changes were introduced which later became a permanent feature of the constitution of the State and Church of Elizabeth I. The reforms of Edward's reign included a new English liturgy: two Books of Common Prayer in the vernacular were published in 1549 and 1552, the second more radical than the first. A new doctrinal statement was published in 1553 consisting of forty-two *Articles of Religion*. With Latin no longer the language of the liturgy, and, with a change in the communion service, there were signs that the Church was being driven in an evangelical direction by Archbishop Cranmer and some of the other bishops, although a minority were courageous enough to speak out for Catholic orthodoxy.

Two measures of Edward's reign had a direct effect on St Winefride's Well and Chapel. The first was the Chantries Act of 1547 (which we will consider below) and the second was a new set of injunctions effecting pilgrimages, relics, miracles, and images. These were virtually a repetition of the directives of the previous reign except for an important addition which showed a distinct departure in a direction away from the medieval Catholic past. There was to be no compromise. Instead there was a determination on the part of the State to get rid of them. The clergy were told:

> … that they shall take away, utterly extinct and destroy all shrines, covering of shrines, all tables, trundles or rolls of wax, pictures, paintings and all other monuments of feigned miracles, pilgrimages, idolatry and superstition, so that there remain no memory of the same in walls, glasses, windows or elsewhere within their churches or houses. And they shall exhort all their parishioners to do the like within their several houses.[12]

These same directives were to be repeated in 1559.

In London, most of the images were cleared from the churches by the end of the year. In a few places outside the capital there was organised iconoclasm at parish level.[13] Much depended upon the desire and ability of local clergy and gentry to enforce the law. The same applied to parts of Wales where there was a tendency to do nothing.

In January 1550, Parliament ordered individuals who had taken any of the above artefacts out of any church or chapel, to destroy them by the last day of June or they would be fined and subsequently imprisoned.

Some evidence of destruction of shrines and images

The following quotation shows how miraculous it was that St Winefride's well, chapel and shrine survived the destruction of the late 1530s:

> Down they came: the canonized saints, Cantilupe, Richard of Chichester, Hugh of Lincoln; the unofficial demi-gods and heroes such as Darvell Gadarn of Wales and John Schorn who conjured the Devil into a boot; down came the alabaster and Purbeck marble shrines at Bury St Edmunds, Winchester and Reading; statues of the Virgin succumbed at Cardigan, Caversham-with all her wax images, crutches, candles and brooches-Southwark, Worcester, Ipswich, Coventry, Penrice, Doncaster, Willesden, even Walsingham; Christ's Rood could no longer be seen at Boston, Boxley, Bromholm or Bermondsey, nor his Blood at Hailes; and all the other English saints in all the other holy places were smashed on the spot or taken on a final journey up to London along with whatever offerings had garnished their shrines.[14]

Government officials were active in Wales and in the diocese of St Asaph Thomas Cromwell's agent was Dr Ellis Price (*c.*1505–94), *Y Doctor Coch* (The Red Doctor), who has been described as 'an assiduous iconoclast in implementing the new laws against the 'superstitious' abuse of images and religious practices.'[15] He knew all about Holywell and showed his ruthless efficiency in the destruction of Derfel Gadarn.[16] Perhaps the defenders of St Winefride knew all about the 'Red Doctor' who had already paid a visit to Basingwerk and paraded his paramor with him when he visited the Welsh religious houses in 1535. They were probably on the look out for him and prepared to oppose anyone who sought to take away the image of their beloved Winefride. Although he had informed his master that he had done his duty by 'expulsing and taking away of certain "abusions", superstitions and hyprocises' in the diocese, but he gave no further details concerning them.[17] Thomas Pennant described him 'as the greatest of our knaves in the period in which he lived.' Elsewhere in Wales, Thomas Cromwell wrote to the local collaborator William Herbert to take down the image of the Virgin Mary at Penrhys 'with quietness and secrett maner as might be.'[18] Some Welsh images were hidden away waiting for the regime to change. This is what happened to *Y Ddelw Fyw* (The Living Image) which was discovered in taking down the old tower of the parish church Mold in 1768.[19]

It is possible to advance reasons for the survival of St Winefride's Well. The locals would not find it difficult, as other communities were to discover, to snuff out the candles and maintain their images and other representations of the legend of Winefride and Beuno in stained glass, decorated ceiling, and carved pendant over the well intact. Any visitors could mingle with the local population as they went to the well to collect their supply of water. They could not be deprived of their water supply and no one was foolish enough to think of destroying the well. It was God's creation and there it would remain until he judged otherwise and as such it continued to be an inspiration to the poets who sang its praises.

However, there are signs, that the number of pilgrims diminished because of the reduction in the value of the oblations. We have more positive evidence of the effect of the injunctions of 1536–8 and fall in numbers as early as 1542 from the lease of Gresford vicarage, Denbighshire, formerly a much frequented pilgrimage centre about twenty miles from Holywell. It laments the loss of offerings of pilgrims who came yearly from 'divers parts of the realm' whereby the church was strongly and beautifully erected and provided with ornaments and replenished with furniture. The profits and advantages brought by the pilgrims aided and favoured the inhabitants of the town and parish 'towards the better sustenation of their living'. There is no doubt that the cause of such loss of income is due to 'certain abusions, by a law abrogate and prohibited.'

There is evidence also that the religious changes made in the reign of Edward VI were effective in another nearby Denbighshire parish at Ruabon (near Wrexham). Here the town constable provided a list.

The new font in Ruabon Church was made by 'lewys mason' and set up on 15
September 1538
On the 17 March 1548/9 the pulpit was made:
On Whit Sunday 1549 mass was discontinued or rather the service was altered
And on 4 January 1550/1 the alter was pulled down
the first silver lost on 12 August 1551.[20]

Mary I (1553–58). A brief return to Papal Supremacy

It was now the turn of Mary the eldest child of Henry VIII to ascend the throne.
She could not forget the suffering and humiliation of her Spanish Catholic mother
Katherine of Aragon and remained throughout her life a devout Catholic and
supporter of the Papacy. The Duke of Northumberland had tried to fix the
succession on Lady Jane Grey thereby ensuring continued religious reform, but
failed after nine days. The people did not want Jane but preferred Mary. Most of
her subjects were prepared to accept the restoration of the Catholic religion of
her father and reconciliation with Rome. There was a price to be paid by the
reformers who were, in the eyes of Mary and her bishops, heretics. Cranmer,
Latimer and Ridley were to suffer martyrdom in the burnings at Oxford and to
wear the same crown as their Catholic countrymen wore in the previous two
reigns.

Putting the clock back and restoring the old ways appeared easy but it took
time and its executants made mistakes. Parliament accepted the return of Papal
supremacy on condition that they received indemnity from the return of Catholic
lands. Church reformers sought refuge abroad to await a favourable time to
return and learn from the continental reformers.

Mary set forth her religious agenda by issuing a set of injunctions with the
object of restoring the old Catholicism. The cost of reconciliation with Rome was
obtained by repeal of all anti-Papal legislation enacted since 1529. All reference
to royal supremacy was abolished, the liturgy in Latin restored, clergy were
forbidden to marry and those who had deprived, heretics repressed and
punished, and diocesan bishops were to set forth a uniform doctrine by homilies
(printed sermons for instruction to be read in divine service). The injunctions
authorised the return to Catholic practice and ordered:

> That all and all manner of processions of the Church be used, frequented and
> continued after the old order of the Church, in the Latin tongue.
> That all such holy days and fasting days be observed and kept, as were observed
> and kept in the latter time of Henry VIII.
> That the laudable and honest ceremonies which were wont to be used, frequented
> and observed in the Church be also hereafter used, frequented and observed.

What may have been done hesitatingly at St Winefride's Well in the uncertain
times of Edward VI could now be celebrated with undisguised joy and, whatever

had been stored away brought out of hiding with the full support of a newly elected Catholic bishop of St Asaph, Thomas Goldwell.

Bishop Goldwell, as a former member of Cardinal Pole's household in Italy, was held in high regard. He eventually took up residence at St Asaph in February 1556 and was there until November 1558. Not long in the diocese Goldwell, played a vital part in preserving the cult of St Winefride. He revived the pilgrimage to the well and prevailed upon Pope Paul IV, to renew the indulgences granted to such, who went to St Winefride's.[21] Although an act of 1547 abolished all chantries and confiscated their endowments, it appears that the chapel of St Winefride survived. This is because it was in the hands of the vicar of Holywell who, after the dissolution of Basingwerk Abbey, became entitled to the oblations of St Winefride's. In February 1542/3 Howell ap David was appointed priest vicar of Holywell and, when he died, Bishop Goldwell collated in his place Magister Gruff' Johnes, LLB as chaplain on 17 September 1557. His title was to 'the free chapel of St Wenefrede near the parish church of Holywell.' A stipend of £10 per annum was to be paid out of the oblations of the said chapel. Whatever remained over and above the said stipend and the vicar's portion was to be expended *in utilitatem dicte Capelle*.[22]

It is possible that the vicar of Holywell, Hugh ap David, appointed in 1542, survived in office until 1593.[23] If this took place, it could be another factor to encourage the retention of Catholic customs at St Winefride's well and toleration for those who continued in the old faith. Further proof of the survival of the cult of St Winefride is a group of records of cures at the well dating from the reign of Mary to that of Charles II.[24] The first cure narrative is brief. It concerns the healing of Harry, a youth of sixteen years of age, who, because he was so crippled, had to be taken to the well on a barrow. After being carried through the water four or five times he recovered. 'In memory of this soe miraculous cure, he was ever after called Harry Guenvrewi, that is to say, Harry St Wenefrides.'[25]

The hopes of a permanent reconciliation of the English Church to Rome ended with the death of Mary I on 17 November 1558. The nation had accepted the return to Papal authority but disliked Mary's marriage to Philip of Spain, found distasteful the burning of heretics, and was stunned by the loss of Calais in France, the last of England's continental possessions. The suddenness of these events, and Mary's unforeseen death, created a political and religious crisis. It had finally been decided that her half-sister Elizabeth, the child of Henry VIII and Ann Boleyn, should succeed to the Crown. The nation was once again faced with the prospect of a new religious agenda and the cult of St Winefride endangered.

However. at the beginning of Elizabeth's reign, miraculously it remained intact. The cult of St Winefride was once again endangered, but it entered the next reign intact. There is no record of damage or destruction to the well, crypt and chapel or its images and furnishings. Indeed there is proof to the contrary. When the

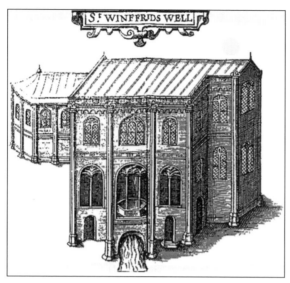

47. *St Winefride's Well as illustrated on John Speed's Map of Flintshire 1610.*

cartographer John Speed published the second part of his atlas *The Theatre of Great Britain*[26] we have the first recorded illustration of the exterior of St Winefride's Well which is the centre-piece of his map of Flintshire. Speed wrote a description:

Fons Sacre. Over the head of the Spring there is built a chapell of free stone, with Pillars curiously wrought and ingraved, in the Chancell whereof, and of glasse window, the picture of the Virgin is drawne, together with the memoriall of her life and death. To the Fountain Pilgrims are accustomed to repair in their zealous, but blinde devotion; and divers others resort to bathe in, holding firmely that the water is of much vertue.

There bee many red stones in the bottome of this Well, and muche greene mosse growing upon the sides; the superstitious of the people holding that those red spots in the stone: were drops of the Ladies bloud, which all the waters in the Spring can never wash away; and that the mosse about he wall was her haire, which though some of it be given to every stranger that comes, yet it never wasteth. But howsoever this be carried for truth by the tradition of time, the mosse itself smells exceeding sweet.[27]

In the post-medieval period St Winefride's Well was recognised as one of the wonders of Wales and John Speed's description gives a Protestant view of the legend and its recognition as a tourist attraction. But the main value of the description is to show that the building was undamaged and visited by pilgrims.

Thomas Pennant the eighteenth century antiquary in his description of the well building records.

On one side of a wall that supports the roof, was painted the tale of the tutelar saint; at present [c.1770s] almost defaced: over it is inscribed, in honorem Sanctae Weneferedae V & M. In another wall is an elegant nich, in which stood a statue of the Virgin Mary; pulled down, as I have been informed, in the year 1635. I have also heard, that there had been another of St Wenefrede …[28]

Notes

1. C. De Smedt, *Analecta Bollandia*, vol. 6 (Brussels 1887), pp. 310–52 – accounts of forty-seven miracle cures.

2. *Valor Ecclesiaticus*, a detailed valuation of church wealth, made in 1535.

3. D. R. Thomas, *History of the Diocese of St Asaph* (Oswestry, 1908–13), vol. 2, p. 190.

4. For the extent of these lands see FRO D/GW/221.

5. A. Jones, 'Basingwerk Abbey,' in *Essays presented to James Tait*, J.G Edwards, V. H. Galbraith, and E. F. Jacob (eds) (Manchester, 1933), p. 172–6.

6. D. M. Robinson, *The Cistercians in Wales Architecture and Archaeology 1130–1540*, Society of Antiquaries (London, 2006), p. 277.

7. G. Williams, *Wales and the Reformation* (Cardiff, UWP, 1997), fn 36, p. 80.

8. D. Williams, 'Basingwerk Abbey', *Citeaux*, vol. 32 (1981), p. 102.

9. J. C. Davies and E. A. Lewis, *Records of the Court of Augmentation Relating to Wales and Monmouthshire* (Cardiff, 1954), p. 96–7.

10. For the documents in this dispute see E. Owen 'The Monastery of Basingwerk at the period of its Dissolution,' *Flintshie Historical Society Publications*, 1919–20, pp. 74–85.

11. i.e. delete, efface, destroy.

12. Injunctions, 1547.

13. See for examples: R. Marks, *Image and Devotion in Late Medieval England* (Sutton, 2004): E. Duffy, *The Stripping of the Altars, Traditional Religion in England, 1400-1580* (Yale, 1992): M. Gray, *Images of Piety The Iconography of traditional religion in late medieval Wales* (BAR British Series, 316, 2000), pp. 73–86.

14. R. C. Finucane, *Miracles and Pilgrims Popular Beliefs in Medieval England* (Book Club Associates, 1977), pp. 204–5.

15 DNB under Ellis Price (*c.*1505–94).

16.Gray, op cit, p. 74.

17. G. Williams, op cit, *Wales and the Reformation*, p.125.

18. Ibid, p. 75.

19. D. R. Thomas, op cit, vol. 2, p. 409.

20. A. N. Palmer, *A History of the Parish of Ruabon* (Bridge Books, Wrexham, 1992), p. 90.

21. Browne Willis, *Survey of St Asaph* (London, 1801), p. 101.

22.. G. M. Griffiths, 'A St Asaph Register of Episcopal Acts, 1506–1571', *Journal of the Historical Society of the Church in Wales*, vol. 1, no. 11, 1956, pp. 36, 38, and 48.

23. D. R. Thomas, op cit, vol. 2, p. 195.

24. De Smedt, op cit, – miracles which occurred between 1556–1674.

25 Ibid, p. 311.

26. 'Wales The Second Part of John Speed's Atlas' The Theatre of Great Britain Book 2, Flintshire, chapter 13, p. 121. edited and printed London, 1676 (S.R. Publishers Ltd, 1970).

27. Ibid.

28. T. Pennant *The History of the Parishes of Whiteford and Holywell* (London 1796), p. 220 – T. Gray Hulse – notes that Pennant seems to have been misled into thinking there had been two images of the 'Virgin'; meaning of course, the virgin St Winefride. The capital 'V' led him to assume the BVM was meant. Pennant does not substantiate his claim.

4. 1558–1603

Introduction

During the long reign of Queen Elizabeth I the pattern for the continued survival of Catholicism in Holywell was established. It is a remarkable story, similar to other small Catholic communities throughout the land who were determined not to surrender their beliefs and practices. But there was more at stake in Holywell: the preservation of the cult of St Winefride. This helped to stiffen the resistance of the local Catholic community towards attempts made by the authorities to destroy the cult. Remarkably, in these years of persecution, pilgrims were not deterred from visiting the shrine and well of the saint to seek consolation from Winefride's prayers and the efficacy of healing waters.

48. Chapter House (left of centre and since demolished), St Asaph Cathedral: Moses Griffiths, watercolour, 1778.

The local Catholic laity kept the pilgrimages alive, always prepared to welcome visitors and provide hospitality. They came from many parts of Britain, members of the ranks of the peerage to the poorest of society. Some of the names of pilgrims and supplicants healed at the well survive in records of government spies and cure records kept by Catholic priests. Going on pilgrimage was a forbidden activity, practising the Catholic faith was illegal, and, later in Elizabeth's reign, to minister as a Catholic priest was a treasonable activity punishable by death.

Ranged against the small Catholic community in Holywell was the law of the land administered by bishops of St Asaph, as members of Her Majesty's Privy Council and Council in the Marches of Wales, with local justices of the peace as their servants. In a small community with Catholics inter-married with Anglicans there was pressure and opportunity for complicity to evade the law and the self-interest to maintain pilgrimages to support the local economy. Whatever the motive for the survival of devotion to the cult of St Winefride there were examples of courage and persistency in times of personal danger and persecution.

No people showed more courage than the spiritual leaders of the Catholic underground resistance movement, the ordained clergy. The previous generation of priests, ordained by the Marian episcopacy or before, either conformed or went to ground. There was a great danger that spiritual leadership would die with them and no one would be available to administer the Catholic rites of passage. They needed to be replaced by a new generation of priests. This happened in the late 1570s and the cult of St Winefride received the benefit of their support.

Father John Bennett (*c.*1543–1625) is the first and one of the most remarkable of Catholic priests to serve in Holywell. His long ministry in the area was spread over forty years of the difficult and perilous years of the reign of Elizabeth I (d.1603) and her successor James I (d.1625). Bennett's courage, heroism, and above all his pastoral work as a priest working in Holywell and north Wales earned him a reputation for sanctity and apostolic devotion. His story is heroic, full of adventure, and part of the unfolding drama which local Catholics shared in these formative years.

The long life of Father Bennett illustrates the changing fortunes of Catholicism from the reign of Edward VI to the death of James I. Bennett went to school in St Asaph in the reign of Mary I, when Goldwell was bishop. His father brought him to St Winefride's Well as a boy and he would have visited other holy wells in the vicinity. He was of the first generation of young men from Wales to attend the Catholic seminary at Douai in France to be trained as a priest for the Mission to England. After ordination he returned to Wales, was apprehended, detained and subjected to interrogation, torture and imprisonment. His ordeal brought him into contact with Sir Thomas Mostyn, the bishop of St Asaph, the Council in the Marches of Wales and the authorities in London, before he was sent into exile three years later. One of his companions in prison, Richard Gwyn, was martyred at Wrexham in 1584. Bennett wrote a record of Gwyn's life and Bennett's life was later discovered in a manuscript at the Star Inn at Holywell.[1] Abroad once more, the young priest was determined to continue his vocation as a missionary. To this end he became a Jesuit to which he was ideally suited and, with his ability to minister in the Welsh language, the Society sent him to Wales in 1590 when he returned to Holywell.

Father Bennett was thus in the unique position of serving in Holywell as probably the first Secular priest and is regarded by the Society of Jesus as the first of its missionary priests. At Holywell he welcomed other Jesuit priests such as Henry Garnet and Edward Oldcorne and ministered to a variety of pilgrims including those who came in the late summer of 1605. Although there is no record of where he lived in Holywell it is probable that his accommodation was provided by the Mostyn family of Talacre. They were resident at the former Basingwerk Abbey and the most influential of Catholic gentry in the neighbourhood. Bennett's life ended in 1625 when, hearing of an outbreak of the plague in London, he requested his superiors to be allowed to minister to the victims. There he died tending the sick, a worthy guardian of the cult of St Winefride, the first of the Jesuit mission who assumed that role at the end of the sixteenth century.

The enforcement of the state religion of Elizabeth I
Henry VIII had renounced the supremacy of the Pope in order to divorce Queen Katherine and marry Anne Boleyn. Elizabeth I was the union of this marriage. The Pope recognised neither this marriage nor the offspring whom he declared illegitimate. Elizabeth's mother had been executed when she was a baby and after this event it took Henry time to accept her as a legitmate successor to the English Crown. Her brother Edward VI became progressively more Protestant and devised the Crown upon Lady Jane Grey. Her sister Mary I, in her turn at religious settlement, reconciled England to the Pope and Catholicism. Excluded from the succession by her younger brother, sent to the Tower by her elder sister, and, when released under constant supervision, Elizabeth regarded her preservation as miraculous. Intelligent, cautious, devout and, like all the Tudor monarchs, with a will of her own, Elizabeth kept her own counsel determined to preserve herself and not burn more heretics. The unity of the nation in matters of religion was her prime concern. Anyone intent upon destroying this unity and failing to recognise the royal supremacy was her enemy.

Much was expected from this young queen from divergent ends of the religious spectrum. The reformers of the Edwardian Church of England, who had fled abroad at the accession of Mary, angered at the burning of the Protestant martyrs Ridley, Latimer and Cranmer, desired to move the Church in the direction of the Calvinists at Geneva. The Catholics hoped that the Church would remain within the Papal fold or at least retain the beliefs of Mary I secured by the marriage of

Elizabeth to a Catholic consort. The new monarch, however, enforced a religious settlement which favoured neither Rome nor Geneva 'but a Church of England truly catholic in all essentials and yet cleansed and reformed from the abuses which had gathered round it during the Middle Ages.'[2]

Hopes were dashed for the restoration of the cult of St Winefride by the publication of royal injuctions in the summer of 1559 and two acts of parliament earlier in the year. The royal injunctions were modelled on those of Edward in 1547. Images, relics and pilgrimages were condemned in the same words used a decade earlier. The condemnation of pilgrimages was further enforced by Bishop Jewel in a *Book of Homilies* to be read by clergy to their congregations in words strongly directed 'Against Images and the worshipping of them'.

> Wherefore, when we see men and women on heaps to go on pilgrimages to images, kneel before them, hold up their hands before them, set up candles, burn incense before them, offer up gold and silver unto them, hang up ships, crutches, chains, men and women of wax before them, attributing health and safeguard, the gifts of God, to them or the Saints whom they represent (as they rather would have it); who, I say, who can doubt, but that our image maintainers, agreeing in all idolatrious opinions, outward rites and ceremonies with the Gentiles idolaters, agree also with them in committing most abominable idolatry?. Wherefore God's horrible wrath and our most dreadful danger cannot be avoided without the destruction and utter abolishing of all such images and idols out of the church and temple of God: which to accomplish God put in the minds of all Christian princes.[3]

The full authority of the Church of England with the Queen as its Supreme Governor and the Episcopal Bench was behind the enforcement of such views. Once again, the cult of St Winefride was in extreme danger.

The back-bone of the Elizabethan settlement were the Act of Supremacy and the Act of Uniformity passed in Parliament early in 1559. Their object was religious comprehension, accommodation between Protestant and Catholic views, moderation and avoidance of strife in the realm. The ecclesiastical legislation of Henry VIII was reasserted. Elizabeth, determined to avoid dissension, chose to be called 'Supreme Governor' rather than 'Supreme Head' of the Church. A new prayer book was introduced which bowed to Protestant pressure with regard to the communion service and restored eucharistic vestments as a mark of catholicity. There appeared to be enough compromise if not to satisfy completely then sufficient enough to maintain peace and not extinguish future hopes of both Catholics and Protestants that reform would come their way later in the reign. The measures met with remarkably little opposition, and in most places there was a desire for toleration. The Queen, more than anyone, desired peace, but was resolved that anyone attempting to disturb this settlement whether Catholic or Protestant, would be treated as an enemy of the state.

The survival of Catholicism

Outwardly Catholicism survived and retained its identity throughout the reign of Elizabeth although reduced in numbers. Closely bound up with this was the cult of St Winefride and its related practices. The government was determined to root out what they saw as Catholic 'abuses and superstitions' and illegal assemblies. The force of law existed and was resorted to at the sign of any political or religious crisis from home or abroad and, as a result, there was inevitable persecution and repression. But such was the inbred nature of these observances associated with birth, death, prayer, and a desperate search for cures often by the incurable, that intervention was unsuccessful. In a peasant society, with a host of religious and social customs woven into the calendar community observances defied all attempts to ban them. That is why people continued to gather in the travelling season at St Winefride's Well. Local people encouraged such activities and participated in them for the same reason as the visitors. Constables and justices turned a blind eye to pilgrimages as long as they did not breach the peace, being unwilling to prosecute their neighbours and kinsfolk. The government, represented by bishops' officials, had to be content to act as police informers. In these circumstances the built-in resistance of traditional Catholic culture throughout rural Wales gave it virtual immunity and protection.

This situation was well described by the Welsh Benedictine Augustine Baker (b.1575).

> At the first, and for some years after the said change made by Queen Elizabeth the greatest part even of those who in their judgements and affections had before bin Catholickes, did not well discern any great fault, novelty or difference from the former religion … save only the change of language … in the which difference they conceived nothing of substance or essence to be. And so easily digested the new religion and accommodated themselves thereto; especially in Wales and in other places from London.[4]

The ordinary laity had no desire to give up their religious habits. They were unfamiliar with and most of them and ignorant of, the new beliefs which were not then available in their own language. A translation of the prayer book into the Welsh language did not appear until 1567 and William Morgan's Welsh Bible appeared in 1588. The abysmal lack of progress in the advance of religion in north Wales was conveyed by the bishop of Bangor, Nicholas Robinson, in a letter of 1567 to the Queen's minister Sir William Cecil.

Robinson reported that there was no lack of good government for 'the people live in much obedience, freedom and quiet, so that toward their prince they are like to continue faithful subjects, and among themselves peaceable neighbours.' The bishop's chief complaint was the people's backwardness in religion, lamenting 'that ignorance continueth many in the dregs of superstition' which he attributed to the ignorance and poverty of the clergy, 'and also upon the closing up of Gods word from them in an unknown tongue'. There were but six preachers in the three counties of his diocese. Apparently the effectiveness of Elizabeth's injunctions had not reached into rural Wales and the bishop reported:

> I have found since I came to this country Images and altars standing in churches undefaced, lewd and undecent vigils and watches observed, much pilgrimage going, many candles set up to the honour of saints, some relics yet carried about, and all the Country full of beads and knots, besides divers other monuments of wilful serving of God.

Robinson concluded his letter to Cecil on an optimistic note hoping that with the progress of reform such customs 'will daily decay,' an enterprise in which he would be assisted by George Bromley, the Chief Justice.[5]

The traditional Catholic practices Robinson described in his diocese in the counties of Caernarfon, Anglesey, and Merioneth were prevalent at St Winefride's Well in Flintshire in the neighbouring diocese of St Asaph. Robinson, as rector of Northop (1562–84), less than ten miles from Holywell, and being related to many of the local Catholic families of Conway, Pennant, Mostyn and others, had in mind the activities at the important Flintshire pilgrimage centre.

The sixteenth- and seventeenth-century records of cures at St Winefride's Well demonstrate that pilgrims continued to observe the rituals and experiences of medieval Catholic precursors. No civil or ecclesiastical authority dared to prevent Catholic religious gestures made openly in a public place for fear of riot. The distribution of the bountiful relics of St Winefride with which nature endowed her sacred well were the common property of the faithful and beyond confiscation.

The same variety of miracle cures continued to be reported[6] as taking place 'by the virtue of St Winefride's water'. Full relief was obtained from rheumatism, paralysis, and weakness of limbs. A deaf woman's hearing returned because she stuffed her ears with 'several stoppels of some of the mosse of the holy well.' 'One Lowry Davies of Carnarvon in the summer of 1617 went on foot in pilgrimage (as the custom in Catholic times was) to St Winefride's well with many others of her neighbours, rather out of pastime than devotion.' On her journey home she scorned the power of the well and was struck blind and taken back to the sacred place in hope of a cure. Her sight returned imperfectly after bathing her eyes and performing penance. In 1607, a young man of eighteen years of age from Lancaster 'being possessed and tormented by a wicked spirit for receiving the blessed sacrament unworthily' came to the feast of St Winefride 22 June' with his exorcists and 'many others to the sacred well with great devotion and the wicked spirit departed from him'. Protestants who experienced healing at the well became 'roman catholiques' and conversions are regularly reported.

It was recorded in 1623 that a man from Henllan, suffering from acute sciatica, in his agony received the assistance of a friend who

> … brought him a relique of S Wenefride inclosed in a stone crystall and silver case, and wished him to apply it to the place of his pain; which he did with all reverence, and withal vowed to go in pilgrimage to the Well of the holy Saint, therein to bathe himself, and morover promised an offering there.

He received lasting relief from his pain. It appears from the account that he was following the example of a woman of his village who, suffering from the same complaint, was healed by following the ritual of applying the relic, making an offering and going on pilgrimage to the well.

It is quite obvious then that many sections of the population did not wholeheartedly obey the government's religious edicts, few fully embraced the new religion, and most merely paid lip service by outwardly conforming and publicly attending the new church services. This did not prevent them from Catholic communal activities or the retention of traditional religious practices such as the use of charms, relics, holy water, and Latin prayers. Gradually, however, distinctions began to be made throughout the country based upon outward religious observance and names were attached to emerging religious groups. Those who rejected the catholicity of the Elizabethan settlement and wanted a more continental Protestant Church were called Puritans. They were persecuted for the threat they posed to the unity of the state. Those whose practices were more traditional and conservative than the Anglican Church permitted, on the whole were tolerated as long as they did not become a danger to the peace of the realm by being seen as the Queen's enemies. They fell into two main categories. The more moderate were known as Church papists.[7] They were those who outwardly conformed by attending Anglican worship at their parish churches. Those who totally separated themselves from the new state religion, deliberately absenting themselves from their parish churches, were called recusants i.e. those who refused and were regarded as enemies of the state because they sought the religious ministrations of Roman Catholic priests, who were banned by law, but managed to function quietly and in secret. A survey of the attitude of magistrates and unpaid justices of the peace made throughout the dioceses revealed them as Church papists, 'outwardly men conformable' and 'only making a good face of Religion.' Many of the clergy were no better and were seen as 'an army of time servers' who had passively and prudently submitted to a settlement. Tanner gave figures which showed that nearly a third of the enforcers of the law were not committed to the Elizabethan religious settlement.[8] This caused alarm in government circles, and the situation turned into crises and repression by a series of events which came to a head in 1570.

Elizabeth's cousin, Mary Stuart, Queen of Scots, a Roman Catholic, escaped over the border into England in 1568 and until her execution in 1587 posed a direct threat to Elizabeth's throne. She became a focus for disaffected Catholics, especially when Elizabeth showed no signs of marriage and slipped beyond child-bearing years. The first sign of unrest came the following year with the open revolt in the cause of true religion of the northern earls Westmoreland and Northumberland: a fact they demonstrated by entering Durham, setting up stone altars, having Mass sung in Latin , and destroying English Bibles. The rumour spread that Mary was to marry the Catholic Duke of Norfolk. Elizabeth brutally punished the rebels

49. Mary Stuart, Queen of Scots.

when 450 were executed. Worse was to come in 1570 when the papal bull *Regnans in excelsis*, deposed and excommunicated Elizabeth by order of Pius V. The Pope had declared war on the Queen of England and given Catholics his blessing for her removal by assassination which placed them in an impossible position.

St Winefride's Well: terrorist safe haven or Holy place?

The second part of the reign of Elizabeth was haunted by prospect of foreign invasion to restore the Catholic Church in England to its former place in the fold of the Universal Church with the Pope at its head. To achieve this end, the assassination of the Protestant queen was the avowed purpose of her enemies. The impact of the papal bull which deposed Elizabeth I in 1570, as the historian Froude declared, 'rendered treason a necessary part of the religious duties of every English Romanist.'[9] The throne and life of the Queen were threatened by

50. The execution of Mary, Queen of Scots, February 1587.

the Pope's legitimatisation of a Catholic crusade to conquer England. Her subjects, both Catholic and Protestant, were affronted by the Pope's temerity to depose her and his denunciation of their sovereign as a heretic and a bastard and resented the idea that they should overthrow their queen.

All places where Catholics gathered were under suspicion and subject to restrictions imposed by law for the maintenance of national security. The survival of St Winefride's Well was threatened not only for its cultic associations but also as a centre for illegal political activities. As such it was regarded as a dangerous place and, in times of crisis, viewed as a terrorist haven rather than a holy place.

The truth of this rather dramatic statement is seen against the background of steps taken by the government to protect the Queen and the national Church of England through the formulation of penal laws against Catholics, and their enforcement by the Privy Council and the local machinery of government. On the other hand, there was the changing nature of Catholic resistance through the training of new priests in European seminaries for missionary activities in the realm of England. A revitalised Catholicism and the deliberate absenting themselves of its members from its worship threatened the Church of England by growing numbers of recusants and dissenters. Catholics and Puritans were nonconformist bodies in waiting. The great majority of Catholics were loyal with no intention of involvement in treasonable activities, and with every likelihood to take up arms in defence of the realm against the Queen's enemies. But with the increase of plots against the Elizabeth's life, hostile relations with Spain, and the infiltration of seminary priests, the government maintained a state of continued vigilance against Roman Catholics.

The reported events from St Winefride's Well from 1570 until 1720 must be viewed against this background and it is from this second period of Elizabeth's reign that a distinct pattern of activity emerges for the survival of the cult of St Winefride during penal times. The holy place becomes a recognised meeting place for the Catholic community with the feasts of St Winefride in June and November occasions for pilgrimage. The well assumes an important place in the Catholic network as a spiritual centre where religious faculties may be obtained from both seminary and Jesuit priests established in Holywell. They became new guardians of the cult of St Winefride, which became a powerful psychological, social, and spiritual focus in the survival of northern Catholicism. With the help of government surveillance records, we are able to observe the persistence of the faithful Catholic community and the frustration of attempts to curtail their activities.

The laws against Catholics
The laws were introduced from the beginning of the reign of Elizabeth to place restrictions on the civil and political rights of Roman Catholics in the realm both lay and clerical. They were designed to detect and discipline the group of

Catholics who refused to attend church, namely the recusants, and were not directed against Catholics who attended worship in their parish churches, the so-called church papists. Robert Parsons, the Jesuit apologist, described the practise of these as commonplace: 'at the beginning of the reign of the Queen, when the danger of schism was not very well realized, for ten consecutive years practically all Catholics without distinction used to go to their churches.' Conformity to the Anglican Church was regarded as a test of allegiance to the Queen and the realm and the papacy identified with an attack on national life.

In 1559, the celebration of Catholic Mass was made illegal and all subjects were to attend Anglican services on Sundays and holy days. Failure to do so, recusancy, incurred a fine of one shilling for each absence. In 1563, upholding the authority of the Pope was made punishable by death for a second offence, and all clergy and office-holders were required to take the oath of supremacy, recognising the Queen as supreme governor of the Church. Most Catholics refused to do this because it meant denying the authority of the Pope in spiritual matters. In 1564, a Papal committee declared that English Catholics might not attend the services of the Church of England and faculties.[10] The concept of a separated Catholic Church united with Rome was developing into which priests and laity were received by reconciliation. There was the recognition of the need for more priests. But whatever was on the statute book there was little active persecution of Catholics and in most places tolerance. Fines for non-attendance at church went uncollected and oath-taking was easily evaded.

The publication of the Papal bull, *Regnans in excelcis,* in 1570 led to the enforcement of previous legislation and the addition of further penal laws which became more severe as the political crisis deepened over the years. 'England had, by 1570,' states a prominent Catholic historian, 'ceased to be a country where the mass of the people were anxious to be Catholics.'[11] The majority of people had accepted the religious settlement and worshipped in their parish churches and resented any threat to national security from Catholic aggressors.

The crisis for Catholics was the difficulty of continuing in their traditional ways through the shortage of priests and access to faculties, that is, the performance of Catholic rites – baptism, marriage, the saying of Mass, the provision of the sacrament of extreme unction to the dying. The imposition of restrictions on education, office holding, employment of servants, and later on travelling, were attacks on their freedom aimed at bringing them into the fold of the national church. The threat of heavy fines and forfeiture of property were to remain on the statute book until Catholic emancipation in 1829.

The new laws were directed at the means for maintaining Catholic religion. The government's reply to the Papal bull of 1570 was to make it high treason to publish it in England and introduce into the country 'crosses, pictures, beads, or such like vain and superstitious things from the Bishop or See of Rome.' The government faced by the infiltration of a new generation of English Catholic priests trained abroad in 1581, classed them as traitors to be punished by death. Fines for non-attendance at Church were raised to £20 per lunar month. A series of further laws of extreme severity were passed against Jesuit priests in the 1580s. In these years the government was reacting to a succession of plots aimed at the life of Elizabeth and establishing as her successor Mary Stuart. She was executed in 1587 and the Spanish Armada defeated in 1588. In 1593, Catholic recusants were forbidden to travel more than five miles from home without a special licence.

Penal legislation thus defined the new Catholic community, the leaders of whom were Catholic gentry. They sheltered the persecuted priests, provided them with a network of safe houses and hiding holes. In return, the gentry received their religious faculties in private chapels and the education of their children before they were sent to the continent. It was these families which provided recruits to a priest-hood continually decimated by martyrdom and persecution. St Winefride's Well was to provide an especial solace for this new generation of the faithful, many of whose families preserved their Catholic identity by inter marriage.

The enforcers of the laws against Catholics

The law was administered by a chain of officials extending from the Queen to the lowly constable in the smallest township of her dominion. For example, Holywell, in Flintshire, was policed by local executive officers, the town Constables, who received their orders from the local justices of the peace acting on behalf of the sheriff. These were town and county officials responsible for maintaining law and order in their locality. Any one charged with an offence was presented at the quarter sessions. If the offence was serious the culprit was housed in the local gaol at Flint. The quarter sessions were part of the system of justice placed under the jurisdiction of the body established for Wales by the second Act of Union in 1543, the Council in the Marches of Wales, presided over by a lord president appointed by the Crown. The Council was a delegative body of the Privy Council, part of whose courts was that of the Star Chamber. It exercised criminal and civil jurisdiction over Wales and the English border shires. The Privy Council, chosen by the monarch, was the chief executive arm of central government made up of the most important officers of State. In this way, Elizabeth was aware of what was going on in the localities and able to take appropriate executive action. An important local example of this is the instruction she gave in Privy Council in June 1579 to the Council in the Marches:

> To discover all Papist activities and recommend measures for suppressing them … to pay particular attention to the pilgrimages to St Winefride's Well and in view of the claim that the water is medicinal to appoint two men to test its properties; if not medicinal the Well should be destroyed …[12]

The Council in the Marches was centred at Ludlow and was the executive body responsible for serving the Crown. It made the royal will known in Wales and selected sheriffs and justices. Alongside the Council was the Court of Great Sessions. The sessions were held in each shire by an assize judge twice a year for six days. Flintshire was placed under the jurisdiction of the justices of Chester, whose circuit included the Welsh counties of Flintshire, Denbighshire and Montgomeryshire. The prosecution of Catholics, priest or laity, would take place either at the local assize, or Ludlow, with the matter on occasions being referred elsewhere and sometimes, if serious enough, to London.

The bishops of the Church of England, employed as executive officers by the Privy Council and Council in the Marches, were usually instructed to gather information about numbers of Catholics in their diocese, administer the oath of allegiance,

51. *Elizabeth I with Burghley and Walsingham. From* The Compleat Ambassador *by Dudley Digges (1655).*

issue instructions to their clergy, interrogate important Catholic prisoners and, on occasion, act as members of the local commission of the peace to investigate matters by visiting troubled spots. Bishops of St Asaph were engaged in all these superior 'policing' activities as overseers of their flock in ways not found in the ordinal at their consecration.

Bishop Thomas Davies (1561–73) exercised his brief in more tolerant times and was an efficient administrator intent on enforcing the religious settlement in his diocese as was apparent in the injunctions issued to his clergy at their first diocesan meeting. One ordered:

> That every of them shall forthwith avoyd, remove and put away, all and every fayned relyques and other superstycyons had withyn ther severall churches, and abolyshe ther autes (altars) yn the same, withyn eight days.[13]

His successor bishop William Hughes (1573–1600) was a more complex character, whose behaviour in his dealings with Father John Bennett was not at all 'fatherly' as we shall see. In his reply to Bishop Whitgift as vice president of the Council in the Marches, Hughes reported in 1577 'that there were no persons within his diocese refusing or neglecting to come to church'.[14] Although accused of neglect of his episcopal duties by the 1590s, he was zealous enough to regularly present recusants of all social degrees in the courts of Great Sessions.[15] In 1582, the report of increase in the number of recusants in the north Wales dioceses of Bangor and St Asaph was blamed on the slackness of the justices, sheriffs and jurors. We have noticed above a certain reluctance to inform on recusants and operate the law against them, but sometimes even the most distinguished enforcer could be thwarted by hostility from traditional Catholics as, Nicholas Robinson, bishop of Bangor, informed the authorities in London when he was accused of showing tolerance towards them. 'Yet thus it is, yt. I have bene divers times in danger of my life in supressing pilgrimages, praying to Images, night watches at tombes of saints and other superstitions.'[16]

Chief among the Queen's protectors was Sir Francis Walsingham, Principal Secretary and Privy Councillor, whose Protestant outlook and travels in France, Italy and Switzerland gave him a European experience. This led to recruitment of a network of double agents and spies. These he employed to inform him of the movement and plans of Catholics in the courts and seminaries of Europe and to keep watch on the movement of priests, the importation of Catholic literature, and to conspire to destroy the Queen's enemies.

His methods of intelligence gathering and use of spies were employed to a lesser degree by the bishops. They had their spies and pursuivants who kept watch on the houses of recusants and those suspected of harbouring priests. Most priests who were captured were taken into custody by local authorities. Walsingham offered reward for information such as that provided by 'a Welshman named Griffiths, who declared that he knew of a cave along the sea-shore in Wales three fathoms deep,' which was a great sheltering place for recusants.[17]

In 1579 the Privy Council issued a warning to bishops that:

> Certain evil disposed persons being sent from Rome and termed reconcilers have crept among her highness' subjects of those parts and seduced many of them from the true religion established in the realm.

This new threat was from the priests of the Society of Jesus. The Jesuits joined other priests on the English mission trained in the seminaries. They became what Eamon Duffy has called the 'storm troopers of the new English Catholicism'.[18]

The new vanguard – missionary priests
It was William Allen, an Oxford don from Lancashire, who was responsible for a new wave of priests of English origin who sustained and reinvigorated the faltering Catholic remnant scattered across England and Wales. For this achievement he was later created a cardinal. On his arrival at Douai University in 1568, Allen, with the help of other exiles, founded an English college and from

this developed the idea of providing 'a continuity of clerical and theological training for when England was returned to Catholic Communion.' The training of these men recruited from English and Welsh Catholics for the English Mission was in the spirit of the reformed Catholicism of the counter-reformation and influenced by the recently founded Society of Jesus. Allen set about training priests to work in a post-medieval climate and face challenges from other beliefs and rigours of state persecution. He brought a sense of urgency and realism to preparation for a missionary priesthood.

The importance of his venture was recognised by the patronage of the Pope and King Philip II of Spain. Allen's intention was to develop a strong spirituality in his recruits for the task of the reconciliation of Catholics and their nurture in the faith. He set out to produce pastors rather than evangelists, to preserve the existing Catholic population rather than convert heretics. The seminarians had daily mass, regular weekly communion, meditation, the mysteries of the rosary, and the Jesuit spiritual exercises. The first ordinations took place in 1573 and four priests were dispatched on the new venture. Other colleges or seminaries were founded at Rome (1579), Valladolid (1586) and Seville (1592). By the year 1580, 100 priests had been sent on the Mission and it is calculated that in the reign of Elizabeth I at least 471 were active. The English government made every effort to wipe out the Mission and at least 294 priests (62%) were imprisoned and a further 116 were executed, 17 died in gaol and 91 were banished.[19]

In 1580, the English Jesuits Edmund Campion and Robert Parsons led the first Jesuit Mission to England. After a year, Campion was captured and executed, and Parsons fled to France. But more members of the Society were to follow and ten years later we see the beginning of a Jesuit Mission in Holywell which continued until 1930. In the closing decade of the sixteenth century, St Winefride's Well was visited by Jesuit priests who were later martyred. From the beginning of the Mission both Jesuit and secular priests worked together, but because there was no defined leadership the relations between the two groups became strained.

The mission to north Wales

Wales was considered to be an important centre for missionary activity because of the strength of traditional Catholicism. This potential for support to the Mission was reflected in the number of Welsh students in the seminaries and the proportion of men who returned to serve in Wales.[20] Cleary estimated that between 1558 and 1642 over 119 Welsh students attended the seminaries with an additional fifty-eight coming from Herefordshire (an English border county in which Welsh was spoken) and forty-one from the rest of the March: a total of 218. Of these fifty-three were ordained priest in the reign of Elizabeth I, of whom forty-six have been traced as serving on the Welsh mission. Of the first fifty-two priests sent from Douai between 1574–78, eleven came from Wales. The number of students ordained at Douai in Elizabeth's reign from the north Wales dioceses

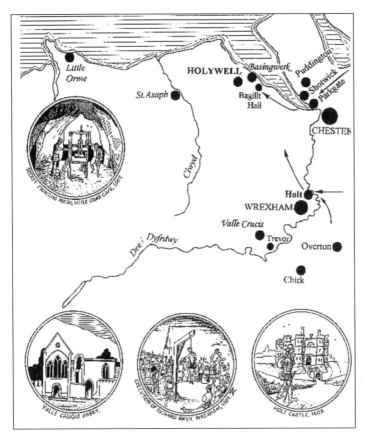

52. *Recusant and Jesuit activities in north-east Wales sixteenth and seventeenth centuries.*

of Bangor were eleven and St Asaph twenty. These numbers fell dramatically in the years 1603–42: two from Bangor and six from St Asaph. Note these figures are for Douai and do not include other seminaries.

We are fortunate in being able to recreate a picture of the hazards of the Mission in north Wales from the circumstances surrounding the experiences of five priests who served there and the recusants among whom they laboured. Their stories reflect the adventures and fate suffered by other priests on the Mission in general in Elizabeth's reign and the help and resources available to sustain them. The shared witness of priests and Catholic laity is seen in these accounts and the importance of St Winefride's Well in their activities.

Catholic lives. Narratives of adventure, imprisonment, suffering, and martyrdom. 1575–1603[21]

The Edwards family of Plas Newydd, Chirk
The most active recusant gentry family in north-east Wales in the sixteenth and seventeenth centuries lived at Chirk, a border parish in the diocese of St Asaph. They were the Edwardses, who were in possession of a number of estates, the chief of which was Plas Newydd where they chose to reside. The house was

secluded, protected by a moat, in the shadow of Chirk Castle (built by Roger Mortimer in the reign of Edward I). Nearer Llangollen they owned Plas yn Pentre, a former grange of Valle Crucis Abbey. The family had been in the service of Sir William Stanley, patron of St Winefride's Well. During the reign of Henry VIII, William Edwards served with distinction at Tournai (1513) and became a member of the king's bodyguard and last steward of the estates of Valle Crucis Abbey, Llangollen. He was well placed to enrich his estates when the monastery was dissolved and the family continued in royal service and received profitable lease of land in the area. John Edwards I (d.1557) fought at Boulogne in 1544 and was sheriff of Flintshire (1546) and Denbighshire (1547). The family had connections with Flintshire through marriage with the Hookes family of Leadbrook in the parish of Flint and also further connections in the area with the recusant families of Conway, Pennant, Salisbury and Mostyn.

The Edwards family traced their ancestry back to Tudur Trefor (*fl*.940) son-in-law of Hywel Dda, the Welsh lawgiver, as did the Mostyn family. They had an inbred ability to survive which, together with an appetite for litigation, aided their determination to remain traditionally Catholic. Wealth, social position and 'safe' houses gave them a certain amount of immunity from prosecution as recusants and they continued to practise their religion undisturbed until they came to the attention of the authorities in the 1570s. From that time onwards they were always under suspicion and faced imprisonment and fines until the outbreak of the English Civil War and the abandonment of their Catholicism. Their first encounter with the authorities came in 1577, and the report gives some indication of Catholic recusancy in north-east Wales and the importance of St Winefride's Well as a meeting place for co-religionists.

In the late 1570s, the government was threatened by attempts by France and Spain to mount an invasion to replace Elizabeth I by Mary Stuart, and the infiltration of missionary priests. North Wales was named as a possible landing place for an invasion force and a Catholic rising. Extra vigilance was required, and this need was strengthened by the appointment of John Whitgift, bishop of Worcester as vice president of the Council in the Marches of Wales, to act in the absence of Sir Henry Sydney, the lord president, now made lord lieutenant of Ireland. Sydney had gained a reputation for slackness and leniency in his dealings with the Catholics. Whitgift's appointment provided the right antidote, impervious as he was to either Catholics or Puritans, and determined to pursue a course designed to protect Elizabeth's religious settlement.

Whitgift was instructed by Burghley, the Lord Treasurer, to write to him personally and inform the Privy Council of events in Wales and the borders. One of the first pieces of intelligence he passed on to them was a memorandum, taken by George Bromley a law officer of the Council in the Marches. It was information given him by two school masters, Thomas Laurence, head of Shrewsbury School, and his assistant Richard Atkyns, which incriminated John Edwards and his family for their involvement in illegal religious activities at his house at Plas Newydd and further afield.[22] They gave damning evidence of the clear intention of the Edwards family to continue in traditional Catholic ways contrary to the laws' demands.

Plas Newydd was an illicit meeting place for 'disorders'. It was reported that Lady Throckmorton, the wife of Mr Justice Throckmorton, and others, heard Mass in the house. It was alleged 'that those that said Mass were five, and so apparelled that they could not be known' and went on to name 'one Hughes as the chief sayer of Mass: and that he came from beyond the seas and that he taught the son of Sir John Throckmorton.' Hughes was Father Edward Hughes a seminarian priest trained at Douai and at work in the Maelor, that detached part of Flintshire not far from Chirk.

It was further alleged 'that these priests, distributed to those that heard Mass certain beads, called "pardon beads", which were little beads of glass; and which they used to tie at the end of their other beads.' They also gave them *agnus dei*, a small wax discs made from the Easter candles, impressed with an image of the paschal lamb and blessed by the Pope, which served as an indulgence. These had been outlawed by parliament in 1571 and to be convicted of possession carried the death penalty.

The priests were also said to be making converts and reconciling others to the Catholic religion, re-baptising children, telling their parents that they should not attend Anglican worship, and conducting burial services at night for those who would not use the *Book of Common Prayer*.

The memorandum made clear the importance of St Winefride's Well in the area for Catholics who were prepared to travel over thirty miles to gather there. George Bromley was informed:

That upon St Winefride's day, Mrs Edwards went to Holywell by night, and there heard Mass in the night season. That they carried thither with them by night in mails and cloak-bags, all things pertaining to the saying of Mass, And that these Mass-sayers used their audience to receive holy water, and come to confession.

It was clear that the seminary priests were making some impact in north Wales and able on occasions to worship together. This was bad news to the Privy Council and on 17 February, 1578 the most senior members William Cecil (Lord Burghley), Robert Dudley (earl of Leicester), Sir Francis Walsingham and others sent their thanks to Whitgift ordering him to take immediate steps to deal with the situation by a special commission of oyer and terminer (to hear and determine) made up of Whitgift and the bishops of Bangor and St Asaph.

Edwards was duly examined and coolly played a waiting game refusing to incriminate himself and promising to send his wife and children, who were then in hiding for questioning before the commission, a promise which went unfilled. The commissioners were ordered to keep him in prison but apparently he was eventually released and fined for recusancy.[23]

Further light was thrown on the activities at Plas Newydd when, in 1834, two images of the 'Bound Christ' and 'St Armel' were found under the floorboards in Plas yn Pentre the other Edwards' residence at Trevor near Llangollen. These figures made of alabaster are thought to have come from Plas Newydd. The Bound Christ measured twenty-five inches and the St Armel table sixteen inches in height . It is thought they 'may have been part of a retable, of which other parts may have been. The Bound Christ if that were so, would have been the central portion;' the writer speculates further 'that it is possible that it was used for private worship by the Edwards family of Plas Newydd and could have been carried around with them on their journeys …'

The two images closely resemble those found elsewhere in former Catholic houses. The alabaster figure of the Bound Christ is similar to that of the wooden figure of the Mostyn Christ now in Bangor Cathedral. The figure was possibly from Rhuddlan Priory at its dissolution and came into the family of Piers Mostyn of Talacre. In order to prevent its destruction it might have been kept safe and treasured by relatives of the Mostyns through marriage to the staunchly recusant family of Pugh of Creuddyn, dealt with below. The figure of St Armel resembles another figure of the saint made of alabaster found at Stonyhurst, the home of Dorothy, the daughter of Sir Richard Shirburn of that place, who married John Edwards (IV) in 1625, and was probably a gift from the Welsh bridegroom.

53. Plas Newydd (New Hall) Chirk. The Edwards residence protected by its moat.

The Anglesey poet Lewys Môn (*fl.*1485–1527), who died at Valle Crucis, wrote in glowing terms of the Plas of William Edwards, the abbey's steward. It was obviously well fitted to be used as a Mass centre in penal times.

> *Islaw'r Waun selerau wyth*
> *Bwrdd a chapel, lle melys*
> *A pharod lle, ffeiriad llys.*

[Under the Chirk mansion eight cellars / Table and chapel, a sweet spot / A place prepared for the mansion's priest.][24]

St Richard Gwyn martyred at Wrexham, 15 October 1584
The details of Catholic activity revealed in the exposure of the Edwards family must have alerted the authorities to an increased vigilance in the apprehension of obstinate recusants and missionary priests at work in north Wales. New evidence was forthcoming less than two years later, which led to the martyrdom of the first Elizabethan Catholic layman in Wales. The victim, Richard Gwyn (also known as White), lived less than ten miles distance from Chirk. In all probability he had worshipped with members of the Edwards family, and there is no doubt of his acquaintance with the priests mentioned as saying mass at Plas Newydd. He is thus an important witness to the hardship and suffering endured by recusants and priests. These are related in the account of Gwyn's trial and martyrdom written shortly afterwards by Father John Bennett, who for part of his incarceration shared the same prison.

Richard Gwyn was born at Llanidloes in Montgomeryshire and followed the profession of schoolmaster at Overton, in Flintshire, and in the Wrexham district of Denbighshire. At the time of his arrest in September 1579, he was married with a number of children. His Catholicism had been noted and the consequent persecution forced him to teach in a barn nearby at Erbistock and go into hiding. Gwyn was a marked man, recognised as an intermediary between the new seminary priests and local Catholic families. He was a man of great ability and wrote religious poetry and his enthusiasm for the Catholic faith made him many friends with the new seminary priests of whom he numbered fifteen.

It is believed that zealous Puritans from Chester, in which diocese Overton then was, resented his Catholic witness and laid information against him to the Bishop of Chester. As a result Gwyn was examined at Eyton (the same place as John Edwards) and transferred to Wrexham gaol from which he escaped only to be re-arrested in July 1580. Henceforth freedom was denied him and he was continually moved, examined and tortured in the places and prisons he was transferred to – at Ruthin, Wrexham, Holt, Bewdley, Bridgnorth and Ludlow, until he was returned to Wrexham for a re-trail, judgement and martyrdom on 15 October 1584.

An account of Gwyn's life was written shortly after his execution by Father John Bennett (who had met him in Bewdley gaol in 1583) to verify the facts of his martyrdom. Pope Paul VI canonized Richard Gwyn in 1970. Another seminary priest known to Gwyn was Father Edward Hughes, who may have taught Robert Jones, SJ, (*c*.1564–1615), the future Jesuit Provincial, who proceeded to Douai in 1582 with the two nephews of John Edwards.

There is a passage in the life of Richard Gwyn when his martyrdom is compared to that of St Winefride's:

54. *St Richard Gwyn.*

> And is it any wonder, the people knew his innocency being well acquainted with the good man's conversation ye space of XXtie years together, they knew his cause to be just and honest being directly for Religion. They knew ye example to be rare, the like never heard of in Wales since the death of St Winefride, traceing therein the happy steppes of his blessed countryman Saint Albano the first martyr of the ancient Britons and proto martyr of this Island.[25]

In pursuit of seminary priests

The long confinement of Richard Gwyn is an indication of the patience and thoroughness of the authorities in their attempt to uncover the activities of recusants and seminary priests. An example of their diligence and anxiety is shown in a letter of May 1582, written by Bishop Nicholas Robinson, to the arch-spy seeker Sir Francis Walsingham. The bishop boasts of his reputation amongst the Catholic exiles, of whom there were some notable ones from his own diocese, as 'a persecutor,' and continues:

> … for that long time I have laid wait for their massing priests and such as hear them, and do make inquisition twice every year through every parish of such, whereby though some times there were many that did withdraw themselves from the Church, yet now in my whole diocese there be but six.[26]

Father Robert Gwyn

Father Robert Gwyn came from Bodfel in Llŷn, in the diocese of Bangor. He graduated from Corpus Christi College, Oxford in 1568 and was taken overseas by Robert Owen of Plas-du, entering the seminary at Douai in 1571. On ordination in 1575, he returned to Llŷn and had an immediate effect. College diaries of the English College in Rome for 1576 note 'that many devout women in Wales were so influenced by Gwyn's words that they put to flight the 'heresiarch and pseudo-bishop' Nicholas Robinson who came to capture their missioner.'[27] He was soon saying Mass in the house of Robert's father, Thomas Owen, a staunchly recusant squire who known to have harboured six priests and was the leader of a Catholic group of 'above four score persons.' Other members of the family lived in exile and played an important role in forming links with secret agents and the governments of France and Spain. At home, the family began to feel the pressure of persecution and financial difficulties. In north Wales the Owen and Pugh families, with others, were members of a network of Catholic gentry who provided seminary priests a rare opportunity for fellowship.[28] Robert Gwyn worked in many parts of Wales including the Maelor and the Usk valley, and eventually found refuge near Abergavenny in 1586, where he appears to have died in obscurity.

It is said that he 'helped his afflicted native land as much through his writings as his actions,' and Gwyn's great contribution to the Catholic community in Wales was the effort he made to compose religious works in Welsh, possible including a Welsh translation of Robert Person's *Christian Directory*. He is particularly remembered as the possible author of *Y Drych Cristionogawl*, a work dealing with 'the four last Things,' part of which was printed in 1586–7 in a cave. Gwyn had met the Jesuits Robert Persons and Edward Campion at a conference in Uxbridge in 1580 to discover the means of publishing Catholic works. As a result, a secret press was set up in the Bangor diocese, by which time Bishop Nicholas Robinson was dead. There is no record of Robert Gwyn's having been imprisoned.

Father William Davies, martyred 27 July 1593.
The ministry of Father William Davies was short and ended tragically with his martyrdom. It was a fate shared by many seminarian and Jesuit priests who worked on the mission. Relentlessly hunted down by a hostile Anglican Church and government, they had to work undercover, but were generally safe and protected in Welsh Catholic areas. Many priests were captured when they had the misfortune to come across a 'fanatic' or over-zealous official who gave them over to the authorities. When this happened, the local populace showed anger and indignation at the way the law operated against their fellow religious.

The work of the priest was built on trust and he had to rely on people not to betray his activities. Suspicions would be aroused when people went off together on a journey to a mass centre or further afield on pilgrimage. Infiltration was an age-old method of detection and informers were rewarded. The priest's task was to reconcile Catholics to their old faith and supply them with religious aids for worship. The Seminarian priests were part of the Catholic Church of the counter reformation, with ideas of reform, and a new spirituality, of which a major vehicle was the printed word. The missionary priests were educated in the main-stream of Catholic learning and the most able of them, like Robert Parsons, became apologists for the faith. There was a need for the translation of some of these works into Welsh and men like Father Robert Gwyn were able to perform that task. The major difficulty was book circulation. How could you smuggle into the country banned books when the ports were continually watched and cargoes searched? The obvious course of action was the risky business of setting up your own secret printing press and this is what they decided to do in north Wales.

The instigator of the scheme was the leading recusant layman Robert Pugh, of Penrhyn Creuddyn, a Caernarfonshire estate bordering on Denbighshire, where he had been high sheriff and member of parliament. His estate lay in the two dioceses of St Asaph and Bangor and he was subject to harassment from both bishops. In 1584, he was reported to Bishop William Hughes as a recusant, together with his wife and ten neighbouring parishioners, and subject to further scrutiny in 1586, when the Earl of Pembroke began his career as lord president of the Council of the Marches in Wales.[29] Undaunted by the authorities, Pugh embarked upon a scheme to outwit them, and set up a secret printing press, possibly under the persuasion of Father Robert Gwyn. Like many recusant enterprises it was ingenious and well hidden. Pugh chose to site his press in a cave at Rhiwledyn on the Little Orme near Llandudno. It was spacious, 'three fathoms deep,' well-furnished with living quarters large enough to be used as a little chapel and accommodating the necessary printing equipment. Pugh, alert to possible detection, provided two entrances, one as an escape route, and arms for defence. The small team assembled by Pugh included his cousin, Hugh Thomas, from Watford, four other anonymous persons and two priests. One of the priests was a Roger Thackwell, a printer, the other Father William Davies, and at one time there were said to have been as many as a dozen priests in the cave.

Their secret enterprise lasted for six months over the winter of 1586–7, during which time they are said to have printed *Y Drych Cristianogal*. In February 1587 Pugh's company were discovered and the authorities informed. The nearest justice of the peace, Sir Thomas Mostyn, of Gloddaeth, was summoned, and took with him eleven men to apprehend the Catholics.[30] Arriving at dusk, he posted a watch and delayed acting until first light the next day. William Griffith, chancellor of Bangor, later reported to Archbishop Whitgift that:

'Thomas Mostyn came to the cave mouth and durst not or took on him not to dare to enter and by the next morning all were suffered to escape …There was found the next day in the cave weapons, victuals and the cave boarded and their altar wainscotted.'[31] The Chancellor reported that they had thrown the lead print into the sea. The Catholic company had eluded capture and became fugitives.

Nothing was heard of Robert Pugh and Father William Davies until their arrest

55. Blessed William Davies: memorial in Our Lady Queen of Martyrs RC Church in Beaumaris, Anglesey.

at Holyhead on 15 March 1592, engaged on making arrangements for the passage of four students to the new seminary at Valladolid in Spain. Here they were detected by a zealous Protestant, Foulk Thomas. Robert Pugh managed to escape, but William Davies, in spite of local hostility, was taken into custody and transferred to Beaumaris gaol. The justices, two judges of assize, examined Father William Davies with the new bishop of Bangor, Hugh Bellot, and others. Davies was found guilty on a charge of treason and moved to Ludlow, where he was again examined and offered his freedom if he would recant. After spending a year in various prisons the brave priest was returned to Beaumaris, and on 27 July the postponed sentenced was carried out. He faced his time in prison with equanimity and courage and his execution caused great grief and anger in the local population, who refused to co-operate with the authorities. Present at the execution was John Edwards of Plas Newydd, who is reputed to have dipped his handkerchief in the martyr's blood, and also received a relic. Father William Davies was the first Welsh priest to suffer martyrdom in the reign of Elizabeth. Robert Pugh continued as a recusant throughout his long life and the number of recusants in Creuddyn in 1611 totalled sixty-three. William Davies's nephew, William Evans, in company with William White, son of Richard Gwyn, sought admission at Douai College on 6 September 1598. The blood of the martyrs was the seed of the Church in this time of persecution.

Father John Bennett (c.1550–1625)
Father John Bennett had a particularly long life full of adventure and service. He survived imprisonment and torture as a seminary priest. Returning from exile as a Jesuit, he narrowly avoided capture in a pursuivant's raid in a priest-hunt and survived for another thirty years. The circumstances of his death in 1625 summed up his character and dedication to Catholicism and the service of others when he died of the plague ministering to victims in London, being sent there at his own request. Bennett came from a Flintshire Catholic family and was born at Bryn Canellan, Cwm, near St Asaph. He was a fluent Welsh speaker which was of inestimable value in his work as a Jesuit missioner in Wales.[32]

John Bennett made an important contribution to the Catholic cause in north

Wales. It is probably through Bennett that we obtain *The Principal Sources for the life of Richard Gwyn*, a full account of the examination, trial and torture of St Richard Gwyn, gained first hand in 1583 from their shared imprisonment. In all probability he is amongst the candidates for the possible authorship of the martyr's life,[33] and for the record of his own imprisonment and brief account of his life which survives in the hand of Father John Hughes, SJ, (*c.*1615–1686), alias John Hugh Owen, the youngest son of Hugh Owen (*c.*1575–1642) of Gwenynog.

The account of Bennett's life shows the love which people felt for him:

Indeed the Faithfull people had an exceedings greate esteeme of him, whome in his life time they comonly called the Sainct. Finally after he had laboured about 50 yeares in the Vineard of Christ wth great proffitt being almost 80 yeares old, he would needs crowne all his Apostolicall Merrits by offering himself a Sacrificial Victime of Charity for ye spirituall weale of his nighbour of dying in the service of the infected with the plague.

Bennett's priestly ministry follows the same pattern as those of some of his contemporaries. From the account of his life we learn more about his brief years as a secular priest from, 1578 to 1586, than the years he spent as a member of the Society of Jesus, 1586–1625. In the Society's lists John Bennett is placed as the first Missioner in Holywell from 1590–1625. As a matter of course he was frequently absent from the town on official matters of the Society such as conferences, and the obligatory annual eight day retreat for renewal of vows. But the evidence given in the account of his Life for his connection with Holywell suggests that this was the principal centre of his Mission after 1590.

And so he soone after returned to his pious labours in Wales, where he spent the rest of his life with greate paines & diligence in the continuall exercise of his Apostolicall function, assistinge for the most part the poore, & meaner sort of people, who about Holywell & elsewhere in North Wales flocked to him in such multitudes to receave the Spiritual Cordialls & Divine food wch he freely & copiously ministred to them, that in the depth of night he used to have an hundred of them in one assembly: wch to him that will consider wth what rigour the Tyrannical Lawes agst Cath. Were then putt in Execution, will seem noe smale wonder.[34]

There is thus a veiled but very apparent reference to the pilgrimages to St Winefride's Well and the function of a priest at such gatherings. These are frequently reported in Bennett's time as we will see.

Between 1578 and 1586, Father Bennett experienced capture, examination, and imprisonment. His is the fullest account we have of a priest from St Asaph diocese experiencing this ordeal, and gives a unique portrait of the behaviour of those responsible for administering the law to seminarian priests.

Bennett was one of the first students at Douai, part of a contingent from Wales. He moved with the college to Rheims in 1578 and was ordained in Cambrai in March the same year, and sent to England on 2 May 1580. Wales was his destination, with some of the other priests mentioned above. But after about two years in Wales he had the misfortune to be captured. Bennett was walking in the vicinity of Gloddaeth, near Llandudno, when he was recognised by a servant of Sir Thomas Mostyn, the local justice, to whom he reported the matter. When challenged by Mostyn he admitted his profession and was sent by him to Bishop William Hughes of St Asaph.

During three days of examination Bishop Hughes attempted to persuade Bennett to conform and offered him a good living in his diocese if he did so. The priest declined such an offer and the bishop, realising his intransigence, had him conveyed to gaol in Flint Castle, but not before Hughes deprived him of his 'Case of holy Reliques that he wore about his neck' which the Bishop proceeded to put round his own neck. It was later reputed to have preserved the Bishop from drowning! From Flint, Bennett was taken to the Court of Great Session being held at Holywell. Here Bennett answered his interrogators in the Welsh language and his courage made a great impression on the local people and gentry of whom it was said that, 'in memory of Catholic Religion and affection thereto did what they could to save his life.' Bennett was loyal to the Queen, as he testified when challenged by the chief justice of Chester, Sir George Bromley, to tell him what he thought about the Queen: he replied 'I am her subject and as my duty is, I pray to God for her and have done so this very day before you were out of your bed.'

It was decided to send Bennett for examination by members of the Council of Wales in the Marches at Ludlow where he was lodged for convenience in gaols at Bewdley and Bridgnorth. Here he was imprisoned with other recusants, including Richard Gwyn. Being regarded as recalcitrant and difficult, the authorities subjected them all to frequent examination with brutal torture in order to try and break them down and extract information sufficient to incriminate them and the Catholic cause. Every precaution was taken to prevent them escaping, and Bennett 'for a long time dragged two iron bolts of great weight fastened to both his legs.' The utmost measures of torture were used in examination and when straightforward questioning failed the prisoners were stretched on the rack. The authorities were seeking information which would reveal the 'underground' movements of the Mission, such vital information as meeting places, recusant houses and acquaintances, persons reconciled to the Catholic faith, and those who supported them by alms giving. On January 15 1584 whilst on the rack Bennett was harangued by the Protestant chaplain and finding this intolerable he besought his torturer:

> … saying that he should in like manner clamp this talkative fellow in iron fetters
> and hoist him up to his own level as they did in the schools so that they might

debate on equal terms, and in the same circumstances.

Bennett was suspended in chains for seven hours and on being let down was so weak that he had to be carried back to his cell. He was allowed to make some recovery before being brought back ten days later and subjected to a similar ordeal by the solicitor-general, John Amyers, being suspended in chains for another three hours. Eventually the Council sent him to London where he stayed before being banished abroad on 14 September 1585. Fortunate to be alive, and undaunted, Bennett set off for the seminary at Rheims before proceeding to Verdun when on 6 September 1586 he entered the Society of Jesus, before returning to England a few weeks later.[35]

56. *'The trial of a Catholic priest in England',
engraving printed in Robert Person's,* de
persecutione Anglicana libellus *(Rome, 1582).*

The Jesuit Mission in Holywell, 1590–1930

Father John Bennett, SJ

The Society of Jesus founded in 1539 by Ignatius Loyola was approved by Pope Paul III the following year. Loyola placed the Society at the disposal of the Pope 'to go anywhere His Holiness will order, whether among the faithful or the infidels.' By the time of his death in 1556 there were over a thousand Jesuits engaged on mission and education throughout the world, in Europe, the Americas, India and the Far East. The first Englishmen entered the Society in 1555, although England was not yet part of the Society's activities.

Ignatius Loyola, a former soldier, organised the Society as an efficient administrative unit, with a strict chain of command, whose head, the superior general, was based in Rome, and to whom the members were answerable through regular reports, and a strict rule of life, Loyola had introduced a new spirituality. The immediate success of the Society in attracting members, and its growth, was based on training, spiritual discipline, and a world-wide administrative network. By 1580, the date of the first English Mission, there were more than 5,000 members.

Cardinal William Allen, who was instrumental in training seminary priests for

57. *Statue of St Ignatius Loyola in St Beuno's College, Tremeirchion.*

the English Mission, wanted Jesuits to be part of the enterprise and decided to convert the English Hospice in Rome (founded in 1362) into a college to educate priests for work in England and approached the superior general, Mercurian, for a Jesuit mission. Mercurian at first was reluctant to accede to his request, fearing that Jesuits priests would be hunted down and martyred as well as causing discontent amongst the secular priests already in England, but after some hesitation, he agreed.

The first Jesuit mission to England left Rome in April 1580. Robert Parsons, designated superior of the mission, was accompanied by Edmund Campion and Ralph Emerson. They were instructed not to get involved in politics or set out to convert Protestants, but that their primary objectives were to strengthen Roman Catholics in their faith and recover those who had left the Church out of ignorance and temptation. The fate these pioneers suffered became all too familiar, and was shared by members of the Society in England for over a hundred years. From the beginning, to be a Jesuit priest in England was an act of treason and to harbour one a capital offence. They were regarded as enemies of the state. Coastal towns were continually on the alert for them as they attempted to enter the country. Suspected Catholics were spied upon, hoping to reveal their whereabouts. Priests were relentlessly hunted down and lay Catholics, the recusants, prosecuted, and their houses searched for evidence of their activities.

The mentality was rather like that experienced in coastal towns in Britain during the Second World War, every stranger was suspected of being a Jesuit and every Catholic of collaborating with them. They were the new enemy, thought capable of performing any terrorist atrocity, particularly those aimed at the life of the Queen. As for the priests they worked 'underground' and were the 'S.O.E.' of the counter reformation, moving about in disguise from one safe-house to another and receiving special instructions from the Queen's enemies, the Spanish, whose invasion was expected to be

58. *Cardinal William Allen founder of seminaries in Europe to supply priests for the Mission to England and Wales.*

imminent. But the intentions and activities of the priests were non-violent. Their mission was to their fellow-Catholics, their object reconciliation not assassination. Unfortunately, the presence of Mary, Queen of Scots, the discovery of a number of plots to kill Elizabeth and the Protestant nationalism of marauding sea dogs with a special liking for Spanish treasure ships, whipped up public opinion. The outcome was inevitable. Edmund Campion was martyred at Tyburn on 1 December

59. The Venerable English College in Rome, formerly a medieval pilgrims' hospice: sixteenth-century drawing.

1581, and Robert Parsons was forced to flee abroad. Throughout the remaining years of the reign of Elizabeth relatively few Jesuits worked on the English Mission. There were eighteen in 1598, of whom four were in prison, and no Jesuit worked in Wales until 1590, when John Bennett was sent.

In 1590, Holywell, with its sacred place of St Winefride's Well, was chosen to be the first centre of the Jesuit Mission in Wales and was to enjoy the privilege of being served by the Society until 1930. Father John Bennett became their first recorded missioner, being accredited as being at Holywell from 1590 until his death in London on 8 September 1625. During these thirty-five years there is a record as detailed as any in Wales of Catholic activity in Holywell in which, by implication, Father John Bennett was deeply involved. He was part of the élite guard of Jesuit priests on the English Mission whose activities became legendary, particularly in the first quarter of a century between the execution of Edmund Campion and those who suffered at the time of the Gunpowder Plot in 1605.

The 1590s were years of uncertainty when Catholics hoped for freedom of worship or some kind of toleration. The disastrous sixteenth century was drawing to a close and, with it, the reign of the last Tudor monarch, and the question of the next occupant of the English throne was causing concern to many at home and abroad. During Elizabeth's final years secret overtures were being made to James VI of Scotland to pave the way for a peaceful succession. But if future

60. St Edmund Campion: Oxford scholar, Jesuit martyr.

prospects seemed more hopeful for Catholics, persecution continued unabated. Evidence of this is seen both in the experience of Father John Bennett in his new role as a Jesuit, and the place of St Winefride's Well as a place of pilgrimage.

Bennett's new career may have ended prematurely when he narrowly escaped capture whilst attending a meeting of priests of the Jesuit English mission in October 1591. All the dozen or so Jesuit priests at liberty on the Mission were gathered at a manor house called Baddesley Clinton in Warwickshire. They were men whose names would become more familiar over the next sixteen years as the government attempted to break the Jesuit underground movement. Many of those attending the meeting were later to suffer imprisonment, exile, and martyrdom. The roll call at Baddesley Clinton in 1591 reflected the heroic quality of the English Mission: Henry Garnet, superior; John Gerard; Robert Southwell; Edward Oldcorne; Thomas Lister; Richard Holtby; John Bennett and others. With them was Brother Nicholas Owen, 'little John,' the brave carpenter and creator of 'priest holes' in the network of safe houses across the country. One such priest hole saved them that day.

John Gerard, one of the participants, left an account of their narrow escape. He won renown for his bravery and dedication, and escaped in 1597 from the Tower of London by swinging on a rope over the tower ditch. Of the gathering he wrote:

> We had held several conferences and the Superior had seen each of us for a talk in private. Suddenly one of us raised the question: what we would do if the priest-hunter broke in without warning? (There were many of us there and an insufficient number of hiding places for all: were nine or ten Jesuits and some other priests besides a few lay men who were forced to live in hiding). 'Yes', said Father Garnet, 'we ought not to meet all at the same time now that that our numbers are growing every day. But we are gathered for God's glory. Until we have renewed our vows the responsibility is mine; after that it is yours.' Up to the day we renewed our vows he gave no sign of being worried; but on the day itself he warned us all to look to ourselves and not to stay on without very good reason, 'I won't guarantee your safety any longer', he told us. A number of the party, when they heard this got on their horses immediately after dinner and rode off. Five Jesuits and two secular priests stayed behind.[36]

Father Bennett was one of those who decided to leave. However, next morning at 5 a.m. the search party arrived at Baddesley Clinton and the remaining priests managed to evade arrest by delaying tactics from the servants, the presence of mind of their hostess and the hiding places constructed by Nicholas Owen.[37] Members of the Mission met in conference twice a year when they renewed their vows. There were other informal meetings when, for example, both secular and Jesuit priests came to St Winefride's Well. Father Gerard left an account of his visit there in 1593:

Once I was there on the 3rd of November, St Winefride's feast, and saw the change that takes place in the well that day. (The water rises a good foot above its ordinary level, and turns red as it rises, but the next day it is clearer than ever.) I myself watched the water moving and turning a reddish colour, water (mind you) that on any other day is so remarkably clear that you can pick out a pin lying on the bottom. It was winter there was a hard frost at the time, and though the ice in the stream had been broken by people crossing it the previous night I still found it very difficult to ford on my horse the next morning. But frost or no frost, I went down into the well like a good pilgrim. For a quarter of an hour I lay down in the water and prayed. When I came out my shirt was dripping. But I kept it on and I pulled my clothes over it and I was none the worse for my bathe.

    These are true facts. Also, there are frequently great and manifest miracles at the well …[38]

John Gerard then goes on to describe the cure experience of Father Edward Oldcorne, a fellow Jesuit and former medical student,[39] which took place around 1600. Garnet relates that:

Father Oldcorne had his heart on visiting the holy well; but St Winefride forestalled him. On his way he stopped at the dwelling of two maiden sisters. They were poor people, but rich in other ways, for they feared God, living and serving Him together, and keeping in their house a priest whom they had looked up to as their father. This good priest had taken from the stream one of those stones sprinkled with blood that I have just described. At the time of Mass he used to place it on the altar with the other relics. When Father Oldcorne noticed it he took it in his hands and kissed it very reverently. Then going aside by himself went down on his knees and began to lick the stone and hold part of it to his mouth. He prayed silently all the time. After half an hour he got up: all his pain was gone and the cancer cured. But he finished his pilgrimage to the well – not to beg a cure from St Winefride, but to make his thanksgiving for it. While he was there he recovered from the anaemia which was thought to be the cause of his cancer, and he came back stronger and healthier than he had for many years. I have told this story in the words that Father Oldcorne told it to me. The priest in whose house Father Oldcorne found the stone, confirmed the facts when I met him at St Omer.[40]

There are accounts of other cures in 1603 and 1604. That recorded in 1606 of Sir Roger Bodenham was celebrated later by a thanksgiving offering made by his daughter-in-law, Mary, who embroidered a beautiful chalice veil which may still be seen at the well.[41] Sir Roger was acting upon the advice of his physician in Herefordshire, Siôn Dafydd Rhys, who recommended him and others 'to go in pilgrimage to St Winefride's well, to see if by the prayers of that Blessed Saint he might obtain that miraculously which was not his to perform'. The cure narrative says that:

The honourable Knight was obedient to the precepts of his physician and went to Holywell where having devoutly bathed himself in the waters of this sacred Fountain, he became as whole and sound and as clean from all manner of scurf and leprosy as a child newly born, and so continued after yielding great thanks to almighty God and Blessed St Winefride for so singular benefit. And this was one great cause of Sir Roger's conversion, being not then a catholic.[42]

Siôn Dafydd Rhys was a talented Welsh recusant who devoted his life to furthering the Catholic cause in Wales. His career went back to the end of the reign of Mary when, as a student of Christ Church in Oxford, he went abroad with other Catholics from the diocese of Bangor. In Italy he earned his living as a tutor and graduated in medicine at Padua before returning to Wales to live with his uncle, Richard Davies (d.1581), bishop of St Davids. Rhys was a noted linguist and assisted his uncle in his translation into Welsh of the *Book of Common Prayer* and the *New Testament*. His contribution to the Catholic cause in Wales was by copying Catholic manuscripts, publishing a Welsh grammar and possibly setting up a secret press in a house he rented in Brecon. He was obviously an influential recusant as well as a reputable and sympathetic physician with a devotion for St Winefride. His Catholicism did not prevent him taking the oath of allegiance to Queen Elizabeth, which was both a test of his loyalty to the Crown and a means of his official practice of medicine.[43]

However beneficial a pilgrimage to Holywell proved, it was still a dangerous place to visit, and was kept under a strict scrutiny by the authorities responsible for security along the north Wales coast. Puritan and Protestant magistrates at Chester were particularly vigilant, and in September 1586, the mayor, Edmund Gamul, sent a report to Sir Francis Walsingham that he

… has received intelligence from Sir Richard Bulkley of two pirates named Wyse and Beare in Pwhelli Road who intend to lie off Holyhead to intercept all ships trading from these parts into Ireland. Two gentleman named Wiseman stayed making a pilgrimage to Holywell for ease of some infirmity.[44]

Evidence of the familiarity of recusants with Holywell may be seen from the examination of two Catholics imprisoned in the Bridewell in April 1593. One was John Upjohn, forty years of age, who is alleged to have 'kept' his companion Edward Hughes, alias Tegon, 'a year', 'and [that] they wash[ed] themselves in St Winefride's well.' Edward Hughes had been active as a seminary priest in north-east Wales since his arrival from Douai in 1578, and his connection with the Edwards family of Plas Newydd as the 'chief sayer of the Mass' there in 1579. He had managed to remain at liberty until his arrest at Fenns Hall in Flintshire, the home of the recusant family, the Hanmers.[45] Edward Hughes spent sometime in prison until his release in 1603 and exile to Douai, from which he returned four years later.

Another seminary priest, Thomas Leek, alias Stamford, from Staffordshire, was arrested with two companions in Chester in August 1601 on their pilgrimage to 'a well called Halliwell.' A search revealed that Leek was probably a priest from the fact that when he was searched he carried: 'a paier of beades, crucifixes and ringes of jett with the picture of Chryst uppon them, and three bookes, one called the Romane Breviary, another the Romane Catichisme.'[46] His fellow pilgrims, Bartholemew Brooksbie and sixteen-year-old son Gregory, tried in vain to protect the identity of the priest and he himself was unable to offer a good reason for his visit to Holywell. The Privy Council instructed that Leeke be sent to London where he was imprisoned in the Clink with other seminary priests until his release in 1603.[47]

It was obviously dangerous to be seen in company or on a journey with a Catholic priest in the last years of Elizabeth I. Many Catholics were secretive about their religion. Dramatists, poets, musicians, and other professional Catholics had to earn a living and some of them found protection and employment at court, like William Byrd. It has been suggested that William Shakespeare was a Catholic, a faith he shared with his father John and daughter Susanna.[48] Whatever the evidence, there is a distinct possibly that when John Shakespeare died in 1601 his hand-written will was of a Catholic formula closely resembling the 'Last Will of the Soul' written by St Charles Borromeo. A copy of such a testament was brought to England by Edmund Campion in 1580. John Shakespeare, as a recusant, would have met Campion at the house of Sir William Catesby at Lapworth near Stratford, and been given a copy to use to compose his own testament. The will refers to Shakespeare senior's reliance upon guardian angels, the Virgin Mary, saints and especially Winefride, favoured by the Jesuit Mission.[49]

The devotion of the Jesuit Mission to England from the time of its inception in 1580 may be seen in the inclusion of the matryrdom of St Winefride in the fresco painted by Pomerancio in the chapel of the Venerable English College in Rome in 1583. The cult of St Winefride had found itself a new guardian in the Society of Jesus.[50]

NOTES

1. D. A. Thomas, *The Welsh Elizabethan Catholic Martyrs* (Cardiff, 1971), p. 317f.
2. J. R. H. Moorman, *A History of the Church in England*, (London, 1953), p. 200.
3. *The Two Books of Homilies appointed to be read in Churches* (Oxford, 1859), pp. 234–5 and 270–1.
4. *Memorials of Father Augustine Baker and Other Documents Relating to the English Benedictines*, Catholic Record Society, xxxiii, 19333, pp. 16–17.
5. See *Bulletin of Board of Celtic Studies*, No. 16, 1933, pp. 77–8, transcribed by David Matthew from SPD Elizabeth 7 October 1567.
6. De Smedt, op cit, p. 311.
7. A. Walsham, *Church Papists* (Boydell, 1999), p. 12.

8. J. R. Tanner, *Tudor Constitutional Documents, 1485–1608* (Cambridge, 1922), p. 41. In the attitude of the justices of the peace towards the proceedings of government in matters of religion Tanner gives the numbers as 431 – described as favourable, 264. Indifferent, neuter, or not favourable, and 157 as 'hinderers or adversaries.'

9. Tanner, ibid, p. 143.

10. i.e. the rites in the Book of Common Prayer such as Baptism and Marriage.

11. P. Hughes, *The Reformation in England* (London, 1954), viii, p. 260.

12. Patent Rolls, 21 Elizabeth, pt 7.

13. D. R. Thomas, vol. 1, p. 89.

14. CSPD, 1547–80, cxviii, 564, 4 November 1577.

15 DNB under William Hughes.

16. CSPD, Elizabeth 153/66.

17. See CSPD c/xiv, No. 59, quoted in Conyers Read, Mr Secretary Walsingham and the Policy of Queen Elizabeth, vii, p. 320 (Oxford, 1925). This probably refers to Rhiwledyn cave under the Little Orme, Llandudno.

18. DNB under Cardinal William Allen – Eamon Duffy.

19. E. Duffy, ibid.

20. M. Cleary, 'The Catholic Resistance in Wales: 1568–1678', *Blackfriars*, vol. 38, 1957.

21. These rely in particular on Cleary and D. A. Thomas, *The Welsh Elizabethan Catholic Martyrs*, op cit.

22. In 1580 George Bromley became Chief Justice of the Chester Circuit.

23. J. Strype, *Life and Acts of Archbishop John Whitgift* (Oxford, 1832), vol. 1, p. 165f.

24. I. Edwards, 'Fifteenth-century alabaster tables and the Iconography of the Bound Rood and St Armel', *Archaeologia Cambrensis*, cxli, 1992, pp. 58–72.

25. D. A. Thomas, op cit, p. 125–6.

26. Quoted by G. Williams, *Wales and the Reformation*, p. 269, from Evans, *Cymm*. xxxix, 180.

27. Diaries of the English College, 228,108, 18 July 1576, quoted by Thompson Cooper, DNB.

28. Cleary, op cit, p. 112–3.

29. A. H. Dodd, *A History of Caernarvonshire,1284–1900*, Caernarvonshire Historical Society, (Denbigh, 1968), p. 58–9.

30. G. Williams, op cit, *Wales and the Reformation*, pp. 274–5.

31. SPD, Elizabeth 200/3.

32. T. M. McCoog, DNB.

33. D. A. Thomas, op cit, p. 80.

34. Ibid, p. 320.

35. Ibid, p. 203f.

36. P. Caraman, John Gerard, *Autobiography of an Elizabethan* (Longman, Green, 1951), p. 41.

37. For an excellent account of the raid see Alice Hogge, *God's Secret Agents* (Harper Perennial, 2006), pp. 150–6.

38. Caraman, op cit, p. 47.

39. DNB.

40. *Analecta Bollandiana*, op cit, pp. 312–5.

41.To be seen in the Well Museum, Holywell.

42. *Analecta Bollandiana*, p. 317.

43. G. Bowen, *Welsh Recusant Writings* (Cardiff, 1999), pp. 25–36.

44. CSPD, vol. 1, cxliii.

45. D. A. Thomas, op cit, p. 43.

46. K. R. Wark, *Elizabethan Recusancy in Cheshire* (Manchester, 1971), printed for the Chetham Society.

47. Susanna was listed as a recusant in 1606.

48. V. B. Richmond, *Shakespeare, Catholicism, and Romance* (Continium, 2000), pp. 82–3.

49. A. Dillon, *The Construction of Martyrdom in the English Catholic Community, 1535–1603* (Ashgate, 2002), pp. 170–242, esp. 214.

5. 1603–60

Introduction

Terror, persecution, and death continued for Catholics openly professing their Faith. Many still came to St Winefride's Well on pilgrimage which marked them out as 'papists' and recusants. This predicament for Catholics whether they should practise their faith openly and refuse to acknowledge the penal laws or conform to the Established Church continued at the centre of religious controversy. It affected the strategy of mission developed by both secular and Jesuit missions and the reaction of the state authorities to their activities which they regarded as illegal.

In these circumstances not only were the lives of Catholics in danger but also the places where they met were threatened with discovery. In particular the cult of St Winefride and her well at Holywell was always in danger of extinction and destruction.

The popularity and survival of the cult obviously depended on the availability of St Winefride's Well to pilgrims and their freedom to travel to Holywell and worship there. The freedom of Catholics to do this could not be taken for granted. Their desire to visit the curative stream and continue to observe traditional medieval rituals and practices in the precincts of the well–crypt and chapel was subject to limitations imposed by laws against Catholics and their enforcement by local officials. In times of anti–Catholic feeling against Jesuits or prodding of the diocesan bishop or justices of the peace by the Privy Council, the controls at the well would be strictly observed, and the concourse of pilgrims checked for priests and troublesome recusants. The first half of the seventeenth century was a period of continuing religious conflict ending in Civil War. The Elizabethan Religious Settlement of 1559 divided Catholics on the right and Puritans on the left until the triumph of the Commonwealth fulfilled the saying of James I 'No bishop, No king'. The Gunpowder Plot of 1605 was a defining moment in the future of the Roman Catholic Church when its mission and organisation was reshaped.

The most mighty and illustrious
Monarcke IAMES by the grace of
God King of great Britaine.
Fraunce & of Ireland &c.

61. James I & VI Window detail: Tremeirchion Church.

The important issues reflecting the cult of St Winefride are fairly well documented for this period and may be discussed by an examination of pilgrimage, Jesuit Mission, and governmental control, all of which were subject to the unpredictability of people and events.

The succession of James I

Much was hoped for when James I of England and VI of Scotland arrived in triumph from his kingdom in the north in the spring of 1603. His dream of riches and power met immediate fulfilment until the money ran out. The statesmen who invited James hoped to impose upon him their own policies, not realising that his Scottish background gave him another perspective on religion and foreign policy. Much was hoped for from the new monarch in the way of religious toleration. Puritans saw him as a king coming from his Presbyterian homeland and Catholics as the son of Mary, Queen of Scots. What went unrecognised was the simple fact that it was the religion of the ruler to which the people conformed. During the next twenty years Catholics experienced some toleration, but still hoped for more. The religious future of all James's subjects was to be settled by events which occurred within the first three years of his reign.

The new king took the initiative in 1604 by summoning the Hampton Court Conference to answer a petition from Puritan clergy requesting moderate changes in liturgy and worship and more equitable Church patronage. Discussions took place between James I, the bishops, and four Puritan clergy in the presence of the council. The king was prepared to make moderate concessions, but the intransigence of the bishops wrecked the conference. As a result, three hundred Puritan clergy were ejected and Puritanism enhanced. The only positive achievement was the decision to prepare a new translation of the scriptures, the 'Authorised Version'.

Unfortunately, the attentions of the new king were drawn to the grievances of the Catholics in a more alarming way. Within the first years of his reign James was confronted by three conspiracies whose object was to obtain toleration for Catholics. None of these plots were sanctioned by official Catholic leadership at home or supported by the Pope or any European power. They were abhorrent to Catholics and were to send some of their members into the arms of the Established Church and others to imprisonment, exile and martyrdom. All the plots involved an attack on the person of the king and his ministers. On their discovery, they were naturally useful propaganda to punish and destroy the recusants, and, as a result, the reputation of Catholics was totally discredited. As a religious institution what remained of the Catholic remnant was disabled, its laity isolated in small communities and its priesthood hunted and driven into hiding. The King's chief adviser, Sir Robert Cecil, (later Lord Salisbury), supported by the government's able prosecutor Sir Edward Coke, conducted show trials to stir up opposition, alienate Catholics, and turn the king against them. But in the long run, the king was remarkably tolerant and by the end of his reign twenty years later the Jesuit Mission had increased in numbers, and large pilgrimages to St Winefride's Well were held annually.

Catholic Plots and Martyrdoms
The first two plots were discovered within six months of each other in 1603–4 on information from the head of the secular Catholic mission, the Archpriest George Blackwell, and Henry Garnet, Jesuit Superior. The first of these, known as the Bye Plot, was hatched by William Watson and a few disaffected Catholics and was revealed to James before its plans were initiated. Watson was half crazy and suffering delusions of grandeur. Its main object was to win toleration for Catholics by removal of penal legislation. To achieve their aims the conspirators planned to kidnap King James, remove ministers associated with the persecution of Catholics, and place Lady Arbella Stewart on the throne. On its success Watson was to be Lord Chancellor.

The second conspiracy, the Main Plot, was a little more sophisticated, and those involved bigger fish. Its leader Lord Cobham managed to implicate Sir Walter Raleigh and others. Cobham was to finance the affair with funds from the Spanish Netherlands supported by troops from the same quarter. This time 'James and his cubs' were to be murdered to make way for Lady Arbella.

Once these plots were discovered inevitable show trials followed with the guilt of the conspirators a foregone conclusion. Two priests Watson and Clarke suffered the full penalty and gruesome death, others including Lord Cobham, were reprieved and imprisoned in the Tower to share the same fate as Sir Walter Raleigh, who may not have been guilty but was conveniently removed by Cecil.

To Cecil's great delight, the trials succeeded in antagonising King James who reacted with characteristic candour angrily condemning the outrages 'protesting his utter detestation of' the 'superstitious religion' of the Papists', and 'that he was so far from favouring it, as if he thought his son and heir after him would give any toleration thereunto, he would wish him fairly buried before his eyes.'[1]

It is against this background that the legendary Gunpowder Treason was revealed in 1605. In view of the events of the previous years and Cecil's determination to remove the Catholic enemy, it is not surprising that he excelled himself in making 'Gunpowder, Treason, and Plot' the greatest show trial in British history. By royal proclamation his success was remembered in the Anglican *Book of Common Prayer* by the addition of a form of service to be used annually in commemoration of the foiling of the plot. Nothing was allowed to erase the enormity of this event from the memory of Protestant England, and in one liturgical event Cecil succeeded in condemning the conspirators, Pope, Catholic community, and Jesuits as traitors.

The official account of the Gunpowder Plot, the traditional story put out by the government was quite straightforward. Guy Fawkes and his fellow conspirators attempted to blow up the Houses of Parliament and destroy the King, Lords, and Commons together, and re–establish a Catholic state. Chief conspirators, Catesby, Winter, Percy, and Fawkes had agreed upon this project in the spring of 1604. In order to put their plans into operation they hired a cellar under the Houses of Parliament and collected a sufficient amount of gunpowder to blow up Parliament together with the king and leaders of state. The luckless Guy Fawkes was to ignite the powder, a signal for his companions to organise a rising of Catholics. More people were drawn into the conspiracy. One of them, Francis Tresham, reluctant to see his brother–in–law Lord Monteagle perish in the explosion, is said to have written the warning note which was passed on to Cecil. Acting on this information the cellars were searched, Fawkes captured, and the rest of the conspirators arrested or killed. In the wave of horror and hysteria which followed the discovery of the plot the authorities arrested the Jesuit priests

A FORM OF PRAYER WITH THANKSGIVING,

To be used yearly upon the Fifth Day of November,

For the happy Deliverance of King *JAMES* I. and the Three Estates of *England*, from the most traiterous and bloody-intended Massacre by Gunpowder : And also for the happy Arrival of his Majesty King *William* on this Day, for the Deliverance of our Church and Nation.

¶ *The Minister of every Parish shall give warning to his Parishioners publickly in the Church at Morning Prayer, the Sunday before, for the due Observation of the said Day. And after Morning Prayer, or Preaching, upon the said Fifth Day of November, shall read publickly, distinctly, and plainly, the* Act *of* Parliament, *made in the third Year of King* James *the First, for the Observation of it.*

62. Book of Common Prayer. Service of Thanksgiving for deliverance 5 November 1605

Henry Garnet, Edward Oldcorne and others on the grounds of their knowledge of the conspiracy. After being tried and found guilty those plotters and their associates were cruelly executed as traitors. The Protestant government created a new generation of Catholic martyrs and an atmosphere of anti–Catholic suspicion that was to last well into the nineteenth century.

It is over three–hundred years since the trial of the conspirators took place and there is no consensus of opinion about its fairness. However, it is generally agreed that evidence taken at the trial has since disappeared, and that some of the remaining evidence was tampered with in the course of the trial. It is obvious that Jesuits would be regarded as being involved in the conspiracy because of their contact with conspir-

63. Henry Garnet, SJ: Flemish engraving.

ators' families, and there is no doubt that Father Garnet had reluctantly learnt of the plot in the summer of 1605, although his warnings went unheeded.[2] But clearly, members of the Society of Jesus suffered a great miscarriage of justice. This they recognised and expressed: 'It well known,' they reported in the Annual Letters 'how much the heretics have striven to render the very name of Jesuit hateful in order to fix upon us the odium of sham–plotting.'[3]

In recent years, the Jesuit historian Father Francis Edwards, SJ, has reinforced the doubts of his seventeenth–century brethren in believing that Cecil, who employed Guy Fawkes as an agent provocateur and some of his fellow conspirators as double agents, engineered 'the traditional story'. They were recruited by government intelligence in exchange for immunity after the Essex rebellion. By the suggestion of the king's destruction by ignited gunpowder Cecil set out to frighten him as a deliberate reminder of the fate of his father at Kirk o'Field.[4]

The Pilgrimage to St Winefride's Well in the summer of 1605

Sir Edward Coke, government prosecutor at the trial of the Gunpowder Plot conspirators, in his questioning of Father Henry Garnett, cast serious doubts on the object of the pilgrimage to St Winefride's Well. By the date the pilgrimage set off, on the 30 August, Garnet admitted under cross–examination, he had knowledge of the powder conspiracy some weeks before, in July. Coke therefore naturally assumed that the pilgrimage was a cover–up for bringing conspirators together to plan their dastardly deed. On their pilgrimage to and from St Winefride's in September 1605 the party called at recusant houses for hospitality and fellowship. But even then, with no knowledge of the plot being planned, Anne Vaux, of Harrowden, sensed that something was in the air. She noted the 'fine horses' in the stables of Catholic houses, later recalling how she had 'feared these wild heads had something in hand and prayed him (Garnett) for God's sake to talke with Mr Catesbye and to hinder anything that possibly he might.'[5] It was not difficult to make out a case for using pilgrimage as an opportunity for discussing the plot, for there were representatives of the three family groups involved either as pilgrims or members of the households visited.

Who were the members of the party who made the pilgrimage to Wales in early September 1605, nine weeks before the State Opening of Parliament? Does their itinerary suggest anything more than the custom of hospitality observed by gentry recusant families in seventeenth century England? What was the object of the pilgrimage?

The pilgrimage and tour began when a small party set out from White Webbs, near Enfield, composed of Father Garnet, Brother Nicholas Owen, and members of the wealthy Vaux family, (their vocation was to provide safe houses for Jesuit priests), Anne Vaux, her sister Eleanor Brooksby, her nephew William Brooksby and his wife Dorothy. Several gunpowder conspirators had visited the house they rented for Father Garnet, White Webbs, that summer. The day before he set off Father Garnet wrote to Father Persons:

> Meanwhile the number of Catholics is greatly increased and I hope that this journey of mine which God allowing I am about to undertake tomorrow – both for the sake of reviving our forces and because my former dwelling has been traced by the diligence of our foes, and I have no reliable abode in town – will not be without opportunity of furthering Catholic interests.[6]

Garnet was optimistic, looking forward to moving away from London, meeting old friends, and reviving his spiritual forces. In his letter he probably gave a veiled assurance to Persons that he would try to exercise some discipline over the hotheads trying to achieve their ends by violence although the phrase 'will not be without opportunity of furthering Catholic interests' might be construed otherwise. Their progress through the Midlands was to add to their number until it reached about thirty pilgrims.

Amongst the houses they visited en route were John Grant's[7] house at Norbrook near Stratford, Huddington Court near Worcester, the home of Robert Wintour,[8] Clopton belonging to Ambrose Rookwood.[9] As they passed through the Midlands the party was joined by a number of small groups of devoted Catholics. Eliza Vaux brought with her two priests sheltered at the family residence of Harrowden, Father John Gerard, SJ, and Father John Percy, SJ. Another group from Gayhurst, Buckinghamshire, were made up of Sir Everard Digby, his wife Mary, and his brother Thomas. The two Digby brothers were recent converts. They had as their chaplain Father Edward Oldcorne, SJ, and his servant brother Ralph Ashley, SJ, and Father Tesimond came too.[10]

The tiny column of baggage carts, riders – cavaliers, gentlewomen, priests and lay brothers – ambled slowly over bad roads travelling about thirty miles a day with Shrewsbury their last stay in England. Crossing over the river Severn into the town they would see the despoiled abbey church which, until 1540, had been an active pilgrimage centre for visitors to the shrine of St Winefride which had housed her relics from 1138 onwards. The bell inscribed in her

64. Holt Castle: from an early print.

honour rang out a solemn mournful dirge as the sun was setting in the west. Next day they set off early and reached the Welsh border. They spent the night by another river, the Dee, at 'a castle in a holt at Denbighshire.'[11] This was the little border town of Holt with its castle, once the home of Sir William Stanley, patron of St Winefride's Well, from which might be seen Wrexham steeple and the place where Richard Gwyn was martyred twenty years previously.

They were near their destination and prepared, as all medieval pilgrims, to walk the last stage barefoot. The gentle Welsh hills to the west, and wide Dee estuary to the north, with ships, cockle gatherers, harvest fields, reapers, and ripening apples, and the speech of the people changing from the blunt, Cheshire dialect to the lilt of the old British tongue, drew them to St Winefride's. A good day's journey completed their coming and brought them to the hill above the straggling town where pathways from surrounding hamlets merged together to descend to the ancient Church and the sparkling stone–work of well, crypt, and chapel. Their servants had gone ahead to arrange accommodation and alert the local Catholics of their arrival.

The pilgrim band gathered beside the stream at the Well to be welcomed by Father John Bennett, SJ, his fellow Jesuits rejoicing at the reunion. Their priorities were those of devout pilgrims down the ages. Penitence, prayer, vigil, Mass, veneration at the shrine of St Winefride and then, making the ritual passage through the curative water, each pilgrim with their particular request. By noon, these exercises completed, votives were made and pilgrims obtained precious relics: ampoules with holy water, sweet–smelling moss, and tinctured stones. The concourse of pilgrims, sick, impotent, and healthy of all degrees, crammed together on the sides of the narrow valley, with beggars, local traders, entertainers, and government spies.

Anne Vaux came to be healed, Father Oldcorne to give thanks for his cure from cancer, Father Gerard offered thanks for good health and escape from the Tower of London, Father Garnet and Father Tesimond prayed that the plans of the Gunpowder Plotters would be aborted, the young couple, Sir Everard Digby and

Mary his wife, for a long and fruitful marriage. All of them prayed for the success of the Catholic cause and offered thanks for the consolations of St Winefride.

Reluctantly they said their goodbyes. Holywell was soon behind them as they turned towards Shrewsbury and home. They returned to the troubled centre of recusant England to face the greatest crisis of post–Reformation Catholicism. They came back by way of Daventry, and Father Garnet, with Anne Vaux and Eleanor Brooksby, spent a night at Rushton Hall, where they learned of the death of Sir Thomas Tresham. His son Francis was to play a fatal part in the coming Gunpowder Plot.

The pilgrimage to St Winefride's Well was over but not forgotten in the propaganda surrounding the Gunpowder Plot. There is no evidence to link it to the planning of the events surrounding 5 November. The discovery of the plot had a disastrous effect on the English Catholic community. It was the 'end of an epoch,' 'it helped precipitate the withdrawal of Catholics from the general concerns of the commonwealth,' and 'clarified the terms on which a Catholic community could come into existence in a Protestant England.'[12] The pilgrim band was decimated and broken by the repercussions of the discovery of the plot: Fathers Garnet and Oldcorne and Brother Nicholas Owen were executed as traitors, together with Sir Everard Digby. Brother Ralph Ashley was sent into exile, Fathers Gerard, Percy and Tesimond eluded capture and escaped abroad. Anne Vaux was imprisoned in the Tower and released in August 1606. She lived for another thirty years. Father Oldcorne is recorded to have called upon St Winefride in the agony of martyrdom. Whatever their fate the Holywell Pilgrimage gave them courage to meet it.

St Winefride's Well, the post–1605 backlash
The government hit back with a series of savage laws against Catholics. The Recusancy Laws were tightened and fines enforced. Catholics were ordered to receive communion in their parish churches, were forbidden to act as doctors, lawyers, and executors of wills, and banished from court. James, in his attempt to distinguish loyal Catholics from potential traitors, presented them with an oath of allegiance in which they were asked to reject Papal powers to excommunicate and condone the murder of princes by their subjects.

The danger was soon over and many of the laws were not enforced. The Jesuit Mission grew in numbers as they struggled to organise the Catholic remnant, of which Flintshire and Denbighshire recusants were part and St Winefride's Well a focal point. The diocesan bishops continued to play a key role as the 'eyes and ears' of government in the localities responsible for reporting Catholic activity. The episcopacy of Bishop Richard Parry of St Asaph (1604–23) almost spanned the reign of James I (1603–25) and his reports to government ministers throw light on gatherings at Holywell.

In August 1605, (a month before the Vaux pilgrimage), Bishop Parry sent alarming news to Robert Cecil, earl of Salisbury, acquainting him with 'the unfortunate and ungodly increase of Papists' in his diocese 'who within the last three years are become 'near thrice as many,' rising from about seven score recusants in 1602 to four hundred in my visitation' concluding by observing that the only remedy was 'the smart of the laws.'[13]

65. 'English Jesuits taken to execution': *engraving 1584, after a fresco in the English College chapel, Rome.*

Taking Catholics to court, making them pay for their religion, was the commonest form of redress. Between 1582 and 1624 the names of twelve–hundred Flintshire recusants are recorded, 'and in the latter year, when one hundred and fifty three were indicted, fines totalling £18,360 were paid into the Exchequer, these being assessed on each person at the statutory rate of £20 per month for each of the six months during which he or she had been absent from the parish church.'[14]

At Holywell, fifty–three recusants suffered for their faith between 1601 and 1621, with the sympathy of at least two of the local gentry, who were church papists, Nicholas Pennant of Brynford and Edward Mostyn of Greenfield. The men hid their Catholicism under the shelter of attendance at the parish church but their wives stubbornly refused to conform and were prosecuted as recusants.[15] Many of the villages around Holywell contained recusants.[16]

As a member of the Commission of Peace appointed by the Council of the Marches, Bishop Parry came to Holywell with Sir Thomas Mostyn in June 1612 to issue a warrant against Raphell Davies, bailiff of Whitford, 'for the redress of some disorders committed about the well'. Unfortunately there are no more details concerning the case, although we know that Davies' wife was a recusant.[17] The bishop's vigilance continued with great vigour as he reported to the Lord President of the Council in 1617:

> We have taken orders for the suppressing of superstitious flocking and resort of your Majesty's subjects unto Hollie Well, commonly called St Winifred's Well, and for dailie service and praiers there; as also for Sermons on Saboths and ffestivall daies. And that the oath of supremacie and allegiance be ordered unto all such strangers (before they go to the Well) as shall refuse to come to church, by which reason whereof the great concourse is stopped.[18]

Neither bishop nor justice could prevent Catholics gathering at the well for the celebration of St Winefride's feast or for sheer customary enjoyment of the occasion. The Catholics came together at their holy place for a mixture of motives: traditional devotion, stubborn defiance, customary seasonal enjoyment, and for healing from the curative stream. A yeoman from nearby Cilcain was fined £10 'for suffring his three daughters, being yong girles, and his maidservants to goe out of his house in the night tyme in superstitious manner to Wenefrids well.'[19] Another indication that the faithful continued to journey to Holywell and gather there on the vigil of feast days as Mrs Dorothy Edwards and her group had come from Chirk in 1577.

John Thomas Griffith, writing in 1609, records celebrating the feast of St Asaph on *Calan Mai* (1 May), enjoying playing during the long holiday at Whitsun, and then, attending St Winifred's Festival 'when all faithful men procede to Holywell.'

> *Gwyl wen frewi ar al hyny*
> *Pob dyn ffyddlon fo a i dre ffynmon.*[20]

A medieval Welsh folk custom prevalent in the vale of Clwyd celebrated May Day with dancing parties and the singing of *Carolau Haf*, summer carols. The groups went around the countryside and probably performed at the local fairs and *gwylmabsant* (saint's days).

The Protestant gentry used the well for their own convenience and amusement. Sir Henry Townshend, justice of Chester, reported to Sir John Wynn of Gwydir, in August 1610, that 'His wife and other gentlewomen of their company do so sweat from Sir John's good cheer and their ill–throwing at dice, that they must needs wash and purify themselves in Holywell.'[21]

In 1617, when Bishop Parry was complaining to the Council in Wales of 'superstitious flocking' at the well a merry band of Catholics came dancing and singing to St Winefride's spring at midsummer accompanied by their own piper on a jaunt from across the Dee in Wirral. The hearty Cheshire folk were reported to their own justices and summoned as recusants.[22]

The family of Plas Newydd, Chirk, was an unmistakable group of long–standing recusants, who gained notoriety through the behaviour of their head, John Edwards. In January 1613, Bishop Parry described him to Archbishop Bancroft as a dangerous recusant who, in his view, should not be pardoned. 'He is a very dangerous ffellowe,' he asserted, 'of as pestilent disposition as eny in all our Contry, and if he get his pardon it may be fearyd that he will doe much mischeef.' Parry was correct, and on receiving his pardon from the king, Edwards continued to be as defiant as ever. But he was still regarded by the justices as 'an obstinate popish convicted recusant and of great power and meanes in those parts,' his 'family of sundry obstinate and seducing recusants hardened in their superstitious opinions and practices'. The sheriff awaited his opportunity and on a Sunday in August 1619, hearing that a large body of papists was assembled at Plas Newydd to hear mass, issued a warrant for their arrest.

John Edwards defiantly barred them from crossing his moated threshold and locked the doors. When the party retreated, he defended himself by writing a letter to the justice of assize saying that only a month previously he had been examined by the Archbishop of Canterbury and the Privy Council touching his religion and had been allowed to depart with no restraint placed on his freedom.[23] Edwards refused to take the Oath of Allegiance, not by reason of disloyalty, but because he was not satisfied with its wording. The obstinate old man soon found himself a prisoner in the Marshalsea over Christmas and was soon begging release.[24]

Towards 1620, Catholics were growing more confident with hopes rising at the prospect of a Spanish bride for Prince Charles, heir to the throne. During negotiations, recusancy laws were suspended and there was the possibility of toleration once the marriage was agreed. This may have been the motive for conveying the information to Spanish authorities on 6 November 1620 that:

> The bishop of Bangor went last week to Saint Winifred's well … it is here that God has worked many miracles that are daily to be seen and the Catholics continue to make this pilgrimage today. Since the bishop desired to stop this, saying it was superstitious, he went in person to arrest the priests and Catholics who resorted there. The people from about the countryside rose up, even though most of them are heretics and seized the bishop and handled him roughly and then threw him into a ditch. They tell me that they would have left him to die if the local justice had not reached him. It is not known as yet what this king will order to be done about this.[25]

This suggests that there might have been unwelcome intervention by Lewis Bayley, bishop of Bangor (1613–31), near 3 November, the feast of St Winefride. The report of the assault, whether or not it was a gross exaggeration, seems to suggest some spirited opposition by the local people to episcopal interference, and a good attendance at the winter feast.

But the government did not welcome a resurgence of Catholic influence or further toleration and attempted to inform themselves of Catholic activities. John Gee, an Anglican clergyman, became involved in this murky world of information gathering. After flirting with the idea of conversion, he became violently anti–Catholic and, in the process, left this account of events at the Well:

> … once every year, about mid–summer, many superstitious papists of Lancashire, Staffordshire, and other more remote countries, go in pilgrimage, especially those of the feminine and softer sex, who keep there their rendezvous, meeting with diverse priests their acquaintance; who make it their chief synod or convention for consultation, and promoting the Catholic cause, as they call it; yea, and account it their chiefest harvest for commodity and profit, in regard of the crop they then reap by absolutions and indulgences. Let me add, that they were so

bold, about mid–summer the last year, 1623, that they intruded themselves diverse times into the church or public chapel of Holywell, and there said Mass without contradiction.[26]

Gee is probably referring to the chapel above the well (not the Anglican parish church which is alongside) which belonged to the rectory of Holywell and was under the patronage of the bishop of St Asaph. Glanmor Williams[27] states that Bishop William Morgan (1601–04) had been 'compelled to abandon Anglican services in the ruined well chapel' because the many Catholics 'were sufficiently numerous and daring' *c.*1600. Williams was incorrect to state the chapel was ruined: it was in a good state of repair when reported on by John Speed in 1610 and the building which illustrates his map of Flintshire shows no signs of disrepair. It is probable that local people turned a blind eye to pilgrims using the building. It was safer to let them in rather than attempt to turn them away – and more profitable.

The Jesuit Annual Letter's claim in 1623 for a total of 2,630 converts was bad news for the Privy Council, although they were probably not surprised. The growth in Catholic numbers came at a time of change all round: on the appointment of John Hanmer, bishop of St Asaph, in January 1624 and the accession of Charles I in March 1625.

Another break with the past was the death of Father John Bennett, first priest of the Jesuit Mission at Holywell, who died of the plague in London on 8 September 1625. The plague devastated the city. In a week in August 4,855 deaths were reported. The month before Sir John Wynn of Gwydir had received a letter from his son informing him that 'men were falling down dead suddenly in the street. It is dangerous to visit any doctor just now, or to buy anything.'[28]

The Jesuit historian Foley wrote of the esteem and affection in which Bennett was held by members of the Society.

> Father John Bennett is said not to have been a man of brilliant talents and learning, but to have abounded in solid virtue, with great sweetness of manner, and a modesty and piety which might be described as angelical. There was a rare spiritual beauty in his expression of face. He had a most mild and pleasing style of address, and above all, a great and ready courage in all events and dangers. Thus furnished, he so successfully laboured for the salvation of souls, he brought the Catholics to such a degree of piety and constancy in profession of their faith, and converted many to the Catholic Church.[29]

The reign of King Charles I (1625–49)
The security of St Winefride's Well in the reign of Charles I was threatened by the effect of the increase in numbers of Catholics and pilgrims. Charles married a French princess, Henrietta Maria, and was tolerant towards Catholics. However, his attempt to govern without Parliament alienated the Puritans and made them

more anti–Catholic. At the beginning of the reign in the late 1620s we have accounts of large pilgrimages, and evidence of official attempts to prevent them. It is clear that the authorities were determined to destroy the crypt of St Winefride's Well, and with it what had miraculously survived the iconoclasm of the sixteenth century.

   We do not know what specific orders were issued for the spoilage of the building in the 1630s but we may speculate that the bishop of St Asaph had something to do with it, acting in league with the Privy Council and officials from the Court of Great Session and justices of Chester. No local group would have dared to vandalise the building without incurring the wrath of local inhabitants both Catholic and Protestant. It is probable that such an official assault on the well crypt was undertaken by forces from outside north Wales aimed at stripping it of all association with medieval and Catholic iconography, and undertaken before the Civil War. A second attack was made some time during the Civil War when more random damage occurred at the hands of Parliamentarian soldiers. There is a record of their rampage in towns and churches of north Wales during the conflict. Hot–headed Puritans in the sect–ridden regiments of Cromwell's soldiery shared a passionate hatred for Roman Catholicism and its entire works and were not slow in showing their feelings. The period is also marked by the success of the Jesuit Mission in establishing a permanent residence in Holywell and attracting financial support for its mission, assisted by the Mostyn/Petre family of Greenfield and the Pennants of Bagillt.

The beginnings of a new Catholic organisation in England and Wales
The organisation of the pattern of ministry in the Catholic community to replace that of the Marian Church took shape within the first two decades of the seventeenth century. The last member of the old hierarchy, Bishop Thomas Goldwell of St Asaph, died in exile in 1585, leaving no one in England or Wales to exercise episcopal powers. At his death there was no recognised ecclesiastical organisation officially established to continue government by bishops. There is no need to go into detail about the painful birth of the system that was eventually set up. It gradually emerged from a series of disputes between secular and Jesuit priests of the English mission. As a result, there emerged two distinct jurisdictions, a Secular Mission and a Jesuit Mission, both of which were later represented in the town of Holywell. Because the Penal Laws banned official Catholic places of worship and priests were outlawed they were forced to hide behind aliases and secular occupations. A frequent disguise was that of inn keeper and in this way two Catholic missions were established in Holywell. The Jesuit Mission operated from the 'Old Star Inn' (now the site of St Winefride's Church) and the secular priests at the nearby 'Cross Keys', less than two–hundred yards from each other. The first priest of the Jesuit Mission in Holywell was Father John Bennett (1590–1625), and the first priest accredited at the Secular

Mission was the martyr, Father John Plessington, some time between 1665 and 1679.[30]

The Secular Mission

The Secular Mission wanted their own bishop and a hierarchical structure of clerical government. At first they had to do with an archpriest, who was later given twelve assistants as his advisors. However, in 1623, William Smith was appointed bishop of Chalcedon, to be succeeded on his death a few months later by Richard Smith. An orthodox structure was set up of vicars–general, arch-deacons and rural deans, with a dean and chapter. The significance of this creation was that it gave an institutional embodiment to the claim that the existing body of Catholic secular clergy in England was legally and historically speaking identical with the *Ecclesia Anglicana* as it had stood before the Reform-ation.[31] This arrangement soon proved unsatisfactory when Bishop Richard Smith exercised his jurisdiction in a manner that alienated the gentry and Jesuit Mission, and was forced to retire abroad.

It was not until 1685, when John Leyburn was appointed the first Vicar Apostolic (a titular bishop), and three more priests were raised to the same rank in 1688, that the organisation of secular clergy became satisfactory, and England and Wales were divided into four districts. This form of episcopal government survived until the restoration of the hierarchy in 1850. In 1688, the Secular Mission at Holywell, with the rest of Wales, became part of the extensive Western District.

The Jesuit Mission

The first notice of Jesuits in Holywell occurs in 1590 with Father John Bennett, SJ, as priest. In order to understand Father Bennett's place in the scheme of things it is necessary to see how the English (and Welsh) Mission operated. The genius of the Jesuits' founder Ignatius Loyola was to organise the society he founded in 1540 primarily as a world–wide missionary body, with each province being organised in the same way.

After surviving the executions and frenzy following the Gunpowder Plot the Jesuit Mission had recovered sufficiently by 1619 to be elevated to Vice–Provincial status. It was designated as the English Province in 1623, by which time ten Jesuits were working in Wales (about 10% of the English Mission) and classified as, *missio Walliae*, the 'Mission of Wales.'

The English Province was divided into twelve districts, each with an immediate superior. Within the districts, called 'missions', there were residences and houses. In some, Jesuits were involved with the education of children. Within each mission there was one house in which the Jesuits could make their annual retreats, renew their vows, and hold meetings. In order to finance their mission, the generous benefactions of aristocracy and gentry were placed in protected trusts to finance their communities.

This was the way in which the Welsh mission was transformed into the college of St Francis Xavier in November 1622. It was located at Cwm, a dwelling house in the isolated parish of Llanrothal, in Herefordshire, overlooking the Monnow, five–miles north of Monmouth, and part of the estates of the earl of Worcester. Cwm had begun as a centre of Jesuit activity in 1605 and was now elevated into the important position of safe house, spiritual community, and school. Its isolation gave it protection as the centre of the Welsh mission until it was sacked as a reprisal during the Popish Plot in 1678. It was not until the 1660s that the Residence of St Winefride was separated from St Francis Xavier as a separate district for mid and north Wales and the English counties of Shropshire and Staffordshire.[32]

When Father Henry Garnet, the Superior of the Jesuit Mission, was executed in 1606, the first choice as his successor was Father Robert Jones (*c.*1564–15), who declined the appointment but accepted office in 1609. Jones was a contemporary of Father Bennett and a fellow countryman, born in the Chirk area, in the diocese of St Asaph. He was successful in setting up the mission in Monmouthshire and along the southern March, and was responsible for the conversion of members of the household of the earl of Worcester at Raglan Castle as well as enjoying the patronage of William Morgan of Llantarnam. Father John Salisbury, SJ, from Rûg, was one of the moving spirits in the formation of the college at the Cwm in 1622. Another Jesuit, originating from the Holywell area, was Father Thomas Pennant. He was born at Bychton near Holywell in 1579, his father, a Pennant and mother a Conway. His early education is interesting: 'I learnt rudiments at two towns: Harden [Hawarden] and Gwaynersco [Gwaunysgor], for about six years and a half; besides having a private tutor for two years at home. I was always a Protestant till my twentieth year.' Pennant entered the English College in Rome in 1604 and was ordained in 1608, later working in and around Wales until his death in 1638.[33]

A Jesuit school at Greenfield[34]

This little episode in the life of the Catholic community at Holywell is the earliest evidence we have of the support given by local families to the Jesuit mission. It also illustrates the strain in relations that began to appear in the 1620s between Richard Blount, SJ, Jesuit Provincial of England and Wales, and Bishop Richard Smith, archbishop of Chalcedon in *partibus infidelium*, and the working of the two parallel jurisdictions of Secular and Jesuit outlined above. The cause of the dispute and its resolution unfolds in a series of four documents relating to the incident.

The first document is a letter, dated 27 January 1626,[35] from Father Edward Bennet, aged about fifty–five years, a native of Whitford, and therefore well acquainted with the area, of whom it was said he bore 'a moderate antipathy towards the Jesuit fathers.'[36] The letter was written in his capacity as archdeacon of Buckinghamshire to Father Richard Blount, SJ, Jesuit Provincial, with information he had obtained from Humphrey Hughes, his fellow archdeacon of north Wales, a native of Denbighshire.

Bennet wrote 'Lately there hath bin a complaint made unto me that one of your Fathers should keep a schoole at Greenfield Abbey, hard by St Wenefreds Well which may breed noe little inconvenience in that place.' Bennet reported that his fellow archdeacon had 'intreated him to desist,' afraid that 'it would not only drawe a persecution upon him selfe but allsoe upon that holy place of pilgrimage,' and 'that the neighbour Justices will knowe of it and they will be glad of any occasion to trouble the Catholicks who live neare them.' Bennet now requests that Blount 'admonish' the schoolmaster 'to desist.'

The next document is a letter from a prominent recusant in the Holywell area, Edward Pennant, of Bagillt, written to Father Edward Bennet under his alias of Mr Edward Ffarington, from Hafod–y–Bwch, near Wrexham on 17 May 1627.[37]

Edward Pennant was an ardent recusant who was regularly fined over a number of years, and between c.1635–40 was paying £250 a year.[38] With a household of ten children to bring up, he desired to find a way of avoiding paying the fines. This is probably the reason for his address being given as near Wrexham. Pennant seems to have been on good terms with the Protestant magistrates in the area, who appeared to be exercising some toleration and prepared to give him the 'tip off' when necessary to avoid trouble. He writes in terms of some familiarity to Bennet, which suggests that they were old acquaintances.

'Good brother, that Mr Pritchard taught at Greenfield, is as sure as there is a schoole at Eaton, and had schollers that mett there to the number of vij this last winter: the same was not privat, but the vicar of the parish (whoe keepes schoole at the church) tooke notice thereof, and grumbled to me therat. And a great magistrat in the neighbourhood, that beares noe affection to the religion complayned to me of great indiscretion and overboldness, for his teachings heretofore at Penrhin …' [Penrhyn Creuddyn].

Pennant is obviously anxious that something is done about the Jesuit school at Greenfield. His letter provided further evidence for Archdeacon Edward Bennet to pursue the matter. Three days later, on 20 May 1627, he finalised his enquiries to send to Bishop Richard Smith by obtaining legal attestation of the existence of the school from four witnesses: Will Johnes, notary; Thomas Pennant, priest; Hugh Thomas and William Parry. This document testified that Mr Pritchard kept a school near Holywell 'from the beginning of November last' and taught some seven scholars, 'till May last', and some four of the same number continued with him 'till this present', which was as well known to 'most Protestants in the neighbourhood as it is to us'. They conclude by stating that if the school continues 'it would breed some trouble to ye country and that holy place.'[39]

The protection of St Winefride's Well is their main concern
The establishment of the school at Greenfield at the former Basingwerk Abbey
may well have occurred following the removal of Father John Bennett to London
and his death there in September 1625. An obvious replacement would have been
Dr John Pritchard (alias Price), SJ, who was in the area at Penrhyn Creuddyn, in
the Catholic household of Robert Pugh. What could have been more natural than
for this learned Jesuit to be welcomed into the Mostyn household, and assume the
position of schoolmaster to the recusant family and their relatives. But the
publicity caused by this event disturbed the delicate balance upon which
toleration existed and activities allowed to continue undisturbed at St Winefride's
Well.

The last letter that survives in the series[40] was written by Sir John Mostyn,
owner of Basingwerk, to Bishop Richard Smith about five weeks after the final
proof had been sent to him with regard to the existence of the school.
Unfortunately, we do not possess the complete correspondence. Vital letters are
unaccounted for: the letter of Bishop Smith to Sir John Mostyn, those between
his Lordship and Lady Mostyn, which her husband describes as:

> … many letters which were writtyn unto yow in defence of Mr Prichards keeping
> of schoole, and all but one of those were written from my wife, yet not with my
> authority or consent but true it is that I might have suppressed it, if soe I would
> but that she sayde it was in defence of her ghostly father (I know not how far she
> would excuse him).

Sir John promises 'by godes leave to avoyd all occasions as that of schoole–
keeping wch was hitherto done without my consent, as any other action that may
bringe disturbance to ye pilgrimage of yt holy place, St Winefride's Well.'
When Sir John next encounters the bishop he promises to give a full explanation
of his wife's conduct. He was attempting, as many other Catholic heads of family
were, to retain his estate and be true to his faith. He hated, as much as many of
the Catholic gentry did, being a Church papist rather than a convicted recusant.
Lady Anne Mostyn[41] behaved as a typical recusant wife in sheltering her husband
and taking the blame on herself for wrong doing or indiscretion. Lady Anne was
a woman of firm conviction and determination, unafraid to practise her religion
and it was typical that the two sons born to Sir John and Lady Anne became Jesuit
priests. When Sir John died (1634) his widow married the Hon. George Petre, of
Ingatestone, Essex, a member of one of the leading Catholic families. They both
made a great contribution to the Jesuit cause in Holywell, and the Mostyn family
of Talacre was a powerful Catholic force in the Holywell district until the estate
was sold in 1920.

Pilgrimage and suppression: 1625–37
The temper of the first parliament of the reign of Charles I in June 1625 was

dictated by the presentation of a petition drawn up by two members, Pym and Sandys, who were intent on denying any toleration to Catholics, and requesting the King to enforce the existing penal laws. Charles I granted their demand and, as a result, the Privy Council acted immediately. They issued a mandate in October 1625 requesting bishops to furnish them with a certificate of all Popish recusants within their dioceses, with further instructions to all deputy–lieutenants to disarm all papists. Parliament was, for the first time making a distinction between 'Popish Recusants' and all others, including Puritans. Religious divisions were beginning to appear.

The Bishop of St Asaph's list of recusants[42] for Flintshire is made up mostly of wives and widows, although a number of men are represented. The surnames of men and women include those of Conway, Hanmer, Morgan, Mostyn, Parry, Pennant, Pugh (of Penrhyn Creuddyn) and Salisbury who were part of the network of recusant gentry families in the county. Some of the recusant names appeared earlier. For example: 'Hugh ap Thomas, gent. of Whitford', who signed the notaries' attestation in 1627 (his wife was Anne Pennant, a great–granddaughter of Thomas Pennant, abbot of Basingwerk); Robert and William Pugh of Creuddyn, married to Mostyn daughters. Others were Elinor Lloyd, widow of John Lloyd, the original owner of Downing, involved in the disorder at the Well in 1612; Ann Hughes daughter of Thomas Hughes of Prestatyn, sheriff in 1611, the wife of Raphell Davies, the Bailiff of Whitford, who was also involved in the dispute at the Well in 1612; and Robert Salusbury of Leadbrook, Flint, married to Mary, a daughter of John Edwards of Plas Newydd, Chirk.

The government relied on bishops as members of the Privy Council to inform them of matters threatening state security. The alarm given in 1625 concerned a threat from Spain and an increase in Catholic strength nation–wide seen in a growing number of converts. The threat of foreign invasion and the anxiety of

parliament led to the enforcement of the Penal Laws. As a member of the Privy Council, the Bishop of Bangor, Lewis Bayly, was keen to prove his competence as a vigilant watch dog in his vulnerable diocese along the north–Wales coast. The first information he conveyed to the government was the usual warning of Papist activity that: 'There is a great concourse of people to St Winefride's Well. In an old chapel near, a public Mass is said continually.'

Once again there was a breakdown in policing illegal pilgrimages and a flagrant disregard of the law. There was nothing new in this. More

66. Charles I.

serious was the bishop's next report in December 1625. It concerned Hugh Owen (*c.*1575–1642) a recent convert and secretary to the earl of Worcester, who the bishop suspected of planning an invasion by Catholic forces.[43] The bishop informed Charles I that:

> About August last a ship sounded the north east coast of Anglesea, and at the same time Hugh Owen Gwenwynog returned for a short period very gallant and full of gold. The Roman Catholics flocked to him, and since then several of them have sold all they had and gone after him. The same party are audacious and a stranger has lately surveyed the havens. The arms and powder at Beaumaris and Carnarvon are totally unserviceable, and 100 men would overrun the Isle of Anglesea. The Deputy Lieutenants and Justices alone abuse their authority to favour their friends, and the country stands in the greatest danger. One of the King's ships would be a great protection.[44]

Sir John Bridgeman's effect on St Winefride's Well

The Privy Council acted quickly in answer to these alarms and used the services of the Chief Justice of Chester, Sir John Bridgeman, appointed by the king in January 1626. His office was answerable to the king and his jurisdiction exercised through the Council in the Marches of Wales in the Court of Great Session. In his power for the next twelve years lay the fortunes of St Winefride's Well. It was to be one of the most significant decades in the well's history.

The Chief Justice of Chester had been responsible for Flintshire since 1284, to which were added, in 1542, the counties of Denbigh and Montgomery. He also enjoyed an important place in the Council next to that of the Lord President, and was in reality the chief executive and judicial official. Bridgeman was hardworking and had the reputation of being 'a grave and learned Judge,' an opinion reflected in the epitaph proposed for him by Ralph Gittins a master of Shrewsbury School whom he had judged too severely. He wrote:

> Here lies Sir John Bridgeman clad in this clay,
> God said to the divell, Sirrah take him away.[45]

Bridgeman, as chief justice, was in a key position as the man in the country upon whom his superiors, the King and the Privy Council, relied to investigate troublesome affairs. They also expected him to enforce their directives and solve the problems in the area under his jurisdiction. Because of the scope his office afforded him, Bridgeman was able to exercise his own considerable power and influence which extended from parish to county level, over the sheriff and justices of the peace. He was there to guide them in their execution of their own business: the mundane operation of the poor law, alehouse regulations, the upkeep of bridges, and the oversight of recusants. His main role was judicial, and this he executed as he rode the circuit of the Court of the Great Sessions in Chester and his three Welsh counties, and during this progress through personal contact he received much information from parish level. It was in this context that Sir John Bridgeman had to make the vital decisions about how to deal with St Winefride's Well.

Within months of assuming office, Bridgeman was confronted with the problem at the well and acquitted himself favourably in the eyes of his masters at the Privy Council, who commended his zeal and judgement:

> Our good Lord the Keeper of the Great Seal did acquaint us with a letter of yours touching some proceedings by you in your circuit against Recusants, wherein as we find great cause to commend your judgement in his Master's service, so we do particularly approve your care to prevent the resort of persons ill affected in religion to St Winefride's Well. And do pray and require you to proceed in taking order for the binding of the Freeholders and other inhabitants thereabouts, where the better sort of Recusants use to lodge, in the same manner as you have done for the Inns and Alehouses, as is intimated in your letter.[46]

Bridgeman had confirmed the worst fears of Catholics at Holywell and the secular clergy that the Jesuit school at Greenfield would do harm to St Winefride's Well. It was the Chief Justice's proud boast that he had succeeded in suppressing the pilgrimages in the summer of 1626 and he outlined his means in a letter to the privy council in October 1626.[47]

The situation had changed. He declared that where there was usually

> … all the summer time usual resort thither of people in troops both men and women, many of them being of note by way of pilgrimage, where Mass was often said … there hath not been any thither this last summer.

Bridgeman attributed his success 'in restraining these persons ill affected in religion from resorting to St Winefride's Well' by enforcing the recusancy laws. He had taken steps to record the names of strangers by requiring all keepers of inns and lodging houses to register the names of their guests and pass them on to the Justices at the next Great Sessions. He required the sheriff to summon recusants to the assize to take the oath of allegiance and conform to the worship of the established church and boasted that 'some have also conformed themselves by hearing Divine Service and sermons in my presence.' He ended on a triumphant note with the report that such was his success that: 'only two in Flintshire and one in Denbighshire being dangerous recusants, and common seducers of others obstinately refused to take the oaths.' As a last resort, the Chief Justice had 'convicted them in a *praemunire*' [the offence of directly or indirectly asserting the supremacy of the Pope over the Crown of England].

It seems that Sir John Bridgeman had won the first round in the contest to turn the holy place into a prohibited area for Catholics. But when the emergency of a threat of invasion and Papist aggression had passed, the authorities relaxed their control and Catholics became more confident and resumed their pilgrimages. This was seen three years later in 1629 when a spy reported the number 'of Papists and priests assembled at St Winefride's Well, on St Winefride's day, 1629.' The informer gave the names of those he regarded as prominent Catholics and simply added at the end of his note:

> ... with divers other knights, ladies, gentlemen and gentlewomen of divers countries to the number of fourteen or fifteenth hundreth; and the general estimation about a hundred and fifty or more priestes, the most of them well known what they were.[48]

If the informers' evidence is correct, then it appears that in the contest for the control of St Winefride's Well between the Catholics and Privy Council, the persistency of Catholics in their visits was proving more than a match for the vigilance of the authorities. There must have been an efficient network involved in secretly advertising the pilgrimage in 1629, and attracting such a large number of laity and priests. The Catholics may have felt reassured with Charles I's French consort, Henrietta Maria, sharing their religion, with freedom to hear Mass and by an increasing number of priests and converts throughout the country. With the King ruling without Parliament there was no longer a public forum for anti–Catholic measures.

Whatever the reason for the Holywell pilgrimage of 1629, judging by the attendance, it was a huge success. The only evidence we have is a single document containing a few of the names, with no further explanation of background or motive. Only thirty pilgrims are named out of fifteen hundred, and so it is impossible to reach any firm judgement of the purpose of the gathering, but some conclusions may be drawn. The two leading names are Catholic grandees; Lord William Howard of Naworth Castle, Cumberland (the aged son of an executed duke of Norfolk) and Lord Shrewsbury (the son of Mary Cavendish a spirited Catholic convert and cousin of the imprisoned Lady Arbella Stuart). These are followed by a list of over a dozen of the Lancashire gentry, and then Lady Falkland, and with her Mr Everard the priest.

Elizabeth, viscountess of Falkland, had recently found her spiritual home in the Catholic religion, and enthusiastically embarked upon her new life. At the time of the pilgrimage she had just completed a book of Catholic propaganda which she dedicated to Queen Henrietta Maria. It was printed at Douai and reportedly burnt on arrival in England in 1630. She came to Holywell with her Jesuit priest, Thomas Everard.

The authorities must have been outraged by the presence of over a hundred and fifty priests at the shrine; many of them were sheltering in the households of the gentry whom they accompanied. For example Sir Cuthbert Clinton, of Lytham and Westerby, came with 'two priests, Anderton and Smith; also Mr

Arrowsmith's clothes and the knife to cut him up are at Sir Cuthbert's house.' Father Edmund Arrowsmith, SJ, was martyred at Lancaster in 1628 at the age of 43, after five years work in the Lancashire Jesuit Mission of the College of St Aloysius founded in 1622. Another priest noticed was the Secular 'Mr Mayfield [? William Maxfield] archdeacon under the Bishop of Chalcedon, of Speake near the sea–side.'

The fact that the majority of gentry named were from Lancashire suggests that the spy may have originated from that county, and it also emphasises the strong attachment of the faithful of that county to the cult of St Winefride, which has continued ever since. William Blundell of Crosby is an example of a squire whose family visited the well regularly through the coming centuries. Others included Sir Thomas Gerard, Sir William Norris, Sir John Talbot, Preston of Furness, Anderton of Clayton, Anderton of Ford, Gerard of Ince, Bradshaigh of Haigh, Harrington of Huyton, Scarisbrook of Scarisbrick, and Lathom of Mossborough.[49] Probably other priests and gentry from the northern and midland counties came with recusant families who were able to make the journey. The total number of Jesuit priests working in England and Wales in 1636 was 178. Only three Catholics were executed between 1625 and 1640, and the martyrdom of Father Edmund Arrowsmith, SJ, the previous year, was out of tune with the times, especially when there were favourable signs of toleration. The Catholic population was on the increase and the total number of Catholics in England and Wales grew by a third between 1603 to 1641, rising from 40,000 to 60,000, and Lancashire had one of highest Catholic populations in the country.

The authorities maintain their watch
We now enter into the critical decade of the first half of the seventeenth century when St Winefride's Well was damaged, and, against all odds, Jesuit fortunes received a notable advance. The authorities maintained their watch with an extra vigilance. Sir John Bridgeman was as opportune as ever in carrying out the wishes of the Privy Council and devising new ways of pleasing them. He was to find a new ally in John Owen, bishop of St Asaph (1629–51). Hostility towards Catholics from the Puritans and the Anglican Church became more vocal in the face of a growing opposition towards the policies of Charles I.

It was a continual complaint of Bishop Owen about pilgrimages to the Well which eventually led to repressive measures. In his reports on the state of the diocese of St Asaph to the Archbishop of Canterbury, Bishop Owen nagged about the Catholic pilgrims at the well until something was done about it. The complaint about the well was presented by the Archbishop to the King, and then discussed in the Privy Council, who then issued their directive to the Council of the Marches in Wales at Ludlow. The Bishop of St Asaph was consistent in his demand for action at Holywell.

1632. There hath been these two last years past, mention made of papists frequenting Holy–Well or St Winifred's well in Wales; and the bishop of St Asaph doth not forget to touch it again in theses words: 'There hath been there all this summer more than ordinary concourse of people, and more bold and open practice of superstition. Where it is not to be forgotten, that at that well a great part of the powder treason was hatched: and therefore my humble opinion is, that serious letters should be directed from your majesty or privy council, to the lord president of Wales and his fellow commisssioners, that at summer next some course should be taken for the repressing of the confluence, being indeed no better than a pilgrimage.'[50]

1633. The bishop of St Asaph returns that all is exceeding well in his diocese, save only that the number and boldness of some Romish recusants increaseth much in many places, and is encouraged by the superstitious and frequent concourse of that party to Holy–Well otherwise called St Winefride's Well: whether this concourse be by way of pilgrimage or no, I know not: but I am sure it hath long been complained of without remedy.[51]

1634. The bishop of St Asaph professes he hath little to return. And that it is a great part of his comfort, in that remote place…but heartily wishes, that they might be as well acquitted from superstition and profaneness.[52]

There is no report I have seen for 1635. The report for the following year is more specific in its detail and suggests that measures had been designed to remedy the matter.

1636. In the diocese of St Asaph there is no complaint but the usual, that there is great resort of recusants to Holy Well, and that this summer the Lady Falkland and her company came as pilgrims thither, who were the more observed because they travelled on foot, and dissembled neither their quality nor their errand; and this boldness of theirs is a very bad construction among your Majesty's people.[53]

On this occasion, the King did take action. He confined Lady Falkland to prison on account of her Catholicism and the upbringing of her children.

Action was also taken sometime between 1636 and 1637 with regard to the complaint about St Winefride's Well, for after that date complaints from the Bishop cease.

1637. … there is nothing but common peace, and universal conformity.

Sir John Bridgeman's actions at Holywell against St Winefride's Well
On 3 February 1636/7 Sir John, writing from Ludlow, confirmed the instructions given to him by the Privy Council on the 9 December previous. He informed them that he was taking steps to carry out their instructions '… to use all means

to hinder the pilgrimages to Holywell' and outlined the measures he proposed. These were virtually a repeat of those he had employed ten years earlier except that, this time, he was to be personally responsible for sending certificates of those of rank or quality who visited the Well on pilgrimage. The authorities had learnt from the scandal and publicity caused by the visit of Lady Falkland. Bridgeman instructed the justices of the peace in the neighbourhood to suppress all unnecessary alehouses the usual haunt of pilgrims ('the usual receptacles of those persons') and to compel:

> innholders, victuallers and others who are used there to lodge strangers there by recognizance to take certain notice of the names and dwelling–places of all such as shall resort to their houses, and to make true certificate thereof, at every great sessions of that county.' Finally they were to keep a strict watch at the Well during the usual time for pilgrimages ('tymes of repayer') to the well, 'which are in spring and in summer.'

He concluded by promising to do more in the week after Easter to view the place himself: 'either by muringe up the head of the spring … or otherwise by all good means I can accomplish his Majesties most gracious command.[54]

We learn from a document in the Royal Library, Brussels, of the measures taken by Sir John at Holywell in April 1637. He now placed the responsibility of 'hindering the pilgrimages' on the churchwardens of the parish. He ordered them 'to take away the iron posts around the fountain (such as had supported pilgrims bathing at the well) and disfigure the image of the Saint, close all the inns except for two, examine all the pilgrims who come there and report their names at the next Assize.'

The churchwardens appeared to disagree about their orders. One of them, William Jones, egged on by his brother Rhys Jones, removed the posts around the well, but not so his fellow warden, William Hughes, who refused to act for the justices and stood by the side of the parishioners in taking no action against pilgrims.[55] When at the Michaelmas sessions in September following, Bridgeman demanded an account of the disabilities undertaken at the well, he was informed that the posts had been removed and the image whitewashed. But the local innkeepers remained uncooperative in refusing to give names of pilgrims and reluctant to betray their faith or ruin their livelihood.[56] There may have been some rough justice as a result, for the house of William Jones was burnt down on the Wednesday in Holy Week.[57]

It can be seen from the present structure of the well that it has suffered damage, particularly around the basin of the spring. The fan vaulting remains intact apart from weathering and loss of coloured decoration. Likewise the robustness of the walls of the crypt are unaffected apart from graffiti, smoke damage, and surface damage and weathering. The major damage occurs to the transoms of the moulded shafts which rise from the well basin into the vaulting, probably as a result of the removal of the metalwork. They shows signs of systematic and deliberate spoilage which may be consistent with an attempt to wall up the well basin to prevent entrance by pilgrims. The only indication that this course of action was contemplated are the words of Sir John Bridgeman to the Privy Council which speak of 'muringe up the head of the springe.'

The earliest and only record of specific damage in the late 1630s is that given in the Brussels document, quoted above. The next reference to damage is made by John Taylor on his visit in 1653.

> It [the well] hath a fair chapel erected over it … which is now much defaced by the injury of these late wars. The well is compassed about with a fine wall of free stone, the wall hath eight angles or corners, and at every angle is a fair stone pillar, whereon the west end of the chapel is supported.[58]

As the image of St Winefride was only whitewashed in 1637, it was removed at a later date, probably during the Civil War.

Damage in the Civil Wars (1642–48)
The Parliamentary soldiers advanced into north Wales and came to Holywell in November 1643. It is impossible to draw any conclusions from the report that:

> At Holywell, the first place we came to, though the town were mostly Papists, we were told they pillaged none but the churches (in want of linen) and the poor curate … It was then time of probationship amongst disarmed people; and you must understand the minister staid, and was a Scotsman.[59]

But it may be that the damage to the Chapel above the Well referred to by John Taylor may have been included in the report:

> About ninth November, Sir W. Brereton and his forces came to Farndon and Holt, and entered through the same to Wrexham, Flint and Holywell, and did pull down the organs, defaced the windows in the churches, and pulled down the Arms and Hatchments.[60]

The establishment of the 'Old Star Inn' as a permanent Jesuit safe–house
Foley gives the background to the building which was to become the permanent centre for Jesuits.

> The Annual Letters of the English Province for 1642–3 record that a benevolent Catholic nobleman undertook to provide a spacious house for the accommodation of the many Catholics who resorted to St Winefride's Well … and he signifies to the Fathers [Jesuits] his intention that they should at all times have admission to this establishment. When this intention became known, some

67. *Interior of St Winefride's Well: George Cuitt's 1813 print shows the seventeenth-century damage to the transoms above the well basin and the empty niche which had contained the image of St Winefride.*

adversaries of the Society began to offer every opposition to the work. They everywhere reprobated the design as highly injurious, especially at the present time [on the eve of the English Civil War], and only calculated to exasperate Protestants. They went so far as to denounce the undertaking to the magistrats, whom they assured that the building in reality was intended for a College of Jesuits. Though they succeeded in procuring a temporary suspension of the work, one large room was completed; and at the ensuing assizes, the Judge applied to the nobleman and obtained the use of it, for holding his court.'[61]

The troublesome background to the building of the Old Star Inn in Holywell can be seen in the archives of the arch diocese of Westminster and has been fully explored by Professor Colleen M. Seguin.[62]

The nobleman referred to in the Jesuit Annual Letters was the Honourable George Petre (b. 1613), the eighth son of William, second Lord Petre, who married Anne, widow of Sir John Mostyn of Talacre, and daughter of Sir Henry Fox, of Lehurst, Shropshire. They lived at Greenfield, in the former abbey of Basingwerk. George Petre had an elder brother, Edward, who was married to Elizabeth Griffiths, of Bagillt. They belonged to a rich and influential Catholic family, of

Ingastone, in Essex who were respected in court circles. Anne Fox/Mostyn, now Petre, had already proved herself a fearless and a strongly committed Catholic who had sheltered Jesuits in her household. Anne's second husband, George, was equally zealous and generous in the financial provision he was prepared to make to further the mission of the Fathers in Holywell and at St Winefride's Well.

It was particularly unfortunate, considering the damage done recently to the Catholic cause by Sir John Bridgeman that opposition to the Jesuits should come from secular clergy in Wales. Bishop Richard Smith (a secular), although he had fled abroad in 1631, remained antagonistic towards the Jesuits, a jealousy which infected many of his clergy. The basis of the quarrel at Holywell appears to have been over the control of St Winefride's Well, an issue which was to re–occur for the next fifty years and involve both priest and people. The provision of Jesuit premises near the Well to house well–to–do pilgrims and a 'College of Jesuits' was too much for the Secular clergy to endure. Not only would they lose revenue from the pilgrims, they could also lose an effective presence at the well.

Alarmed at such prospects, they hit back by making a complaint which reached King Charles I, and on 7 July 1640 his secretary of state sent orders to the sheriff of Flintshire that 'for reasons of State, best known to His Majesty that you forthwith upon receipt hereof repair to Holywll and there give express command that the building aforesaid immediately cease and be no further advanced.'[63]

It was suspected that the King prohibited further building work at Holywell because of information supplied to him by George Gage, an influential Secular priest. Gage's cousin was Anne Petre whom he had visited at Greenfield. In retrospect he appeared to have come as a spy for the Seculars, intent on discrediting the purpose of the work in hand. Dissatisfied with the information he received from his cousin Anne, he exaggerated the cost from £400 to £2,000, and told the authorities that the building would contain a chapel for Roman Catholic worship.

On receiving the sheriff's instructions to cease building their hostel for pilgrims and Jesuits, George and Anne Petre contacted friends in London, and, as a result, it was arranged that the building be inspected by government officials. The surveyors reported that they could not 'by the eye find any outward appearance of church or chapel, for such Romish use,' and stated that the Petres' inn was not immediately adjacent to the well as had been alleged.[64] Morever they observed that the house of Father Williams, an old Secular cleric, was much nearer the well and concluded:

We conceive that this cloud burst out into a tempest against Mr Petre. For apprehending that his house might prejudice their benefit, we think they did out of malignity calumniate him with such imputations.[65]

Apparently the loyalty of lay people was divided in support of the two clerical parties. A partisan of the Seculars,

> … a Mr Roberts, informed the authorities, that their opposition was not against Mr Petre but the Jesuits. A secular priest had informed [the government] that the said building was to be 'a college of Jesuits,' and that the new building would prejudice Mr Williams, who was an ancient priest and lived in that place by the gains he got [from pilgrims] in the summer season.[66]

After viewing the building and listening to local opinion, the prohibition was revoked and new instructions conveyed to the sheriff to inform Mr George Petre:

> Whereas I lately signified His Majesties pleasure to you to cause stay to be made of a building in Holywell now being erected by Mr Petre, there having been some Suspicion that the same was intended for a place of devotion or meeting for Roman Catholics His Majesty now being fully satisfied as well by certificate from some Gentlemen of those parts as also by security given by the said Mr Petre, that the said building was not intended nor shall be converted into any such use, his (will is) that they shall have liberty to go on with the work. Drury Lane: 12 Sept 1640.[67]

Catholics at the court of Queen Henrietta Maria were displeased by the behaviour of the Secular clergy and Count Rossetti, the Pope's representative, believed that those involved were 'de facto excommunicated'. Unfortunately the Civil War prevented the Count taking further action.[68]

The Civil War was to affect the fortunes of all involved in this dispute. George Petre died at Wexford on 26 September 1647, aged 34, 'who for the Roman Catholic faith and loyalty to his Majesty left his country.' Father George Gage who became Vicar General for London and south–east England, was arrested in 1650 and died in prison in the summer of 1652.[69] Anne Petre lived to see not only the Restoration of Charles II in 1660 but also the creation at Holywell of a new Jesuit district in 1666–7, the Residence of St Winefride. The building erected by George Petre served for the next one hundred and fifty years as a mission house, an inn for pilgrims, and an unofficial chapel for visitors and local Roman Catholics. Later, the Secular clergy followed suit, and housed their mission almost next door to the Old Star Inn at the Cross Keys. The Mostyn family at Talacre and Greenfield enabled the Catholic community at Holywell to gradually concentrate their buildings on the Holywell stream around St Winefride's Well and on the street which leads up the hill into the town. Anne Petre's two sons by her first husband, Sir John Mostyn, entered the English College in Rome. Edward, the eldest, gave the following account: 'I have two brothers in Flanders, now studying at the English College at St Omer. I have four sisters, two in the English Convent, Antwerp, and two in England.' He returned to England two years later and was created a baronet in 1670. By his first wife, Elizabeth Downes, he had five

```
                    IESUS ~ MARIA
    HERE ⌀ LYETH ⌀ TH ⌀ Y ⌀ BODY ⌀ OF ⌀ GEORGE ⌀ PE
    TRE ⌀ LATE ⌀ OF GREENFIELD ⌀ IN ⌀ FLINT,
    SHIRE, ESQ. SONE TO ⌀ W. ⌀ LORD PETRE
    BARON ⌀ OF ⌀ INGLESTON ⌀ IN ⌀ ESSEX ⌀ &
    MARRIED ⌀ ANE ⌀ Yᵉ ⌀ RELICT ⌀ OF ⌀ JOHN
    MOSTOIN ⌀ ESQ. ⌀ BEING Yᵉ DAUGHTER
    OF HENRY ⌀ FOXE ⌀ ESQ. ⌀ WHO ⌀ FOR Yᵉ ⌀ RO
    MANE ⌀ CATHOLIQUE ⌀ FAITH ⌀ & ⌀ LOYAL-
    -TY ⌀ TO HIS MAᵗⁱᵉ ⌀ LEFT HIS ⌀ COUNTRY ⌀
    & SPENDING ⌀ HIS TIME Wᵗ GREAT ⌀
    EDIFICATION ⌀ OF ⌀ HIS ⌀ NEIGHBOURS
    DIED ⌀ AT ⌀ WEXFORD Yᵉ 26 DAY OF SEP.
    AN. DO 1647 AGED 34.
```

68. *Monumental inscription to George Petrie, d. 1647: it was formerly at Basingwerk Abbey.*

sons and three daughters, two of whom, namely Elizabeth and Anne, became Teresian nuns at Lierre and three of his sons entered the English Province of the Society of Jesus.

The second of Anne's sons, John, entered the English College in Rome in 1650, and later proceeded to the University of Padua to study medicine. The Mostyns of Talacre were the leading Catholic recusant family in Flintshire until 1920 when they left the district. It was their allegiance to the Catholic cause in Holywell and the position they held as leading landowners that made them outstanding guardians of the cult of St Winefride during the remainder of the Penal period.[70]

NOTES

1. Quoted in J. R. Tanner, *Constitutional Documents of James I, 1603–25* (Cambridge, 1930), p. 83.
2. DNB under Henry Garnet.
3. Annual Letters, Foley Collection, part 2, p. 1036.
4. F. Edwards, SJ, 'Still Investigating the Gunpowder Plot', *Recusant History*, No. 21, 1992.
5. TNA, SP 14/216/200.
6. G. Anstruther, *Vaux of Harrowden A Recusant Family* (Newport, Monmouth, 1953), p. 276.
7. Conspirator in the Gunpowder Plot, executed.
8. Conspirator in the Gunpowder Plot, executed.
9. Conspirator in the Gunpowder Plot, executed.
10. For Father Tesimond's responsibility for passing on knowledge of the plot to Father Garnet see Antonia Fraser, *The Gunpowder Plot* (Phoenix, 1999), pp. 156–7.
11. *The Life of a Conspirator being a biography of Sir Everard Digby by one of his descendants* (London, 1895), p. 100.

12. J. Bossy, 'The English Catholic Community 1603–1625' in *The Reign of James VI and I* ed. A. G. R. Smith, p. 96 (London, 1973).

13. Hist. MSS Comm. Salisbuy, pt xvii, 1938, HMSO, p. 374, 1605 Aug 15.

14. E. G. Jones, 'Catholic Recusancy in the Counties of Denbigh, Flint and Montgomery, 1581–1625' *Transactions of Hon. Soc. Cymmrodorion*, 1945, p. 120.

15. Ibid, p. 121.

16. Ibid, pp. 129–133.

17. NLW, Great Sessions, Flintshire Gaol Files, Wales, 4/976/4/35. I am grateful to Mr K. L. Gruffydd for this reference.

18. C. A. Skeel, *The Council in the Marches of Wales* (London, 1904), p. 150.

19. G. D. Owen, *Wales in the reign of James I* (Boydell, 1988), p. 10.

20. T. H. Parry-Williams, *Canu Rhydd Cynnar* (Caedydd, 1932), lxxi, 353. I am grateful to Mr K. L. Gruffydd for this reference.

21. Calendar of Wynn (of Gwydir) Papers, 1515–1690, ed J. Ballinger (Cardiff, 1926), No. 544, 9 Aug 1610.

22. TNA, Che 21/21/3.

23. E. G. Jones, op cit, p. 118.

24. CSPD, James I 1619–1623, vol. cxi, 89, 23 Dec, pp. 104–5 and 1620, 8 Jan, vol. cxii.

25. A. J. Lorrie (ed.) 'Spain and Jacobean Catholics II; 1613–1624, *Catholic Record Society*, 68, 1978, p. 140.

26. T. H. B. M. Harmsen, *John Gee's Foot Out of the Snare* (1624), (Nijmagen, The Cicero Press, 1992), pp. 121–2.

27. G. Williams, *Renewal and Reformation Wales c.1415–1642* (Oxford, 1993), p. 478.

28. *Calendar of Wynn Papers*, op cit, Nos 1348, 1361.

29. H. Foley, *Records of the English Province of the Society of Jesus*, vol. 4, p. 497 (Burns & Oates, 1878).

30. P. Hook, 'The Catholic Registers of Holywell, Flintshire', *Catholic Record Society*, vol. 3, pp. 105–134.

31. J. Bossy, op cit, p. 97.

32. T. M. McCoog, 'The Society of Jesus in England 1623–1688', Ph D thesis, University of Warwick, 1984, and T. M. McCoog 'The Society of Jesus in Wales; The Welsh in the Society of Jesus: 1561–1625', *The Journal of Welsh Religious History*, vol. 5, 1997.

33. Foley, vol. 4, p. 519, McCoog, 'The Society of Jesus in Wales', p. 12.

34. This account depends upon the article by J. M. Cleary in *Worcestershire Recusant*, No. 32, 1978 'Recusant Schools in north Wales, 1626–1627', and is based on four documents in the archives of the Archbishop of Westminster for which permission has been given to quote.

35. AAW, series 'A', vol. 1,9 p. 391, No. 11.

36. Cleary, p. 13, see fn 34.

37 AAW, series 'A', vo.l 20, No. 82, p. 291.

38. Recusant documents from Ellesmere MS, ed. A. G. Petti, CRS, 1968, p. 257.

39. AAW, series 'A', vol. 20, No. 83, p. 295.

40. AAW, vol. 20, No. 93, p. 325.

41. Daughter of Henry Fox of Lehurst, Shropshire.

42. H. Taylor, 'Popish Recusants in Flintshire in 1625', *Journal of the Chester Archaeological and Historic Society*, vol. 5, pt. 3 (1898), pp. 304–16.

43. The son of Hugh Owen, alias Father John Hughes, SJ. He later served in the mission at Holywell.

44. CSPD, Chas I, p. 172, vol. xi, 37, Dec 8 1625.

45. W. R. Williams, *The History of the Great Sessions in Wales, 1542–1830* (Brecknock, 1899), p. 35.

46. FRO D/GR/1465, extract from Privy Council Register, 25 April 1626.

47. CSPD, Chas I, vol. xxxviii, No. 73, 1626, Oct 23, quoted in Foley, vol. 4, p. 534.

48. CSPD, Chas I, v cli, No. 13, 1629, quoted by Foley, ibid, pp. 534–5.

49. J. A. Hilton, *Catholic Lancashire,1559–1991* (Phillimore, 1994), pp. 29–30.

50. *The Works of William Laud* (Parker Society, Oxford), 1853, vol. 2, pp. 310–11, Archbishop Abbot's

account of his Province to the King for 1632.

51. Ibid, pp. 320–2.

52. Ibid, p. 329.

53. 'My Lord of Canterbury's returns to his Majesty's instructions for the year 1636', J. P. Kenyon *The Stuart Constitution 1603–1688 Documents and Commentary* (Cambridge, 1966), p. 163.

54. CSPD, Chas I, 1636, vol. ccxlvi, No. 25, endorsed Feb 10 1636, 'From Sir John Bridgeman concerning pilgrims to Holywell' quoted in Foley, vol. 4, p. 535, op cit.

55. Swift, op cit, *The Life of St Winefride*, pp. 73–456.

56. Ibid p. 74, taken from a document in the Royal Library Brussels.

57. Ibid.

58. 'John Taylor, a short relation of a long journey, London to Wales, July 1652 – September 1653', from John Chandler (ed.) and selections *The adventures of John Taylor the Water Poet* (Sutton, 1999), pp. 260–1 and 268–9.

59. J. R. Phillips, *Memoirs of the Civil War in Wales and the Marches*, 2 vols (Longman, London, 1874), vol. 2, p. 111.

60. Harleian MS 2125, fol. 135.

61. Foley, op cit, vol. 4, p. 536.

62. C. M. Seguin, 'Cures and Controversy in Early Modern Wales: The Struggle to Control St Winifred's Well', *North American Journal of Welsh Studies*, vol. 3, 2 (Summer, 2003). The discussion which follows relies on this study, especially pages 12–15. I am grateful to the Archdiocese of Westminster for permission to quote from their archives.

63. TNA, Sp/16/459/49.

64. It is on the same site as the Holywell Presbytery, about three or four hundred yards from St Winefride's Well.

65. AAW/A, vol. xxix, No. 114, 359–60, and Seguin, op cit, p. 14.

66. AAW/A, vol. xxix, No. 131, 419, and Seguin, ibid, p. 14. This mention of Mr Williams is the first mention of a Secular priest by name in Holywell. It is impossible to say who he was although Ansruther, *The Seminary Priests*, vol. 2, gives two possibilities – Lewis Williams (b. Monmouthshire, 1585), or Thomas Williams (b. 1577).

67. TNA, SP/16/467.

68. AAW/A, vol. xxix, No. 131, 420–421, and Seguin, op cit, p. 15.

69. George Gage, entry in DNB.

70. Foley, vol. 4, pp. 523–52,7 op cit, for an account of the Mostyn family of Talacre.

6. 1649–88

Introduction

The cult of St Winefride had survived the dramatic political changes of the one hundred and twenty years from the religious reformation of Henry VIII to the execution of Charles I on 30 January 1649. The Roman Catholic faith had refused to disappear from the religious landscape in Britain. In spite of constant persecution it steadfastly persisted in small groups in many areas and Holywell was one of the strongest centres in Wales. Here its continuity was maintained by the attraction of St Winefride's Well, and the devotion of Jesuit and Secular priests, with support of faithful recusant families.

For the next sixty years there were new challenges to be met and dangers faced created by unpredictable events. A tantalising effect on Catholic hopes for toleration over the period was that the four Stuart kings – two James's and two Charles's – had Catholic queens. An unpredictable feature of the period was the struggle between a ruler who believed in the Divine Right of Kings and a Protestant parliament which frustrated attempts towards an absolute monarchy by financial control. In his attempt to get round this financial difficulty, Charles II concluded the Secret Treaty at Dover with the King of France, Louis XIV, which promised toleration for Catholics, and support against the Protestant Dutch in return for cash.

In the tension caused by this struggle, attention was invariably diverted to the Roman Catholics at times of political unrest. This situation was further affected by the conversion to Catholicism of James, Duke of York, the heir to the throne, who had a potential Protestant contender in Charles II's illegitimate son, the Duke of Monmouth. Amongst great animosity, Charles II was forced to prorogue Parliament in order to prevent their passing legislation designed to exclude a Catholic successor.

And, when James II did succeed to the throne, he exercised neither restraint nor wisdom by pursuing too quickly a policy of toleration, which threatened to overturn the existing religious settlement. The Protestant backlash, when it occurred after these national crises, was to have serious repercussions on the Catholic community.

A little more is known in this period of the identity and work of Jesuit and Secular priests who served the mission in Holywell and their influence on pilgrims who came to St Winefride's Well. The most important event in this period was the establishment of the Residence of St Winefride in 1666–7, with Holywell as one of its four districts, carved out of the northern half of the Residence of St Francis Xavier.

The Commonwealth, 1649, to the Restoration of Charles II, 1660

From February 1650, the religious life in Wales was controlled by the Act for the Better Propagation and Preaching of the Gospel in Wales, enforced throughout the country by seventy-one commissioners. They were responsible for the institution of a Puritan ministry throughout Wales and the establishment of a number of schools to be paid for out of the funds of the Anglican Church. Bishops of the Church of England were abolished, the clergy in Wales were subject to the approval of the new commissioners, and, if found wanting, removed. This is what had happened in the parish of Holywell, when vicar Evan Lloyd was deprived by sequestrators, and a Puritan intruded into his place. Oliver Cromwell pursued some form of toleration for Catholics in England and Wales for most of his governance which is demonstrated by an increase in the number of Catholics, presented as recusants in Flintshire.

The visit of John Taylor, 1652

In spite of these disturbed times, there is evidence that travellers and pilgrims came to St Winefride's Well, with some being fortunate enough to be healed. The first account we have is that of John Taylor (1578–1653), called the 'Water Poet', an eccentric, gregarious, ebullient and self-educated literary character, who spent most of his life as a waterman on the Thames. Through this occupation, rather like a modern 'cabby,' he became acquainted with many of his 'fares,' some of whom were writers. His lively wit led him to devise a series of exotic adventures to Germany, Scotland, and England, a record of which he published, with other works of satirical verse and nonsense writing.

His last adventure was published as *A Short Relation of a Long Journey from London to Wales 13 July 1652 to 7 September 1653*.[1] At a time when he kept The Crown alehouse in Westminster which name, after the King's execution, he changed to 'The Mourning Crown.' His journey, made on his faithful steed Dun, took him to Chester and then on a tour round the Welsh coast. He was greeted warmly by the cavalier gentlemen, but viewed with suspicion by the parliamentary garrisons and was afraid of being arrested as a spy. His observations are those of a curious traveller rather than a devoted pilgrim, with a mind lively enough to leave an interesting account of the well.

Saturday, the last of July, I left Flint, and went three miles to Holywell, of which place I must speak somewhat materially. About the length of a furlong, down a very steep hill, is a well (full of wonder and admiration), it comes from a spring ... from it doth issue so forcible a stream, that within a hundred yards of it, it drives certain mills, and some do say that nine corn mills and fulling mills are driven with the stream of that spring: it hath a fair chapel erected over it called Saint Winifred's Chapel, which is now much defaced by the injury of these late wars.

The well is compassed about with a fine wall of free stone, the wall hath eight angles or corners, and at every angle is a fair stone pillar, whereon the west end of the chapel is supported. In two several places of the wall, there are neat stone stairs to go into the water that comes from the well, for it is to noted that the well itself doth continually work and bubble with extreme violence, like a boiling cauldron or furnace, and within the wall, or into the well very few do enter: The water is crystalline, sweet and medicinable, it is frequented daily by many people of rich and poor of all diseases, amongst which great store of folks are cured, divers are eased, but none made the worse.

The hill descending is plentifully furnished (on both sides of the way) with beggars of all ages, sexes, conditions, sorts, and sizes, many of them are impotent, but all are impudent, and richly embroidered all over with such hexameter prouded ermins (or vermin) as are called lice of England.

The next morning Taylor again set off.

When the day begun, I mounted my Dun, having hired a little boy (to direct me in the way) that could speak no English, and for lack of an interpreter, we travelled speechless eight miles to Rhuddlan, where is an old wind and war-shaken castle;[2]

The visit of Sir Francis Throckmorton August 1658
Sir Francis Throckmorton of Weston Underwood, Buckinghamshire, visited the well in consecutive summers in 1657 and 1658. As a member of a famous Catholic family with branches mostly in the Midlands, he came as a pilgrim and his memories are as such. There is no mention of Throckmorton female cousins who were married to local north-Wales gentry. The record of his visit is based on the ledger book kept by his steward, James Smyth, and gives an exact account of the expenditure expected from a wealthy Catholic pilgrim.[3]

The party rode on to Holywell after their supper. The poor there, 5s. 6d. certainly came off very well in comparison with other places where Francis had always remembered them, but then those other places were not comparable with the shrine of St Winifred of Holywell, to which they went next day and which was always particularly infested with beggars. This happened to be August 15th, the Feast of the Assumption of Our Lady. Here the woman that kept the chapel was given 1*s*. 6*d*. 5*s*. 8*d*. was paid for more burnt wine when they went into the well and 1*s*. 6*d*. for moss and stones (note: taken back to Weston) and to the man that kept clean about the well. The visit to the well was repeated the next day.

This priceless piece of information reveals that the reception of pilgrims and the services provided for them at the Well was continuing as usual. During the closing years of a Puritan regime the Catholics were openly observing at Holywell the feasts of the Church and that the chapel above the well was open in 1658 in spite of what Taylor had observed five years earlier. The Parish Church was under the control of an intruded Puritan minister and yet the ritual at the well continued as usual, with 'relics' of St Winefride, stones and moss, readily available.

What kept the cult of St Winefride alive during this most strongly Puritan episode in British history? There may have been some official toleration but what is most probable is that the local recusant population, under the leadership of the Petre family and others, had developed an understanding with local constables and justices to allow their activities to go unmolested, using the persuasive argument that the economic welfare of the town was dependent on pilgrims. They had learnt the lesson that outside interference, as happened in the Bridgeman years, was detrimental to the town's affairs.

Cure narratives of visitors to St Winefride's Well, 1640–74
Accounts of pilgrims visiting St Winefride's Well from all over England and Wales and sometimes further afield seeking a cure occur throughout the period.[4] Not surprisingly, the least recorded time is that of the Civil War. Afterwards numbers begin to increase. The accounts give a sense of normality to the events at the well, since business appears to be as usual. There are references to the effect of the Civil War and Puritan rule, to the wide variety of the social background of pilgrims who are able to travel in relative freedom, and to Catholic devotion which encourages the sick to make the journey. Once they have arrived pilgrims often linger at the Well following the ritual of bathing a number of times, until they have the confidence and health to make the return journey.

These cure narratives kept by Jesuits eventually found their way to Stonyhurst and were published in 1886 by the Bollandist fathers.[5] The series began in 1556 and ended in 1674.[6]

The accounts in some cases seek to establish the primacy of St Winefride's Well over Bath in Somerset as a healing centre. Most of the cures are experienced by Catholics, either through their own devotion or those of friends and relatives. Two Quakers from Bromsgrove were healed and one of them became a Catholic. Not so Henry Herbert of Colbrook (Coalbrook, Shropshire?) described as 'a Parliament man,' whose father had recently died, being eaten away by a 'canker' which was judged to be 'a just punishment from heaven for the tyranny and oppression he had persecuted the poor Catholics of his neighbourhood.' His son Henry Herbert made the journey of over eighty miles to the Well, and after his return home sent a horse with panniers to bring him some bottles full of Well water. But it was ineffectual and he died soon after, 'and it was no wonder it availed him no more, being a schismatic and heretic he wanted (in a very great measure) faith, which is always necessary for the obtaining of supernatural favours.'[7]

It was recounted that when Catholics came to the Well for healing, they made every effort to be in a state of Grace. This is seen in the case of Mrs Francis Fortescue of Northamptonshire who, having received no relief after being at Bath for six weeks, came to Holywell in August 1657. Here she found the water extremely cold and was somewhat overcome by the shock of it, but she was determined to venture again.

> For next day, having first by the receiving of both the usual holy sacraments disposed herself to gain the plenary indulgence (then lately granted to that holy place) and withal having distributed some alms both to good men and others, thus very well armed, she entered confidently again into the Holy Well and (to the honour of God be it spoken who is pleased to be glorified in his Saints) she found herself a palpable recovery' and on returning home made a full recovery.[8]

The healing power of St Winefride's continued to be extolled in the seventeenth century throughout the Catholic world. In 1660 a male servant, a Catholic, of the English Benedictine sisters at Ghent came to England looking for an improvement in his heath. He first went to Bath and was then directed by the Provincial of the Society of Jesus to come to Holywell. Francis Reeve, the son of a servant of the Throgmortons in Warwickshire, when 'no human help availed', decided to trust in the merits and intercession of St Winefride, and after bathing in the well was cured. Other sufferers were healed of rheumatics and another of leprosy by immersion. The spring water brought relief and improved vision to those with eye troubles.

The Jesuits regarded the recording of cure narratives at Holywell as part of their mission. Of equal testimony to the faithful and hopeful was the obsolete collection of crutches.

The continued persecution of recusants
Before the Civil War the penal laws were in times of crisis put into operation against those refusing to attend worship in their parish churches. The Great Rebellion changed all this for during the Commonwealth, Anglicanism counted for nothing and Puritans and Sectaries were permitted to worship in their own way. The two main bodies who suffered as recusants in the 1650s were the Quakers and Roman Catholics, whose names begin to appear in greater numbers.

There were fifteen Popish recusants presented at the Flintshire Great Sessions in 1655; the number increased in 1657 to sixty-nine, and peaked in 1658 at seventy-six, by which time the period of toleration appeared to be at an end. In 1660, the year of the restoration of the monarchy, the number dropped to thirty-three Popish recusants. In these county lists there were a number of names from the Holywell area, many of them already familiar, and showing that the old recusant families had remained faithful through the hard years of the troubles. These included Anne Petre and Hugh Totty from Greenfield; both Edward Pennant the elder and younger of Bagillt; Edward Conway and John Foukes, gentlemen, from Ysceifiog; Raphael Davies, gent from Whitford; and the wives of tradesmen (joiner, cobbler, tailor, weaver, and husbandmen) from the town of Holywell – a cross-section of the Catholic community.

More significant than the names of recusants presented at the Great Session of September 1657 was that of Peter Griffiths, Constable of Holywell, who was charged with the escape of a seminary priest. We have no knowledge of the name of the priest or the outcome of the case but it does raise the question about the name of the priest in charge of the mission at Holywell during this period.[9]

Priests who served the Jesuit Mission in the seventeenth century
The names, whereabouts, and length of time spent in one place by Jesuit priests are difficult to establish with accuracy because of the need for secrecy in penal times and the use of aliases. The identity of priests serving in Holywell is more difficult because it was one mission out of others in a larger district or residency. From 1622 to 1666 Holywell was part of the College, or Residency, of St Francis Xavier, centred at Cwm along the border in Monmouthshire and south Wales. Priests served the Holywell mission under the direction of a superior and could be moved about. In 1666, the original residency of St Francis Xavier was divided into two and a new college or residency established, known as the Residency of St Winefride, made up of four missions of which Holywell was one.

But the surviving lists of priests[10] provide a general indication of the Jesuit priests who served the mission in Holywell until 1930 although they do not give exact years for their presence there. The names, which find general agreement for the seventeenth century, are:

> Father John Bennett, SJ, (1590–1625).
> Father William Wright, SJ, 1609.
> Father Richard Whitely, SJ (alias Wright), (b.1583, d.London 1651; at the College of St Francis Xavier, 1641?).
> Father Humphrey Evans, SJ (alias Brown), (b.c.1598, d. 14 January 1679). Said to have been in Holywell for six years – 1656–62.
> Father John Hugh Owen, SJ (alias John Hughes). (b. 1615, d. Holywell 1686)
> Father Roderick or Thomas Roberts, SJ, (b. 1640s, d. June 26 1721). Residence

of St Winefride 1672–6, 1678–96, Superior 1687–96.

Father Edmund Thorold, SJ, (b.1657, d. Holywell June 26 1721).[11]

Throughout the seventeenth century, the existence of penal laws and hatred of Catholics, in some cases genuine, in others stirred up for propaganda purposes, continued. Both Secular and Regular priests like the Jesuits were always in danger of arrest and imprisonment, and had to adapt their life styles accordingly. This created difficulty in serving Catholic congregations either in urban or scattered rural areas. There was always danger of detection, betrayal and infiltration by spies. To protect themselves, priests dressed as laymen, worship was conducted behind locked doors, in barns, upper rooms, and even out of doors, in woods in summer time. Travelling was hazardous, laity could be arrested for sheltering priests, and in times of crisis search parties forced their way into suspects' houses. In order to protect themselves some priests lived together in small communities, as for example those who served the Residence and District of St Francis Xavier at Cwm. The Old Star Inn in Holywell was used for those working in north Wales in the same way as the house at Cwm. Secular priests dwelt in cottages provided for them by the laity, and other priests found refuge as chaplains and tutors in gentry houses. Here they were virtually in hiding, their identity known only to the members of the household in which they sheltered, and in the last resort forced to hide in the priest hole. For many of them it was an isolated precarious vocation and few escaped imprisonment at some time or other, as we see in the lives of those who spent time on the Holywell mission.

Father Humphrey Evans, SJ, (alias Brown), (b. Caernarfon 1598, d. 14 January 1679)
Father Humphrey Evans spent fifty-eight years as a Jesuit and may have succeeded Father Bennett in 1625.[12] Like John Bennett he was Welsh speaking and served his countrymen in the north and south of the principality as well as in England. For six years he was superior of St Winefride's Residence, and was twice rector of St Francis Xavier's College and south Wales District. He may have been the unnamed seminary priest whom Peter Griffiths, constable of Holywell, allowed to escape from his charge in 1657. Father Evans is reputed to have come 'to Holywell about 1656 and remained six years.'[13] He died tragically in prison on 14 January 1679, during the Popish Plot persecution.

Whilst at Holywell, in 1664, Father Evans received for safe-keeping a relic of St Thomas Cantilupe (1218–82) from a fellow Jesuit, Father Cuffaud, of Hereford. The relic of the former bishop was the right arm-bone (tibia) nine-inches long. It was until the Reformation enshrined in his cathedral at Hereford and was then secreted away to be venerated by local Catholics. The relic remained at Holywell until 1835 when it was taken to Stonyhurst. It has now been returned, and is on display in the Well Museum. Father Evans' successor at Holywell promoted the cult there of St Thomas of Hereford in a Welsh language primer *Allwedd neu Agoriad Paradwys i'r Cymry* which he published in 1670.

Father John Hugh Owen, SJ, (alias John Hughes) (b. Anglesey 1615, d. 1686)[14]
Father Hugh Owen's main sphere of activity was the Welsh missions of the College of St, Francis Xavier where he played an important role, both at Cwm and Holywell. He provided an interesting link through the reigns of four Stuart kings from James I to James II, contributing to Welsh language devotional writing by the compilation of *Allwedd neu Agoriad Paradwys i'r Cymry*… (*Key to Paradise for the Welsh people, that is Prayers, Devotions, Instructions and godly Doctrines seeking to open the Gate to go to Heaven, collecting from many godly books and compiled by I. H).*[15] 'a rendering into fine Welsh of extracts from the Gospels and Catholic catechisms.'[16] Father Hugh Owen was the son of Hugh Owen (1575–1642), of Gwenynog, Anglesey, whom Bishop Lewys Bayly accused in 1625 as being 'a felon and a Romish recusant.' Hugh Owen, the elder, left the island and became secretary to Henry Somerset, Lord Herbert, at Raglan Castle, a household with strong Catholic sympathies. When he died in 1642 he bequeathed all his books and writings to his son. In 1684, Father Hugh Owen (alias John Hughes) published his father's translation into the Welsh language of the religious classic *De Imitatione Christi* (the Imitation of Christ) by Thomas à Kempis (*c*.1380–1471) as *Dilyniad Crist* (following of Christ).

It was probable that Father Hugh Owen was priest at Holywell on more than one occasion. The first may have been in the 1660s for it is said that he was there during the same time (1660–66) that his cousin, George Griffith, was bishop of St Asaph. At the end of Owen's codex of miracles is a letter dated 26 June 1674 written in guarded terms to his Superior Father William Morgan then at Powis Castle. It appears to refer to the celebration of the feast of St Winefride four days earlier. Apparently there was no open celebration:

> … by advice of the Great Ones hereabouts no use was made of the Closett on ye 22nd hereof, but the new suite sent from the Noble Lady wth you, was fix't on the frames and wth the other best dresses sett up: the most eminent of those who then were here, were in the evening permitted to go in to see all & say their devotions, & nobody else:

Possibly this refers to the celebration of Mass. Then follows a list of names: 'Madam Lumley (ye Lors mother) & her daughter, Madam Ploydon [Plowden?] & her daughter, Mr Lewis Barlow out of Pembrokeshire, &c., but the most famous was the Lady Green (Don Carlo's mother) as well as others.'

The final document referenced 'L' is a short note about St Beuno.[17] Father Hugh Owen was obviously a scholar priest devoted to the Welsh language as well as to the Catholic faith and the cults of St Winefride and St Thomas of Hereford.

CATECHISMVS
AD PAROCHOS
EX DECRETO
CONCILII
TRIDENTINI EDITVS.
ET PII V. PONT. MAX.
juſſu promulgatus.

Sincerus & integer, mendiſque iterùm
repurgatis operâ P. D. L. H. P.

*A quo eſt additus Apparatus ad Catechiſmum, in quo
Ratio, Auctores, Antiquitas, Approbatores
&, vſus declarantur.*

PARISIIS,
Apud NicoLAUM Pepingouɛ', in ſuâ Palatij primariæ,
è regione Cameræ Conſultorum Iuris, ad
inſigne Solis aurel.

M. DC. LXXII.

69. The Catechism of the decrees of the
Council of Trent.

Coincidental with his first period at the Holywell is *A Catalogue of the Bookes belonging to the Society of Jesus in my keeping at my lodging at St W this 12th day of March 1663/4.*[18] There are about a hundred titles listed of works in Latin, Welsh and English. It is the working library of a Catholic missionary priest to help his own devotional life, and more particularly to encourage a flock which varied from visiting pilgrims at St Winefride's Well to Catholics scattered across Flintshire and north Wales. Many of the Catholic gentry would have their own libraries and Father Hugh Owen may have had access to the extensive Mostyn library. He would certainly have inherited books as well as manuscripts from his father, and have used the library of the College of St Francis Xavier, which was shamelessly ransacked by Bishop Herbert Croft of Hereford in the autumn of 1678. Father Hugh Owen's collection was probably similar to the library at Cwm albeit on a much smaller scale.

The Holywell library contained for example: *Martyrologies; the Life of Bishop Fisher; S Wenefr Lives* (bound in leather) – 54 copies; the same (in vellum) – 47 copies; *The Glorie of St Ignatius* 19 copies; *Tridentine Canons*; and *De Imitatione Christi*, Thomas à Kempis. For his pastoral work there is a *Vade Mecum; Bellarmines Little Catechisme*, 5 copies; *Keyes of Paradise* by John Wilson, 8 copies.[20] There is also the reminder that both Hugh Owen the elder and younger were from north Wales and part of the renaissance movement for the revival of the Welsh language and publication of works in the same tongue and it is not surprising to find texts to remind us of this. For example, a Welsh dictionary, either William Salesbury's of 1547, but most probably Dr John Davies' *Dictionarium Duplex* (1632); a Welsh *Book of Common Prayer* and Welsh *Bible* would probably be the 1630 edition, published with generous financial help from the Puritans, Sir Thomas Middleton and Rowland Heylin; *Trefn Ymarweddiad y Gwir Gristion* by Edward Wynn (1618–69), of Bodewryd, Anglesey, chancellor of Bangor Cathedral, is a collection of Welsh prayers, the catechism, and a selection of metrical psalms; *Arhravaeth Gristnogavl* by the controversial Morys Clynnog

(1525–81), is a short Welsh catechism an adaptation of one by the Spaniard Ioannes Polanco (d. 1574) the first secretary of the Society of Jesus. The existence of this working-, cum lending-library, helps us to build up a picture of how the cult of St Winefride was sustained during the perilous years of the last half of the seventeenth century. This had much to do with the high calibre of priests who served at Holywell.

From the time of his ordination Father Owen had the reputation of being 'a man of remarkable patience and excellent behaviour.' His death at Holywell in December 1686 at the age of seventy-one years is said to have been accelerated by an accidental fall from his horse, when returning from administering the sacraments to the family of Mr Salisbury, a recent convert. He was a holy man of very mortified habits.[21] Besides the accustomed Friday fast, he abstained from food until Sunday at noon, never went abroad for mere recreation and never played cards.

The establishment of the Residence of St Winefride in 1666–7
In 1666–7 north Wales was separated from the College of St Francis Xavier, and incorporated as a new district of the Jesuit Province, with the title of the Residence of St Winefride. It became a distinct residence, passing occasionally under the aliases of 'Mrs North Wales," and "Mrs Flint," and included the whole of north Wales, with Shropshire, Holywell, Welshpool, Powis Castle and Plowden Hall as its principal missionary residences.

At this time the finances of the College of St Francis Xavier were surveyed and investigated in order to decide what portion of the portfolio should be assigned to the new Residence of St Winefride.[22]

In order to support the ministry of priests, which was its chief object, the funds of the Society of Jesus were allocated so much per head. The amount allocated was very meagre — £10 or £15 per annum. Catholic peers and gentry were generous but eventually crippled by recusant fines and financial support for the Royalist cause in the Civil War. Whatever money the Society received had to be carefully protected through the use of trustees. According to the Chantries Act of 1547 and Elizabethan legislation against Jesuits and seminary priests, any legacy given to Popish or superstitious uses was forbidden and liable for forfeiture to the Crown.

However, by the middle of the seventeenth century it was judged that there were sufficient endowments to support a residence in north Wales. By this time the Society possessed a number of small properties, land and tenements in the parishes of Tremeirchion, Caerwys, and Whitford, in the county of Flintshire, of about one hundred and forty acres, to which was later added a farm of ninety acres at Llanfechain in Montgomeryshire. In addition, there was land and property in Holywell.[23] The Star Inn, whose erection caused a storm in the 1640s, was the principal building, to which were eventually added stables, gardens, and

Jesuit districts 1623
Later sub divisions

St. Aloysius

St. Winifred   St. Chad

St. Francis Xavier

Based upon J. Bossy

70. Creation of the Residence
of St Winefride 1666/7.

tenements through the judicious management of trustees and generosity of local laity.

By the beginning of the nineteenth century, the Catholic community in the Holywell area had accumulated enough property to enable it to meet the needs of Catholic emancipation and a growing Catholic population. It had sufficient land in the vicinity of St Winefride's Well on which to build a chapel, schools, hospice and convent. Some of the land in Tremeirchion parish, with superb views over the vale of Clwyd, was the site of a new Jesuit theolgate – St Beuno's College. Thus, eleven hundreds years later, Winefride's teacher and mentor was duly commemorated.

The Titus Oates Plot, 1678–9

The Titus Oates Plot, otherwise known as the Popish Plot, was the second calamity to strike the Society of Jesus in the English Province in the seventeenth century. The consequences of the plot were arguably more devastating than that of the Gunpowder conspiracy over seventy years earlier. By the 1670s, the Society was more organised and had recovered from the consequences of the Civil War. The plot, one of the great political dramas of the seventeenth century, had a disastrous effect on Catholic confidence. Its most disastrous consequence was that of stirring up fear and hatred of Catholics, and Jesuits in particular. Oates succeeded in arousing a national hysteria which at the time was greater than that of the Gunpowder Plot of 1605. For over twelve months the enormity increased of Oates capacity for false testimony and character assassination as he revealed more and more unlikely stories which condemned innocent Catholics to the gallows.

Oates was barely thirty years of age when he announced the news of the plot, apparently manufactured by his imagination from the details of his murky past and unstable character. Uncouth, of coarse temper, odd life style, with a dubious history as a failed under-graduate, Anglican clergyman, and seminary student, he was expelled from

71. *Charles II.*

all these institutions when his superiors discovered his unscrupulous character. His villany and capacity for lies increased from each set-back, fired by instability, fantasy, fanaticism, and a desire for vengeance. These unfortunate traits were stimulated by his companions Dr Israel Tonge, a former clergyman and fervent anti-papist, obsessed with the Jesuit menace, and William Bedloe. In league with these unfortunates Oates began to manufacture his plot. To make it more convincing, he embellished it with his personal knowledge of Catholic insti-tutions and information gathered during his flirtation with the Society of Jesus and acquaintance with two superiors of the English Province. When inevitably his accusations led him to be called upon as the chief prosecution witness he quickly became a master of perjury and an instant manufacturer of damning evidence.

Oates's poisoned imagination implicated the Society of Jesus, Catholic peers, and anyone he felt inclined to accuse, including the Queen, and Edward Coleman, secretary to the Duchess of York. No one was safe: many innocent men were condemned to painful deaths, and the whole nation was whipped up into a frenzy of fear and persecution.

The plot told the public what they wanted to hear that the Pope, the Jesuits and English Catholics were said to have plotted the murder of Charles II and planned to enthrone his brother James, duke of York, as successor. A Catholic government was to be installed, Protestants massacred by rebellions in England and Scotland, and the French were to invade Ireland. Oates claimed to be privy to secret correspondence and to have been present at a secret conclave of Jesuits in London in April 1678 when the plot was discussed.

It was hatched at a time when the Earl of Shaftesbury was pursuing his own policy of seeking to exclude the Duke of York from the succession and bring discredit upon Catholics and prevent their involvement in public life. Oates credibility was further supported when it was revealed that Danby, Charles II's chief minister, was in secret negotiations with the French to restore the Catholic religion in England and wage war against Dutch Protestants.

Although London was the main theatre for the enactment of the plot, the Catholic community in Wales and north-west England suffered from the brutal persecution which followed. These events were felt in Holywell through its association with those who suffered. All Catholic priests were at risk on account of their orders, and Jesuits in particular because of detailed allegations against the Society. The Privy Council gave instructions to local magistrates for a priest hunt,

72. *Titus Oates in the pillory encircled by some of the Jesuit victims of the Popish Plot: Dutch engraving.*

which resulted in the martyrdom of clerics and laity. Some of these tragic stories were reported in a letter written by Father William Morgan, chaplain at Powis Castle, to a Jesuit at Rome, in 1679.[24]

Father William Morgan (1623–89) was no stranger to violence and sudden death, having served with Royalist forces at Naseby in the Civil War. He was a Flintshire man, born at Cilcain and educated at Westminster School. He joined the Society of Jesus in 1651 and eventually became professor of Philosophy and Hebrew at the seminary at Liege, returning to north Wales in 1672 as superior of the Residence of St Winefride. Morgan's account of the effect of the plot on the Society of Jesus, both in the England and Wales, is a very comprehensive catalogue of the calamity of events to the autumn of 1679 and begins with an assessment of the effects of the plot.

> Our afflicted Province, is now so reduced by the hands of the present persecution that it scarcely bears the resemblance of a Province. More than thirty-five of our Fathers are either dead or in prison on this occasion. Six of them were sentenced to death and died by the hands of the executioner as guilty (innocent though they were) of the pretended plot.

He then recounts the deaths of the six at Tyburn.[25]

Later in the letter he laments that 'Some died in the prisons themselves; others under their sufferings and miseries incurred in their constant shifting up and down to avoid the pursuivants.' These were the professional priest-hunters who, accompanied by magistrates and soldiers, arrested many of the accused. Oates had a troop of soldiers to accompany him on these searches. In the winter of 1678–9, Bishop Herbert Croft of Hereford, a former student of the Jesuits, acting on the orders of the Privy Council, descended on the College of St Francis Xavier at Cwm in south Wales. In reporting this incident Father Morgan simply stated: 'The College of South Wales is totally rooted up.' Fortunately, the Jesuit residents were warned and escaped with their altar equipment and vestments, but failed to rescue their library. This became the prize of the bishop who, in the process of looking for incriminating papers, removed the college records and books in several 'horseloads' to the famous Hereford Cathedral library. Amongst these were some 'Welsh popish books lately printed.'

Two priests with former associations with Holywell were discovered by pursuivants in Cheshire. On 28 December the priest catcher, Thomas Dutton, raided the house of the Masseys at Puddington Hall and took into custody Father John Plessington (1636–79) on suspicion of being a Roman Catholic priest.[26] Plessington was tried and found guilty at Chester Castle on 12 May following and, after nine weeks imprisonment, was dragged on a hurdle to his execution at Gallows Hill, Boughton, on 19 July 1679. Tradition has it that when soldiers brought his body to Puddington after execution the hostile villagers stoned them.

73. *St John Plessington martyred at Chester 1679 a victim of the Popish Plot – devotional print.*

74. *St John Plessington stained-glass window St Winefride's RC Church, Holywell.*

The martyred priest was associated with Holywell as a Secular priest serving in the mission operating from the Cross Keys some time between 1665 and 1679.[27] He was canonised by Pope Paul VI in 1970 as one of the 'Forty Martyrs of England and Wales'. The custodians' house at St Winefride's Well is named in his honour and there is a window depicting him in St Winefride's Church, Holywell.

Father Morgan had probably worked with Father Humphrey Evans whom we noted above. The sick and aged priest, now being cared for in a gentry household, was a greatly loved and highly respected member of the Society, and his unfortunate death was a matter of great sadness. Father Morgan describes the scene of his detection similar to others throughout the country.

Father Humphrey Evans, for a long time bed-ridden, had the happiness of procuring an acceleration of his death by the ill-treatment of the officers, who last Christmas morning entered with great violence, the house of a gentleman called Sir James Poole, Bart. of Pool Hall, Cheshire, and casting down walls in every direction, finally laid open the room of the good and aged man, and flinging themselves into it with drawn swords and harquebuses in hand, threatened death to a man who through paralysis had lost the use of speech. So they insolently commanded the lady of the house to draw him forth from his bed, but she answered with great courage: 'Do what you will, I certainly will have no part in the death of this servant of God.' Finally, the officers having ill-treated the family for many hours, bound over Sir James Poole, under heavy penalties to produce the Father when summoned. A few days after, all the family were cited to appear at Chester, and although no one had mentioned this order to the Father, he who was speechless, as I have said, through paralysis, somehow exclaimed with a loud voice: 'Take me in your company' and having said this, he shortly afterwards died.[28]

More deaths were to follow:

It is certain [continued Father Morgan] that Father David Lewis, alias Charles Baker, being one of those priests newly condemned to death for their priesthood (also Father Philip Evans) although the news of their death has not yet reached us.

Father David Lewis (1617–79), alias Charles Baker, was superior of the mission of St Francis Xavier, and was affectionately known as '*tad y tlodion*' 'the father of the poor.' His arrest in November 1678 on the sole charge of being a priest was due to an informer. He was sentenced to death at Usk the following March and executed there on 27 August 1679.[29] Father Philip Evans (1645–79), a young Jesuit Priest, ordained four years earlier, was also betrayed by an informer and imprisoned with Father John Lloyd in Cardiff Castle. Both were condemned to death on 9 May 1679 and executed together by being hanged, drawn, and quartered on 22 July. They were canonised on 25 October 1970 by Pope Paul VI. The two men were of great assistance to each other in prison and as they prepared to die on the gallows. Cleary describes the fortitude of Father Philip Evans:

… it thus came about that the notice of execution was brought to Fr Evans while he was playing tennis near S. John's church. His remark: 'what hurry is there? Let me first play out my game', is memorable, as are his other words spoken from the ladder of the gallows: 'Sure this is the best pulpit a man can have to preach in'. He returned to the prison and sang to his own accompaniment on the harp.[30]

Dom Bede Camm, OSB, has suggested[31] 'that two martyrs' skulls preserved at St Beuno's (they are now in the museum attached to St Winefride's Well) which cannot now be identified' are probably those of St David Lewis, SJ, and St Philip Evans, SJ, 'One of them has a hole in the cranium made by the pike on which it was exposed; with them are the bones of a leg which were found wrapped up in a child's jacket in which they were evidently hidden when rescued by some pious and daring Catholic from the gate or public place where they had been exposed.'[32]

According to Father Morgan the situation created by the Popish Plot was showing no signs of improvement:

As to the present condition of the Kingdom, matters daily go from bad to worse, without any sign of improvement, and we are all in such confusion that no one can conjecture from the events of the present day, what is to happen on the morrow. It is true that the deaths of our Fathers produced some good feeling in the people, and had this been seconded by favourable measures the wheel may have been gradually reversed; but if any one writes that our affairs are mending, he does not penetrate beneath the surface.

Previously he had made mention of Holywell:

We of the North [The Residence of St Winefride] have fared a little better thus far, but God knows how long it is to last, for we live in constant fear and peril, only three of us remaining, viz., Fathers Hugh Owen, William Bianchi (White), and Thomas Roderick Roberts.

The events during the next decade (1679–89) were to show the 'wheel' of fortune turning forwards as well as backwards for Father William Morgan and the Jesuit and Secular Priests who served in Holywell. The persecution of Catholics continued unabated until suddenly, with the death of Charles II in February 1685, the situation changed. Father Huddleston, the priest who had hidden him in his flight after the battle of Worcester, had secretly received Charles II on his deathbed into the Roman Catholic Church.

The reign of King James II, 1685–88. A break in the cloud of persecution
After vigorous efforts to exclude him from the throne, James II succeeded his brother Charles II unopposed, the first openly-confessed Roman Catholic to wear the crown since Mary I died in 1558. He was received warmly by a loyal nation, although they regretted his religious beliefs, preferred peace to civil war. It appeared to be understood that, if James II had respect for the laws of the land and parliamentary government, he should be allowed to govern in peace. Unfortunately, James II's good qualities of courage and dedication were over-shadowed by obstinacy, lack of common sense, and a belief in a divine right of kingship that allowed him to show toleration to Catholics without the backing of the law of the land. James refused to listen to those who advised restraint in his rapid pursuit of a policy to restore Catholicism, and, in the process, alienated the Church of England. The climax came in June 1688, just over three years after his accession, when the birth of a Catholic heir to James II coincided with the imprisonment of seven of the bishops of the Church of England in the Tower who were awaiting trial for opposing the power of the King and the birth of a son to James II who would continue the Catholic succession. By this time the patience of those who mattered in government was exhausted, and they had as a willing candidate a Protestant prince, William of Orange (who was married to Mary, the Protestant elder daughter of James). William, with an invading army, landed unopposed at Torbay on 5 November and on 11 December, when his power evaporated, James the last Catholic king of England, fled to France.

King James II, Queen Mary of Modena and St Winefride's Well

In 1687, James II presented St Winefride's Well to his queen, Mary Beatrice of Modena, who immediately gave it into the keeping of the Jesuits. James came to the well in 1687. In a dispute over the custody of the well, the Seculars were dispossessed in favour of the Jesuits, who began to repair the building. Going into exile in 1688, both James II and Mary of Modena found consolation in their prayers to St Winefride and through possession of one of her relics. This renewal of royal interest and patronage in the Well and cult of St Winefride proved to be a false dawn before a return to severe penal laws against Catholics after the Revolution of 1688.

The Progress of the Duke of Beaufort, August 1684

We are fortunate in having a drawing and description of St Winefride's Well and Chapel made by Thomas Dineley, the chaplain to the Duke of Beaufort (Lord President of the Council in the Marches of Wales) less than two years before the accession of James II. Dineley left a memorable account of his master's vice-regal progress through the principality in the summer of 1684[33] and St Winefride's Well was one of several buildings and occasions he thought worthy of illustration.

Henry Somerset, formerly earl of Worcester, was a member of the family who had provided the Jesuits with their headquarters for the district of St Francis Xavier at Cwm and sheltered Catholics at Raglan Castle. It was almost fifty years since the Council in Wales had taken steps to destroy the cult of St Winefride and it was ironic that the Lord President should find time to pause in his progress to allow his company to pay their respects at the well.

Beaufort's tour through the principality lasted five weeks and was conducted with great pomp, ceremony and display. Accompanied by trumpeters and uniformed and liveried supporters, there was more than a touch of the medieval magnate in the duke's progress. After witnessing a display of military exercises at the hall of Colonel Sir Roger Mostyn, the progress on their return stopped at the well.

Thomas Dineley did not disappoint and made an invaluable sketch of the well building and its precincts to which he added quotations from Ovid and Horace. The line from Ovid captured the effect of the water on the visitor at midsummer who viewed the well from the point of view of a classical scholar rather than a Catholic pilgrim: 'And the shining stream, more transparent than glass, the sacred fountain, which many think has its own deity.'[34]

Dineley added a note of his own:

… see the penitentiers douch themselves, and receive some of the Moss, which they say by keeping becomes more and more fragrant. The Cavalcade being numerous & thirsty ye water inviteing, and the people unprovided with glasses for ye haste, some lay down & drank as the Poet hath it under the title *Alios alia delectant'* [another form of pleasure].

A long quotation from Horace speaks about 'the tranquillity of rural retirement' and the man 'who is not averse to full cups of old wine, taking a part from the entire day to indulge, at one time stretched out under the green wild straw-berry tree, at another by the placid head of some sacred stream.' To which Dineley adds: 'And the whole fountain is sacred from its source; its whispering entices sleep.'[35]

At the bottom of his sketch Dineley turns from the sacred to the secular and states that: 'This Mir-aculous spring within less than a stone's cast from its Source keeps in employ two mills.'

75. Sketch and account of St Winefride's Well made by Thomas Dineley, chaplain to the Duke of Beaufort on the occasion of his progress through Wales in 1684. Compare with Herald's sketch of 1670.

A dispute between Seculars and Jesuits for control of the chapel over the well

The Jesuit Annual Letters for 1688 summed up the dispute at Holywell in a rather bland way.

> Here was an ancient and most beautiful chapel, about the right to serve which a dispute arose. The Fathers of the Residence of St Winefrid claiming it as having been given them by the Queen, to whom it was said to belong; on the other hand, such was the celebrity of the place, that some of the secular clergy put in a strong claim for it as their right. Seeing that the Queen was inclined towards the old missioners of the Residence, they sought the intervention of a nobleman of that country, who was in favour of their claim to the right of the patronage to the chapel. Upon this the King and the Queen referred the matter in dispute to the law judges, who adjudicating in favour of her Majesty's right, she was pleased to present it to the Fathers.[36]

The dispute was over the right to use the chapel over the well. The building was part of the rectory of Holywell, which had come into lay hands at the dissolution of Basingwerk Abbey in 1536. It was to remain in lay hands until it devolved to the Church in Wales at the time of the disestablishment and disendowment of the Church in Wales in 1920. The occasion of the dispute occurred because the lay rector Mr Davies had allowed the Catholic Secular clergy to use it for their own purposes. His right to allow the Seculars to use the chapel was overruled by King James II – on what grounds we do not know. James gave the chapel to the Queen and the Secular clergy were turned out of occupation to be replaced by Jesuits.

The correspondence relating to this change of fortune sheds light on the relationship between Catholics and Protestants in the Holywell area and the continued rivalry of the two priestly establishments.

The first attempt to gain the use of the chapel over the well for Catholic purposes was made early in the year of 1686 when James II was pursuing a policy of toleration for Catholics and Protestant dissenters. In 1685 the Pope appointed John Leyburne, bishop of Andrumetum, to supervise Roman Catholic secular clergy in England. All over the country Roman Catholics were hoping to use ancient chapels for their worship, and St Winefride's Chapel was an obvious example, enjoying as it did, an historic link with medieval pilgrimage. The secular clergy in Holywell felt that the time was opportune for them to gain entrance to the chapel they had lost at the Reformation.

A report on their progress to achieve this purpose was made by Roger Kynaston, vicar general of north Wales, to his dean, John Perrot. It revealed that Kynaston and the local priest, Father John Brian, had lobbied the lay rector Mr Davies and his Protestant relation Madam Pennant, who appeared to be

76. *Drawing of Holywell Parish Church, St Winefride's chapel and well. In the foreground may be seen bathers in the water of the stream issuing from the spring and on the right (F). Copy of a drawing in the Herald's Visitation Papers for Flintshire, 1670. [M. Powell Siddons (ed),* Visitations by Heralds in Wales, The Harleian Society, *new series, vol. 14, (1996), p. 144]*

A: Holywell
B: The Cloyster of the well
C: The water pownded up to drive the mill.
D: Holywell Chappell.
E. The parish church of Holywell.
F: The Little Spring for the cure of sore eyes.

favourable to the arrangement. The difficulty was the opposition of William Lloyd, bishop of St Asaph, who overruled Mr Davies because it 'raised a scruple in his conscience.' It was now suggested that Dr Bonaventure Gifford (the new vicar apostolic of the Midlands district) should approach the King to 'signify his pleasure to Mr Davies and in addition Sir Edward Mostyn should be asked to make representations to him as his kinsman.'[37] These manoeuvres were successful and the Seculars were granted the use of the chapel until turned out in June 1687.

> Mr Brian, chaplain at Cross Keys in Holywell town, gave me an account on June 22 1687, that after he had procured a lease of Holywell Chapel and the possession given him by the landlord, the Jesuits' agents demanded the key of Mr Brian; but he refused to deliver it. Whereupon they broke open the door and delivered possession therof to the Jesuits. For redress of this wrong done to Mr Brian he had recourse to the landlord, who fairly owned that his lease was good and duly executed, but withall declared that in regard it was the Queen's pleasure that the Jesuits should have the chapel for their use, he was not willing to incur her displeasure by opposing their proceedings.[38]

The Queen was in no doubt what her pleasure was when she had written to Colonel Sir Roger Mostyn a few weeks earlier.

> It having pleased the King, by his royall grant, to bestow upon me ye ancient chappel adjoining to St Winefrede's Well; these are to desire you to give present possession in my name, of the said chappell, to Mr Thomas Roberts, who will deliver this letter into your hands. It being also my intention to have the place decently repaired, and put to good use, I further desire that you will affoard your favour and protection, that he may not be disturbed in the performance thereof. You may rest assured, that what you do herein, according to my desire, shall be very kindly remembered by.

Colonel Roger Mostyn (1624–90), after years of careful economy, had recently finished nursing back his estates from the enormous debt of £60,000 they had incurred during the Civil War. The old cavalier, a Protestant with a Catholic wife, was embarrassed by the request. He told his son that he 'could have been very well satisfied without it if it had pleased her Majsty to order some body else to do it,' and, two days later (18 May), he informed him that he had consulted the bishop of St Asaph, Mr Davies, Pyrs Pennant and others, and 'I went & turned out Mr Brian & putt in Mr Roberts, changing a secular for a Jesuit. Bishop did approve of my obedience to Her Authority, Mr Davies and Pyrs Pennant did the like. If I shall be liable to the Censure of the Country, my Loyalty must bear the blame.'[39]

1. Castell and upper part of Holywell stream by J. Ingleby, c.1790. from A History of Whitford and Holywell by Thomas Pennant.

C2. St Winifred's Chapel , Holywell. Watercolour by John 'Warwick' Smith, c.1790. [NLW PE919 [FR] SR/215]

C3. *St Winefride's Well, lithograph by T. Bailey, c.1810. An unusual artist's impression which shows how the well was used
pilgrims for healing (notice the moss), tourists for bathing and local townsfolk for their domestic water supply and washing.*

77. St Winefride's Chapel. [Crown copyright RCAHMW.]

The visit of King James II to St Winefride's Well and Chapel

On 29 August 1687, about half way through his reign, James II paid a visit to Holywell. In this period he was using every opportunity to further his policy of re-establishing a Catholic nation. In pursuit of this object the king appointed a number of Catholic councillors, introduced Catholic fellows and heads of colleges at Oxford and Cambridge, and granted army commissions to the sons of Catholic peers and gentlemen. He unsuccessfully attempted to force through a relaxation of the Penal Laws and the Test Acts; Catholic and Protestant dissenters were named as justices of the peace, Catholic chapels and schools were opened. James wanted the Pope to elevate to cardinal one of his closest advisers, the Jesuit, Father Edward Petre. Being alarmed by the speed of James' pro-Catholic actions, the Pope refused. In order to make a Catholic restoration and succession permanent, James needed a male heir. This was to be granted as a consequence of the events of August 1687.

His queen and second wife, Mary Beatrice of Modena (1658–1718), was an Italian Catholic, whom he married following the death of Ann Hyde in 1672. None of the children born to Mary had survived. The king and his queen, desperate to produce an heir, were determined to do anything that would make such an event possible.

After her mother's death, Mary Beatrice, on the advice of her doctors, decided in August 1687 to go to Bath, where she was joined by James, the royal couple spending four days together. The king attended a service at the abbey where he touched for King's Evil[40] and heard a Jesuit exhort the congregation 'to an immediate change from the errors of Protestantism to the true faith from which this country had apostacised.' The queen bathed every morning in the Cross Bath to the strains of an Italian orchestra.[41]

Leaving his wife at Bath, James continued on his royal progress through the Midlands until he arrived at Chester on Saturday, 27 August, where he stayed until the following Thursday. The account of the days spent in the city and the visit to Holywell left his subjects in no doubt of his determination to create a Catholic Kingdom. Their reaction was that of the majority of his subjects, deeply loyal to James as their King, attached to the Anglican Church, and stubbornly against repealing anti Catholic legislation.[42]

Saturday 27 August 1687 — King James 2nd came to Chester, and was received by the corporation in their Formalities, placed on a Scaffold, near the Barrs in Foregate street: His Majesty was sumptously entertained at the Pentice, where there was prepared for him a Throne or Canopy of Crimson-Velvet. The King lodged at the Bishops Palace.

Sunday 28th August — He walked thro' the City (the Mayor, bare headed carrying the Sword before him) to the Castle and heard Mass in the Shire-Hall.

He went into the choir of the Cathedral at nine o'clock where he healed 350 persons. After which he went to his devotions in the Shire Hall, and Mr Penn held forth in the Tennis Court, and I [Bishop Cartwright] preached in the Cathedral.

Monday 29 August — The King rose at six and was in the saddle by 7.30 en route for St Winefride's Well at Holywell' 'where he was presented with the shift which his great-grandmother, Mary Queen of Scots, wore when she was beheaded.

The Annual Letters for 1688 adds to this account:

… the King on occasion of a visit of devotion which his Majesty made to the holy well, which was beneath the said chapel, was pleased to make a donation to the Fathers who resided at Holywell of about one hundred and forty scudi (about £30) for the purpose of reparations and decorations, to render it fit for Divine worship, which was accordingly done, to the great increase of piety and devotion in the Catholics. But it was used again for its former purpose (a Sessions House) in the time of the Revolution.[43]

Thomas Pennant recorded that the King gave 'as marks of his favour, golden rings with his hair plaited beneath a crystal.'

On Tuesday he returned to Chester, and the day following closetted several Gentlemen both of the City & County in order to prevail with them to approve of the Repeal of the Penal Laws, and Tests, but met with very little satisfaction as to that affair;

On Thursday His Majesty left Chester, not at all pleased with the Deposition of the People. … before he left, James expressed his displeasure that there was no loyal address forthcoming from Chester.

Burne's account, taken from Bishop Cartwright's diary, is that 'James left Chester next day [30 August], after he had had mass in the presence chamber where he did eat. From thence I attended him into the choir, where he healed 450 people; from thence to the penthouse [Pentice] where he breakfasted under a state [sic], and from thence took horse about ten of the clock … The King left £20 to the house servants.

The bishop of Chester, Dr Thomas Cartwright, owed his appointment to James, and supported the king in his measures to win toleration for the Catholics and dissenters. Fellow Anglicans regarded the bishop's stance as betrayal, and one writer has described him 'as the primary clerical quisling under James II.'[44] The bishop, who went into exile with the king in December 1688, remained an Anglican, and died in Ireland in April 1689.

He was throughout his episcopacy openly friendly with local Catholics; for example, on 12 September 1687, the bishop recorded in his diary: 'I went to Holywell with my wife, son and daughter, (and others); dined at the Star with them and Mr Roberts the priest.'[45]

Earlier, when Bishop Leyburne, the new Catholic vicar apostolic came on his confirmation tour to Chester, Cartwright housed him in his episcopal palace, and in the summer of 1688, Cartwright was one of the bishops who sided with James against his seven colleagues.

Queen Mary Beatrice of Modena and St Winefride

On Christmas Eve 1687 it was publicly announced that the queen was with child.

The priests attributed this to the intercession of St Winifred and to a pilgrimage which her mother the Duchess of Modena had made to Loretto just before she died. The less devout credited it the efficacy of the Bath waters; and the Earl of Melfort placed a large baroque monument in the Cross Bath as a thank-offering for the happy consequences of the Queen's treatment.[46]

Old wives, charlatans, and the superstitious speculated about the birth. Lord Macaulay wrote about them:

The impudent zealots who dwelt on these tales foretold with confidence that the unborn infant would be a boy, and offered to back their opinion by laying twenty guineas to one. Heaven they affirmed would not have interfered but for a great end. One fanatic announced that the Queen would give birth to twins, of whom the elder would be King of England, and the younger Pope of Rome. Mary could not conceal the delight with which she heard this prophecy; and her ladies found

78. The birth of James, Prince of Wales, heir to James II, on 10 June 1688: engraving Rome, 1688.

that they could not gratify her more than by talking of it.[47]

At Chester a priest announced confidently that the baby would be a boy. Asked how he knew, he replied that St Winifred invariably granted all or nothing, and since there was to be a baby, it would certainly be a son.[48]

Others refused to believe that the queen was pregnant. When a son was born on 10 June 1688, James Francis Edward Stuart (the 'Old Pretender'), disbelieving Protestants said that he had been smuggled into the palace in a warming pan. But there was no doubt about his legitimacy. The new prince of Wales was entrusted into the hands of the marchioness of Powis, a devout Catholic. Her husband's estates were centred at Powis Castle near Welshpool, one of the districts in the Residence of St Winefride. It was the marchioness who who gave the queen a relic of St Winefride (one of her fingers) and on the death of her mistress in obedience to her wishes sent the relic to the college at St Omer. Lewis Sabran, principal of St Omer, later sent it to the English College in Rome.[49]

The end of the Catholic dream. The Flight of James II December 1688
The birth of a son to James II took place two days after the king had committed seven of his bishops to the Tower for protesting against reading a declaration of indulgence which suspended the penal laws against Roman Catholic and dissenters. They were found not guilty of conspiring to diminish royal power. The king, whom one Protestant described as more Catholic than the Pope, had gone too far. It was now the turn of 'The immortal seven' influential politicians

to issue an invitation on 30 June to the Protestant Dutch prince, William of Orange, to come to England and investigate the circumstances of the birth of the prince of Wales and the condition of English liberties.

Answering their call, William of Orange landed at Torbay on 5 November in command of a large invasion force. James II appeared to lose his nerve and there was no military confrontation before the king took flight to France in disguise. When aboard ship without money or clothes, exhausted and distraught, he is said to have 'broke down completely and wept and began to ramble on about St Winifrid's Well, and to deplore the loss of Saint Edward's Cross one of his most treasured possessions.' The sailors, unaware of his identity, subjected him to indignities, and called him 'an old rogue, lean-jawed, hatchet-faced Jesuit. Popish dog, etc.'[50] Although he did not realise it at the time, he had lost his throne and the succession for his male heirs.

The first priority of those who assumed power after the king's unprecedented flight was to call the Convention Assembly to decide what action to take. The elected members made their position clear with the resolution that it was 'inconsistent with the Safety and Welfare of the Protestant Religion, to be governed by a Popish Prince,' and after a great deal of debate, William and Mary were offered the throne. Eventually, in 1701, the Act of Settlement decreed that the succession should pass through Sophia of Hanover, granddaughter of James I, next in line after princess Anne. This did not prevent the heirs of James II, the 'Old and New Pretenders,' from attempting to regain the throne for the house of Stuart in the so-called Jacobite rebellions of 1715 and 1745. Thus, for the next fifty or sixty years, Catholics were under suspicion as being sympathisers of and supporters of the Jacobites, and suffered accordingly from the severity of the penal laws.

79. James II's flight from London, 11 December 1688. Dutch engraving P. Pickaert and A. Schoonebeeck.

NOTES

1. C. Hindley (ed), *Old Book Collector's Miscellany*, vol. 4 (London, 1873), pp. 6–8. And John Chandler (ed) *The Adventures of John Taylor, The Water Poet* (Sutton, 1999), pp. 260–1, 268–9.

2. Hindley, ibid, pp. 7–8.

3. E. A. B. Barnard, *A Seventeenth Century Gentleman* (Cambridge, 1949), pp. 47–8.

4. Counties of Northants, Warwick, Staffs, Salop, York, Carmarthen, Flints, Monmouth, Montgomery.

5. *Analecta Bollandiane*, op cit, pp. 331–51.

6. It is not proposed to discuss these twenty-four narratives (between 1640–74) in detail .

7. Ibid, p. 335.

8. Ibid, p. 340.

9. I am grateful to Mr K. Lloyd Gruffydd for generously providing me with information from Gaol files, Flintshire of the Court of Great Sessions at the NLW.

10. Letters and Notices 1911 and 1931, and P. Hook, *Holywell Registers*, The Catholic Record Society, 1903, pp. 105–134; and T. G. Holt, S. J. "Jesuits in Montgomeryshire 1670–1873, *The Journal of Welsh Religious History*, vol. 1, 1993, pp. 66–80.

11. There is no evidence that they served in Holywell for the whole period they are listed.

12. Foley, vol. 5(b), pp. 937–8.

13. *Letters and Notices*, vol. 31, 1911–12, p. 181.

14. Foley, vol. 7(b), 1883, *Collectanea*, p. 560, and G. Bowen, *Welsh Recusant Writings Writers of Wales*, ed M. Stephens and R. B. Jones (Cardiff, 1999).

15. Bowen, ibid, p. 72.

16. M. Stephens compiler and ed, *The Oxford Companion to The Literature of Wales* (Oxford, 1986), p. 450.

17. *Analecta Bollandiana*, op cit, pp. 351–2.

18. AAW, xxxii, 99. I am grateful to Father T. McCoog, SJ, for the information and Dr E. P. Roberts for her observations.

19. Probably copies of J. Falconer,S.J, *The Admirable Life of Saint Wenefride* (1635).

20. Which he acknowledges in his own compilation.

21. Foley, vol. 7(b), p. 560 and vol. 4, p. 518.

22. T. McCoog, 'The Society of Jesus in Wales', *Journal of Welsh Religious History*, vol. 5, 1997, pp. 1–27.

23. Discussed in chapter 7.

24. Foley, 5 (b), pp. 937–9.

25. Five were Jesuit priests executed together on 20 June, 1679.

26. P. Phillips, 'St John Plessington Priest and Martyr', *Recusant History*, vol. 28, CRS, 2007.

27. P. Hook, *Holywell Registers*, CRS, 1903, vol. 3, p. 105.

28. 14 January 1679.

29. Under David Lewis, DWB, p. 549.

30. Under Philip Evans, DWB, p. 1120.

31. Dom Bede, *Camm Forgotten Shrines, an account of some old Catholic Halls and families in England and of Relics and Memorials of the English Martyrs* (St Louis, 1910), p. 368.

32. The writer adds that 'Father Morris found the skeleton of a mouse inside one of the skulls. It had apparently made a nest there, and when the skull was placed in the box, the mouse could not escape.'

33. T. Dineley, *The Account of the Official Progress of the First Duke of Beaufort through Wales*, 1684 , ed R. W. Banks (1888).

34. Ibid, p. 93, Mr J. B. Lewis kindly translated this quotation from *Ovid Epistulae ex Ponto 1*.

35. Ibid, p. 93, Mr J. B. Lewis kindly translated this quotation which is from a superscipt (f) added by Dinely to Horace's text.

36. Foley, vol. 5(b), series xii, 1879, pp. 934–5.

37. Anstruther, op cit, vol. 3, p. 123, letter dated 30 March 1686.

38. C. Tootal, Ushaw Collection, 1, 369, 1687, 22 June.

39. Lord Mostyn and T. A. Glenn, *Mostyn's of Mostyn* (1925), pp. 147–8.

40. It was believed that scrofula could be cured by a touch from the monarch.

41. M. Hopkirk, *The Queen over the Water* (Murray, 1953), pp. 112–13.

42. James II's Chester itinerary is pieced together from a number of accounts – the events recorded in the Cowper MS, Crewe Cowper Collection, Cheshire Record Office, DCC/2, form the outline. Other details are from R. V. H. Burne, *Chester Cathedral* (SPCK, 1958).

43. Foley, op cit, vol. 5(b), p. 935.

44. M. Mullett, DNB.

45. *The Diary of Dr Thomas Cartwright, Bishop of Chester*, Camden Society, 1843, p. 27.

46. Hopkirk, op cit, p. 118.

47. C. H. Firth (ed), *The History of England from the Accession of James the Second* by Lord Macaulay, 6 vols, 1914, vol. 2 p. 962 .

48. Hopkirk, op cit, p. 119.

49. G. Holt (ed), *The Letter Book of Lewis Sabran*, CRS, 1971, p. 102, and Foley, 5, p. 532–3.

50. F. C. Turner, *King James II*, p. 456.

7. 1689–1829

Introduction

The 'long eighteenth century' saw changes which gradually transformed British society from anything that might have been imagined in 1688. By the end of the period considered in this chapter the nation was in the midst of an industrial and agricultural revolution and had contested a number of European wars, lost the American colonies, and gained a new empire in India, Canada, and Australia. The major political revolutions in north America and France had its effect on political reform in Britain which led to the removal of penal laws against Catholics and Dissenters. These various economic and political revolutions, and the gradual change from religious persecution to toleration of dissenting churches are reflected in the variety of events which occurred in the Holywell Catholic community.

The first thirty years from 1688–1718 witnessed hostility and open acts of aggression against the Catholic community in Holywell. One example of this attack on the Catholic community was the attempt by William Fleetwood, bishop of St Asaph, to deny the existence of St Winefride and the curative qualities of her well. He failed, and, there is no evidence that her cult suffered from his arguments, or that visitors and pilgrims declined in strength. There is evidence on the other hand that the number of Catholics increased in Holywell. Through the quiet and unspectacular ministry of a succession of Secular and Jesuit priests the Holywell mission kept alive the cult of St Winefride and her well.

Holywell and its Catholic Community, 1688–1718

In December 1688, the month James II and his family fled to France, the Catholic community left behind feared they would be massacred. The new government reacted violently against the Catholics. The Penal Laws were strengthened, and for a while many priests were subject to persecution and went into hiding. In these circumstances, it is difficult to determine the names of priests specifically serving the mission in Holywell, although we are more certain of those working in the Residence of St Winefride. The Jesuit *Annual Letters* report accounts of

80. *St Winefride's Well at the beginning of the eighteenth century: print first published in 1713.*

persecution which are supported from other sources. What appears to have happened in these uncertain times is that the clergy moved within the Residence of St Winefride from the mission in Welshpool to the mission at Holywell, although we cannot give precise dates. The stories of the persecution of two of these priests will show the dangers they faced.

Father Thomas or Roderick Roberts, SJ, (1645–1721) was the priest in residence at the Star Inn at Holywell in 1687. He received the use of the Well Chapel for the Jesuits and greeted James II and Bishop Cartwright on their visits. It appears that when the Orange revolution began at the end of 1688, Father Roberts was at the mission in Welshpool and was the target of the mob. His story was reported in *Annual Letters* for 1688.[1]

> 'In the Residence of St Winefrid, lived Father Roderick Roberts, who laboured as a missioner with a great fruit of souls until 1688, in which year, after the retirement of King James II, a mob from the adjacent parts, excited by an increasing but false rumour of a threatened onslaught and plunder of the English by the Irish soldiers, rushed straight to the house where the Father lived, which they searched, and then made for the chapel, which they plundered, almost entirely stripping it of the sacred furniture. Part of the plunder was shared in common, and amongst the other objects burnt was a crucifix, which they dragged along the ground to the market place, and cast it into a slow fire. The Father's library shared the same fate. A few days after, a company of soldiers marched that way and halted at the place for some time, and forty men of the troop, who happened to be acquainted with the Father were ordered to the house, which they both searched and watched for a space of six weeks by day and night, robbing it of the greatest part of the furniture which they carried off.
>   Meanwhile Father Roberts, who could find no place of sufficient security, was compelled to hasten hither thither, living one while in half–ruined huts on the tops of hills, at another concealed by day in dykes and woods. During the greater part of two summers he lay by night in the fields, and yet through a signal providence of God his health did not suffer. He had many hairbreadth escapes from falling into the hands of the heretics. On one occasion, when information had been given to two officers that he lay concealed in a certain house they sent a company to seize him; but the Father warned of the danger, got safely off, even after the house was beset, and so escaped their hands ...'[2]

Father Edmund Thorold, SJ, senr (1657–1715), was a contemporary of Father Roberts in the Residence of St Winefride and served at Welshpool and Holywell, and was superior at Holywell c.1696–c.1706[3] and died at Holywell on 7 November 1715.

From the 1670s until 1747, there were Jesuit chaplains at Powis Castle and Edmund Thorold was one of them. William Herbert (d.1696) was created marquess of Powis by James II and went with him into exile, where he was raised to a duke; his wife Elizabeth Somerset (d. 1691) was royal governess and gave the queen the relic of St Winefride. Their eldest daughter, Winefride, Countess of Nithsdale, aided her husband in his escape from the Tower after the 1715 Rising. During the reign of James II, Catholicism flourished in the Welshpool mission as was reported in the *Annual Letters*:

> In a town commonly called Welshpool we had a chapel and public school; also some boarders who lived in our house. The then Earl but now Duke of Powis greatly favoured these beginnings by whose patronage by the beneficence of his most pious wife this place in a short time would have been able to make great progress and would have become exceedingly useful to the whole of that district.[4]

Neither the school nor the chapel survived the mob violence of the revolution of 1688 as we have seen from the account of the privations of Father Roberts. He escaped imprisonment but not so Father Edmund Thorold, who was arrested whilst travelling with William Christopher, a lay brother, in mid–winter 1688; both were imprisoned for nine months.

Their examinations make interesting reading.[5] They show the caution of the Catholic religious at the time and their difficulty of movement between mission stations.

> Edmund Thorwell aged 31 years or thereabouts being brought before us and examined saith, that he belonges to the Ld. Montgomerie of Powis Castle, and was left there to overlloke to the sd. Ld. Montgomeries servants and horses, and confesseth, that when he was searched, there was a silver box of oyles (having three partitions) with a Case to enclose it, found in one of his pockests, and says it belongs to a popish priest, but denies himself to be a priest. The sd Edmund Thorold) being further examined by us upon oath, whether he was a recusant, confessed himself to be recusant, and refused to take the oath of allegiance being duly tendered to him, and this deponent being further examined declareth, that he designed to go along with the aforementioned William Christopher to Holywell and to stay there some time and afterwards to return to his friends in Lincolnshire, and further saith not. (he signed his name – Edmund Thorold)
> Sent to prison for refusing to take the Oath of Allegiance.
> Taken before us Edw. Brereton, Ellis Lloyd.

> The examination of William Christopher taken before us the 17th December 1688. The above mentioned examinant aged 32 years or thereabouts saith, that near five moths past, he the sd. Examinant hath been employed as steward under one William Conway, late schoolmaster of the popish school in the Town of Poole in the County of Montgomerie, and confesseth, that there was found about his neck one silver box with popish relicks in it, and likewise one rod of his discipline,

with some other trifling baubles; and thereupon the sd William Christopher being further examined upon oath, who then he was a recusant; and hath refused to take the oath of allegiance being duly tendered to him, and this deponent declareth also, that he was in the companie of one Thorwell, (Thorold) when he was apprehended, and that they both designed to goe for Hollywell and further saith not.

[He signed his name William Christopher]

The priest and lay brother were fortunate not to have been tried as Roman Catholic religious for which the penalty was death. There was sufficient incriminating evidence: the box of 'Popish relics' worn about his neck by Brother Christopher, and the 'silver box of oyles,' the chrism for baptism, carried by Father Thorold. The court accepted their evidence that they were not religious, but recusants, and imprisoned them because they refused to take the oath of allegiance. Such an action by Catholic school masters and priests was made an offence liable to imprisonment for life by an act of parliament of 1699.

The local magistrates probably imprisoned them to keep them out of the way of the mob. Montgomeryshire Quakers were also imprisoned in the county. On release from prison Thorold probably remained in the Welshpool area as he is shown in 1692 as 'resident at Powis Castle with a cure of £10 per annum to serve the poor of Montgomeryshire and of the Welsh borders of Shropshire' before he took up residence in Holywell. Brother Christopher, too, came to serve there, for on 15 March 1703, Nicholas Blundell entered in his diary: 'I gave 2/6 to Brother Christopher towards ye repair of ye cover over Holy–well.' Apparently the Jesuits were still allowed to have use of St Winefride's Chapel.

The Franciscans had some kind of presence in Holywell in the last years of the seventeenth century. Father Michael Russell was Preses[6] of St Winifride's, Holywell, in 1687 and a Provincial Chapter was held there towards the close of the century.[7]

Father Henry Todd succeeded as superior at Holywell in 1710 and died on Christmas Day, 1712, aged 46.[8]

Years of unease: 1689–1718

The thirty years from the departure of James II to 1718 were unsettled for the Jesuit and Secular missions in Holywell. It was impossible for the Catholic community in Britain (and so in Holywell) to be left in peace whilst it continued to be associated in the nation's mind with the Jacobite Cause. The attempts of James II (d. 1701) and his son 'the Old Pretender', James Frances Edward Stuart (1688–1766), and grandson Charles Edward Stuart (1720–1788), 'the Young Pretender,' to regain their throne left little impression in Flintshire. If there was any support for 'King over the Water' it was from a drinking club, 'Cycle of the White Rose,' with a membership of opposition Anglican squires. Although regularly toasting the Stuarts, they did not follow them into rebellion.

The proximity of Holywell to Catholic Lancashire and its convenience on the sea–route to Ireland increased suspicion of it being tainted by Jacobite plotters. Little was alleged about local disloyalty and nothing was ever proved, but on rare occasions, in times of alarm, punitive measures both legal and arbitrary were taken against the local Catholics. But, in contrast to the sixteenth and seventeenth centuries, St Winefride's Well in the eighteenth century did not suffer damage and although the devotion of pilgrims did not decrease, the sacred spring grew in popularity as a spectacle for tourists.

The Star Inn was well known as a rendezvous for Catholics in north Wales and as the headquarters of the Jesuit mission. In the 1690s, a government informer George Wilson gave it the distinction of reporting it as a meeting place for Jacobites planning an invasion from Ireland in 1689 and from France in 1692. It was alleged in evidence given against Colonel John Parker in the 'Lancashire Plot' that he was present '… at the signe of the Starr, an inn in Holywell, in Flintshire and about twenty gentlemen from Ireland., where he saw Parker deliver commissions to Mr Pue of Pendrell, to be a Captain of horse and to several others.'

Wilson's evidence of meetings in Lancashire and north Wales was spread over four years from 1689–92, and implicated over a dozen of the Lancashire gentry, and some from north Wales, including Captain Pennant of Bagillt. In 1694, some of those implicated were brought to trial at Manchester, and others at Chester and all acquitted. In 1757, a chance discovery of papers written in cipher later proved that the statements by the informer were most probably accurate. If this is correct it is probable that the Jesuit mission house, the Star Inn, was used as a meeting place for disaffected Catholic gentry from Lancashire and north Wales.[9]

The raid on the Cross Keys and Star Inn Holywell in 1718

In 1718, Catholics in Holywell experienced the indignity of having their places of worship disturbed by a troop of dragoons from Preston in Lancashire. This violent intrusion was the last recorded incident of persecution in the history of the two Catholic missions in the town. Although other places in the kingdom were later to experience riots when there was prospect of Catholic emancipation, Holywell remained quiet because of the general sympathy of the local population. After the Jacobite rebellion of 1715, the government were determined to root out support they believed had been provided by the Catholic community, and introduced legislation designed to inflict crippling fiscal penalties. Flintshire with the rest of the counties was required to make a register of every Papist estate.

The visit of the soldiers in 1718 to the two mission headquarters was the result of information supplied to the Commissioners of Forfeited Estates who were seeking to 'discover' property given for superstitious uses which included support of Popish chapels. On 27 June 1718, Richard Hitchmough, an apostate

Catholic priest, gave to Francis Foote, secretary to the Commissioners at Preston, details of the two Catholic inns at Holywell.

Richard Hitchmough (1674–c.1724), had an erratic career as a Catholic priest. He was a drunk, and the verdict of the Lancashire Ccergy was that 'he was cracked.' These weaknesses of character led to his expulsion from the priesthood after a varied ministry of about ten years. He launched himself on a new career as an informer against the Catholic community, and eventually obtained an Anglican benefice in Yorkshire with which to support a wife and several small children. The Commissioners gave rewards for information leading to a 'discovery', with £100 the rate for the apprehension of a Catholic priest. Hitchmough's career as a priest had provided him with information he utilised to gain reward. He had spent time as a priest at the Jacobite court of St Germain in France, served as chaplain to the Vicar Apostolic of the Midland district, and after his removal from that office served in southern Lancashire from where he made a visit to Holywell in 1709. This acquaintance with the two mission chapels in the town enabled him to give a thorough description of their contents, which he listed in his deposition.

They are remarkable for their detail. The information relating to the Star Inn for example mentions relics and the worship available in the chapel:

> ... the house in Holywell town, commonly called the Star, which is let by the Jesuits at £60 per annum, belongs to that Society, Mr Griffiths[10] being the present resident Jesuit there; and another house called the Cross Keys, belongs to the secular clergy, Peter Bodwell, alias Girin,[11] resident priest there.

The informer gave an inventory of the church plate at the two missions.

> At the Star: six large silver candlesticks, with a large silver crucifix on the altar. For solemn feasts, six large candlesticks with a crucifix, said to be of gold, with other plate answerable. On the middle of the altar, a large silver tabernacle, in which were kept a golden remonstrance, in which the Sacrament was exposed on great days: a large ciborium, out of which the priest communicated the people, one large gold chalice and paten, one large silver chalice and paten double–gilded and well–carved, with two others of a smaller size: a large silver basin, six silver cruets and four plates, which belonged to the side table by the altar: two silver thuribles, with which they incensed the Sacrament when exposed. In the middle of the chapel hung a large silver lamp before the tabernacle: in the vestry were lodged the shrines and large reliquaries which contained, as they affirmed, part of the bodies of several saints, with which the altar was adorned on great days, besides rich copes, vestments, antependiums, and all church linen suitable, and also a library of books. At the Cross Keys, for common use, six tall candlesticks and crucifix of Corinthian brass, said to be as valuable as silver. Six large silver candlesticks and crucifix. In the tabernacle which was ebony, were kept a large

silver chalice well gilt, which was said to weigh three pounds, two silver chalices of a smaller size, a large remonstrance for exposing the Sacrament, and a ciborium in which the Sacrament was kept, besides cruets and other plate belonging to the altar. Two silver lamps hung constantly before the Sacrament, and there were two thuribles to incense it with. In the great chest and press in the vestry were reposited the Mass–books, vestments, and all other utensils for church use.'[12]

Impressed by this evidence, Foote, secretary of the Commisioners, wrote immediately to 'Hugh Dreisdale, esq., Major of Rgt. of Dragoons, commanded by Sir Charles Hotham.'

Information having been laid before us that there are two Popish Chappels at Holywell, in the co. of Flint, in which are a great quantity of plate and other valuables given to superstitious uses, we have directed our Precepts to Hitchmough, clerk and others to seize and secure the same; and we adjudging it be for the service of the Publick that our officers should be supported in the execution of the said precepts desire you would detach such a number of the soldiers under your command for the purpose as you shall think proper. Town Hall, Preston, 27th June, 1718.[13]

Receiving their orders on Friday a detachment of Dragoons from Preston arrived in Holywell on Monday. A report of their excursion summed up the affair.

The Commissioners of Enquiry having Information on Oath, that here were two *Popish* Chappels at *Holy Well*, in which Mass was publicly perform'd, and that there were great Quantities of Plate, and other valuable *Things*, sent two of their Messengers to seise the same; and being also informed, that many of the *Popish* Noblemen and Gentlemen were at this Time there, being near the Feast of *St Winifred* (which is kept with an Octave) and that the Inhabitants, and the vast Number of Miners in that Neighbourhood were *Papists* sent one of their chief Officers and a Detachment of Dragoons, out under Pretence of going to *Chester* to fetch Powder and came so secretly and expeditiously to *Holy Well* on Monday the last day of *June*, that at the *Cross–Keys* Chappel they found a priest at the altar at Mass. Without any Disturbance they seised and took away their Trinkets which are not of any Value, compared to the Writings and Deeds which discover Estates settled to superstitious Uses. The Priest was left with *Mr Evans*, A Justice of the Peace at *Flint*.[14]

Although the report doesn't mention any intrusion by Hitchmough and his dragoons at the Star, they visited it. The Jesuit priest, Edmund Gage, alias Plowden, reported to Thomas Eberson, SJ, on 1 August that 'the *Star* had pretty good luck, and got most of the effects out of the way in time. An old gentleman Mr Wilmot, was taken at the Cross Keys, but soon bailed.'[15]

The justice of the peace, Mr Thomas Evans, wrote to the Master of the Rolls on 11 July that William Wilmot 'was brought before me and charged with being a popish priest, which was proved upon oath before me by one Richard Hitchmough who knows him to be such as he swears.'[16]

Apparently, John Seison[17] another secular priest was taken into custody at the Cross Keys. News reached Rome on 28 July 'Last post brings news that one of our priests, and, I think Mr John Seison, has been taken at Holywell, Flint saying mass in his vestments by some dragoons sent for that purpose.'

The report given above suggests that Hitchmough and his dragoons found what to them was more important than Popish treasure, that is 'Writings and Deeds which discover Estates settled to Superstitious Uses.'

The evidence given on 10 July by the examination of Thomas Parry, inn holder of the Cross Keys, provided the information the commissioners were looking for, namely, the ownership of the premise being used as a Popish chapel (i.e. for superstitious uses). This evidence is the most comprehensive statement of the ownership and use of the Cross Keys inn we possess. The building was sold in 1802 and the funds, together with the secular mission, were transferred to Monmouth.

Thomas Parry stated that he took over the inn by arrangement with Captain Peter Pennant of Bighton [Bychton], the landlord, sixteen years previously (1702), at a yearly rental of £11 13s. Captain Pennant stated that in 1704, he let the Cross Keys to Sir Pyers Mostyn (of Talacre and Greenfield, the leading Catholic nobleman in the area) and Mr Roberts of Nerquis (a prominent Catholic squire and a relation of the Parrys of Twysog) for a fine of £50.

Mr Wilmot, the priest, Parry said, came to the Cross Keys two years ago (1716) and boarded there paying £6 a year. He was a very poor man and 'had but fifteen shillings in the whole world' when he was taken into custody.

Thomas Parry stated that, when Hitchmough and the dragoons entered the Cross Keys with a warrant:

> … there was nothing taken a way save only a pair of sheets which was immediately returned to Parry's servant, and that he hath not heard that anything was taken away from the Starr, save only the furniture of the chapel there, nor hath he heard of any complaint of any loss of goods in the town or of any misbehaviour of any of the officers that seized the same or of the soldiers that came with them, and that the civil and quiet deportment of the officers and soldiers during their stay at Holywell is the frequent discourse of the inhabitants there.[18]

There is no surviving evidence of visitors remaining in Holywell for the octave of the Feast of St Winefride. The priests at the two missions must have been troubled by the intrusion of dragoons in their mission chapels, and two of them died soon afterwards: Father George Griffith on 2 August 1718 and Father William Wilmot on 2 August 1720.

The battle of the books 1713
In 1713, the bishop of St Asaph, Dr William Fleetwood (1656–1723), denied the existence of St Winefride and any connection of her with the well. His attack on Winefride and Holywell came in a book with the long title of *The Life and Miracles of St Wenefrede, together with her Litanies, with some historical observations made thereon.*[19] Fleetwood brought out his work as a firm rebuttal of the claims made by the Jesuit missioner at Holywell, Father Philip Metcalf, in his new version of the *Life of St Winefride*. Metcalfe had published it the previous year as a completely new retelling of Father John Falconer's *Life*. Falconer's *Life* of 1635 was based on a translation of the Latin *Life of St Winefride* by Robert of Shrewsbury and was advertised as *The Admirable Life of Saint Wenefride Virgin, Martyr; Abbess*. Metcalfe changed the title of his work to *The Life and Miracles of S. Wenefride Virgin Martyr and Abbess Patroness of Wales*. Bishop Fleetwood, recently consecrated bishop of St Asaph, took this opportunity to strike at the heart of papist practices in his diocese, and deny the credibility of the cult of St Winefride and her associations with Holywell.

The two Jesuit fathers published their *Lives* to honour the saint's immortality: 'her memory is worthily honoured amongst men, whose soul is passed to the joys of angels' proclaimed Falconer, for which Metcalfe substituted 'God is wonderful in His Saints.' The seventy–seven years between the two editions had not changed the missionary motive or strategy of the Jesuit fathers. Their aim was 'for the edification and comfort of Catholics', 'not to gratify curiosity but to promote piety and devotion', to relate the life of St Winefride and 'the place of her martyrdom famed for miraculous cures both of soul and body.' St Winefride's shrine and the curative fountain at Holywell provided an ideal vehicle to emphasise traditional beliefs and practices. *The Admirable Life of St Winefride* contained such material for didactic and proselytizing purposes and was widely circulated and found in many Catholic households.

The Jesuit Fathers were used to

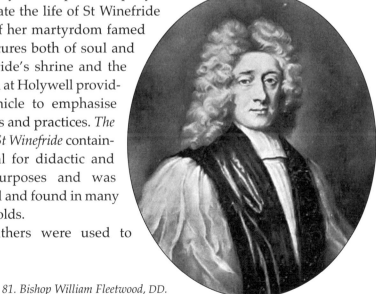

81. Bishop William Fleetwood, DD.

censure from the Established Church, but they had the advantage over Bishop Fleetwood by reason of their continual presence at Holywell. Through the care of the priests, the whole area around the shrine of St Winefride and the curative spring quickly came alive to the sensitive response of pilgrims. The Sword of State had failed to evict them from the sacred site in former centuries, and the Protestant pen of the bishop in this instance was unlikely to move them from their position.

William Fleetwood was consecrated bishop of St Asaph on 6 June 1708 and translated to Ely on 18 November 1714. He denounced the existence of St Winefride in 1713, the year before he left for a wealthier bishopric under the patronage of Queen Anne, who called him 'my bishop.' Fleetwood was an able classical scholar, an antiquarian of repute, an anti–Jacobite Whig politician and a Protestant bishop who denounced Roman Catholic beliefs. He brought together these gifts of scholarship and firmly–held political and religious views to deny any claims for the existence of St Winefride. Fleetwood attempted to demolish the reputation of the saint who had been held in such esteem in the fifteenth century that she was placed next to the patron of the diocese, St Asaph, and the holder of the see on the seal of the cathedral chapter.

Fleetwood wrote in a fluent style and presented a thorough and formidable attack on the life of the saint and her miracles. He brought to his purposes a zealous dedication determined on success of purpose. 'I set myself,' he declared, 'the hard task of procuring whatever had been written concerning her by any author.'[20] His first intention had been to translate the *Cotton Life*, Prior Robert's, into English, with a larger chapter of historical notes and a chapter on 'the superstition of the waters' and another 'of the growth of miracles.'

Fleetwood reviews the Bollandist/Jesuit rules 'concerning the credibility of history' although he judges that Prior Robert, the author of the *Life of Winefride* 'was not wise,' he was 'sure he was over credulous.' He quotes Bollandist opinion of the British saint Gildas (6th century): 'that in the lives of the British saints there are abundance of things that he could make nothing of, that could be brought under no chronology, and were above all belief.' A view he was all too ready to apply to Winefride.

The Bishop takes notice of the Bollandists' reference to miracles at Holywell.

There is a great concourse still to St Wenefrede the virgin's well in the extremist part of North Wales, of such as seek a cure for their diseases and distemper. And that the Jesuits had been told that Protestants 'neither cared nor minded what their ministers prated in the pulpit; they very well remembered that the water of that well were used to do good both to themselves and to their cattle, and to cattle of their fathers, and that they used to impute this benefit to St Wenefrede or to God the author of all good.' To which statement Fleetwood retorts, 'we are no enemies to miracles, but we desire to be assured that they were wrought before we believe them'.

And continues:

> I do not, for my part, believe, that any miracles have been wrought at Holywell,
> either before or since the Reformation, because I see none proved: but if there
> had, it would not have followed, that St Wenefrede had had any hand therein …
> It is true that many of those whom the Jesuit and his person of quality call heretics
> do also resort to this well, to seek help. It is a very cold spring, and is good as
> other cold springs are, in many cases; but the heretics seek for help from God and
> nobody else; and if they find it by the means of those waters, they return God
> thanks, and no body else, and bless his holy name for having given such salutary
> virtue to that well …

He attacks the Catholic claim that 'St Wenefrede is our sacred patroness.'

> I would not choose such a saint as Wenefrede, of whose very being there is no
> manner of certainty left to us. I would not pray to one, of whom I find no mention
> made for full 500 years after the time wherein she is said to have lived. I would
> not go on a pilgrimage to a saint's well, whose history is only told by a poor
> monk, that lived so long after her as 500 years, and brings no one writer of name
> or credit to vouch for anything he says concerning her all that interim, except a
> few loose scraps of paper or parchment in the church chest, or the relations of
> some honest old priests, who told him what the stories of the country were about
> her. Such a tradition as this is not ground sufficient for a Christian to build a
> patronage upon.[21]

Fleetwood adds his condemnation of Holywell:

> Holywell is a fountain of great superstition; and as ridiculous and idle as the fable
> may appear to protestants, it does not, as yet, appear so to the papists: and it is
> for their sake and service that I have taken the pains these observations cost me;
> and for their sake would take much greater, if I knew I could be useful to them
> in so doing.[22]

The Anglican bishop warns his readers against the Catholic religion and the
claims of the Old Pretender, the child of James II and Mary of Modena:

> The enemy we have to deal with grows more numerous, is active, vigilant, and
> daring, daily pushes on his conquests, is in good heart and under no
> discouragement but that of laws rejoices in our unconcernedness, confirms us in
> our indolence, and tells us, if we suspect them, we are unreasonable. And for
> these reasons I should be glad to see men somewhat more afraid of their
> inveterate enemy talk somewhat louder against popery both from the pulpit and
> the press, and tell the people, that if that superstition ever settles here again upon

the throne, there is an end of the religion, liberty, and property, and every thing besides that life is worth the living for.

The attack on the credibility of St Winefride by Bishop Fleetwood in 1713 marks a watershed in post–Reformation history of the well. Politically, the days of persecution of Catholics and enforcement of penal laws were virtually over. The Act of Settlement ensured a Protestant succession, made certain by the succession for the next hundred years of four Hanoverian kings named George who were in firm control of parliamentary government. The Catholic threat subsided and the failure of the 1745 rebellion was the end of their dream of return. The hopes of Catholics were no longer centred upon the return of the house of Stuart, but modestly and realistically upon relief of penal legislation, which inevitably came, when necessity demanded. As the eighteenth century progressed Catholic communities became more visible and less restricted.

At Holywell, the Mission at the Star continued to operate in spite of the suppression of the Society of Jesus by the Pope, which affected its members between 1773 and 1814. The Secular Mission left the Cross Keys, Holywell, in 1802, with its funds transferred to Monmouth. With more information available, it is possible to see a number of trends developing which act as a prelude to the great awakening of activity at the well and in the Catholic community at Holywell from the 1850s onwards.

The first trend is seen in written accounts made by visitors to the well in the eighteenth century. Pilgrimage and curiosity attracted Protestants, Catholics, and tourists. This is reflected particularly in the draughtsmanship of topographical artists, who left not only a record of St Winefride's well, but of the industrial revolution powered by the stream originating in the same fountain.

The subtle changes made to the buildings around the well reflect a more tolerant accommodation made to its users. Protestants and Catholics shared the site in peaceful co–existence. The tourists regarded the continued traditional Catholic usage of rituals, feast, and pilgrimages no longer as a threat, but more as a curiosity. Protestants continued to visit the well for curative purposes.

Holywell town prospered and its population grew rapidly as water power provided the first engine of industrial revolution in Wales, to drive the manufactories along the Greenfield stream. Improvements in communications, the development of a limited but impressive Georgian townscape and regular markets in lead and cattle accelerated an early growth spurt in population, which had a dramatic effect on Catholic numbers.

The Catholic Population of Holywell, 1681–1809

The number of Catholics resident in the Holywell district increased during the eighteenth century, as metal and textile industries were attracted by water power along the Greenfield stream. Information for the number of Catholics is derived from registers of baptisms and burials kept from 1730 onwards at the two missions, the Star and the Cross Keys. Thomas Pennant gave a speculative comparison between baptisms in the Anglican Church at Holywell with Catholic baptisms for the same years, as far as they were recorded. He worked out averages for five specific years (1770, 1780, 1787, 1790 and 1794), with Protestant 160 to 8 Catholic a ratio of 20 to 1 at the end of the eighteenth century.[23] A third source for the number of Catholics in Holywell and district is found in the returns made by the vicar of Holywell to the bishop of St Asaph at fairly regular intervals throughout the eighteenth century.

Although there was a frequent 'turnover' in the bishops of St Asaph in the eighteenth century (fourteen between 1703 and 1802) the vicars of Holywell remained longer. Ellis Price was vicar of Ysceifiog (1704–63) and Holywell (1711–63) and had a wide knowledge of the Catholic population and their foibles observed over a period of fifty–nine years. John Lloyd, Thomas Pennant's antiquarian friend, followed him between 1774–1807.

The information provided by Anglican clergy at Holywell is more reliable than any other, and is a good indication of both the strength of the Catholic community and the way it was regarded by the Established Church.

In the 1680s, Bishop William Lloyd made a census of population of parishes in his diocese which is known as *Notitia*, after the details required by the return. This included the names of the heads of household, the number of souls in the family without names, and the ages of all under 18 without names, and the names of all Popish recusants. The form for Holywell dated 1684[24] records the number of families as 283, 1,153 people – 'souls', and 'the names of ye Roman Catholicks in ye parish of Holywell.' Fifty–seven names are given on the return from Greenfield, Holywell, Bagillt and Brynford. The Greenfield names are headed by those of Mrs Elizabeth Mostyn and Mrs Dorothy Davies; those from Holywell by 'Mr Throp [? Thorpe] & his wife, Mr Standish & his wife.' Figures from the neighbouring parishes with strong Catholic affiliations are those of Llanasa which in 1681 was of comparative size in population with Holywell, 231 families, 998 souls, 33 Popish recusants above the age of sixteen years (names include those of Mostyn of Talacre),[25] and the parish of Bodfari with 136 families, 609 souls and 28 Popish recusants.[26]

A letter from Peter Evans, curate of Holywell, to Bishop Thomas Tanner[27] on 31 October 1732 gives information on the strength of the Catholic community in Holywell during the first half of the eighteenth century. Evans explained to the bishop that he had been employed as a curate by Mr Price, the vicar of Holywell, for the last eight months and was now able to provide him with firm proof 'How that Popery gains ground here in Holywell.' He informed his lordship:

That in this Town are two Popish Chappels most richly adorn'd where Mass is said by two resident priests, the one a Jesuit, & t'other of the Secular Order, who by particular artifices & gilded baits have of late perverted above forty families out of about seven score that this Town contains.

I have a list of above thirty Children that have not been baptized in the Church. I examined the Parents about the reason for that neglect, who openly declared that they were baptized by these Priests.

Marriages are frequently performed by them without either License or Banns, not regarding what (religious) profession, for several Protestants have been married by them at any hour day or night.

And they exercise all Priestly Offices with such freedom & liberty that their Converts take occasion thereof to despise & reproach our Holy Religion, as Heresy, the Professors thereof, Hereticks, & Loyalty to his sacred Majesty King George is little regarded by them.

All which flagitious & abominable proceedings excited me to this great presumption, for which I earnestly implore your Lordship's pardon; trusting that you will, out of your great Wisdom & Prudence, order some means for the regulating thereof.'[28]

Bishop Tanner and Vicar Ellis Price in their wisdom and prudence probably decided to take no action because they hesitated to enforce recusancy laws in a community marked by mixed marriages between Catholics and Anglicans, which had set their own boundaries of toleration and dwelt together in peace.

Irregular marriages frequently occurred in places where there was a strong presence of Catholics. Lord Hardwicke's Marriage Act of 1753 for the 'Better Preventing of Clandestine Marriages' required them to be performed in churches and chapels of the Church of England, and registered in a prescribed form. Evidence of irregularity in Holywell was given in 1775 when Mary, the widow of a miner who died in Whitford, on seeking Poor Relief, testified that:

she was married to her late husband by Mr John Gwllym a Popish Priest late of Holywell deceased (died 1763) in a Chappel belonging to a house then called the Cross Keys 22 yrs ago; that her Settlement was in Holywell by serving the said Mr Gwllym as a yearly hired servant for two to three years; that she believes there was no licence obtained from the Ecclesiastical Court; that she has ten children and is now with child.[29]

Vicar Ellis Price shared his observations on the Roman Catholic presence in his parish on at least three occasions with the Bishop of St Asaph in his replies to the bishop's visitation queries. In 1738 he reported:

Above 500 families in the parish of whom 140 persons rek'ning Men, Women & Children may be Papists. I have as occasion has offered and received them in the Spirit of Love & Meekness. They wd shun Me, if the Design were suspected; & where I could get at the Speech of 'em. they would turn a Deaf ear, declaring themselves satisfied; & unmov'd from their present Settled Persuasion.[30]

Ten years later, he reported a general population increase and spoke of the effect of mixed marriages on church membership and Catholic mission centres. In 1745:

> Families 537 of which 50 other – more may be partly Popish being but few that are entirely such. In some ye Husband not ye Wife, in others ye Wife and not ye Husband: ye Children also divided, ye sons going one way & ye daughters another.

His reply about Catholic places of worship was that there were:

> Two Popish Chapels & have been I doubt not Since ye Reformation: one at ye Star for Regulars only. Before ye present Popish Priest, whose name is Williams (John Williams died 1761) there used to be two Jesuits constantly resident at ye Star Inn. The other chapel is for a Secular Priest only known by ye name of Gwillym. There are Prayers twice a day among them. Service twice a day Sunday & Holy Days, Wednesday & Fridays.[31]

Ellis's last return was made in 1753 when he reported one Jesuit priest at the Star and Father Gwillym, at the Cross Keys with daily Mass said in both chapels: 'the Numbers resorting to them appears to be but few'. He concluded:

> I've been informed there is another Priest in the widow Lady Mostyn of Greenfield's Family, but whether a Regular or Secular I know not. He that lived in her Family, when at Talacre, was a Jesuit.[32]

Vicar Ellis probably learnt to respect his Catholic contemporaries and they him, and this was probably based upon an acknowledgement that they would not be swayed in their views. Interestingly, there is no mention of practices at St Winefride's Well in the bishop's queries or the vicar's answers. The information recorded is sufficient to give the impression of an established Catholic community with traditional links through marriage to the stronger Anglican Church before the emergence of Nonconformity in the 1780s.

The most valuable information relating to Catholic population was provided by the Return of Papists 1767. These were numbers of Catholics received from Anglican bishops of the dioceses of England and Wales.[33]

The information for Holywell was collected by Vicar Benjamin Havard for Richard Newcombe, bishop of St Asaph, who signed the diocesan returns on 21 November 1767. The information lacks only names and addresses of Papists, and provides details of their sex, age, family relationship, and occupation. Some of the incumbents in the diocese failed to submit returns, it being supposed there were no Papists resident in their parishes.

The return shows that there are 362 Papists in the diocese, 176 (48.6%) from Holywell, with 47 at Llanasaph, 37 at Pool (Welshpool) and 17 at Guilsfield in Montgomeryshire, all of these places part of the Residence of St Winefride.

There is a marked decline of Catholics in villages surrounding Holywell: Bodfari (8), Caerwys (1), Flint (2), Halkin (7), Whitford (9) although at Mold (21) and Nercwys (10) with the Roberts and Giffard families, there is a stronger presence. The 234 Catholics in Flintshire and 56 in Montgomeryshire were the responsibility of the Catholic priests at Holywell . All Catholics in the diocese probably had a strong attachment to St Winefride's Well and represented the wider constituency of Catholics associated with Holywell since the Reformation.

The Holywell return shows a community in transition from an agricultural to an industrial society, with Catholics represented in a broad cross–section of occupations. Extractive industries are represented by ore workers, miners, mine agent, coal jagger, pumper, collier, white washer, budler (buddler), ore washer, smelter, calamy (zinc ore) dresser. The new copper industry is represented by wire drawers; traditional trades supporting the growth in the townscape by glazier, stone sawer, joiner, and labourer; tradesmen by occupations such as tanner, weaver, cordwainer, blacksmith, clockmaker (Winstanley family), malster, inn keeper. There are two priests, two gentlemen, gentlewomen, a surgeon, apothecary, schoolmistress, midwife, and farmer. Two washerwomen, laundress, breeches maker, sempstress, perukemaker, staymaker, a parish apprentice, three paupers, and several servants. The age grouping shows sixty–one members of the population aged twenty years or under; twenty–seven aged sixty years or over, and eighty–eight (50%) between twenty one years and fifty nine years.

Another return of 'Papists or reputed Papists' was made to the House of Lords in 1780. The figures show a severe and inexplicable decline in numbers of Flintshire Catholics down from 362 to 210 and Holywell numbers down from 176 to 149,(70.95%).[34]

Reliable population figures exist from 1801 on the introduction of the government census. The following numbers are for Holywell parish. 1801: 5,567; 1811: 6,394; 1821: 8,309; 1831: 8969.

John Jones, vicar of Holywell, noted in his answers to the bishop's queries in 1809 a general increase in the total population of the parish and a decline in the number of Catholics.

> Numbers of houses about 1146, inhabitants 5567. There are 113 Papists in this parish, including 56 children & 5 servants, None have lately been converted to Popery; on the contrary they have greatly diminished in numbers. They have a Chapel where they regularly assemble; but no school nor has Confirmation or Visitation been lately had by any Papal Bishop.[35]

St Winefride's Well in the Eighteenth Century

Travel became gradually easier and less restricted, and by the end of the eighteenth century, became a fashionable pursuit of the gentry and emerging middle classes. A growth in trade and prosperity encouraged road improvements paid for by turnpike trusts. Scientific invention gave birth to a revolution in the agricultural and industrial life of the nation. A new reading public devoured newspapers and journals for sensation, curiosity, and wonder. 'The printing press', claimed Lewis Morris enthusiastically in 1735, was 'the Candle of the World, and the Freedom of Britain's sons.'[36]

Father Metcalfe's new impression of the *Life of StWenefred* in 1712 and the attack it provoked from bishop Fleetwood the following year publicised the well. New travel books and road atlases made it an essential place to be included in the tourist itinerary. In the nearby expanding port of Liverpool handbills were printed advertising St Winefride's Well to its immigrant Catholics population. The view of St Winefride's Well became a popular subject included by topographical artists with Edwardian castles in north Wales. Pilgrimage, devotion, and curiosity attracted a cosmopolitan variety of visitors in a new age of freedom.

The visit of Celia Fiennes in 1698

Celia Fiennes (1662–1741) was a thirty–six–year–old spinster when she visited St Winefride's Well in 1698. She had decided to travel to regain her health by 'change of air and exercise' and visited Chester and Holywell in 1698 as part of her 'Great Journey to Newcastle and Cornwall.' Celia Fiennes came of a family of noted dissenters who had supported the Commonwealth. She was the granddaughter of William Fiennes, first viscount Saye and Sele. On leaving Chester she visited her cousin at Hawarden who was married to the rector. They saw that she arrived safely at Holywell.

More interested in commercial life than antiquitiy, she gave a good account of St Winefride's Well which showed a critical but mild scepticism of Catholic practices:

> St Winfreds Well is built over with stone on pillars like a tryumphall arch or tower on the gates of a Church; there is a pavement of stone within ground 3 sides of the Well which is joyn'd on the fourth side by a great arch of stone which lies over the water that runs off from the Well, its many springs which bubbles up very fast and lookes cleane in a compass which is 8 square walled in with stone; in the bottom you see as clear as Chrystall are 9 stones layd in an oval on which are dropps of red coullour some almost quite covering the top of the stone, which is pretended to be the blood of this holy saint whose head was struck off here, and so where her body laid this spring burst forth and remaines till now, a very rapid current, which runs off from this Well under a barre by which there are stone stepps for persons to descend which will bathe themselves in the Well; and so they walke along the streame to the other end and then come out, but there is nothing to shelter them but are exposed to all the Company that are walking about the Well and to the little houses and part of the streete which runs along by it; but the Religeuse are not to mind that; it seemes the Saint they do honour to

in this place must beare them out in all things, they tell of many lameness's and aches and distempers which are cured by it; it's a cold water and cleare and runs off very quick so that it would be pleasant refreshment in the sumer to washe ones self in it, but its shallow not up to the waste so its not easye to dive and washe in; but I thinke I could not have been persuaded to have gone in unless might have had curtains to have drawn about some part of it to have shelter'd from the streete, for the wett garments are no covering to the body; but there I saw abundance of the devout papists on their knees all round the Well; poor people are deluded into an ignorant blind zeale and to be pit'd by us that have the advantage of knowing better and ought to be better; there is some small stones of a reddish collour in the Well said to be some of Winifreds blood also, which the poore people take out and bring to the strangers for curiosity and relicts, and also moss about the bancks full of great virtue for everything–but it's a certaine gaine to the poore people, everyone gives them something for bringing them moss and the stones, but least they should be in length of tyme be quite gather'd up they take care to replensh it dayly from some mossy hill and so stick it along the sides of the Well– there is good streames runs from it and by meanes of steepe descent runs down and turns mills: they come also to drinke of the water which they take up in the first square which is walled round and where the spring rise, and they say its of wonder full operation; the taste to me was but like good spring water which with wine and sugar and leamons might make a pleasant draught after walking amongst those shady trees of which there is a great many and some straight and tall like a grove but not very uniforme, but a sort of iregular rows.

As an afterthought, Celia Fiennes adds a disapproving note on the local population:

… at Holly Well they speake Welsh, the inhabitants go barefoote and bare leg'd a nasty sort of people, their meate is very small here, mutton is noe bigger than little lamb, what of it there is was sweete; their wine good being neare the sea side and well provided with fish'[37]

The visit of Henry Prescott 1716

Henry Prescott was deputy registrar of the Chester diocese and often had official business which took him to St Asaph. He was an affable and gregarious lawyer whose diary is full of gossip of local interest. This brief extract records his visit to the town of Holywell in September 1716:

… pass Northop about 12 proceed the tedious 4 Miles in a deep and rude road and severe rain to Holywell. We came there about 1. Wee see the Well and are teazd by its Beggars, we have a sordid dinner of suppitious Mutton in a cold room at the Starr, which yet costs me 4s 2. We go for and find relief at the Crown.

Celia Fiennes also found it difficult in travelling from Chester to Holywell, 'with all its washes over the marsh ground' and 'sands which makes it very difficult for strangers to passe without a guide.'[38] Prescott took a route along the higher ground. Pilgrims from Lancashire would be guided across the Dee, and many guides from Bagillt found employment in this way, usually fishermen familiar with 'the sands of Dee.' William Blundell and other Catholics from Lancashire regularly made a pilgrimage crossing the estuary to the well. The river Dee was canalised as far as Wepre in 1737, but there were still hazards to be overcome on the remaining seven miles of the journey.

The visit of Daniel Defoe in 1724

Daniel Defoe (*c.*1660–1731) was another experienced Protestant traveller whose powers of observation were sharper than most having been employed as a master spy by the government. As a nonconformist and pamphleteer for the cause of religious freedom, he was quick to notice the toleration enjoyed by Catholics at Holywell. Defoe was interested in antiquities and the beginnings of commercial transformation, and, as the author of *Robinson Crusoe*, in travel and tourism. His description, like Celia Fiennes, shows an emphasis on curiosity, and social and cultural differences in Britain.

> From hence we come to Holly–Well: The stories of this Well of S. Winifrid are, that the pious virgin, being ravished and murthered, this healing water sprung of her body when buried; but this smells too much of the legend, to take up any of my time; the Romanists indeed believe it, as 'tis evident, from their thronging hither to receive the healing sanative virtue of the water, which they do not hope for as it is a medicinal water, but as it is a miraculous water, and heals them by virtue of the intercession and influence of the famous virgin, St Winifrid; of which I believe as much as comes to my share.
>
> Here is a fine chapel cut out of a solid rock and was dedicated to this holy virgin; and numbers of pilgrims resort to it, with no less devotion than ignorance; under this chapel the water gushes out in a great stream, and the place where it breaks out, is form'd like a basin or cistern, in which they bathe: The water is intensely cold, and indeed there is no great miracle in that point, considering the rocks it flows from, where it is impregnated by divers minerals, the virtue of which, and not of the saint, I suppose, work the greatest part of the cures.
>
> There is a little town near the well, which may, indeed, be said to have risen from the confluence of the people hither, for almost all the houses are either publick houses, or let into lodgings; and the priests that attend here, and are very numerous, appear in disguise: Sometimes they are physicians, sometimes surgeons, sometimes gentlemen, and sometimes patients, or any thing as occasion presents. No body takes notice of them, as to their profession, tho' they know them well enough, no not the Roman Catholicks themselves; but in private, they have their proper oratory's in certain places whither the votaries resort; and

good manners has prevail'd so far, that however the Protestants know who and who's together; no body takes notice of it, or enquires where one another goes, or has been gone.[39]

The visit of William Statham 1731

William Statham (1694–1738), a Derbyshire man was a Catholic convert from Anglicanism. Apprenticed to a wine merchant in London, William was sent to Lisbon where he was influenced by the Roman Catholic devotions he observed there. On his return to England, he became part of the congregation of Jesuits at Spinkhill in Derbyshire. He eventually became an assistant to one of the duke of Norfolk's agents and took a house near Hathersage in Derbyshire and was confirmed as a Catholic in the duke's chapel in Sheffield in 1727. He visited St Winefride's Well in August 1731 and his Diary entry recounts his experience and devotion to St Winefride:

> Bathing in Wales on Saturday about eight in the evening Augst 7. I Bathed that night & on Sunday & Munday each time staying in about one hour, it is the cleanest & most beautiful imaginable almost impossible to foul or muddy it & its waters so strong. I think no person can sink down to be drowned in it.

Statham gives a description of the stone of St Beuno:

> There is a large piece of a Rock stands up called the wishing stone, people kiss it & wish, & tho' its top be but about half a yard or hardly so much below the surface it is with great difficulty to bring your face so low as to salute it & get hold of it with both my arms & so forced my head down that way.

He describes the scene around the well in words which are a reminder of the daily activity of the local washerwomen who relied on the stream for their water supply.

> All the people are every day washing & rinsing their cloth I never heard any one falling in was drowned. The moss growing about it smells very fragrant & so doe the stones taken from the bottom of the Well (if they have the red tincture upon them). Laying them to dry in the sun, the moistness smells as violets or perfume. These waters of honour are intirely free to all strangers & Passengers whatever.

He gives a clear indication of the opportunities for bathing at the well with none of the inhibitions expressed by the Protestants Fiennes and Defoe.

> After I had bathed me in the outward Well I courageously said (to myself) the waters be no Master I will venture into the Holy Well; & so resolute & stepping in I being the only person that I saw amongst so many hundreds which had the

curiosity to go in there, indeed I had a mind to see the appearance of blood which remains exceeding natural upon the stones in the Holy Well. I took them up & could not but admire their beauty especially when I turned them & found the colour not passing into the stone but only remaining upon the face some as in streames out of vaine & others in spots promiscuously dashed upon them. I examined them one by one.

Statham marvelled at the wonder of the St Winefride's Well.

This the strongest Spring that ever I beheld rises up with so great force amongst these Stones as if the Earth was a Prison to its waters & as if its beginning has some sudden surprize to cause the violent hasty bursting out of the current flowing as it were wth joy to cure all our maladies. The breaking of these chaste floods was in the seventh century, especially & by all having their original from pure & preserved chastity.

In his efforts to express his wonder his language verges on the ecstatic. Statham is obviously overcome by his experience and veneration of St Winefride.

Oh you Kings, Queens, Princes & Nobles of those days, Crowns Sceptres Jewels of that age you are not buried in oblivion, but the White Lady of Chastity & Illustrious Angelical purity is not for ever to be blotted out.
   Over this renowned Well of British Chastity is a building of curious work; & altho in its plundered State from the liberality of the founder & devotion of Antient days, over its fine arched roof was a Catholick Chapel now defaced & made an English School; debased, deformed devoured but virginity is for ever glorious & shall never be deflowered.'
   I left this place of admiration on Wednesday August 11th.[40]

Statham's diary entry has echoes of other accounts St Winefride and her well for example the description by the poet Michael Drayton in 1612 who imagines 'the *Devian* Nymphs' leaving 'their watery bowers':

To see her whom report so greatly should admire
(Whose waters to this day as perfect are and deere.
As her delightful eyes in their full beauties were,
A virgin while she liv'd) chaste Winifrid: who chose
Before her mayden–gem she forcibly would lose,
To have her harmlesse life by the leud Rapter spilt:
For which, still more and more to aggravate his guilt,
The livelesse tears shee shed, into a Fountain turne,
And that for her alone the water should not mourne,
The pure vermillion bloud, that issu'd from her vaines,
Unto this very day the pearly Gravell staines;

> As erst the white and red were mixed in her cheeke,
> And, that one part of her might be the other like,
> Her haire was turn'd to mosse; whose sweetness doth declare,
> In liveliness of youth the naturall sweets she bare:
> And of her holy life the innocence to show,
> What–ever living thing into this Well you throwe,
> Shee strongly beares it up, not suffring it to sinke. Etc. etc.[41]

St Winefride's Well continued to serve as a place of pilgrimage to the Catholics of Lancashire. It was of great comfort to the Blundell family of Crosby, who gave sons and daughters to the priesthood and convent and generation after generation regularly made the journey to Holywell.[42]

Nicholas Blundell's marriage to Mrs Francis Langdale produced a bevy of daughters but unfortunately a son and heir did not arrive, a desire for which was probably a poignant petition in their intercessions when they made their almost annual visits to St Winefride's well around the date of her summer festival. These usually lasted two or three days, when they stayed at either the Star or the Cross Keys. The difficulties of the journey are seen in the following entries:

1721 July 8. My Wife and I began our Journey towards Holy–well but no Ferry Bote being on this Side I hired the Sower–Milk Gallay, she Carried us & our three Horses over at twice & landed us at the Wood–Side, thence we went to Shotwick & so to Holly–Well where we Lodged at the Starr. My wife went into the Well.
9. My Wife & I went into the Well, I was much out of Order after I came out and Continewed so for Hours. I went with my Wife to Mrs Crews, who walked out with us to a pleasant sort of a walk.
10. We came from Holliwell to Flint where we baited awhile at the Signe of the Ship thence to Shotwick where I rode over without a Guide and came back again with one to fetch my Wife over, than to Eastom (Eastham ferry).
Wives Journey & mine to and from Holly Well £2 2s. 3d.
To Priests there & Elce–where   8s. 6d.[43]

The wonder of St Winefride's Well

Scientific curiosity and the making of wagers by Anglican clergy and gentry was a new innovation at the well, but in the spirit of eighteenth century deism and enlightenment a group of gentlemen assembled on 12 July 1731 to wager on the volume of the water in the well and the time it took to fill. They were:

Mr Price, the Rector of Holywell, Mr Wynne, Dr Taylor, and several other gentlemen when, to the surprise of the company, the well filled in less than two minutes; which proves that St Winefride's spring raises more than one hundred tons of water in a minute. The Bason is six feet deep, and yet the water is so clear, that a pin may be seen in the bottom … In the bottom of the bason are several large *pepple* (pebble) stones, which to the eye, appear as if besprinkled or besmeared with blood.

Ellis Price was vicar of Holywell (1711–63) and a graduate of Christ Church, Oxford. He was also master of Holywell Free School held in the chapel above the well. Price was eminently qualified having been in his younger days an assistant at Westminster School under the celebrated Dr Busby.

Forty years later, on 3 August 1774, Dr Samuel Johnson, accompanied by Mrs Hesther Thrale, drove over in a coach to the well. Johnson's diary makes no mention of St Winefrede, and is chiefly interested in seeing the various industrial undertakings, which followed the stream to Greenfield. He recorded in his diary of the tour:

> Holywell is a Market town neither very small nor mean. The spring called Winifred's Well is very clear, and so copious that it yields one hundred tuns of water in a minute. It is all at once a very great stream which within perhaps thirty yards of its eruption turns a mill and in a course of two miles eighteen mills more. In descent it is very quick. It then falls into the sea. The Well is covered by a lofty circular arch supported by pillars, and over this arch is an old chapel now a school. The Chancel is separated by a wall. The bath is completely and indecently open. A woman bathed while we all looked on.[44]

By contrast, Mrs Thrale's journal gives more space to the well and St Winefride.

> Wednesday, 3rd August. On this day we were carried to Holywell, where we saw the devastation committed by Puritanism, which in its zeal had battered poor Saint Winifred and displaced her statue, broken three of the columns surrounding the Well which had any effigies upon them, and left nothing but the stone at the bottom of the water which bears any mark of ancient superstition and is spotted with red in two or three places, and the Roman Catholics believe from their hearts that it was stained by the blood of their favourite Virgin martyr. The spring is so

82. Textile mill below St Winefride's Well in the late eighteenth century

83. Dr Samuel Johnson.

84. Mrs Hesther Thrale.

clear and pellucid that it tempts one to jump into it, but the wonder is in the thoughts of its throwing up 100 tun in a minute. When you look, however, at the rapidity with which the water throws itself off, you wonder no longer, and are willing to believe on the spot that which at a distance seemed wholly incredible.[45]

Mrs Thrale left no prudish comments about the indecency of public bathing. Bathing garments had been available in the seventeenth century. Richard James had noted them in 1636 as 'The smocks which now for bathing we doe hire.'[46]

In 1761, Thomas Pennant, as a justice of the peace at the Flintshire Quarter Sessions examined Mary Jones, a washerwoman, when John Griffiths of Holywell was accused of theft. She informed him she served persons who came to the well in Holywell for bathing, with linen, the property of Richard Barthur, of Bagillt, labourer. It was her practice to hang the wet bathing garments to dry about the churchyard above the Well Chapel. On the Sunday next after St James's tide (July 25), a witness, Anne Williams, said that she saw John Griffiths of Holywell, tailor, 'take either a shirt or shift from the churchyard wall and stoop to the ground as if he was for gathering it up in a lump clandestinely, and take the shirt and shift with him.'[47]

Sometime the bond of trust existing between bathers and those who looked after their clothes was broken. A case not proved was that against John Parry of Holywell in the summer of 1783. He was accused of the theft of two guineas from the clothes entrusted to him by Midshipman James Buchan of the frigate HMS *Richmond*, whilst bathing in the well one evening between eight and nine o'clock.[48]

The obvious source of information relating to the well in the eighteenth century

C4. Rolfe banner depicting St Winefride.

C5. Rolfe banner depicting St Gregory.

C6. Rolfe banner depicting St George.

C7. Rolfe banner depicting St Augustine.

C9. Reliquary of St Winefride in the Well Museum, Holywell.

C.8 Bishop Edwin Regan, HRH The Duchess of Gloucester and Mr David Schwarz at the Holy Well, 16 October 2005.

C10. HRH The Duchess of Gloucester being presented to two volunteers, Sister Aidan Hayden and Mrs Betty Lloyd, 16 October 2005.

C11. HRH The Duchess of Gloucester being shown the richly-embroidered mitre of the bishop of Wrexham which depicts St Winefride, by Tristan Gray-Hulse.

is from Thomas Pennant, of Downing. He was a noted antiquary, tourist, correspondent, ornithologist, and zoologist of European repute. Amongst his correspondents was Father Thomas Daniel, alias West, SJ, an antiquarian who wrote the *Antiquities of Furness*, a popular *Guide to the Lakes*, and left behind notes on many subjects. He was in Holywell *c.*1760 and had entrance to the libraries of the local gentry. Thomas Pennant went on a grand tour of Europe and published an account, *Tour on the Continent, 1765.*[49] He took the opportunity of visiting members of local Catholic gentry families who had entered the religious life, and other Catholic acquaintances. At the College of St Omer he met his neighbour Sir Pyers Mostyn, and whilst in Louvain he supped at the

85. *The antiquary Thomas Pennant of Downing: engraving from a portrait by Thomas Gainsborough.*

English Convent and visited Ursula Townley 'sister to Teresa, married to Sir George Mostyn of Talacre 4th Bart, d.1746, sister to Lady Mostyn, a Nun in this house; saw also at the gate an Aunt of Mr Jones of the Cross Keys and another of Mr Parry of Twysog.'[50] At Bruges, he visited the English Augustinian nuns, and saw there a sister of Mr Blundell. He visited the English Jesuits, 'I asked after Mr Watson, late of Holywell, who I know was sent to Cassel to do penance. They denied him pleading ignorance, tho' I am certain he is among them.'[51] The same month he visited the Benedictine nuns at Dunkirk and saw the abbess, Mary Winifred Englefield, a daughter of Mr Mostyn of Segroit, Denbighsire.

In 1795 thirty years later in his *History of the Parishes of Whiteford and Holywell*, Pennant noticed the decline in pilgrim numbers.

The resort of pilgrims of late years to these *Fontanalia* has considerably decreased; the greatest number are from Lancashire. In the summer, still a few are to be seen in the water in deep devotion up to their chins for hours, sending up their prayers, or performing a number of evolutions round the polygonal well; or threading the arch between well and well a prescribed number of times. I am sorry to say that this excess of piety has cost several devotees their lives. Few people of rank at present honor the fountain with their preference.[52]

He gives an explanation of the curative effects of the Well water in a typical eighteenth century Protestant down to earth manner:

> The waters are indisputably endowed with every good quality attendant on cold baths; and multitudes have here experienced the good effects that thus result from natural qualities, implanted in the several parts of matter by the divine Providence, in order to fulfil his will. Heaven for a short period deigned to convince a dark and obdurate age with a series of miracles; which were delivered down to succeeding times, as incontestable proofs of the reality of the divine mission. Without them, a sufficient ground of trust and reliance upon the Supreme Being has long since been established. Second causes innumerable are dispersed throughout the universe, subordinate to the FIRST. Every element proves to us a medicine or a bane, as suits His unerring dispensation. We cannot want, we cannot have the mediation of poor departed mortals. The supposition would be bestowing on them the attributes of the Deity; omnipresence and omniscience.[53]

The Catholic community in Holywell, 1750–1840

The period between 1750 and 1840 was a decisive watershed in the history of the Catholic community in Britain. The disastrous reign of James II and subsequent uncertainty of hopes for a Jacobite return demoralised the Catholic population and meant no early relaxation of penal legislation. The situation was made much worse by the Suppression of the Society of Jesus in 1773, the consequences of which were felt more on the Continent. Religious suppression reached its height during the French Revolution and Napoleonic Wars (1789–1815). This is true of

86. Upper cotton works, 1796.

87. St Winefride's Well. An unusual artist's impression which shows how the well was used by pilgrims for healing (notice the moss), tourists for bathing and local townsfolk for their domestic water supply and washing.

the Jesuit Mission in Holywell which experienced a similar progress through the threat of shipwreck and the doldrums of suppression and decline in numbers to emerge in full sail in the 1830s.

The storm was weathered through the perseverance and devotion of able priests who managed to survive the suppression of the Society of Jesus with the support of the Secular clergy and vicars apostolic. A pastoral ministry was maintained to parishioners and pilgrims in Holywell town. The work of the mission increased with the rapid industrialisation of the area in the second half of the eighteenth century. The legal standing of Catholics was recognised by the removal of penal legislation in 1778 and 1791, and Catholic emancipation in 1829. Persecution was ended, but prejudice continued unabated throughout the nineteenth century. However, the Mission in Holywell was strengthened, reinvigorated, and became more confident through a welcome emergence of middle class support from incoming laity like the Sankey, Roskell and Potts families. They were an important paternalistic influence in the lives of poor immigrant Catholic families. The return of the Mostyn baronets to Talacre in the 1820s came in time to support building projects such as a new church and school in the area. They were important allies in the local debate for Catholic emancipation against Protestant opposition and professional laity were of great assistance in the consolidation of Catholic property in the Well Street area and in safeguarding Catholic interests in the administration of St Winefride's Well.

The Catholic mission
Within thirty years two major decisions affected the Catholic mission in Holywell. The first came in 1773, when a brief of Pope Clement XIV[54] suppressed the Society of Jesus, which was to last until its restoration by Pope Pius VII in 1814. One effect of this was a fall in the number of members of the Society, when the mission at Holywell had to make do with the services of one, rather than two, priests. The other disability was the administration of Jesuit property, the income from which financed the mission. The Jesuit priest at Holywell, Michael Moseley (*c*.1762–77), took over administration of Jesuit property in north Wales, and at his death named Sir Pyers Mostyn as his executor. The worthy baronet, believing that the Jesuits would never be restored, transferred the funds of the district of St Winefride's and its real property to the trusteeship of two Vicars Apostolic. Although this expediency safeguarded the funds, it later created difficulties in releasing funds for the building of a Catholic chapel and schools in the town.[55]

   The other major decision was taken in 1802, when the secular mission at the Cross Keys decided to remove to Monmouth. Its property was sold and funds transferred there by Bishop Sharrock of the western district. In these years of distress there is evidence that the two missions supported each other. The vicars apostolic came regularly to carry out confirmations: Bishop Walmsley, 1786; Bishop Sharrock, 1799; Bishop Collingridge, 1810 and 1813; and Bishop Briggs, 1833. The last of the Secular priests, Father George Thomas Gildart resided with Father Edward Wright, SJ, at the Star from 1800–02.

   Only a few years earlier, in 1795, Thomas Pennant described the Star and the Cross Keys:

> Both of their cures are endowed with land vested in trustees. Each of their houses has a species of hotel, probably designed for the reception of pilgrims of better rank … I remember at one or other of these, Edward Duke of Norfolk, and other visitors of distinction.[56]

The ground and building which formed the Cross Keys property must have been fairly extensive. When the house and chapel were taken down, a large house, a factory, and several cottages were built on the premises, and in about 1860 the property came into the hands of the Jesuit mission and was obtained by Father Mann for his hospice.[57] In 1799–1800, a great part of the Star Inn was pulled down and a new building erected with a chapel.[58]

The survival of the Catholic community in Holywell from 1750 to 1840, and its adaptation to political and religious changes, and industrial and demographic growth, was due to some extent to a continuity of ministry provided by four Jesuit priests from 1762–1842. Before a review of their contributions an account book from the Star Inn is examined.[59]

Star Inn account book, 1748–54

The priest at the Star during this period was John Williams, SJ, (b. *c.*1691 Monmouthshire, d. Holywell 1761). Although there is nothing of note in the accounts, they provide some insight into the life of the mission and it is the only local information we possess. The accounts are mainly a record of housekeeping expenses, which, although on the whole mundane and monotonous, give a sense of rhythm to the life of the mission. Most of the household goods were purchased in Holywell, a bustling town of shopkeepers and weekly market–stall holders, and centre of the local lead industry, full of pilgrim visitors in season. The Star Inn was about a hundred yards from the town centre down Well Street, with St Winefride's Crypt further down.

The priest gave his housekeeper cash to purchase provisions in the town, and other commodities came by carrier from Chester or were bought in bulk locally: measures of malt, corn, wheat, and hops for brewing. A brewing woman and a washerwoman were employed regularly. Mr Vickers, the nurseryman, provided 'things from the garden,' and coals came from Mostyn. Regular items of purchase were cheese, sugar, butter, potatoes, and candles. A rare buy was a box of oranges for 4s.6d, and raisins and nutmeg were used to spice the drink. During Lent sturgeon, oyster and salt fish were obtained locally, or from Chester. There is no mention of the purchase of meat, poultry, or eggs. This came from land nearby, farmed as a small–holding to supply these necessities.

It is perfectly clear, however, that Thomas Pennant's statement that the Star was a 'species of hotel' was correct. The large and spacious house, with its chapel, stables and grazing land, was ideal for letting rooms to gentry, some of whom were in residence for long periods. Thomas Mostyn of Talacre and his Lady were continually resident from 23 March 1748/9 until August 1752, and maybe longer. It was agreed that they pay sixteen pounds per head a year for bed and board with meals, and they were to find fire and candles, tea, and coffee and furnish their own room and the room next to it, and also the little parlour. Mr Mostyn paid an extra three shillings a week for stabling his horse, and grazing in

Brochnallt, land adjoining the Star to the west. The Mostyns must have been comfortable and satisfied with the service they received for it was noted that they persuaded the maid at the Star to go into service with the family:

> Nelly Onsworth went from my service & to Mrs Mostyn's on ye 9th of Jan. 1753 for whose board Mrs Mostyn is to pay £8 *per ann.*

A Mr Turner, his family and four servants stayed at the Star for the month of June/July 1750, for the summer celebration of St Winefride's feast. Grazing land at the *Brochnallt* provided a steady income and a fresh milk supply. The Star Inn was an ideal mission centre to minister to pilgrims, to provide long and short term accommodation, and was self sufficient, providing an adequate income to support the Jesuits.

The primary purpose of the Star was as a Jesuit mission residence, but, with its plentiful accommodation, it could always muster attendance at its devotions in the chapel. A notice written by a priest (John Williams?) for the feast of All Saints, Tuesday I November 1754 reads:

> Tomorrow being ye feast of All Souls I shall begin ye office of ye dead at eight o'clock, and Mass at ½ after 8, at which I recommend to all yt. can conveniently to be present to offer up their praises and Suffrages for ye release of ye souls in Purgatory: Thursday is ye feast of St Winifred Patroness of North Wales, Holy day of obligation. I give you all notice yt there is a Plenary Indulgence granted by his present Holiness Pope Benedict XIV to be gained any day within this octave of All Saints, yt. is from this day till Tuesday next inclusive by those yt. shall perform on their part ye conditions required.[60]

These two small records which have survived, although they provide a mere glimpse of the Jesuit mission centred at the Star, give evidence of its activity in the middle of the eighteenth century. We are more certain of the careers of the priests who follow Father John Williams. Father Michael Moseley, SJ, (b.1720, died at Holywell 29 November 1777), was at the Residence of St Winefride when the Society of Jesus was suppressed in 1773 and attempted to safeguard its local funds and property by placing them with Sir Pyers Mostyn of Talacre. Moseley's successor Father Joseph Tyrer, SJ, gave twenty–one years to the Holywell Mission and died in his bed there on 22 December aged sixty–four years. These two priests enabled the mission to survive in years of uncertainty. During Father Tyrer's ministry in Holywell two important measures of government legislation for Catholics were passed. They were a sign that the threat from the House of Stuart, which caused such alarm by the Jacobite Rebellions in 1715 and 1745, had become completely ineffective, and that liberal opinion was demanding the removal of ferocious penal laws. The Roman Catholic Relief Act of 1778 began the process of removing legal penalties and a movement towards religious freedom.

Bishops and priests were now tolerated and no longer guilty of felony. Priests and laymen could keep schools, inherit and purchase land, and possess property as private individuals. In 1791 another Relief Act gave Roman Catholics the freedom of worship and education, and allowed them to build their own schools and places of worship. These reforms were welcomed by Catholics, everywhere but were resented enough in some communities to cause an occasional riot.

Father Joseph Tyrer's ministry, like that of his contemporary at the Secular Mission at the Cross Keys, Father Philip Jones (b.1722, d.1800), was to ensure the survival of the Catholic community in Holywell. Father Jones was at Holywell from 1763 until his death in 1800.

The work of the Jesuits and Seculars is measured to some extent in the Holywell Registers.[61] The Revd Mr Jones's Register October 1763 to August 1798 has 144 entries of baptisms, including some at gentry families at Twysog, Bryn Madin, Talacre, Bodfari, Gwespyr, and Nercwys. Mr Tyrer, his contemporary at the Star from 8 June, 1778 to 31 January 1798 baptised 46 and his successor Father Edward Wright baptised 169 candidates between 3 February 1799 to 15 June 1825. Two confirmations took place: the first at the Star in 1786 by Bishop Walmesley, vicar apostolic of the Western district when there were 13 candidates, and the second, in the same chapel, by Bishop Sharrock, his successor, when 15 candidates were presented. These statistics show that the Catholic community in Holywell district was stable and supported by a number of faithful local families as it entered into a new century.

They were fortunate in the contribution made by Father Edward Wright (b. 1752, d.1826), who served at Holywell from January 1799 until his death there on 9 April 1826 at the age of seventy–four years. At the time of the suppression of the Society in 1773 he was one of the masters at the Jesuit College which had been transferred from St Omer to Bruges. He lived to be able to renew his vows to the restored Society (1814).

The ministry of Father Edward Wright, SJ, 1799–1826

The twenty–five years' ministry of Father Edward Wright, beginning in 1799, laid a solid foundation for the subsequent growth in the strength of the Jesuit mission in Holywell. Besides the uncertain position of the suppressed Society of Jesus, Father Wright had to contend with the vigour of new challenges he found at Holywell. The economy of a town in the middle of an industrial revolution struggling to satisfy the wartime demands imposed on its metallic industries of lead, copper, and brass, and subsequent painful post–war adjustment when they were no longer needed. The extension of religious toleration granted to Roman Catholics brought them into the open, and placed them on terms of equality with other dissenting religious bodies. The variety and number of these in Holywell increased rapidly after 1780 as a result of Welsh religious revival, population growth and industrialisation. Although they shared in common a position outside the privileges offered by membership of the Established Church of England, a new element of competition was introduced, if not necessarily for souls, at least for space. New places of worship had to be accommodated in the townships to provide freedom of worship. The eventual equality, brought about by the recognition of religious toleration, introduced a new element of *laissez fair* into the expression of religious views. This freedom was exercised not only in tin tabernacles but also through the printed word, public meeting and newspaper. Open religious debate in which Catholics were fully involved, became one of the features of the nineteenth century society.

As soon as he arrived at the mission in Holywell, Father Edward Wright set about coping with these developments. His first resolve was to obtain a licence and open a public place of worship and build an elementary school for the education of poor Catholic children. The few local aristocratic and middle class Catholics continued with their loyal financial support but, Father Wright was anxious to discover what property or funds the mission had in trust and how these could be realised. This he did in 1803 when he acquired a full account of the property belonging to the district of St Winefride which information provided full details of land, acreage, and buildings. rental, and tenants in Holywell, Tremeirchion, Whitford, and Caerwys, in Flintshire, and a farm in Llanfechain in Montgomeryshire. There were about 140 acres of land in Flintshire producing a rental of *c.£70 p.a.*, together with a farm of 90 acres at Llanfechain valued at £80 *p.a.* and property in Holywell consolidated in small portions in the Well Street area. The Holywell estate, although small, was valuable from a strategic point of view, and brought in an income of around £60 p.a.[62] This property later provided the resources for the building of a new Catholic chapel at Holywell in 1833 and the Jesuit Theologate of St Beuno's, Tremeirchion, in 1849.

The Catholic Chapel, *c.*1800

Wright achieved his first objective by 1808, if not earlier, when a new Catholic chapel received a licence at the Flintshire Quarter Sessions on 14 July when:

> A certain Chapel at Holywell was recorded as a place of Congregation or Assembly, for religious Worship for persons professing the Roman Catholic Religion, pursuant to the Directions of "An Act to relieve upon Conditions and under Restrictions the persons therein described from certain Penalties and Disabilities, to which Papists or persons professing the Popish Religion, are by Law Subject.[63]

The new chapel was of a modest size (31 feet x 19 feet x 26 feet), built on the same site as the Star Inn founded by George Petre in 1640. Father Wright pulled down part of the old house and built a new house and chapel. The original chapel of the Star (or 'Old Star') remains, and is the kitchen of the present presbytery.

The chapel may have been built a few years earlier.[64] Evidence that it had been built by September 1801 is given in an account of a visit to Holywell by John Bryan, a Wesleyan Methodist preacher. On this occasion an event happened which became part of the folklore of the Methodists, and an early example of nineteenth–century antipathy between Protestants and Catholics in Holywell. It probably arose because the Methodists were resented as intruders encroaching on territory Catholics had long regarded as their own.

The incident took place opposite the new Catholic chapel at the top of Well Street at the end of September 1801. It was the Methodists' second visit: a fortnight previously it was alleged that they had said something which offended the Catholics in a sermon preached in the open air in a place called the 'Five Courts,' almost opposite the new Catholic chapel. This was an open space near the Antelope Inn, a piece of ground used for fights between the local drunks. When John Bryan reached the nearby village of Halkyn, he was warned that the Papists were determined to avenge the words he had spoken against them previously, and that they threatened to murder him if he attempted to preach in the town that day. They implored him not to go there. But Bryan, ignoring this advice, proceeded to the 'Five Courts'. He was warned again, this time by Robert Morris, landlord of the Antelope Inn: 'don't think of preaching here to day, the Papists are sure to murder you. Don't go there; a relation of the priest has his gun loaded, and he will surely kill you.' But Bryan pressed on regardless, and as the yard became crowded, and the hearers were enthused by his fervour, their worship was rudely disturbed by a barrage of stones thrown over the wall into their midst. No record exists of the outcome, apart from the fact that the Methodists opened a chapel in Holywell at the other end of the High Street in 1808.[65]

The registers show that Father Wright baptised 169 candidates between 3 February 1799 and 15 June 1825. Bishop Peter Collingridge, vicar apostolic of the Western District confirmed candidates in the new chapel in 1810 and 1813. The chapel at the Cross Keys was sold in 1802 when the Secular mission removed to Monmouth.

The reminiscences of a Catholic retold his experience of worshipping at the Cross Keys in 1800 shortly before the departure of the Secular Mission.

My father and I used to ride eight miles on Sundays to prayers in a small upstairs room of the old Cross Keys, which was then in an enclosed court yard and gates, and fine old trees between it and the street. Old Mr Jones, the priest, used to come himself, and sitting under the trees, was delighted to see us boys amusing ourselves at play.[66]

There were always a number of Catholics visitors in Holywell. For example, in 1811 it was recorded that there were 11,000 who went to the well, a marked improvement since the time of Thomas Pennant. This increase in numbers may have been the result of travel restrictions imposed by the continental wars against Napoleon. The school, whether it was opened by Father Wright or his successor, was situated in New Road on the hill on the west side of the parish churchyard. During his last year at Holywell his namesake, Father Henry Wright, assisted Father Edward Wright. He took charge of the Mission on the death of the old priest in April 1826, and remained until the arrival of Father Francis Lythgoe who took charge on All Saints' Day following.

The ministry of Father Francis Lythgoe, SJ, 1826–42

Father Francis Lythgoe (b. 1796, d.1873) was the ideal person to succeed Father Wright. The elder man had brought stability, wisdom and patience to the Jesuit Mission, and saw it restored. His pastoral ministry gave his successor something to build on. Lythgoe was young, energetic, and enthusiastic: a nineteenth century man, at the dawning of a new age for Catholicism, and his sixteen years at Holywell was marked by major changes which were to transform the Church there. The granting of Catholic emancipation, the building of a new St Winefride's Church, close contact with the Jesuit Mission through his cousin Father Randall Lythgoe, English Provincial of the Society stimulated progress. He (Randall) was responsible in 1848 for the foundation of St Beuno's College on land at Tremeirchion belonging to the Holywell mission.

Catholic Emancipation, 1829

Catholic emancipation was granted in April 1829. This gave Catholics the right to be admitted to Parliament. Prime Minister Wellington and Home Secretary Peel were forced, by the actions of O'Connell in Ireland, to persuade George IV to give his assent to the measure. The nation was divided on the issue, which was forced through because of the fear of Irish revolt. Protestants on the whole were appalled and angry, and gave expressions to their feelings in large gatherings.

   The churchwardens of Holywell were responsible for convening an anti–Catholic meeting at the Bell Inn on the 18 February 1829 to sign a petition against the measure which requested Parliament to refuse concessions to Catholics. The gathering was a rowdy affair attended by five hundred people of whom four hundred signed the petition. The press described it as 'uproarious', and Father Lythgoe failed to get a hearing because it was 'contended that the meeting was not assembled for the purpose of discussion, but for that of petitioning,' and he couldn't be heard in the uproar. The petitioners declared that 'they respected the laws and clung to the religion of their forefathers in which they hoped to live and die,' and that 'they viewed with apprehension and alarm the recommendations for Catholic Emancipation,' and stated that 'the adoption of such a measure we sincerely believe to be incompatible with the security of the State and the ascendancy of the Protestant religion.' This was the view of the majority of the speakers, and the feeling of most of those present, although a small minority who advocated views to the contrary made themselves heard. One who protested against the petition was Mr Francis Jones who was reported as saying:

> The Catholics were as worthy a body of men and as loyal and trusty as any other class of his Majesty's Subjects; and he felt exceedingly sorry that any Clergyman of the Church of England could be found to prepare an address expressive of contrary sentiments towards them. He was not a man to be put down by clamour. He would again assert, in the face of this meeting, that the Catholics were so, and he appealed to the experience his townsmen had of those Catholics among them. He had hoped to see the Clergy of the Established Church cementing the bonds of peace and order, and not pointing out a valuable sect of fellow Christians to obloquy and ignominy.

The press noted that at this point the uproar became absolutely deafening, and Mr Jones was compelled to give way. Mr Richard Addison failed to be heard when attempting to introduce a counter petition expressing satisfaction with Catholic Emancipation. The report of *The Chronicle* concluded: 'We are confident that deducting the Roman Catholics themselves, nine tenths of the population are unfriendly to Catholic concessions.'[67]

What mattered, however, was that Catholics had regained most of the freedoms they had lost at the Reformation, and could now begin a process of reinstatement in society, which would no longer be obstructed by legal penalties but dependent upon religious toleration. This process of Catholic recognition and growth in Holywell is the major underlying assumption in their history in the nineteenth century.

Household accounts, 1826–7

Household accounts from the Catholic presbytery indicate that Father Lythgoe travelled much on horseback throughout Flintshire, visiting the small villages on the Mission and a new church at Denbigh. He bought a map of north Wales for his own guidance, and Fleury's *historical catechism* for instruction of others. He purchased a whip, double–bridle, and horseshoes. He rode to Stonyhurst and Scarisbrick, and began to negotiate for the two thousand pounds required for building a larger Catholic chapel and opening an elementary school in New Road. He paid Isaac Taylor, surveyor, for mapping the estate. Sanitation was improved at the presbytery, and the house renovated. A variety of fish and meat was purchased, including a live pig, which was later killed. Money was spent on the wear and tear of clothes after hours spent in the saddle. Lythgoe's great coat was mended, a new suit of clothes, shirts, and trousers were made. There was a variety of drink: rum, brandy, whisky, ale, porter, buttermilk, tea, and coffee. Ten shillings and sixpence was subscribed to the Holywell newsroom and the indispensable Molly received seven guineas a year for running the household.

St Winefride's Church, 1832–3

In October 1828 Father Lythgoe enquired of the Revd C. Brooke: 'Perhaps you can give me some information as to what amount of money you can advance towards building the chapel. Perhaps also Mr Scott might get something handsome from some of his charitable friends in London for the same purpose.'[68]

The cost of building the new chapel was paid for by subscriptions raised by Father Lythgoe and money advanced by the funds of the Society of Jesus. Probably each of these two sources raised a thousand pounds. Tŷ Coch farm at Llanfechain in Montgomeryshire provided the security for an arrangement by which the Jesuits in the North Wales District borrowed a thousand pounds from the Society in the Lancashire District on the strength of the payment of two–thirds of the revenue from the farm, with the remainder of the rent continuing to support the Holywell mission.[69] In the meantime, Father Lythgoe began collecting donations. In December 1830, Lord Shrewsbury replied to his appeal that he 'felt happy to allow his name to be put down as a subscriber of £100 to my new Chapel and School.'

Father Lythgoe built a larger chapel on the same site to replace the one erected by Father Wright thirty years earlier. It was one of the earliest church designs of J. J. Scoles (1798–1863), and was built in what has been described as 'dignified Neo–Classical with a west front of ashlar and a pedimented central projection.'[70]

The chapel ,dedicated, to St Winefride, was opened for public worship on Wednesday 13 November 1833 by Dr Briggs, co–adjutor bishop of the Northern District. The ceremony included a Pontifical High Mass. Present were 'a numerous body of Catholic Clergy', a choir and vocalists from Liverpool assisted by others from Chester. After the gospel, Father R. Sumner of Stonyhurst gave a homily in the presence of 'some of the most influential gentry of the neighbour-hood.' The opening of the Catholic chapel was reported in a letter to the editor of the *Chester Chronicle* by a correspondent who appeared to have been overcome by the occasion. The writer lamented the deprivation since the time of the Reformation of so many impressive ceremonies which he had witnessed on that occasion: 'the splendid procession, the gorgeous attire of the clergy followed by a bishop wearing a mitre decorated with embroidery of gold and silver, and studded with jewels, bearing in his hand a golden crosier.' A collection for Catholic charities in Holywell realised the sum of £70.[71]

Such a note worthy occasion was an opportunity for Catholics in the District of St Winefride to celebrate the freedom brought them in 1829 by the granting of Catholic emancipation. The following day, Bishop Briggs ministered the sacrament of confirmation to an impressive number of candidates drawn from the parishes around which included forty–one candidates from Holywell, one from Wrexham, and eight persons of the Talacre Catholic congregation.[72]

The Mostyn family return to Talacre, 1823

The confirmation candidates from Talacre were the first fruits of the return of the Mostyn family to their estate where they erected a chapel in 1829, dedicated to Our Lady of Mount Carmel. In 1823, Sir Edward Mostyn, Baronet (1785–1841), succeeded to the Talacre estate on the death of his father and decided to take up residence there whilst retaining his estate in Worcester. This was a matter of great rejoicing in the Holywell area, and when he returned home in December 1823 twelve thousand people turned out to welcome him. They escorted him to the White Horse Inn in the town led by the band of the Flintshire militia. Sir Edward, to mark his intention of living amongst his tenants, decided to build a new mansion at Talacre. The foundation stone of this was laid in July 1824, and the house destroyed by fire in September 1827, but immediately rebuilt by the architect Thomas Jones of Chester, in the Tudor–Gothic style. It was reported in 1841 that, on the morning of his death, Sir Edward was up early and proceeded to the performance of his religious duties in his chapel, following which he had a fatal seizure at the breakfast table. Until the family sold the Holywell estate in 1920, they exerted great authority in the area to the benefit of the Catholic cause.

Father Lythgoe became involved in the affairs of the town and was above all determined to protect the Catholic interest in St Winefride's Well.

NOTES

1. C. David, op cit, attributes this incident to Holywell, although Foley in his discussion of the Residence of St Winefride places this report under Welshpool. Wherever it took place it shows the anti Catholic reaction at this time. Foley, 5, p. 943.
2. Foley, op cit, vol. 5, p. 943.
3. *Letters and Notices*, vol. 31, 1911–12, p. 182.
4. Quoted in T. G. Holt, 'Jesuits in Montgomeryshire 1670–1873', *Journal of Welsh Religious History*, vol. 1, 1993, p. 72.
5. Great Sesions Denbighshire, 4/34/23/86, NLW. Reference from Mr K. Lloyd Gruffydd.
6. Priest.
7. *Daffodils under the snow*, Franciscans in Wales, p. 21.
8. Letters and Notices, op cit, p. 183.
9. J. A. Hilton, *Catholic Lancashire*, (Phillimore, 1994), p. 48, and J. H. Hodson, *A History of Cheshire Restoration to Industrial Revolution 1660–1780*, (Chester, 1978), p. 19, and HMC, 14th Report, appendix, part iv, pp. 301–04.

10. Born Flintshire in 1668, probably at Holywell, *c.*1703 died there 2 Aug 1718.

11. Born Caernarfonshire, was at Cross Keys in 1702 and *c.*1715 resident there.

12. J. Morris, *Catholic England in Modern Times* (Burns & Oates, 1892), pp. 13–14.

13. J. O. Payne, *Records of the English Catholics* (Burns & Oates, 1889), p.123.

14. *The Political State of Great Britain*, vol. xvi, July 1718, p. 69.

15. Foley, 4, p. 529.

16. Anstruther, op cit, vol. 3, pp. 181–2. William Quatermain, alias Wilmot, secretary to Bishop Leyburn in 1685, died at Holywell, 2 August 1720.

17. Ibid, p. 199.

18. Payne, op cit, pp. 99–100.

19. *The Works of the Right Reverend William Fleetwood, DD* (Oxford, 1854), vol. 3.

20. Ibid, p. 221.

21. Ibid, p. 239.

22. Ibid, p. 251.

23. Pennant, op cit, *Whiteford and Holywell*, p242 and incumbents visitation returns to the Bishop of St Asaph and Rural Deans Reports at regular intervals in the eighteenth century see Schedule St Asaph Diocesan Record, NLW.

24. SA/Misc/1353, NLW.

25. SA/Mis/1368, NLW.

26. Ibid.

27. Bishop of St Asaph, 1731, d.1735, author of *Notitia Monastica*.

28. SA/Let/1061, NLW.

29. FRO, Holywell Overseers records.

30. SA/QA/1/171, NLW.

31. SA/MB/58, NLW.

32. SA/QA/5, NLW.

33 E. S. Worrall (ed), *Returns of Papists 1767*, vol. 2, Dioceses of England and Wales except Chester, Catholic Record Society (1989), pp. 180–2.

34. HL/PO/10/10/7/620, Nov 11 1780.

35. SA/QA/15, 1809 NLW.

36. G. H. Jenkins, 'Literature, Religion and Society in Wales 1660–1730', *Studies in Welsh History* (Cardiff, 1978), p. 230, quoting Lewis Morris.

37. C. Morris (ed), *The Journeys of Celia Fiennes* (Cresset Press, 1967), pp. 180–1.

38. Ibid, p. 179.

39. D. Defoe, *A Tour through England and Wales* (Dent, London and Toronto), No. 821 Everyman' Library, vol. 2, p. 66

40. I have to thank Dr Marie Rowlands for this reference and Sheffield Archives for permission to publish this extract from the diary of William Statham of Hathersage reference MD 6853, pp. 136–138

41.J. W. Hebel (ed), *Polyolbion*; M. Drayton, op cit, vol. 4, pp. 204–5

42. *The Great Diurnal of Nicholas Blundell*, 3 vols (1968, 1970, 1972), edited by J. J. Bagley and transcribed and annotated by F. Tyrer, The Record Society of Lancashire and Cheshire

43. Ibid, vol. 3, pp. 49–50.

44. A. Bristow, *Dr Johnson & Mrs Thrale Tour in North Wales, 1774* (Bridge Books, Wrexham, 1994), pp. 40–41.

45. Ibid, p. 104.

46. R. James, *Iter Lancastrenses; A Poem Written 1603*, Chetham Society 7, (1845) old series, p. 8.

47. FRO QS/SR/46/18, 1761. Epiphany reference from K. L. Gruffydd.

48. NLW 4/1010/10/28, reference from K. L. Gruffydd.

49 Thomas Pennant, *Tour on the Continent 1765*, edited with notes by G. R. De Beer, Ray Society, 1948.

50. Ibid, p. 167–8.

51. Ibid, p. 172.

52. Thomas Pennant, op cit, *History of Whiteford and Holywell*, p. 230.

53. Ibid, 230–1.

54. Bull, 1773, *Dominus ac Redemptor*, 1814. *Sollicitudo omnium Ecclesarum*.

55. Holt, op cit, 1993, Montgomeryshire, p. 75.

56, Pennant, op cit, *History of Whitford and Holywell*, p. 244.

57. Letters and Notices 1869, miscellaneous paper, *History of the Mission of Holywell*, Father Lythgoe, SJ, p. 280.

58. *Letters and Notices*, vol. 31, 1911–12.

59. There are two sets of accounts (i) 1748–1754, FRO, MF 34, and (ii) *c*.1827–8, FRO, RC/30/2.

60. Wrexham Diocesan Archive, nd (*c*.1870) from MS *History of Holywell*. Benedict XIV granted the four Plenary Indulgences in 1753.

61. Hook, op cit, *The Catholic Registers of Holywell*.

62. FRO, MF/6.

63. 31 Geo 3, c.32 (1791).

64. 1800 is the date given in the anonymous *History of Holywell* in the Wrexham Diocesan Archives. Quarter Sessions Licences were often issued retrospectively.

65. D. Young, *History of Methodism in Wales* (London, 1893), pp. 472–4.

66. *Flintshire Observer*, 11/6/1869.

67. *Chester Courant*, Feb 1829, *Chester Chronicle*, 27/2/1829.

68. FRO, M/F5.

69. Holt, *Journal of Welsh Religious History*, vol. I, 1993, p. 76.

70. E. Hubbard, *Buildings of Wales, Clwyd*, op cit, p. 374. A Certificate of the Registration of the new Chapel was obtained from the clerk of the peace of the county of Flint on 6 April 1837 see FRO, RC/30/7.

71. *Chester Chronicle*, 22/11/1833.

72. Ibid, Registers.

SECTION THREE

1830–1930
Recovery and Rejoicing

Introduction

This final section shows Catholic recovery and reinstatement in British society after repeal of penal legislation which had deprived them of their freedom from the middle of the sixteenth century. St Winefride's Well and the Jesuit Mission in Holywell showed remarkable signs of recovery and a return to large pilgrimages. There was overwhelming evidence of cures to pilgrims who came in thousands for healing, a phenomenon which earned Holywell the title of 'the Lourdes of Wales.' An element of celebration and rejoicing eventually found expression in processions led by newly commissioned banners and statues of the Blessed Virgin Mary and St Winifred. The Catholic community in the neighbourhood benefited from the foundation of the Jesuit College of St Beuno in 1848. The marriage of Louisa Pennant, heiress of Downing, to Viscount Feilding, heir to the Earl of Denbigh, and their conversion to Catholicism established a Franciscan friary in the neighbourhood at Pantasaph in the 1850s. The Mostyn family of Talacre and the Feildings of Downing were now chief landowners in the town of Holywell until their estates were broken up at the beginning of the twentieth century. One of the Mostyn sons, Francis, was appointed vicar apostolic in 1895 and first bishop of Menevia in 1898 and later archbishop of Cardiff.

The story was not without its moments of drama and surprise. There was an ongoing dispute about the ownership of the well and chapel, on occasions antipathy between Catholic visitors and local Protestants erupted in violence; a Lancashire entrepreneur caused dismay when he proposed bottling the well water; an itinerant artist and writer named Corvo quarrelled dramatically with the Jesuit Father Beauclerk; the well ran dry in 1917 and had to be re–supplied. Throughout these adventures the chief focus was on St Winefride and her well, which continue into the twenty–first century to maintain their attraction to pilgrims, visitors, and those who seek their consolations. In 1930, the Jesuits surrendered their mission (which had begun in the 1590s) to the diocese of Menevia,

The first themes discussed in this final section is the rejuvenation of the well in the nineteenth century.

8. The Rejuvenation of St Winefride's Well

Introduction

The word 'rejuvenation' is employed to suggest renewal, principally in terms of the acquisition of new vitality, but also to indicate the combination of various aspects of such restoration. There were efforts to improve the well and chapel building in the physical sense of improvement, repair and the provision of facilities for pilgrims. There was the obvious renewal and demonstration of the Catholic presence at the well in terms both of the medieval pilgrimage experience and a desire to celebrate the freedom to march in procession with banners and statues. And there was a subtler impact of a new vitality in the approach to the curative qualities of the well and the explanation and interpretation of the evidence of reported cures. This combination of effort to respect and enhance the sacred space of St Winefride's Well succeeded because of the dedication and sincerity of those who espoused, presented, and reported the cult of St Winefride from the beginning of the nineteenth century. The commitment and expectation of pilgrim and guardian contributed to this process of rejuvenation and was blessed by the vision of exceptional individuals.

Bishop John Milner and the cure of Winefride White, 1805

In 1805, Bishop John Milner published a pamphlet, *Authentic documents relative to the miraculous cure of Winefrid White of Wolverhampton at St Winefride's Well on the 28th of June 1805*. Milner was vicar apostolic of the Midland District (1803–26), a recognised and able religious controversialist, well–respected within the Catholic community, whose voice and authority carried beyond its bounds. He brought a rigorous and systematic method of enquiry to the cure of Winefride White, aimed at silencing sceptics.

Winefrid White was twenty–six years of age in 1805, and having suffered for three years it was apparent to her physicians and herself that they had failed to cure her or provide any relief. She was pronounced incurable, and was practically bedridden and unable to work because a severe affection of the left hip and the back bone, apparently a paralysis from a curvature of the spine. She was only able to walk with the aid of a crutch under her right arm, and used to drag her whole left side as if it had been dead. Finding herself in this helpless condition Winefrid White came to Holywell and was cured.

Hearing about her cure, Bishop Milner set about proving its veracity by collecting information from witnesses of the event and people who had known her during her illness and following her cure. Milner's energy and desire to get at the truth led him to Wolverhampton, Manchester, Liverpool, and Holywell, mostly in September 1805, where he gathered sworn statements, 'authentic documents' which provided him with proof of the 'miraculous cure.' Four months from the date of the cure he had collected the necessary evidence and published it.

He first interviewed Winefrid White and 'took it down from her lips in writing.' In her sworn declaration she described the nature, length, and progress of her illness, and the treatment she received from two medical men, Dr Underhill and Mr Samuel Stubbs, and its ineffectiveness. On its failure:

> Winefrid thought of applying to Almighty God for supernatural relief; and as she had read and heard of many miraculous cures that had been performed by his power and goodness, at Holywell, in Flintshire, through the prayers of the blessed Virgin Mary and St Winefrid, she felt a strong inclination to get herself conveyed thither.

Aided by encouragement from her Catholic mistress, Mrs Withenbery, with whom she was a servant, she set off alone from Wolverhampton by the Shrewsbury stagecoach, and eventually arrived in Holywell. She described to Milner what happened on the following day.

> The next morning, the 28th of June, about seven o'clock, having performed those daily acts of devotion which she had constantly performed ever since she formed the first design of visiting Holywell she left her lodging, which was situated at the house of Mrs Humphreys in Well Street, and with the utmost difficulty crawled down to what is called St Winefrid's Well in company with a Mrs Midghall and the two Mrs Bromleys, ladies who had arrived from Liverpool at Holywell the same day that she did. One of the latter, she says was so charitable as to assist her in bathing. She describes the effect of the water, upon her being immersed in it, as so much surprising and overpowering her, that she was unable to recollect herself, or attend to the state of her health, till she began to change her bathing dress in the adjoining cabin, belonging to a Mrs Needham who attends at the well, when she found herself able to stand upon her left leg as firmly as upon her right leg, and that the excruciating pains in her back, and her other pains and maladies had quite left her; in a word, that she was in every respect perfectly

88. *Facing page: Interior of St Winefride's Well by J. Ingleby, c.1790. [NLW]*

well. She says, that remaining a fortnight longer at Holywell, she bathed two or three times more in compliance with custom and to satisfy the importunity of her friends, but without any sensible benefit to her health, as in, in fact, she was perfectly cured at her first bathing, and enabled to walk, run, or work as ever …

Isabella Midghall of Liverpool described what happened after the visit to the well.

Upon being dressed she walked with me and my companions home (Mrs Humphreys in Well St), with the greatest strength and liveliness, having left her crutch behind her in testimony of her cure. After breakfast she walked with us to Greenfield Abbey, the distance of a mile or more, and back again, and ran down one of the hills, to show that she was perfectly cured …

Mrs Jane Needham testified to Bishop Milner that Winefride White:

… came to this Well in a very languid state, and all in a flutter, and to my thinking, helpless on one side. She bathed after which I saw her walking and running up and down the steps in my house, as it were rejoicing at the recovery of her health. She left her crutch here, with the mark of her name, and seemed perfectly cured.

Father Edward Wright gave the bishop a written certificate stating that he had seen the young lady when she arrived:

… supporting herself on a crutch; and, on the following day, about ten in the morning, she again presented herself to me perfectly upright, having been released from her infirmity after bathing in St Winefrid's Well.

Samuel Stubbs, her surgeon, who had last seen Winefrid White two or three days before she set out for Holywell, met her on return to Wolverhampton at the end of July, and told Milner:

I met her in the streets, to my utter astonishment, walking with as much firmness, vigour and agility as any other young persons of her age. All the above mentioned fatal symptoms, as she declares, and I have reason to believe, have disappeared. The ligaments of the vertebrae are contracted and firm, as I ascertained yesterday (Sept. 10), though a certain small enlargement of them is discernible, being rather a mark of her past weakness, than any present inconvenience; she holding herself perfectly erect, and moving, in every respect, with the vigour and activity of perfect health. These changes so extraordinary, compleat, and performed in so short a time, I am unable to account for, by any principle of medicine I am acquainted with, or by any experience I have had in it.[1]

After presenting the written declarations of Winefrid White and fifteen other witnesses to her 'miraculous cure,' Bishop Milner gave his conclusions. The evidence would have satisfied the criteria of the learned Bishop Fleetwood! Milner asserted that he did not hear any witness contradict or invalidate the reality of the reported fact, and that the witnesses perfectly agreed together and their depositions supported each other. It added weight to the evidence that the greater part of the witnesses were unacquainted: they came from different places, were of different stations in life, and were a mixture of Protestants, Catholics, English and Welsh. From their evidence he was led to conclude 'in plain terms an EVIDENT MIRACLE has been wrought amongst us.'[2]

Bishop Milner then gave an authoritative endorsement of the healing power of St Winefride's Well which is worth quoting in full because it stated the official Catholic opinion regarding cures at Holywell. It was a useful position to re–establish at the beginning of the nineteenth century. Bishop Milner added authority to the statement, and for many Catholics and Protestants it provided a reasonable argument to use against sceptics who might be led to support the conclusions of Bishop Fleetwood.

Milner was anxious that St Winefride's Well should be regarded as more than a cold bath 'endowed with a natural salubrious quality.' He did not wish 'to deny the natural efficacy of cold–bathing, and drinking of cold water, either at Holywell or anywhere else.' He went further in his claims for the nature of cures recorded at Holywell.

> But I think I am warranted in maintaining that these, as *natural remedies*, never yet cured a patient in the lamentable situation of this young woman. Thus much I am perfectly sure of, that whatever considerable good effects have ever been produced by these or other natural remedies, have taken place *gradually* and by a *repetition* of them. But here, observe, is the case of a young woman who is restored from the most desperate state of illness to the most perfect state of health in a *minute*, at her *first immersion in the fountain*. At the same time, I am very remote from questioning that other cures as extraordinary as the one in question have hitherto been performed at Holywell. On the contrary, I am convinced, not only from authentic records [*Milner refers the reader to 'see in particular the miraculous cure of Sir Roger Boddennham'], but also from the testimony of the subjects of them, or of other living witnesses, that such miraculous cures have actually taken place.
>
> But then I maintain, that on all such occasions the cures have been sought for and obtained, as on the present occasion, by supernatural means, namely by prayer, and a strong faith in the omnipotence of God, with hope in the prayers offered up to God by the blessed Virgin Mary and St Winefrid.[3]

Bishop Milner takes the opportunity of stating the view of Catholic theologians on the continuation of miracles uninterrupted down to the present time. He states that Catholics believe in modern miracles: 'such events happen from time to time, and of course the present prodigy, in our opinion does not stand alone.'[4] His pamphlet closes with a statement which could not fail to attract pilgrims to Holywell.

> For every known miracle is the voice of God proclaiming to men his infinite power, goodness, and providence in their regard. It calls therefore for a renewal of our profound homage, of our ardent love, and of our entire confidence in him, under all the accidents and sufferings that we do or may experience. Every miracle is moreover a divine sanction of the religious worship or devout practices, for the sake of which, or by means of which, such supernatural communications with man has taken place. Hence the present miraculous cure, obtained of Almighty God by the prayers of the Blessed Virgin and of St Winefrid, who had been invoked for this purpose, at a place consecrated to the memory of the latter for more than a thousand years ago, ought to confirm us in our faith …[5]

The importance to the status of St Winefride's Well of the investigation of the cure of Winefrid White and the publicity which Bishop Milner gave it, has been seen as 'taking Holywell back into the public imagination. It was sufficient to breathe new life into a declining religious cult which was suited to the temperament and spirituality of a large proportion of nineteenth century Englishmen.'[6]

The cure of Sister Mary Ann Wood, 1809

Another cure associated with St Winefride's Well took place at the Franciscan Monastery at Taunton three years later, when Mary Ann Wood, a lay sister, made a remarkable recovery from a serious injury to her arm. The manner in which the cure was confirmed suggests familiarity with Bishop Milner's pamphlet about the 'miraculous cure' of Winefrid White which had by this time gone through a number of editions.

Sister Wood, when opening a sash window in March 1809, slashed the tendons of her arm and as a result lost the use of her hand and the injured arm and hand began to wither. All attempts by the surgeon to restore the limb failed, and he declared that she would never regain complete use in her hand. Sister Wood, however, did not lose hope and 'with the approbation of the Reverend Mother Abbess determined to make a *Novena* in honour of St Winefride.' The report of the cure made it clear that:

> … she had no idea of asking for a miracle, but confidently believed and hoped that He who made the arm would restore to her, through the intercession of the Saint, some small use of it. On the 6th of August she put on it a piece of moss from Holywell & began the Novena: after this she suffered excruciating pain in it, so that she was tempted to take off the moss, till she reasoned with herself that

it could not possibly be the cause of such pain. She continued particularly recollected all that evening, praying mentally, without taking notice of her arm. To her great surprise when she got up the next morning she found it perfectly cured.

There was some perplexity about publicly making it known that Sister Wood had been healed in such a dramatic way. The cure was apparent to the surgeon who had so unsuccessfully treated her for over five months. An eminent London surgeon, when presented with the facts confirmed that there was a cure, which in his eyes was inexplicable and contrary to medical experience. The vicar apostolic of the Western District, Dr Collingridge, having heard the evidence, gave 'as his detailed opinion that the cure was supernatural & an evident miracle.' Once again weighing up authentic evidence a Catholic bishop had investigated the 'miraculous cure' of a woman whose faith and devotion led her in prayer to call upon God and to St Winefride to intercede for her. Moreover Sister Wood had used moss from the holy well as a poultice on the limb which was healed.[7] Mr Charles Weld wrote years afterwards that the cut, though healed never closed, so that 'you could put your finger in it between the divided tendons, and yet she could use her hand and arms, as if they were entire.'[8]

The cure of Mary White, 1830

Mary White, it was reported by a Catholic priest in December 1830, 'has by the blessing of God, obtained a complete and miraculous cure of her maladies.' These were serious consisting of cancer of the face and a resultant loss of sight. Her condition was pronounced incurable at Salisbury Infirmary and by her surgeon, Dr Wates. In these circumstances Mary White was fortunate to receive help from Lord and Lady Arundell, head of the noted recusant family at Wardour. On hearing of her condition, they instructed their priest Father Parker to apply to St Winefride's Well for a supply of water and moss to apply to the face cancer. When Father Parker received these gifts he made clear their purpose.

We explained to the patient that she was not to consider the application as any charm or medical remedy, but to be used and applied in the prayer of faith, confiding in the goodness of God and the powerful intercession of His saints. On the first application the patient declared she found the pains which she had so long suffered ceased. She continued to use the application of the moss and water for a considerable time. The dreadful wound gradually healed, and now I am happy to inform you that the cancer is perfectly cured.

Parker informed his readers that Mary White had regained her sight and completely recovered from her maladies. Bishop Baines had been informed, and those who had witnessed the cure 'have every reason to give thanks to Almighty God for this signal instance'.[9]

89. 'St Winifred's Well' (note the neglect of the chapel roof): engraving by H. Wallis after H. Gastineau, 1830.

The joyful and moving accounts of the 'miraculous cures' of three devout Catholic women (two Mary's and a Winifred), all of them authenticated by three vicars apostolic, must be seen as a remarkable attestation of the cult of St Winefride. Each of the women's cure narratives re–emphasised the particular devotion inspired by the Saint. Their stories showed that the ritual of bathing at the well had not changed over the centuries, nor the peculiar effect of water and moss as simple objects associated with the curative spring of St Winefride's.

The development of the precincts of St Winefrides Well, 1836–73

The only information we have for the care and upkeep of the well in the eighteenth century is derived from a number of engravings of artists whose illustrations are liberally used in this text. They were produced to satisfy aristocratic patrons, and advance the careers of a new generation of topographical artists who found a new inspiration in the picturesque, the discovery of the beauties of Cambria, the poetry of the bards and legends of Welsh saints. The only major work to the well in the eighteenth century was undertaken sometime between 1710 and 1740. It was the construction of a plunge bath immediately in front of the entrance to the well crypt as approached from the north.

There is very little evidence of repairs to the well crypt or the chapel above it. An isolated entry is in the Vestry Book: 'Lay'd out on the new Stairs to ye Well £2 4s. 9d. May 9th 1716.' Another reference to remedial work, to reinforce support for the chapel was discovered in 1938 when the well crypt was inspected. The architect[10] noted in his report:

The western pier of the arcade between the nave and the north aisle of the chapel, supporting the main northern wall of the nave and the roof, rests on a stone lintel. This lintel rests at its northern end on a pier supported on the centre of an arch over the entrance to the steps descending into the well. The lintel has proved insuficient and has broken through its centre. A stone pillar, 1' 0" x 9", has been erected under it. This pillar bears the date 1754 and probably was constructed at that date when the lintel threatened to collapse.[11]

The well crypt and chapel were under the management of the vicar and churchwardens. It was recognised that repairs to St Winefride's Chapel were met out of the churchwarden's accounts, and repairs to the well crypt and other works in the precincts, particularly those relating to the public water supply, out of the rates levied by the vestry. The vestry appointed and paid a well keeper who lived in a cottage in the precincts. The account of the cure of Winefride White in 1805 gave an insight into the well–keeper's duties at the beginning of the nineteenth century. There were probably other arrangements in place to accommodate Catholic pilgrims, with persons hiring bathing dresses, to control access to the well and to take charge of the communal system of water supply.

What is most apparent, however, is the distinct lack of care for the building and its immediate precincts. The ownership of land in the vicinity of the well was divided in two by the stream issuing from it: that on the west side, together with riparian rights to the water, belonged to Sir Pyers Mostyn, Bart, of Talacre; land on the east bank to the Grosvenor family (later the dukes of Westminster), who inherited the lordship of Holywell at the beginning of the nineteenth century.

90. An unusual view of St Winefride's Well: aquatint by J. Havell after a print in
E. Pugh, Cambria Depicta, *1816.*

91. *St Winifred's Well. William Latham, 1824. The drawing shows the mill, brewery, waterpower for industrial purposes and overcrowding by adjacent buildings. [Manchester Archives and Local Studies, NFF741 L25]*

Their main concern, and those of other industrialists, was to exploit the force of water issuing from St Winefride's Well. Corn mills had jostled with the well site for a thousand years. Brewing and a cotton mill, all dependent on the same rapid watercourse whose power was harnessed immediately it left the shadow of the fountain, to drive a number of mills and works down stream.

This neglect, overcrowding, and unplanned arrangement of the precinct to St Winefride's Well has been depicted by artists in a multitude of ways. An engraving in the *Gentleman's Magazine*, August 1804, shows a cottage erected at the doorstep of the entrance on the north side of St Winefride's Chapel. A view from the south by William Latham in 1824 has as its subject an entroughed watercourse with a mill and brewery alongside. Another engraving, taken from Edward Pugh's *Cambria Depicta*, is a view from Greenfield Street, with Smalley's cotton mill in the foreground. W. Wallis in 1831 portrayed the sacred space of St Winefride's Well serenely nestling in the midst of these dark satanic mills, its exterior bathing pool neatly railed off.

St Winefride's Well, the source of the town's water supply
Water was the dominant issue in Holywell local government throughout the nineteenth century, and continued until the 1920s. Treffynnon (Well Town), had an inadequate water supply, and spent a hundred years debating the best means to provide a public water supply. As one writer has so graphically put it, 'the story of cholera in Wales was the story of the Welsh marinating in their own filth.'[12] Cholera visited Holywell in 1832 and killed around a hundred people, and again in 1849, when another forty–six were victims. One critic, at the end of the century, went so far as to rename the town 'Sewers end.'[13] Throughout the nineteenth century a public supply of water was available from a cistern near St Winefride's Well, from where it was pumped and carried by townsfolk, whilst others were supplied by Joe Barker, the blind water seller, from his donkey and cart. A letter from 'a ratepayer' in 1861 commenting on the plight of women stated that he was:

> … grieved with the perpetual sight of females breasting the hills from St Winefride's Well, the Roft toft and other places with large tins of water on their heads particularly because the limited number of houses available compelled large families to live in overcrowded conditions, which necessitates the greatest regard for cleanliness.

The writer urged that a meeting of the Holywell vestry be summoned to discuss the possibility of finding an adequate water supply.[14] Five years later, during the cholera outbreak, the Roft toft well was contaminated with sewage and caused the death of eighty–eight people.[15]

Whenever the question of the provision of a public water supply was discussed,

92. Blind Joe Barker carrying water and selling it from door to door c.1910.

it divided public opinion, inflamed tempers, and, on more than one occasion, the dispute was finally settled in the House of Lords. As the nineteenth century advanced, more people became involved in discussion through the reform of local government. When the great Parliamentary Reform Act was passed in June 1832 the bells rang, cannons fired, and thousands marched in procession to celebrate, accompanied by bands and banners, from Flint through Holywell to Mostyn. In the midst of this triumph came the cholera. The visitation was remembered years later.

> Many of the leading townspeople, were seen walking in the streets in the morning and were carried to their graves at eventide. Scores of them were fatally attacked. It was a remarkable fact that the majority of those who died were among the poorer class of the population, while, in the year 1849, the bulk of the fatal cases were among the well–to–do portion of the community. So serious was the aspect of things that the chapels were crowded at five o'clock in the morning.[16]

Reform gradually introduced improved living conditions and began to tackle social problems through the devolution of powers to localities through a succession of local government measures which culminated in the creation of Holywell Urban District Council in 1894. An early example of this was the new Poor Law of 1834. In 1838–40 the elected Board of Poor Law Guardians built a Union workhouse, which conveniently moved the poor out of town. Ratepayers were granted power to elect representative bodies, beginning with the vestry, and from 1862 the local board. These elected boards were divided into committees to implement parliamentary legislation. St Winefride's Well was managed through one of these committees, and its affairs became the concern of the meetings of the local board and on occasions at specially convened public meetings.

Public health reform became one of the cornerstones in the creation of a new society in Victorian Britain. It began the crusade for the eradication of dirt and disease, the removal of the 'great stink' and provision of sewerage schemes, slum clearance and notification of infectious disease. The availability of an efficient modern water supply was the only means to carry out public health legislation and meet the demands of industrial and domestic consumers. St Winefride's Well was the only local natural water supply, and therefore became the focus of every new initiative for an improved supply.

In making decisions about water supply the people of Holywell acted from a simple premise: 'St Winefride's Well is our water'. It followed from this starting point that they were responsible for all other related questions, such as, who is allowed to use the water? How do we safeguard our interests as a controlling authority? What regulations do we make for the use of the water? How do we decide what actions to take? How do we raise money to pay for improvements? Unfortunately, events were to prove that the simple assumption by the Holywell townsfolk that 'St Winefride's Well is our water' was to be challenged for the next hundred years. Disputes had to be settled about the ownership of St Winefride's Well and the chapel buildings. Boundary disputes occurred over land in the precincts of the well. The townsfolk, in safeguarding the water supply, found themselves in opposition to a powerful mining company whose drainage scheme had a disastrous effect on the well. Anglicans and Roman Catholics had to learn to live side by side and not disturb each other's devotions. The story of St Winefride's Well from 1836–1936 revolves around these questions.

The first scheme proposed for the improvement of St Winefride's Well, 1836–8
In 1836 a meeting was summoned by a majority of Protestant ratepayers to discuss the revival of the traditional Catholic pilgrimage centre. Ironically, after three hundred years of persecution and suppression, the first resolutions to inaugurate improvements were proposed by the Jesuit missioner, Father Francis Lythgoe, SJ. A major change in outlook had taken place since he was shouted down seven years earlier at a meeting on the eve of Catholic emancipation.

In 1836 the townspeople decided

> … to determine upon some plan for the immediate restoration of the beautiful edifice [and that] the first step to be taken in this praiseworthy project was to endeavour to obtain possession from the Most Noble the Marquess of Westminster of the waste land contiguous to the Well, and also two cottages,

which have for many years been allowed to interfere with and disgrace the architectural order of this ancient building. For this purpose a deputation was appointed consisting of the Rev. Francis Lythgoe, SJ, Cofner Oldfield Esq., and Mr Churchwarden Simon, to wait upon his Lordship and explain to him the improvements the parishioners were desirous to effect. The deputation was kindly received and most hospitably entertained at Eaton. The noble Marquess applauded the design, and immediately removed the first obstacle to its accomplishment by liberally offering to secure possession to the town by lease both of the cottages and land at a nominal rent.[17]

On 15 July 1837, at a general vestry meeting, it was proposed by Father Lythgoe, seconded by Mr Brighouse:

First: that it is the opinion of this meeting that the erection of Commodious Baths near St Winefride's Well is likely to be a convenience to the inhabitants, an attraction to visitors & a benefit to the town and neighbourhood.

Second: that the nobility & gentry of the neighbourhood be solicited for donations to restore the ancient building to its original state, and for the erecting of baths and convenience for the poor, that they may have the privilege of Bathing free of charge.

Mr Henry Hughes, seconded by Mr Turner, proposed further resolutions:

Three: that a public company be now formed for the erection of the Baths, according to the plans and drawings submitted to the meeting and a subscription for shares – 2,000 of £1 each.

Four: that Messrs Douglas & Smalley & Co. to be Bankers of the company, to whom the money shall be paid.

Five: a committee of fourteen was appointed of which Father Lythgoe was a member.

Six: Mr Thomas Crofts be appointed Secretary.

Seven: that the Marquess of Westminster be respectfully requested to allow his name to stand as patron.

Eight: Trustees be appointed who included David Pennant, Esq., of Downing and Sir Edward Mostyn, Bart, of Talacre.[18]

Notice of the new company appeared in the *Chester Chronicle* in the form of a prospectus[19] which enlarged upon the original resolutions of the committee and introduced a new theme into the project stating that:

93. *Facing page: John Welch's Plans (1837) for the development of the Well precincts. Note the stream marks the boundary between the land of Mostyn (Talacre) and Grosvenor property. The Well and the 'plunging bath' are not included.*

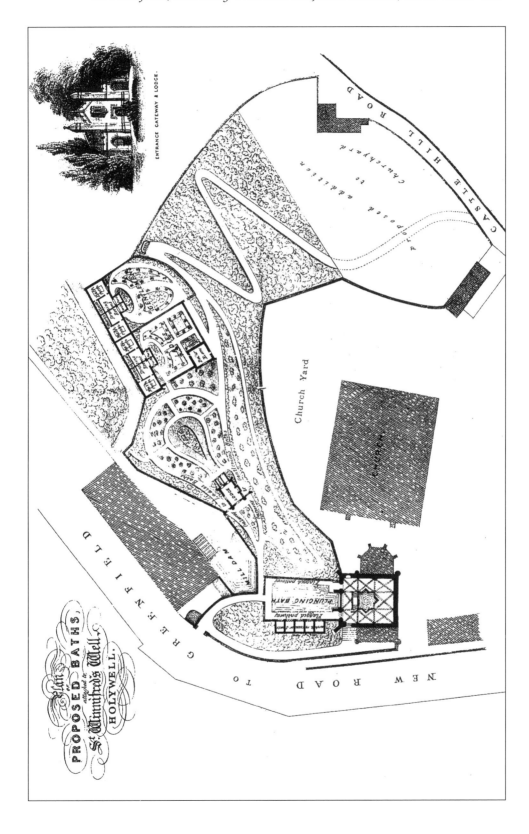

It is evidently the interest of the landowners, and all persons engaged in trade in Holywell and the neighbourhood, to promote the undertaking, as there is every reason to believe these Baths will prove as attractive as any others of great and fashionable resort. The celebrated Well of St Winefred may fairly compete with the Waters of Cheltenham, Leamington, Harrogate, Buxton, Scarborough, Tunbridge, or Beulah, for the invigorative and restorative qualities of its waters; whilst if quantity were to decide their respective merits, it far surpasses them all. If scenery be the attraction, North Wales, with her stupendous mountains, trout streams, lakes, and delightful valleys, will vie with any part of the United Kingdom; and short excursions within a round of ten or fifteen miles, will convey travellers to St Asaph, Rhuddlan, Rhyl, Newmarket, Denbigh, Flint, Northop, Mold, the Vale of Clwyd, and other intervening spots, where there are innumerable objects affording pleasing historical reminiscences, associated with so many fine castles – the scenes of chivalrous deeds in bye–gone days.

The regulations to the shareholders looked forward in the future 'to create additional shares to erect Cottages suitable for visitors of the baths.'

The plans for this ambitious and comprehensive scheme of improvements were drawn up by the architect John Welch (1810–55), who was born at Overton in Flintshire and established himself in business at St Asaph.[20] His plans show modest proposals for an ornamental entrance gateway and lodge in the gothic style which leads through a garden to the south to a walled area with two separate bathrooms each, with dressing rooms and water closets, for ladies and gentlemen. There is no indication where the poor would bathe. Two small shrub-bed enclosures outside each bathing area lead into a walkway through the grounds of the Well into an addition to the churchyard. The area around the 'plunging bath' was to be flagged and an arched recess provided.

The patron, Robert Grosvenor (1767–1845), second earl Grosvenor, and first marquess of Westminster (created 1831) brought by his marriage to the Hon. Eleanor Egerton, the lordship of Holywell, Fulbrook, and Greenfield to the Grosvenor estates, and began the family's involvement with St Winefride's Well. On 31 March 1838 he granted the trustees a lease for forty–one years of two cottages in Greenfield Street in the occupation of William Needham and Richard Jones, and land adjoining the well.

The lessees to undertake to erect, on the site, within five years, good and commodious baths and appropriate buildings to be attached thereto – the baths and premises to be built with brick or stone or both and covered with good slate – and to expend thereon £600 or upwards.[21]

Unfortunately the scheme foundered because Douglas & Smalley and Co.'s bank, in which all the money had been collected, including £60 subscribed by the patron, was declared bankrupt. The only improvement achieved before bankruptcy was that the cottage that had been built at the front of the well was taken down. All further proceedings were suspended and the plans aborted.

Leigh's *Guide to Wales & Monmouthshire*[22] stated that:

Small cabins are built for the convenience of persons wishing to bathe, and attendants are always at hand, with bathing dresses, and drinking glasses for those whose curiosity may induce them to taste the water.

Undeterred by the setback in fortune in 1839, the locals continued to advertise what Hemingway[23] described as 'an ornament to the town' in a handbill dated 1844,[24] with a further edition of 1850, which stated that:

A plain stone cistern at the gable–end of the corn mill, has been erected by Sir Pyers Mostyn, Bart of Talacre, for the purpose of supplying water to the Inhabitants during the hours that the Well is closed for bathing. The water is conveyed to this cistern by pipes direct from the main spring.

At the bottom of the handbill is the notice:
The Inhabitants are requested not to carry water from the Well between 9 o'clock and 12 in the forenoon and 6 o'clock and 9 in the evening, that strangers and visitors may be permitted to bathe in private.

A list of donations amounting to £207 had been subscribed by 13 September 1844.

94. St Winefride's Chapel, 1942 – exterior from New Road. [Crown copyright RCAHMW]

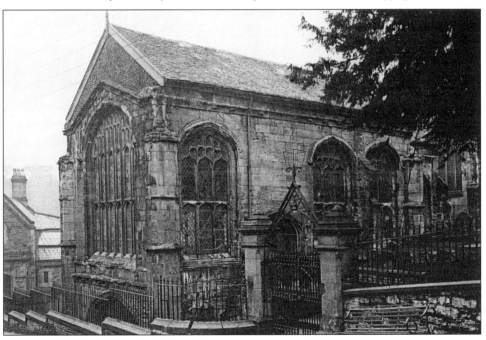

In June 1848, a correspondent complained in a letter to the editor of the *Chester Chronicle,* that Holywell was a 'deserted village' through unemployment, the end of stage–coach traffic to the town since the coming of the railway to Greenfield and poor trade in the market and shops. He closed his dismal catalogue with an observation on the situation at the well:

> There is one source in particular from which the town might derive great benefit, provided the management of it was in proper hands, which is now in so shameful and disgraceful a state, although so much money has been uselessly expended, in what might absurdly be termed 'garnishing the dish before the fish was caught.' If the money which has been so uselessly expended, had been, as originally intended, laid out in erecting warm baths on the flat adjoining the Well, or even in paying a man to look after the Well by keeping off the noisy and abusive fellows who now make the Well their common play ground, thereby driving the respectable people away not only from the Well but the town, it would have been of service, and would have been the means of bringing in an ample revenue to the committee to enable them to repair and beautify the edifice, and render it a source of much greater attraction to the stranger, and a benefit to invalids, who are now driven away with disgust.[25]

Whether or not the committee heeded that complaint efforts were made to improve conditions at the well. In the season of 1851, Mr Vickers, a draper in Holywell, provided canvas which, as the newspaper reported:

> Secured to the bathers greater privacy and comfort. The large Well is now nearly covered over with canvas, thereby screening from public view those who are enjoying themselves in its cold and invigorating stream. The committee have also put in force a bye–law which has long been neglected, viz. 'That no person will be admitted into the Well during any portion of the day when parties are bathing, unless for the same purpose.' It is gratifying to perceive the beneficial results of this regulation, by the increased number of bathers.[26]

The use and repair of St Winefride's Chapel in the nineteenth century
The chapel ceased to be used as an elementary or free school by the Anglican Church when the National School was opened in the parish in 1819. From 1841, until the first part of the twentieth century, it was used for religious services in the Welsh language, and a Sunday school. Other meetings were held in the chapel until the 1970s.

In 1841, William Carey, bishop of St Asaph, being satisfied that 'St Winifred's Hall' belonged to the vicar and churchwardens, licensed the building for divine service.[27]

A year later, when the windows of the chapel were glazed at a cost of £4 5s., a note was made in the vestry book that the bill was 'paid by the Church Wardens,

95 & 96. St Winefride's Chapel, 1942, showing the chapel after restoration in the nineteenth century It was used by the Anglican parish until the 1970s. Above: interior of chapel looking east. Below: interior of chapel north arcade from south west. [Crown copyright RCAHMW]

97. St Winefride's Chapel, 1942: the interior of chapel looking north west.
[Crown copyright RCAHMW]

the Hall being part and parcel of the property of the Parish.'[28]

Work of restoration continued the following year, when an appeal in the *Chester Chronicle* indicated difficulties by the Church authorities in raising money to pay for the repairs. They told the readers that:

> We have on several occasions noticed in our columns the progressive and judicious improvements which have been made in and about this beautiful and ancient structure. The committee have been lately engaged in restoring the large western window, a work for which correctness of style, and entire execution, reflects the highest credit on John Welch, Esq., architect, and Mr Richard Davies, stone mason, Brook Street Chester.

They begged the public to follow the 'noble example, of the local gentry, and come forward with additional pecuniary aid,' and explained that:

> Much remains still to be done; the present roof destroys the order of the building, and ought to be replaced by a flat leaden roof; the surrounding houses are most unsightly objects and should be immediately removed; the grounds contiguous to the well require laying out and planting: but that which especially presses itself upon the attention of the committee is the state of the foundations of the octagonal well. It has been lately discovered, that through the continuous and

immense body of water which is thrown up, the foundation has been gradually removed, and is now undermined to such an extent, that fears are entertained for the safety of the whole building. It is contemplated that the sum of £50 would enable the committee to complete the work of securing the foundation & otherwise materially improving the Well.[29]

The work of securing the foundations was not carried out until 1859. The delay was probably caused because of the restraints of the economic depression in the 1840s, and the deaths of the vicar, Arthur Gardner, and David Pennant of Downing in 1844. Eventually the well and chapel structure received attention in the late 1850s. An account of this will be given below. Before examining later schemes for the improvement to the well it is interesting to look at a suggestion which was made in 1848.

The proposal in 1848 to develop St Winefride's Well as a water–cure centre
Thomas Croft, secretary to the well committee, probably planted in the minds of tourists and invalids the vision of the well as an ideal watering place. This idea was originally expressed in Croft's prospectus for shares in the company for the erection of *The Baths at St Winefride's Well*. The handbill, published in 1844, boasted that the well could compete with the main watering places in the country. Such notices probably attracted the attention of Captain Mervyn Richardson of Rock Ferry, in Cheshire, who came to Holywell to see for himself.

The captain saw the possibility of St Winefride's Well becoming a hydropathic centre, where medical treatment by means of the water–cure could be developed. He looked the place over, and to his delight, discovered that the existing lease of the well facilities by the Marquess of Westminster to the townspeople was soon up for renewal. Richardson acted quickly and wrote to the marquess requesting a tenancy to develop the well for the practice of the water–cure.

Enclosed in the captain's correspondence to the marquess was the January number of *The Water Cure Journal*, and *Hygienic Magazine* in which was a letter from him addressed from 'St Winifred's Well, Holywell, Dec. 2nd, 1847'. The letter sets forth the captain's aspirations:

When I want change of air and scene, with splendid mountain walks of unequalled beauty and variety, in a country teeming with springs of the purest water, and when I want a plunge bath of surpassing efficacy, I come here. This is the poor man's hydropathic establishment; and if those in authority in this place had their wits about them, and the interests of the town sincerely at heart, they would erect a suitable and convenient building, to suit persons of moderate means and the poor of the land, without the loss of a moment of time.[30]

The captain's letter to the marquess a few weeks later repeats his ideas as expressed in the *Journal*. He asked for a lease of the facilities at the well and

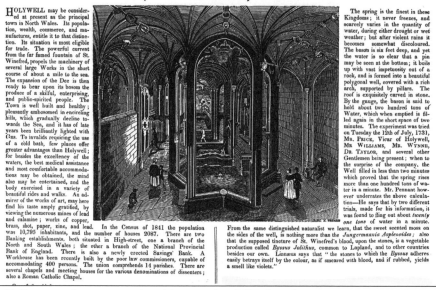

98 & 99. *Two examples representative of the many handbill's, issued to promote St Winefride's Well in Liverpool and Holywell from the late eighteenth century onwards.*

AN HISTORICAL DESCRIPTION OF

ST. WINEFRED'S WELL;

AT HOLYWELL, FLINTSHIRE, NORTH-WALES,

WHICH SPRING PRODUCES, EVERY MINUTE, NIGHT AND DAY,

ONE HUNDRED TONS OF WATER!

And Bathing therein cures many Distempers, and strengthens in an extraordinary manner all such as have had the Small-pox, or any other severe Disorder.

See the waters ever-flowing, Fresh from her sacred gore; Virgineal mercies shewing, A thousand year ana' more.	Ye British muses aid the lay, The *Winefreds* shall rise; Over the Well and all the way, Singing " eternal joys."	The silver streams shall cease to flow, And hoary ocean roll; The groves to sing, the flowers to grow; And stars desert the pole.
Fair life and precious health Adorn these living springs; Without them what's all wealth Of Princes, Lords, and Kings?	See faith divine, and holy grace, The fairest progeny of heaven, Enhance the lustre of this place, With many helps and blessings given.	While *Winefred* shall live Beyond the blast of time; The mould'ring rocks survive, The honor of our clime. *Daniel's Ode to St. Winefred.*

expressed his willingness to act as superintendent in such a scheme. He emphasised the advantages of the water–cure and the necessity for a scientific approach.

I am much disposed to agree with the late Mr Pennant that many poor creatures cause their illness Bathing in the Holy Well. In order to remedy this Evil and to make it a means of unequivocal good the first step to be taken is to provide accommodation on the spot for Patients who resort there for their restoration to Health. When that is done in a complete manner, there will be no lack of Medical Skill at hand to direct, since it will differ from all other spots it having existed in a rude form for centuries and already commanding a sufficient trade to tempt the most skilful to venture on the market.[31]

The marquess tactfully declined to assist the captain, pleading as his excuse that 'My property in the immediate neighbourhood of Holywell is extremely small, and I have just had the misfortune to lose by death the services of the very valuable Agent who manages my Welsh property. I can therefore take no steps upon the subject of your letter, at this unfortunate juncture.'

The captain in reply thanked the marquess with a final observation that:

An establishment at Holywell cannot fail to prove highly beneficial and remunerative since the great body of the Invalids of the Middle Classes are excluded from attending the more expensive Establishment at Malvern & elsewhere. If the report of Patients be correct the two leading Establishments at Malvern, are dividing between them nearly £30,000 as clear yearly profit.[32]

1857 – St Winefride's Well proposed as part of the town improvement plan

The policy decisions taken in 1857 on behalf of St Winefride's Well proved a turning point in the management of the building and have influenced its development ever since. The well found a new patron and champion in Richard Grosvenor (1795–1869), second marquess of Westminster. His patronage and leadership until his death in 1869 was instrumental in carrying out major changes in the town of Holywell. He was the midwife who ushered in an effective scheme of local government to oversee responsible management of the affairs of Holywell town and St Winefride's Well. The marquess was in the ideal position to assume this role, for as well as the prestige which went with his title, he was the lord of the manor of Holywell, and it was thought that he owned the freehold to the well. His great wealth and generosity made him an excellent patron. Together with Sir Pyers Mostyn, he owned the land and buildings within the precinct of the well. Their holdings encircled the well and were divided by the stream issuing from it, as may be seen on the plan (see p.257). This shared occupancy of the well precincts between the Catholic baronet and Protestant marquess meant that disagreements had to be ironed out before schemes for improvement were undertaken, and they sometimes were aired by their respective supporters in meetings of the local board.

The first object of the marquess was to commit the ratepayers of Holywell to a programme of improvements which would include St Winefride's Well. He realised that any major improvements would require outside funding and a strong local elected representative body to oversee the work. The marquess decided to submit his proposals to the people of Holywell by means of a public meeting held at the King's Head Hotel on the 20 October 1857.[33] The meeting attracted a large gathering of landowners and gentry, professional men and tradesmen. Although unable to attend, the marquess presented a detailed set of proposals by means of a memorial addressed to the assembly. Viscount Feilding chaired the meeting, and Captain Mostyn of Calcot Hall spoke as a representative of the marquess. He was also a relative of Sir Pyers Mostyn, who was present.

The proposals of the marquess were designed to encourage the local populace by personal generosity, practical proposals, and a positive programme of action. His personal generosity included the offer 'that for the establishment of a Market House my claim to a Toll in the open market as Lord of the Manor which I hold from my ancestors should be abandoned.' In order to improve St Winefrede's Well it was stated that:

> Lord Westminster is willing to give up any charge of the Well, and he will make over to the Well Commissioners, the Buildings belonging to him adjoining the Well, to be pulled down; and he will surrender of his Ground on the opposite side such space as may be required for the completion of three new Baths.

It was announced that 'Lord Westminster will subscribe £500, provided he is met by a liberal contribution from others, and that these objects are effectually carried out.'

The practical proposals suggested by the marquess for the implementation of the scheme of works were adopted by the meeting, and a few weeks later a notice appeared in the local paper outlining a private bill to be immediately presented to parliament, 'for supplying the inhabitants with water and gas. For establishing and regulating a Market and Market Places and Baths and Wash–house therein.' The bill had powers to vest in the commissioners St Winefred's Well and the basement storey of the structure to enable them to repair or restore the building:

> And also the cottage and land adjoining on the west and north east sides of the outer basin or plunging bath and to enable the Commissioners to convert the cottages and land into public baths, or to construct and make new baths and other conveniences for bathing upon such other site as shall be agreed upon.[34]

The bill gave the commissioners plenty of scope for improvement to the well but, unfortunately, although the public meeting in October 1857 had agreed to these proposals being implemented by commissioners, the adoption of the Act was rejected by the ratepayers by a majority of thirty–two votes. The ratepayers of the township of Greenfield were mobilised into opposition in November 1859 by the local industrialist William Keates to defeat the legislation. Their only reason was that they did not wish to be overburdened by the payment of increased rates for amenities which would mainly benefit the neighbouring township of Holywell.[35]

After this failure, responsibility for the well remained in the hands of the vestry through its own committee, although the marquess exercised some influence over them as he explored means of implementing improvements at the well. Early in 1857 he was in consultation with the committee, and the architect T. H. Wyatt[36] who had prepared plans for the construction of two new baths. Wyatt was also in correspondence with the vicar over repairs to St Winefride's Chapel.

Wyatt's proposals for the well were outlined at the public meeting in October 1857 and the bill published the following month. They consisted of making three plunging baths by constructing a new bath either side of the existing bath, about thirty feet by twenty feet each, with dressing rooms. The central one was for the public, those on either side for the separate use of ladies and gentlemen. The baths were to be hid by a light screen from the well, the old building to be repaired and restored. The spring was to be protected with iron railings and kept to itself, but accessible to all visitors, and not to be used as a bath, or in any other way. The spring water to be conducted by pipes to the drinking place, as now, on the outside in the street, and into the three reservoirs prepared for baths.

However there was local opposition to Wyatt's scheme, and the marquess informed him in December:

> I have had an occasion of concurring with Gentlemen connected with the place – & I fear the objections & difficulties to carrying out such a Plan as has been proposed are almost insuperable.[37]

It appeared that poor Wyatt also failed to satisfy the vicar, Hugh Jones, in his report on St Winefride's Well, and probably, because of difficulties in raising funds, the architect received no contract. He estimated that at least £500 'could I think be the least required to repair the stone work of the Well & lower portion of the building inclusive of the carving but exclusive of the chapel above. The stone work is in a very dilapidated condition.' Wyatt needed to make a more detailed examination of the building before he could arrive at a realistic estimate for the cost of repairs.[38]

A dramatic description of repairs to the well in April 1859

Twelve months after Wyatt's inspection his doubts about the state of the well building were confirmed by an inspection made by the architect Thomas Penson of Chester[39] who pronounced it in a very unsafe condition. Dramatic repairs had to be undertaken in April 1859 by Mr Thomas Hughes, a tradesman from Chester Street, Holywell.[40] The contractor conducted the repairs working overnight to accomplish them. The work attracted a large number of spectators hoping to see the well yield up its secrets. A fascinating account of the operation 'which produced no small excitement in our quiet town', was reported in the *Flintshire Observer*.

Mr Thomas Hughes had contracted to underpin the octagonal Well with ashlar stone, 3ft. 6in. or 4ft. deep, and 18 or 20 inches wide, and fill with paving stones, 3 feet deep. To flag the small well, under the arch (commonly called the ladies' well,) and the plunging well, with self–freed flags, squared 2in. thick. Having made his necessary preparations, on Thursday the 21st inst. At noon an examination of the octagonal well was made, that if necessary stays and props might be fixed to render the working safe for the men. This however was thought unnecessary.

At 6 o'clock the water was let off from the well, and several of the gentry of the neighbourhood, and the inhabitants of the town were present, to witness the lower flood–gate opened below the old mill pool, which had not been done for many years; and here occurred the first difficulty. The masonry which filled up the culvert was first removed, which allowed but a slender stream to shew itself; but after an hour's battering at the wooden door, the watercourse was made clear, and the mill pool soon emptied. An opening was then made below the flood–gate of the plunging well, to lower the water at the spring head, and from 8 at night on Thursday, till seven on Friday morning, relays of men, five hours at a stem, worked, nearly up to their middle in water, cutting a course that the stream might be below the level of the spring.

During the night the work was visited by many of the inhabitants. The place lighted up with workmen's lamps. As soon as the water was sufficiently lowered, the masons descended and began to underpin the octagonal well, and at eleven, others were set on to make a culvert to enable the water to pass below the plunging well, whilst that was being flagged. The foundation of the columns in front of the Well and under the arch, were found to be almost gone, and in a most ruinous condition, and had it not been for the peculiar construction of the building, it was deemed impossible for it to have stood so long. This was all made good, and during Saturday the plunging well was partially flagged. Monday morning early, the work was resumed, so that at about five o'clock the water was allowed its accustomed channel. Finally by noon on Tuesday the work was completed by the repair of the aqueduct leading from the mill pool to Messrs Hill's flannel mill.

The plunging bath has been flagged, making a depth at the arch way from the spring, of 5ft., graduating to 3ft. 6in. at the flood gate, and the sides painted with cement. More than 100 cubic feet of ashlar stone for the foundation, and 120 square yards of flags were used in the repairs. Thirty men divided into stems of 5 hours each, were employed. A space of 1613 cubic feet was filled with water in 2 minutes, making 806.5 ft. in one minute. The water thrown up by the Well is estimated as 22.56. tons per minute.[41]

It was originally planned by the well committee to remove 'St Beuno's stone' which lay at the foot of the stone steps on the right hand side of the bath and as the newspaper reported 'a warm altercation took place in the Well between the contending parties both lay and clerical on both sides.' Eventually common sense prevailed and the stone was allowed to remain undisturbed.

At the ratepayers' annual meeting in June 1860 the recommendations of the well committee were accepted that the well be placed at the disposal of the working classes for bathing on Saturday from 2p.m to 9p.m. without charge, providing they bring their own bathing dresses. There was a hiring charge of one pence for these. The well was now being used by the town as a public wash–house, and it was the question of the use of the well for public–health purposes which led to the following question being asked in the local newspaper: 'St Winefride's Well, whose is it?' The question arose because of recent parliamentary legislation, the Nuisances Removal and Diseases Prevention Amendment Act 1860, proposed setting up sanitary committees under the jurisdiction of the local Board of Guardians. There was a fear that the well committee might lose control, which would pass from the vestry. On the other hand, the Marquess of Westminster believed that he had the freehold. When a new authority, the Local Board, came into being in 1862, they immediately established a well committee, which they regarded as a successor to the vestry.

The Holywell Local Board, 1862–95

From the 1860s until the beginning of the twentieth century there was a great deal of uncertainty about ownership. The Local Board regarded the well as being held in common by the ratepayers as it was their local water supply. The Marquess of Westminster, who owned half the land adjoining the perpendicular crypt and chapel, believed that being lord of the manor entitled him to the well and he had his agent draw up a lease for the Local Board as tenants. More confusion was caused when neither party signed the lease and the tenants disregarded their annual rent.

The defeat of the adoption of the Act to appoint commissioners for improvement in 1859 did not deter those ratepayers who wanted to save their town from decay. In May 1862, at a meeting of churchwardens of the parish of Holywell, it was resolved that the Local Government Act of 1858 be adopted within the township of Holywell, and the Local Board came into being.

The Local Board operated in Holywell from 1862 to 1897 becoming the town government. There was no charter of incorporation, instead it was composed of twelve members elected by the ratepayers and presided over by a chairman. It met regularly in open session as a body, and was divided into specialist committees which were responsible to the board, who made decisions on their recommendation by the vote of the majority. Their proceedings were reported in detail by the press, chief of which were the *Flintshire Observer* and the *County Herald*, who both had offices in High Street. From their regular weekly and differing points of view it is possible to obtain a detailed picture of the affairs of the town from the 1850s onwards. Information concerning St Winefride's Well, and events relating to the Catholic community, are frequently featured, and often the subject of the leader page and correspondence column.

Major improvements at St Winefride's Well, 1867–71

A detailed picture of the course of the improvements made to St Winefride's Well between 1867 and 1871 and the background which led up to them emerges from the local newspapers. In these we read that, in its early years, the decisions of the board were influenced by the chief landowners and local patrons: the Marquess of Westminster, Sir Pyers Mostyn of Talacre, Viscount Feilding (later Earl of Denbigh), of Downing, all of whom were substantial property owners in the parish and neighbourhood. The pressure they exerted affected decisions, and conflicts of interest along sectarian lines sometimes emerged in the discussions. The leasing of land, the appointment of architects, the acceptance of plans and tenders took time. The implementation of improvement schemes was dependent on the availability of funds.

The land and money which enabled the Local Board to improve the well came from three main sources. The major source of revenue was through rateable income. Financial assistance was also obtained from loans from national government for specific purposes such as public health. This money was lent on security of property, and repayment of loans from the rates. In the case of money borrowed for improvements to St Winefride's Well, the sum was based on the entrance fees from visitors. The third source of assistance came in the form of patronage, and from the grant of leases and property in the immediate vicinity of the well. The architect's plans agreed to by the Local Board reflected the utilitarian objects of the age, and the expectation of Victorian social legislation to improve living conditions. Features and services such as a public washhouse, and private warm and cold baths were introduced. More space and paved areas were needed to meet the needs of large parties of excursionists and pilgrims. This was a way of generating income to pay a well keeper, heat the warm baths and pay off the loan.

The land within the precincts of the well was owned by Sir Pyers Mostyn, of Talacre, a leading Catholic, and by the Marquess of Westminster, a tolerant member of the Anglican Church. The area bordering on the well and to the south was the Anglican parish church and churchyard. When decisions had to be taken over the acceptance of improvement schemes, both Sir Pyers Mostyn and the Marquess of Westminster usually made their consent conditional on approval of the choice of architect and his plans. In this way, for example, Sir Pyers Mostyn was able to safeguard Catholic interests.

The first Holywell Local Board was elected on 18 July 1862, and one of its first actions was to choose a crest and seal of office, which depicted St Winefride's Well. The Board was anxious to make up for time lost by the failure to adopt the Act, appointing improvement commissioners. In January 1863 they appointed a sub–committee to enquire into and report on the state of St Winefride's Well. Six months later Captain Mostyn informed the clerk to the Local Board of 'the interest being shown in "the Well question" by the Marquess of Westminster'. Heartened by his support, the board resolved to spend £1,000 on the erection of bathhouses and called a meeting of ratepayers to sanction the expenditure.

The process of modernisation was to take eight tortuous years of decision making, delays and disagreements. Its achievement was significant in the history of St Winefride's Well. It put the building in the public sphere, to obtain funding for the upkeep of its fabric. From this time onwards the precincts to the Well were seen as an integral part of the well crypt and chapel, and the acquisition of additional space a priority, when it became available. The Local Board and its successors developed a pattern of administration, with a resident well keeper whose presence was beneficial to the interests of the employing authority, visitors, and leaseholders. By virtue of a renewable lease, which has extended unbroken since 1873, St Winefride's Well was in the guardianship of the Jesuit Mission until 1930, and from then on was taken over by the local Roman Catholic diocese. In this way both the pilgrimage and cure traditions have survived.

Significant decisions were taken with regards to improvements to the well in the second half of 1863. The Local Board decided to borrow £1,000 which was to be expended on the erection of baths, and a public meeting of ratepayers increased the sum to £3,000. They were confident of financial support and advice from the Marquess of Westminster. Sir Pyers Mostyn promised he would consider selling the vacant mill and brewery which would open up the area round the well, subject to his approval of the plans for improvements, and reservation of control of water power through his riparian rights.

In this spirit of optimism the Board decided in October to advertise for plans 'from architects and others.' But already doubts and differences of opinion appeared between members of the Board and their patrons. The clerk reintroduced John Welch's plans of 1837 (see p.257), which the Board instantly dismissed as an 'exceeding artistic and ancient design'. Doubts were expressed about the viability of the construction of two side baths, one each side of the 'plunging' bath immediately in front of the Crypt building. Board members were reminded that the Marquess of Westminster had shown his disapproval of this ordering when put forward by T. H. Wyatt in 1857, and they were reluctant to lose the £500 he promised on approving the scheme. The Marquess expressed his opinion in November that the placing of a side bath on the church side of the well would be too dangerous; neither did he think it advisable to pay Sir Pyers Mostyn £1,000 out of the rates for his mill and brewery.

In November the Board received the plans for which they had advertised. Out of four sets of plans they chose two identified by *nom de plumes*: 'Dertiminatia', by Robert Scrivener (1812–78), an architect from Hanley, was given nine votes, and 'Faveat Fortune', by Robert Morris, an architect from Chester, received three votes. In December, the two patrons showed themselves divided in their opinions. The Marquess approved of Scrivener's plans, but eventually judged them too expensive to pursue. Sir Pyers Mostyn 'wholly disapproved of Scrivener's plans,' which he pronounced as 'totally out of character with the Well.'

No further progress was made until the autumn of 1864 when, as a compromise, Robert Morris was appointed architect, and in December Sir Pyers Mostyn expressed himself willing to give a portion of the mill premises as part of the improvement scheme. The Catholic baronet made his gift and approval conditional on the fulfilment of four pledges:

> 1st – That the improvements should not interfere with the narrow well next the octagon well, generally used by cripples;
> 2nd – That the small eye–well, outside the plunging bath, be not removed;
> 3rd – That the charge for bathing in the plunging bath, be not increased, but remain as hithertofore;
> 4th – And providing the tenants of the Mill and Brewery be willing to give up the property.[42]

However it was not until 21 September 1866 that the plans of the Chester architect, Robert Morris, were adopted by the Board, and a thousand pounds was borrowed to put them into effect. This became known as the 'first scheme.'

The First Scheme, 1867
The first scheme was designed to clear the area around the well of dilapidated buildings and cottages, to define and strengthen boundary walls, and rebuild dressing boxes. The tender to builders advertised for works for masons, carpenters, plumbers, painters, and iron founders. It required them to take down premises adjoining St Winefride's Well, erect new boundary walls to the well, and rebuild the walls to the present 'Plunge Bath Entrance, Dressing Boxes, Girders, and Overhanging Roof.'[43] In May, Messrs Anderson of Liverpool were appointed contractors to the project. The churchwardens of the parish church co–operated by taking down the old hearse house and ruinous cottages extending to the church gates. A comment in the local press suggested that an appeal be made to the Earl of Denbigh and Sir Pyers Mostyn, to create a park or pleasure ground on the opposite side of the road to the well 'by the removal of cottages which would open out a most picturesque rocky glen.' Nothing came of this imaginative idea; neither did any difficulties prevent the first scheme being successfully completed.

The Second Scheme, 1869–71
The second scheme cost about £2,000 and was financed by the Holywell Local Board by means of a loan from the Public Works loan office, 'for a loan for baths and wash–houses,' in June 1867. The second part of the improvements was more

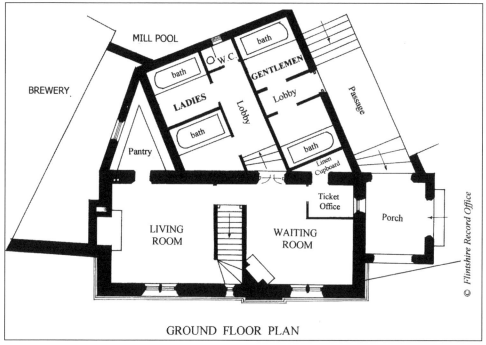

GROUND FLOOR PLAN

100. K. Lloyd Griffiths' copy of Scivener's plans for the new baths in the Well precincts.

ambitious than the first. The scheme included a house for the keeper of the well, ladies' and gentlemen's swimming baths, and hot and cold baths. The Local Board was anxious to attract visitors to Holywell, and provide a warm bath in the town; otherwise they would go to either Chester or Liverpool to find similar facilities.

In December 1868, plans were received from Robert Morris and Messrs. Scrivener (and in addition Mr Crofts, of Liverpool, on behalf of Mr Anderson, the contractor to the first scheme). The public of Holywell was given the opportunity to inspect the various architects' plans, and Scrivener's were chosen.

After much clarification, some dispute, 'and removal of obstacles' work began in August 1869. In the winter 1869–70, Anderson found himself in financial difficulties, was declared bankrupt and the work was completed by Holywell tradesmen Thomas Hughes, John Jones, and Pierce Lloyd.

A description of the two schemes of improvement
This account is based on the report which appeared in the *Flintshire Observer* 28 April 1871.

The old unsightly cottage and tumbledown dressing boxes have disappeared and the ground so encumbered has been laid open and judiciously utilized by the erection of tastefully designed dressing cabins surrounded by handsome masonry. This portion of the improvement took place some three years ago. These

101. The three-storeyed Well House erected c.1869.

alterations were followed by others of a more important and imposing character which have within the past month or so been completed.

A very beautiful Well house has now been erected three stories high, of a most picturesque design in general keeping with the architecture of the Well building. Its porch or portico is a gem of architectural beauty, and the building constitutes the residence of the Well–keeper in which are also incorporated the hot and cold baths for ladies and gentlemen. These baths are constructed upon the most modern principles and in all respects are replete with every comfort and luxury. They are light and airy, and scrupulously clean.

The most important of the alterations was

… that of the new swimming bath, which rejoices in the noble name of the 'Westminster Bath,' in consideration of the munificent sum subscribed by that late Marquess of Westrminster, to carry out the Well improvements. This bath is truly most magnificent being 62 feet long and 25 feet wide. It is enclosed by substantial walls of masonry, and a roof of iron and glass thrown over it. Along one side there are erected seventeen most beautifully constructed dressing cabins; and with a view of suiting the requirements of every class of bathers, the bath is so constructed to admit of four depths viz: – 3 feet 6 in; 4 feet; 4 feet 8 in; and 5 feet 7 in. The bottom of the bath is lined with white tiles.

The old plunge bath remains as of yore, with the exception of the placing of beautiful dressing boxes in lieu of the unsightly structures that formerly existed.

Overcome by the nature of the improvements, the editor compared St Winefride's Well with the English watering places. 'The mineral springs of Bath, Buxton and elsewhere had a monopoly – and however beautiful and efficacious they may be – we believe we may safely say, that our own Well will bear honourable companion with them.'

Unfortunately, one of the patrons of the improvements and benefactor to the town of Holywell, Richard Grosvenor, second marquess of Westminster, died in 1869. He had been a driving force in encouraging an uncertain Local Board, and a figure who commanded respect. His place was taken by his son Hugh Lupus Grosvenor, third marquess (1825–99) and soon to be elevated to first duke of Westminster. He came with his sons on the 20 April 1871, 'and minutely inspected the late improvements, with all of which his lordship expressed himself highly pleased.'

New management

The position of well keeper was advertised in December 1870, to be paid a salary of £40 a year, with house and coal. He was later given permission to let a bed for a lodger. Out of twelve applicants, Walter Owen and his wife were appointed, and commenced their employment on 13 March 1871.

The Local Board's well committee named the individual baths and set payment charges. The new plunge bath was known as 'Westminster Bath', payment 4*d*.; and the old plunge bath as 'Winifred', payment 3*d*. with a reduced rate of 1*d*. on

102. The improved entrance to the Well. Note the variety of people waiting to be admitted.

103. The wall erected in the 1860s to enclose the plunge bath. The wall was removed in the 1990s.

Saturday. Visitors to the well were charged 2*d*., with ratepayers admitted free of charge. Private warm baths were charged at the rate of 1*s*., cold or shower bath, 6*d*.; and a Saturday warm bath the same rate. Mr Scotcher, a local shopkeeper, contracted to supply bathing drawers, dresses, and towels, for hire, some white and others blue. The well keeper was ordered to purchase a thermometer for the warm bath, at a cost of less than 5*s*. To count the numbers of admissions and regulate entrance, a turnstile was installed.

104. The view in 1986 with the Well and plunge bath obscured.

The Local Board entrusted publicity to E. J. Davies, who prepared a pamphlet and an advertisement in the local press which was addressed:

To Tourists. St Winefred's Well, Holywell, Flintshire, North Wales
This world–renowned Well has of late undergone very great and considerable Improvements, and while in its primitive days it could well pride itself as being one of the greatest attractions of the Principality, it may now be safely said that it certainly has no rival. The Well, as it now appears is truly a great ornament and acquisition to the town, and Holywell may certainly boast of having Baths – hot, cold, plunging and swimming – second to none in the Kingdom.

The advert continued with a description of the recently completed improvements.[44]

The Well Committee dealt with a variety of management problems. In July 1872 a complaint was made by Miss Letitia Crowther, of Cheltenham, regarding the behaviour of the bath keeper. Early one summer morning at 7.15 a.m. a group of enthusiastic visitors knocked on the door of the well fronting the street, seeking to gain admission. It was not until ten minutes later that a disgruntled well keeper appeared to open the gate, and began to curse the visitors who had disturbed him. The well keeper was dismissed.

It was too much of a temptation for members of the Anglican Sunday School, who met in St Winefride's Chapel, to resist throwing stones on the glass roof covering the Westminster Bath. The caretaker who tended the chapel and church heating was also guilty of throwing the ashes over the churchyard wall on to the well premises. On the other hand, the Catholics were accused by Anglicans of disturbing their Sunday services by singing at the well. In spite of occasional friction, the two old protagonists maintained a strained co–existence.

A fight between excursionists to the Well and local 'roughs' of Holywell, June 1869
This extract from the local newspaper gives some insight into the way in which excursionists to St Winefride's Well organised their outings, and the hazards which might await them.

On Tuesday last the annual visit to our town was made by the Holy Cross Society of Liverpool being the second excursion made during the season by the Roman Catholic Societies of Liverpool and Birkenhead. Considerably over 1,000 persons, men, women and children–chiefly natives of the Emerald Isle, and denizens of the distinguished locality of Marylebone, Liverpool, arrived early in the morning, accompanied by bands of music.
A field had been engaged for them belonging to Mr Williams, Tŷ Coch, situate at the back of Greenfield Hall. The holidaymakers enjoyed themselves in their usual manner during the day, hackney and donkey carriages being in high

105. The site of the Westminster Bath (1869); now the exhibition centre, repository and entrance.

request amongst the party conveying them to their destination of St Winefride's Well, or to the famous monastery at Pantasaph. A tent was erected in the field and refreshments in the way of beer, porter, &c. supplied by Mr Vickers, of the Royal Oak Inn. Games and sports were also indulged in, but we are sorry to have to add, that a disturbance arose, deplorable in itself and disgraceful to all who took part in it, and at one time promised to lead to very serious consequences. As the evening wore on a quarrel arose between the roughs of Holywell and the excursionists over a game of football, and two or three fights took place, which, owing to the police of our town being engaged at Mold, there was no one in authority to prevent.

Eventually the Welsh were very strongly reinforced by colliers from Holywell, Greenfield, Mostyn, and Tai Trevor, including several of the men at present on strike, who each were armed with sticks and staves. Those who were not so equipped furnished themselves with hedge–stakes, and a regular pitch battle ensued, which lasted for some time. The Welshmen took possession of the lane and an opposite field, whilst the excursionists retained their ground. Stones, of which there were plenty at hand, were flying through the air like a snow storm, coming from all directions, and blood was freely shed, some of the tourists being very severely cut about the head. Mr Fanning of the Constabulary Office, who happened to be present endeavoured to dissuade the men, and to a certain extent his efforts partly succeeded. Mr William Freeman, one of the parish constables, also exerted himself in quelling the riot.

A pool in the locality served the colliers as a means of punishing their adversaries, and we are told that a Priest who accompanied the excursionists, was rather unceremoniously driven into it. One young man in a light suit of clothes was actually immersed in the water, and kept there for a considerable time; and others of the excursionists shared the same fate. Whilst the fighting was going on, women and children ran bewildered and screaming to any place where they could find shelter from the stones, and Mr Bowden, excise officer, made a gap in the hedge to facilitate their escape.

When the excursionists were proceeding to the station they were followed by a dense mob, which completely filled the station road, and the shopkeepers had to put up their shutters for safety. The fight was here again renewed, and another Priest received rough treatment at the hand of the mob, while a third took refuge in Mr Evans' houses, from whence he was escorted to the station by Mr Fanning. The rioters at this stage of the proceedings seemed bent on mischief, and armed as they were the greatest fears were entertained. Some were seen to fill their pockets with stones, and it was anticipated that the fight would be continued after the excursionists had entered their train, but some of the Welshmen advised their comrades to refrain from attacking the train, unless its occupants first opened fire. One foolhardy fellow threw a stone at the train, and was taken into custody by Walker, the company's police officer at the gates, but his companions rescued him, and Walker received a severe cut on the side of the head, with a bludgeon, for his interference. As soon as the prisoner got released he made off as fast as his legs could carry him, and the indignation of his friend was aroused against Mr Bowden because of the cane of that gentleman coming into collision with the miscreant's head.

The train left the station at about eight o'clock without further molestation, but party spirit soon displayed itself, as out of most of the carriages streamers of green ribbon &c. were flying. The members of the society declared that this should be their last visit to Holywell. Several persons both Welsh and excursionists were injured in the melee, but none dangerously, all being able to proceed homewards.[45]

St Winefride's Well and the future of the town water supply
Part of the Act for the appointment of commissioners for the improvement of Holywell in 1857 anticipated supplying the inhabitants of Holywell with water, and the construction of works and pipes for its distribution. In November 1871 a notice for a scheme to carry out these intentions appeared in the press. It proposed the construction of Holywell waterworks for supplying the town and district. The water works included erecting an engine, pumping, and boiler house to the west of Greenfield Road in the township of Greenfield. This was situated on the property of Sir Pyers Mostyn. Linked to the scheme was the construction of a reservoir to the south–west side of Whitford Street, on the property of the earl of Denbigh with the necessary service pipes. The public water supply was to be taken from St Winefride's Well. The amount was not to exceed one and a half million gallons per week, to be 'drawn by the undertakers from the said Well on Sundays between midnight on Saturday night and midnight on Sunday.' This was the beginning of a series of schemes and discussions which were to last for the next fifty years.[46]

The consideration of this scheme is another sign of the importance of St

Winefride's Well to the town of Holywell. It proposed the well be put to another secular use in the interests of public health. We have seen in the schemes for the improvement of the well that as far as possible the Catholic lay people of Holywell and district strove to maintain their loyalty and devotion to St Winefride.

1873 the Jesuits become tenants of St Winefride's Well

The Catholics in Holywell had held no long–term period of tenure at the well crypt and chapel since their eviction at the dissolution of Basingwerk Abbey and the injunctions of King Henry VIII in 1536. Remarkably this was changed in 1873 when they began a lease of the well crypt[47] which, at first tentative and uncertain, was to be renewed by the Local Board and its successors to the present day. In this sense the rejuvenation of the well, both in the physical sense, and the restoration of the care of pilgrims visiting the shrine of St Winefride, was complete. The way the new tenants and their patron reacted to this change of fortune was expressed in a broadsheet which is worth quoting in full.

HOLYWELL ST WINEFRIDE'S WELL

The Rev. J. B. DI PIETRO wishes to inform the Visitors coming to Holywell for their health, that he has taken the Well under his own management, by lease from the Local Board. Mr and Mrs JUKES – both Catholic – are appointed keepers of the Well, and no care will be wanting on their part in attending to the comfort and convenience of Visitors. A spacious field and orchard has been secured opposite the Presbytery for the use of the excursionists, and hot and plunge baths will be continually in readiness, both Winter and Summer, all the year round.

The annual expense of the Well, including £162 for rent, will amount to at least £250. Catholics are invited to contribute to this truly pious and charitable undertaking, on which God has been pleased to bestow so many and such continued proofs of special favour through the admirable intercession of St Winefride.

The EARL OF DENBIGH has been very kind to publish the following letter in the *Tablet*, ON THE 22nd Feb., 1873:

Sir, – Those of your readers who have a devotion to S. Winifrede, will be glad to hear that through the spirited exertions of the Rev. J. B. Di Pietro, SJ, of Holywell, the management of the Well and Baths attached to it has been secured in Catholic hands for three years. Those who have been as pilgrims to bathe there will know what an advantage this will be to all such. This has not, however, been accomplished without incurring much risk. The revenue of the Well, &c., last year amounted to £170 in Protestant hands. Fr di Pietro has engaged to pay the Local Board of Holywell £162 per annum. Besides this he has to pay his Well keeper £1 per week, and the purchase of furniture, bathing–dresses, and cost of coals, gas, &c., will run the expenditure to about £250. I earnestly hope that many, when they read this, will consent to send him some little donation towards defraying these expenses, so that he may not in his charity be a loser by this undertaking. The Hospice is now I am happy to say doing well, and it has been of great value to those respectable pilgrims who are above the common lodging–houses, and yet cannot afford to pay for separate lodgings. The assiduous care shown them by the good Sisters who have charge of the establishment is admirable.

I am, Sir, yours faithfully,

Denbigh.

Newnham Paddox, Feb. 17, 1873.

NOTES

1. J. Milner, *Authentic documents relative to the miraculous cure of Winefride White of Wolverhampton at St Winefride's Well on the 28th of June 1805* (Wolverhampton, 1805), p. 13.
2. Ibid p. 22–4.
3. Ibid pp. 22–6.
4. Ibid p. 33.
5. Ibid p. 39.
6. J. F. Champ, "Bishop Milner, Holywell, and the Cure Tradition" W. J. Sheils (ed) *The Church and Healing Studies in Church History*, vol. 19 (Oxford, 1982), pp. 153–164.
7. 'Franciscana. Annals of Nuns at Taunton', *Catholic Record Society*, vol. 24, 1922, pp. 110–11.
8. Father H. Thurston, SJ, *The Life of St Winefride*, Catholic Truth Society, 1922, p. 98.
9. Ibid, pp. 98–100.
10. Harold Hughes, Bangor Diocesan Architect.
11. FRO P/30/1/147. The Holywell churchwardens acounts are missing until 1759.
12. R. Davies, *Hope and Heartbreak. A Social History of Wales and the Welsh, 1776–1871* (Cardiff, 2005), p. 190.
13. Frederick Rolfe.
14. *Flintshire Observer*, 1/3/1861.
15. R. Davies, op cit, p. 192 and fn 213, p. 480.
16. B. Hughes, 'Reminiscences of Holywell from the year 1830', *County Herald*, 19/2/1904.
17. *Chester Gazette*, 29/12/1836, quoted in *Letters and Notices*, vol. v–vi, 1869, p. 252.
18. FRO, P/30/1/147.
19. *Chester Chronicle*, 19/9/1837.
20. FRO, D/GR/1449, plan dated July 1837.
21. FRO, P/30/1/147.
22. 4th edition, 1839, p. 178.
23. J. Hemingway (ed), *Panorama of the Beauties, Curiosities and Antiquities, etc* (London 3rd ed, 1845), p. 183.
24. FRO, D/GR/1467.
25. *Chester Chronicle*, 28/6/1848 under correspondence.
26. Ibid, 16/8/1851.

27. D. Thomas, op cit, p. 27.

28. FRO, P/30/1/205 May 16 1842.

29. *Chester Chronicle*, 11/8/1843.

30. FRO, D/GR/1451.

31. Ibid.

32. Ibid.

33. *Flintshire Observer*, 30/10/1857.

34. *Flintshire Observer*, 13/11/1857.

35. The poll took place in the vestry room. The result was 117 for the adoption of the Act and 149 against.

36. T. H. Wyatt (1807–80) was responsible for the design of many churches in Flintshire including the Friary Church at Pantasaph 1849 and Brynford and Gorsedd Churches built to replace Pantasaph.

37. FRO, D/GR/1452.

38. FRO, P/30/1/147.

39. Probably Thomas Mainwaring Penson.

40. *Slater's Directory*, 1856, describes him as a bricklayer.

41. *Flintshire Observer*, 29/4/1859.

42. *Flintshire Observer*, 16/9/1864.

43. *Flintshire Observer*, advertisment, March 1867.

44. *Flintshire Observer*, 24/5/1872.

45. *Flintshire Observer*, 11/6/1869.

46. *Flintshire Observer*, 24/11/1871.

47. It was recognised that the well crypt was the responsibility of the Local Board and their successors whereas the chapel above the well crypt remained in possession of the Anglican parish of Holywell.

9. The strengthening of the Catholic Community

In the middle of the nineteenth century the local Catholic community was strengthened and given a new vitality, both in the town and neighbourhood of Holywell, by the arrival of influential supporters and the creation of new religious and educational institutions. This gave local Catholics a sense of confidence that enabled them to openly celebrate and practise their faith. There was an increase in the number of pilgrims, which advanced the cause of St Winefride and her well. The establishment of the College of St Beuno at Tremeirchion strengthened the Jesuit Mission. As a result of these developments the medieval cult of St Winefride was revived in all its splendour and demonstrated by a series of remarkable events and an increased number of reported cures.

Catholics become masters of Downing

Downing, one of the great estates in the county of Flintshire, situated in the parish of Whitford and beyond, with extensive property in the town of Holywell, passed through marriage and conversion into Catholic hands. The Catholics in Holywell were given strong lay and aristocratic champions in Lord Rudolph Feilding and his bride Lady Louisa, both fearless and zealous on behalf of their new faith. Their conversion to Roman Catholicism coincided with the restoration in 1850 of the Catholic hierarchy of bishops, an event greeted with horror and disapproval by the majority of the population. Anti-Catholic protests in the neighbourhood about so-called

106. *Rudolph, Viscount Feilding, later eighth Earl of Denbigh.*

283

107. Downing Hall, Flintshire, the ancestral home of Louisa Pennant.

Papal aggression found a local centre of abuse in the conversion of the Feildings and the special circumstances surrounding the event. Bishop Short of St Asaph, supported by the local Anglican clergy, led a crusade against them, and effigies of the Pope and Lord Feilding were burnt in the villages of Flintshire.

The marriage between Rudolph William Basil Feilding (b.1823), Viscount Feilding, eldest son of the seventh earl of Denbigh and Desmond, of Newnham Paddock, Warwickshire, and Louisa Pennant (b.1824), daughter and heiress of the late David Pennant, Downing, Flintshire, in the parish of Whitford, took place in the Anglican church of St Nicholas, Brighton, on 18 June 1846. Louisa Pennant was a great-grand-daughter of the famous antiquary Thomas Pennant (d.1796), and a descendant of the last abbot of Basingwerk. Her estates in Flintshire consisted of about 4,500 acres, which included extensive property in the town of Holywell.

Both bride and bridegroom were devout members of the Anglican Church at the time of

108. Louisa Pennant.

their marriage, and as an act of thanksgiving decided to a build a church on the Downing estate at Pantasaph in the parish of Whitford. This action was in accord with the wishes of the bride's lately-deceased mother, Lady Emma Pennant. It followed previous efforts of the Pennant family to provide Anglican places of worship where needed in the outlying parts of their estates. Lady Louisa's late parents had built St Mary's, Bagillt, largely at their own expense, consecrated in 1839. Similarly, the Pennant family had given generously to Christ Church, Mostyn, consecrated in 1845, and were donors of a mortuary chapel, St Peter's, and burial ground, in the town of Holywell, consecrated in 1847.

109. *Henry Edward Manning, in 1844 when Archdeacon of Chichester; was received into the RC Church in 1851.*

The foundation stone of the Feildings' church of St David's, Pantasaph, was laid on 16 August 1849. The ceremony at Pantasaph was preceded by a service in Whitford Parish Church. Henry Edward Manning, then archdeacon of Chichester,[1] preached at both places. The Feildings had made the acquaintance of Manning on their visit to Rome at the beginning of 1848, and he became their confessor and spiritual director. Manning left an account of the proceedings in his journal:

> …went to Downing, then to Pantassa for the laying of the first stone of St David's Church; met at the Schools about 60 clergy, Bishop and Dean of St Asaph; long procession – banners, cross stars, *fleur-de-lis* green and blue, vestments crimson, cross gold – leading up a green lane into a field with broken ground, and a high hill looking down upon it; the clergy went first, the choir chaunting the *Te Deum* in Welsh. Lord and Lady Feilding laid the stone, Lord Feilding read the copy of the inscription. The bishop said a few words, then Mr Pugh and Mr Owen in Welsh. Very strange and striking to hear a priest in the open air, and in a surplice, speaking in an unknown tongue.

Manning's description of the weather on that August day was an omen for the shape of future events.

> A thunderstorm came on, gathered and formed in a way and advanced, black and close; then lifted up, and the sun came from beneath it; then it wheeled about and went off, 'lifted up its hands and fled away.' A strong gust blew over just as the stone was laying …[2]

A year later, on 28 August 1850, the feast of St Augustine, bishop of Hippo, the Feildings' were received into the Roman Catholic Church at Edinburgh, by Bishop Gillis, vicar apostolic of the Eastern District. Lady Louisa was showing alarming signs that she was consumptive. Time was short, and the Feildings made the decision to give the unconsecrated and uncompleted church of St David's to the Roman Catholic Church.

The great 'row' between the Bishop of St Asaph and Lord Feilding
Nothing could have been more appropriately designed to raise the wrath and disturb the slumbers of the Anglican clergy in the neighbourhood, than the news in the autumn of 1850 of the Feildings' conversion.[3] The consequent alienation of their gift of St David's Church, Pantasaph, and the announcement by Pope Pius IX, making England and Wales an ecclesiastical province, with a hierarchy consisting of an archbishop and twelve suffragans with ecclesiastical titles.[4] Reports of these events were like thunderbolts from heaven, the clamour of which reverberated throughout the diocese, with the eye of the storm over Holywell. Those most concerned were the Right Reverend Vowler Short, bishop of St Asaph; Richard Briscoe, vicar of Whitford and his neighbour at Holywell, Canon Hugh Jones.

On the transfer of Pantasaph church from the jurisdiction of the Anglican bishop of St Asaph into the hands of the newly-proclaimed Roman Catholic bishop of Shrewsbury, T. H. Wyatt, the architect-in-charge, 'declined to continue his professional services in superintending the internal fittings and decorations of the Popish Church … and now finding that Lord Feilding intends it for a Popish Mass-house, he will have nothing further to do with it.'[5] The unfinished work was given to A. W. Pugin, a Catholic and the most famous decorative architect of his time, to complete.

The Bishop of St Asaph was determined not to let the church fall into the hands of the Catholics. He immediately wrote a letter of protest to Lord Feilding and on receiving an unfavourable response made public the correspondence. The Bishop reminded Lord Feilding of his public declaration to bestow 'a large sum of money in funding a Church and all things belonging to it and his invitation to join in the laying of the foundation,' and that 'we received the Lord's Supper together with this understanding'. He further alleged that the late Lady Emma Pennant his wife's mother left the funds for the building of an Anglican church.

Lord Feilding replied to the bishop 'that were I to carry out under present circumstances the intention which I undeniably had of giving up S. Dewi's to the "Church of England," I should be sinning in the face of God, and acting inconsistently before men.' He added that 'I have taken time to obtain the opinions of many whom I have considered capable of giving sound and just advice.'[6] Amongst these was their friend Manning, who was fully and intimately acquainted with the motives which had induced them to build the church. 'His judgement was, that, as owners of the building, they were bound in conscience not to hand it over to the services of a church in which they no longer believed and had formally renounced, but to devote it to Catholic uses.'[7] Feilding repudiated the bishop's charge that he had used money left by Lady Emma Pennant to build the church at Pantasaph, stating that 'none of the £10,000 devoted by me to St Dewi's has been drawn from her funds.'

Admitting his failure to retain the church at Pantasaph under his own jurisdiction, the Bishop of St Asaph, with the joint co-operation of the vicars of Whitford and Holywell, launched an appeal on 30 November 1850, for subscriptions 'to build and endow a District Church, and to erect a School-room and Parsonage, to supply the spiritual wants of the District now

110. Bishop Thomas Vowler Short of St Asaph who dedicated the Church of St David's, Pantasaph.

threatened with the intrusion of the Romish Schism.' This plan was revised three months later when it was decided to create two new Anglican districts out of the parishes of Whitford and Holywell. A new appeal was launched in February 1851, and the large sum of £8,566 was collected for the erection of two churches at Brynford and Gorsedd, with their respective parsonages and schools. Such was the uproar caused by the Pantasaph affair that twenty-five churches in the diocese responded to the appeal, as did persons throughout the United Kingdom. One of Lady Feilding's trustees, the Earl of Cardigan, gave £150, her relative Mrs Pennant, of Brynbella, St Asaph, and Dean Luxmore gave £500 each,

The success of the bishop's appeal reflected the intense anti-Catholic feeling aroused by the Feilding's alienation of the church, which often became heated in a number of largely-attended public meetings held in the autumn and winter of 1850. Two meetings indicative of the passions aroused were held in Holywell on a Thursday towards the end of November. It was reported that:

> On Thursday morning last week about six hundred of the gentry, clergy and other influential persons, ratepayers of the parish of Holywell and its neighbourhood, assembled at St Winefride's Hall, for the purpose of adopting an address to the Queen relative to the recent Popish attack upon her prerogative …. The evening meeting which was conducted in the Welsh language, was held at the Calvinistic Chapel, Whitford Street, which contained about 1,800 persons.' Amongst the speakers were the local Anglican clergy, vigorously led by Hugh Jones, Vicar of Holywell, the local Wesleyan minister, and an outspoken opponent of Catholicism, Thomas Owens, of St Beuno's cottage. The greatest unanimity was

THE THIN END OF THE WEDGE.

DARING ATTEMPT TO BREAK INTO A CHURCH.

111. The reaction of Punch *to the restoration of the Catholic heirarchy.*

reported between Anglican and Dissenting clergy and 'the auditory frequently in rapturous bursts of applause manifested their true Protestant feelings. After the meeting several large bonfires were lighted up in Holywell; and effigies of His Holiness the Pope, and another Noble personage (Lord Feilding) connected with North Wales were 'tarred up', and burnt to ashes, amidst the hurrahs of the multitude.[8]

The anti-Catholic protest reached a higher level at the county meeting of Flint, called in November 1850 at the County Hall, Mold, on 4 December. It was the duty of the High Sheriff, who happen-ed to be Lord Feilding, to summon the meeting on behalf of the Lord Lieutenant, Sir Stephen Glynne, 'for the purpose of addressing a memorial to the Queen expressing their astonishment and indignation at the late ecclesiastical appointments by the Pope in these dominions … and to consider the effect of the late ecclesiastical arrangements of the Catholic Church in this country.' Lord Feilding did not attend the meeting and apologised for his absence. The motion was carried overwhelmingly, and signed by eight peers and nearly a thousand freeholders.[9] The newspaper report added that:

> … relative to the church at Pantasa, the noble Lord's effigy has been burnt in several villages in Flintshire and he himself been hooted and hissed when attending the Roman Catholic chapel in the neighbourhood of his residence. To compensate the loss of his Lordship's friends and neighbours, Lady Feilding has, it is stated, received a most flattering autograph letter from the Pope, in which his Holiness expresses the pleasure it will give him to receive at the holy city two such illustrious converts to the Papal faith.[10]

The sight of two new Anglican churches with schools and parsonges, being built in the neighbouring villages of Brynford and Gorsedd, eventually replaced noisy protests. Both churches were consecrated in 1853. The *Chester Chronicle* could not resist making comparisons in favour of the Anglicans when it commented on the laying of the foundation stone at St Michael's, Brynford on the feast day 29 September, 1851, that:

> The ceremony was performed most solemnly and impressively, and we could not but admire the simple and unostentatious manner in which all was conducted, especially when we call to mind the ridiculous and miserable imitation of popish procession that took place, on a similar occasion at Pantasa in 1849.[11]

The summer of 1852 was the last the Feildings had together. They had been sustained by their devotion to each other and by the spiritual consolations of their newly-embraced religious beliefs. Their Catholic neighbours, the Mostyns of Talacre, gave them their friendship at home, together with other old Catholic households. In Italy, where they went hoping for an improvement in Lady Louisa's health, they received unfailing comfort and support from the highest quarter. At home in Downing, and in the town of Holywell, their tenants, and many of the Catholics and townspeople, rekindled their loyalty and affection for the last of the Pennants. When the harvest was gathered in and the swallows had taken flight, the Church of St David was ready for dedication. A. W. Pugin, before he died of overwork, gave the finish to the building begun by T. H. Wyatt. The High Altar, the Lady Altar, the Shrine of Our Lady, the font, the pulpit, and various statues designed by him for the adornment of the church were conspicuously exhibited in the medieval court of the Great Exhibition of 1851.[12] Two accounts of the church and its dedication survive[13] from which the following account is collated.

The church was dedicated on St Edward's Day, 13 October 1852, six months before Lady Louisa Feilding would be laid to rest in a vault within it. The ceremony took place on a most beautiful golden autumn morning, ideal for those converging across mountain and common land. The dedication service was presided over by two members of the hierarchy of the recently-created Province of England and Wales: the diocesan, the bishop of Shrewsbury, Dr James Brown, assisted by the bishop of Newport and Menevia, Thomas Joseph Brown, a Benedictine, who preached the sermon on the occasion. The storms of prejudice and bigotry which had raged over the country were stilled. There was more than a cease-fire, for goodwill had replaced enmity, in Holywell at least. If many came out of curiosity, more came to thank God for the fulfilment of the purpose of the founders, Lord and Lady Feilding, in opening a Catholic church for the benefit of the their tenants, as the correspondent of the *Tablet* reported:

The church of Pantasaph, though only two miles from Holywell, stands I might almost say, in a wilderness, in the midst of an ill-cultivated district, sprinkled with cottages tenanted principally by miners. It was for the benefit of these poor creatures that Lord and Lady Feilding, even before their own eyes were opened to the light, had determined to expend their bounty; and it was for the salvation of these as well of many others that the Almighty was working when He vouchsafed to take that illustrious pair by the hand, and lead them to the knowledge of His truth.

The correspondent was further carried away by his eloquence when he expressed his opinion on the religious beliefs of the indigenous population. It was just as well that none of them chose to read the *Tablet*.

Gathered as they were from all the country round of all those various denominations in which this poor land abounds, accustomed at best to the empty services of a Protestant Church, the assembled multitude beheld for the first time one of those glorious ceremonies which the Church has established to console her children, and to teach them the dignity of the worship of God.

The reporter mistook the innate good manners and politeness of the non-Catholic native-Welsh members of the congregation to be a sign of assent to what they were witnessing:

The brilliancy of her ornaments, the splendour of her sacred music, and the solemn ceremonies of the Holy sacrifice, were all new to them, so calculated to produce an impression, that it was no wonder the whole crowd behaved with decency and respect.

Although the local vicar had told his parishioners not to attend, they arrived in their Sunday clothes. It was observed that 'a great proportion of them were Protestants of the highest respectability. The church which was calculated to receive six hundred persons with ease, was crowded to excess, and considerable numbers, unable to enter the church.' Lord Feilding was pleased with the behaviour of the mixed congregation, and wrote to Catherine Berkeley at Spetchley Park that the church was 'crowded with Cats and Prots. The latter behaved on the whole most decorously and I should hope many a good seed was sown that day.'[14]

112. *Blessed Pope Pius IX, restorer of the English Hierarchy; he presented to the Feildings the relics of St Primitivus now enshrined in St David's Church, Pantasaph.*

The donors and patrons of the church, Lord and Lady Feilding were present, surrounded by prominent Catholic laity, who included members of the Mostyn family of Talacre and the Blundells of Crosby. Amongst the leading Holywell Catholics, who would eventually find their resting-place in the churchyard, were Roskells and Sankeys. Present also was Edward Pugin, son of the distinguished architect, who had furnished the church but had died in September. Pugin's contribution was to furnish and decorate the structure designed by T. H. Wyatt. The correspondent of the *Catholic Standard* gave perhaps the best description of the church.

> It is a gothic edifice, a complete parish church, with steeple, chancel, nave, and one aisle. The chancel is adorned with richly stained glass windows, the great window over the high altar representing the principal mysteries of the life of our Saviour. It is paved with coloured tiles and shut in by a light oaken screen, surmounted by a large rood with the figures of Our Lady and St John the Evangelist. Stalls line its sides right and left of the high altar. At the eastern extremity of the side aisle is a neat little altar to Our Lady, and beside it an exquisite statue of the Blessed Virgin, almost as large as life. To the left of the principal entrance is a font elaborately carved with designs emblematical of the Sacrament of Baptism.

On 4 January 1851, Pope Pius IX had presented Lord Feilding with new-found relics of the Roman martyr St Primitivus, and these were placed under the altar in the Lady Chapel.[15]

The impressive service began a little after eleven o'clock, when the procession of clergy commenced from the presbytery, headed by cross and banner, with priests in dalmatics and copes, in a long line of about forty clergy. Benedictine fathers in their habits, canons bearing the insignia of their rank, with Jesuit professors and students of the neighbouring College of St Beuno, and finally the mitred bishops with pastoral staff, proceeded through the grounds to the great door of the church, singing the litanies in the solemn Gregorian chant. As they entered,

> The effect at this moment within the church was thrilling; all was a death like stillness, and the candles and lamps were lighted in the Sanctuary, and the sun then shone with redoubled splendour through the stained glass windows.

High Mass was sung by the choir of St Chad's, Birmingham, concluding with the *Te Deum*.

On the Sunday following the Jesuits of St Beuno's College assumed responsibility for the services at St David's, whilst awaiting the arrival of a community of Capuchin friars who had been invited to settle in the presbytery. The account in the *Catholic Standard* closed with the observation:

It is to be hoped that Catholics will not leave all the burden on the shoulders of the generous individuals who have already done so much, but will come forward to assist in establishing our Holy Faith in a locality blessed by the martyrdom of the glorious Winefride, and even at this time famous for a succession of miracles worked at her shrine.

The death of Lady Louisa Feilding

Lady Louisa Feilding died on 1 May 1853, in a small villa above Naples, aged twenty-nine years.[16] Her remains were brought to Pantasaph to be interred in a new vault prepared under the altar of the chapel. The last of the Pennants returned to Downing, and was honoured by the locality to which the family had given four hundred years of distinguished service. The shops in Holywell were partially closed for a week before the funeral and did not open on the day of the interment. Many of the townsfolk attended the funeral, and in order to show their collective mourning it was decided that forty of the town's tradesmen should join the funeral procession and escort it the last two miles to the church. On arrival at the gate of Pantasaph church the hearse was met by the bishop of Shrewsbury, Dr Brown, and the bishop of Southwark, accompanied by twenty-six priests, the Capuchin fathers and a choir composed of ten boys from Mr Skellon's Academy in Holywell and members of St Beuno's College. The celebrant at the Mass was the Jesuit, Father Lewis, and the deacon and sub-deacon, Capuchin friars Fathers Seraphin and Anthony. An address was given by Bishop Grant of Southwark, followed by interment in the vault.[17]

113. St Beuno's College, Tremeirchion.

New Catholic institutions,

The Feilding presence in Flintshire from the mid 1840s marked a remarkable expansion in Catholic institutions which gave support to the cult of St Winefride. Their establishment was an enlargement of Catholicism, an expansion rather than a mere revival of former institutions, an introduction of new forces which strengthened the old religion.

The College of St Beuno, Tremeirchion, near St Asaph

The College was erected in 1846–9 to the design of J. A. Hansom, and built in the local white limestone in a gothic style described as 'Pugin-inspired collegiate.'[18] The choice of the site was made by Father Randal Lythgoe, then Jesuit Provincial, on land which belonged to the residence of St Winefride, the district of North Wales. The rector of the college became the district's superior, and as such played an important part in the Holywell mission. It was built for a Theologate, or House of Divinity, and trained Jesuit priests many of whom were acquainted with the town of Holywell. Their professors often officiated in the church of St Winefride and at services at the well. They provided ideal platform support in times of controversy between local Catholics and Protestants.

The most famous student at St Beuno's College was the poet Gerard Manley Hopkins, who on occasions walked to Holywell to visit St Winefride's Well. He was captivated and inspired by the spring; which devotion he expressed in his writing. In the autumn of 1874 he noted in his journal:

> Bright and beautiful day. Crests of snow could be seen on the mountains. Barraud and I walked over to Holywell and bathed at the well and returned very joyously. The sight of the water in the well as clear as glass, greenish like beryl or aquamarine, trembling at the surface with the force of the springs, and shaping out the five foils of the well quite drew and held my eyes to it.
>
> Within a month or six weeks from this (I think Fr di Pietro said) a young man from Liverpool, Arthur Kent (?), was cured of rupture in the water. The strong unfailing flow of the water and the chain of cures from year to year all these centuries took hold of my mind with wonder at the bounty of God in one of His saints, the sensible thing so naturally and gracefully uttering the spiritual reason of its being (which is all in true keeping with the story of St Winefride's death and recovery) and the spring in place leading back the thoughts by its spring in time to its spring in eternity: even now the stress and

114. Father Gerard Manley Hopkins, SJ

buoyancy and abundance of the water is before my eyes. (J, 261)[19]

Mr Skellon's Academy for Catholic Boys, Holywell

This was a Catholic boarding school which existed in the 1850s and 1860s, and is listed in the trade directories. Ten boys of Mr Skellon's Academy, Holywell, formed part of the choir which sang at Lady Feilding's funeral. This was the school described by John Duck,[20] one of three brothers from an old Catholic family from Yorkshire who attended the school. John Duck was seven-years old when he started boarding at the school together with others from Wigan, Portsmouth, Liverpool, and two Spaniards. His memories are those of a small boy who had fond memories of his time in Holywell. His reminiscences were made in 1916, when he was probably about seventy-four years of age. They do not say anything about the subjects taught in the school, which were probably of a preparatory nature, for John Duck eventually proceeded to Stonyhurst to complete his education, before taking up a career in the army. We do however learn some interesting things about Catholic education in Holywell, and some information about the school.

Mr Duck remembered that Holywell Academy was held in two old 'roomy houses' next to each other in Pen-y-ball Street. The school numbered perhaps twenty boys and girls, who boarded in a house that was shared with the master's parents. Perhaps Mr Skellon senior may have taught in the school advertised twenty-five years earlier. His daughter taught the girls in the school, and his son the boys. Mr Skellon junior was rather a mournful man, but kindly. There is no mention of ill treatment, or complaints about food, accommodation, or unjust punishment, and neither is there any mention of the master having a sense of humour. He remembered that his schoolmaster had studied for the Jesuit priesthood in Belgium, that he was gloomy, and that religion was an important part of the schooldays. After morning prayers, there was study followed by breakfast after which:

> We all left the house, and walked in pairs to the chapel [St Winefride's Church] to attend Mass. We formed most of the congregation, and I can only remember two elderly ladies beside ourselves, who seldom missed going to Communion. Later on, a school presided over by a Mr Stanhope, a sort of poor school consisting of day scholars only, also came. I think they would be the children of the poorest people in the neighbourhood, possibly of Irish labourers. There were about twenty of them and they used to sing sundry hymns in English with a strong Irish accent. On going to the chapel and returning thro' the little town, we were often hooted and jeered by the boys of the place, who used to shout 'Papists, Papists'. But there was no overt act of hostility because the principal magistrate of the place, Captain Mostyn, was a Catholic. It was well understood in the town that we were under his direct protection and we thus avoided being molested.

115. The Community at Pantasaph: left, original presbytery; centre, monastry; right, St David's church.

The boys were often taken up Pen-y-Ball and walked over Brynford Common to Pantasaph. It was an exciting adventure for them, who imagined they were in the Wild West as they mounted the grazing donkeys, riding bareback 'across the range.' They began their walks during the time St David's church was under construction, and continued to visit Pantasaph eventually making friends with the Capuchins. This is the most moving part of the old soldier's narrative for his encounter with the friars made a lasting impression :

As time went on we became acquainted with the Capuchins, and often made visits to the monastery where we were always welcomed by the good fathers, in their long rough brown robes tied round their waists with a length of rope from which suspended a rosary, and their sandals, and bare feet. We always liked them for they were always good to us, and we came to think of them as the incarnation of all holiness and goodness. For their superior Father Louis we entertained feelings of awe, and looked upon him as a living saint. A stooping figure, bowed not with age or physical weakness, but the figure of one who had lost all the pride and vanity of man, and taken on himself the burthen of the Cross.

When he left the calm and sanctuary of his monastery he laid aside his monastic habit, and appeared in what he perhaps thought was the garb of civilisation. He wore a tall black hat on the back of his head and much too large for him, black trousers very much too long, ordinary boots, and carried a big bulging umbrella. To the man in the street no doubt he appeared ridiculous, but we only saw the holy saint of God, the gentle Franciscan monk, and we should have fiercely resented any show of disrespect or derision. Years have rolled away and snows of sixty winters have melted on the bleak summit of Pen y Ball, yet in the hearts of those of us who may now survive there remains only a great love and profound veneration which time itself cannot weaken or efface.

This is an example of the religious influence brought into the Holywell district through the Capuchin presence.[21]

The Capuchin Franciscans at Pantasaph

The decision to invite the Capuchin Franciscans to Pantasaph was made by Lady Louisa and Lord Feilding in *c.*1852. At first they lived in the house originally intended to be the Anglican parsonage, until the erection of the friary. The Capuchins arrived shortly after the dedication of the church on the 25 October. Confused and tired after a long journey, they were discovered late in the afternoon peering through the drawing room windows at Downing. They settled in and tackled a multitude of tasks, transforming the mountain-side into a calvary, supervising the building of the friary, and acting as missionaries over a wide area from nearby at Flint and Saltney, to other parts of north Wales, and Chester. They were involved with Holywell and the churchyard of St David's became the resting-place of Catholic laity and Franciscan friars. Soon a visit to Pantasaph was regarded as an integral part of a pilgrimage to St Winefride's Well. Thousands of visitors from the industrial towns of England and Wales delighted in being conveyed up the hills, across the common, to the medieval atmosphere of the Franciscan Friary, together with the biblical experience of toiling up the Calvary.

The first community consisted of Fr Louis, its first superior (the Franciscan beloved by the young boy Duck), and Fathers Emidius, Anthony, and Laurence. The following January they were joined by Fr Seraphin, superior from 1853 to 1856. A remarkable expansion took place under Lord Feilding and his second wife, Lady Mary Feilding. A convent, three separate schools, an orphanage and a Franciscan novitiate provided a strong Catholic centre in remote northern Flintshire.[22] The spheres of influence of Jesuits and Franciscans in the Holywell district, although separate missions, were complimentary and of mutual benefit to the growth of Catholicism in north Wales. The religious experience available to visitors in a day's outing to Holywell was probably unparalleled in the United Kingdom. The visitors and Catholic community were doubly blessed by such graces.

Lord Feilding, defender of the Faith, 'Protestantism and Popery'

The zeal and ardour of Lord Feilding for the Catholic cause continued unabated in his second marriage, performed by Cardinal Wiseman in 1858, to Mary Berkeley, a member of an Old Catholic family. The event was the occasion of reconciliation between the heir and his father, the Earl of Denbigh, who had disinherited him on his conversion. Feilding succeeded him in 1863 as eighth earl, and took up residence at Newnham Paddock, in Northamponshire. He was frequently at Downing and was regarded as an important figure in Holywell affairs as an officer in the Flintshire Militia and spokesman for the Flintshire Catholics.

One such occasion occurred shortly after his second marriage. The bride and bridegroom, as an act of thanksgiving on their return to Downing, made a pilgrimage to St Winefride's Well to ask for a blessing on their union. Shortly afterwards the vicar of Holywell preached a sermon in the parish church which caused great offence and scandal.

Hugh Jones, vicar of Holywell (1844–68), was a former fellow of Jesus College Oxford and future canon and archdeacon of St Asaph. By this time he had been vicar for fourteen years, and was well aware of the Catholic presence. Of perhaps more significance, he was chairman of the committee which administered St Winefride's Well. He had been involved in the controversy which surrounded St David's Church, Pantasaph, and had spoken out in the anti-Catholic public meetings held in Holywell a few years earlier.

Whatever his motive for preaching the sermon, it was clear that his anti-Catholic sentiments had hardened. In his sermon on 7 November 1858, he launched a full-scale attack on Catholicism calculated to offend the local Jesuit mission. The vicar denied the existence of St Winefride, the miraculous powers of the holy well, and the validity of post-Gospel miracles. He denounced the teaching of the Roman Catholic Church, in particular intercession of saints, and their veneration. He was scathing about Papal claims and the Holy Office. The sermon was a characteristic piece of anti-Catholic propaganda. It sought to condemn all that the well had represented to Catholics in past centuries, and undermine their present teaching and practice by denying any proof for the life of St Winefride, miraculous cures at the well, and the nature of pilgrimages to Holywell. The vicar had managed in one sermon to deny the reason for the origins of his own parish, and caused anger and offence to his Catholic neighbours by making statements they regarded as insulting, virulent, unnecessary, and historically and theologically untrue. When the sermon was published in print and circulated, the Roman Catholic community had no alternative but to defend themselves in public.

The sermon became known as 'Lying Wonders', from the full text from 2 Thessalonians 2, verses 9, 10, calculated to give the maximum offence, which read:

> Even him, whose coming is after the working of Satan with all power and signs and lying wonders, And with all undeceivableness of unrighteous in them that perish; because they received not the love of truth, that they might be saved.

Their defence was organised by the newly-appointed Jesuit missioner in Holywell, Father Maurice Mann. He had taken up residence shortly before the vicar preached his sermon. The vicar probably misjudged the reaction of the Catholics and most certainly had not anticipated the opposition of a scholarly, energetic Irishman from Tipperary, with a dedication and devotion to the cause of St Winefride to match that of his predecessors. The vicar had given Father

Mann the opportunity to prove himself, and he immediately assembled as defence counsel an able team for a debate to be conducted by the respective adversaries through a series of public lectures in the town and in the pages of the *Flintshire Observer*.[23]

Viscount Feilding assumed the patronage of the defence. His friendship with Pope Pius IX and Cardinal Wiseman gave him a position of authority to preside over their lectures. He was supported by Captain Mostyn, of the Talacre family; Father Seraphin, guardian of Pantasaph; and by Father Lambert, rector of St Beuno's. The Jesuits from St Beuno's College, Tremeirchion, provided forensic and intellectual skill, with Thomas Dykes, SJ, professor of dogma as their spokesman. The vicar in a lecture on 2 November answered Catholic lectures held on 24 March and 30 June. All the lectures received full coverage in the *Flintshire Observer*, with the debate continued in the correspondence columns until the editor brought it to a close on the 23 December 1859 24.

The lectures were crowded with Catholics and Protestants. They were serious, good-humoured, polite, with no physical violence, or unruly behaviour. The vicar, Hugh Jones, in his denial of the existence of St Winefride, used the arguments employed by Bishop Fleetwood in 1713, and also relied on him for his statement on miracles. Professor Dykes defended miracles much as Bishop Milner had done in 1805, by alleging corroborative evidence from reports of cures made by the Jesuit missioners to the present day. Dykes was more informed than the vicar about the historical evidence surrounding the lives of St Winefride and St Beuno. He lampooned the vicar's attack on the Pope, and ridiculed the ignorance he displayed of Catholic dogma, and the historicity of St Winefride. The Jesuit professor had the last word in the *Flintshire Observer* at the conclusion of the coverage, when he wrote:

> In reading Mr Jones' sermon, Lecture, or letters, I have been often sorely puzzled which most to admire: the sublime ignorance he displays as to what it is Catholics really believe, or the blundering or perverseness with which he contrives to misrepresent whatever little he does happen to know…He gravely assumes that a Catholic is bound to believe every account of a miracle which any ancient legend or any private Catholic writer, no matter who, may have recorded, with as firm a faith as if it was an article in his creed, or a plain declaration of Holy Scripture. It is sickening to have to deal with such stupidity …let me tell Mr Jones what every little ragged Irish urchin knows, that no Catholic is bound to believe anything whatever, unless God has revealed it.[25]

The year-long debate gave the Catholics an opportunity not only to defend their religious views in public, but also to enhance the reputation of St Winefride and her well. They had defended the pride of the citizens of Holywell, and demonstrated the unity, which existed between local Catholics and the support received from the Jesuits at St Beuno's and the the Capuchin Franciscans at Pantasaph. A valuable partnership had been forged between Lord Feilding and

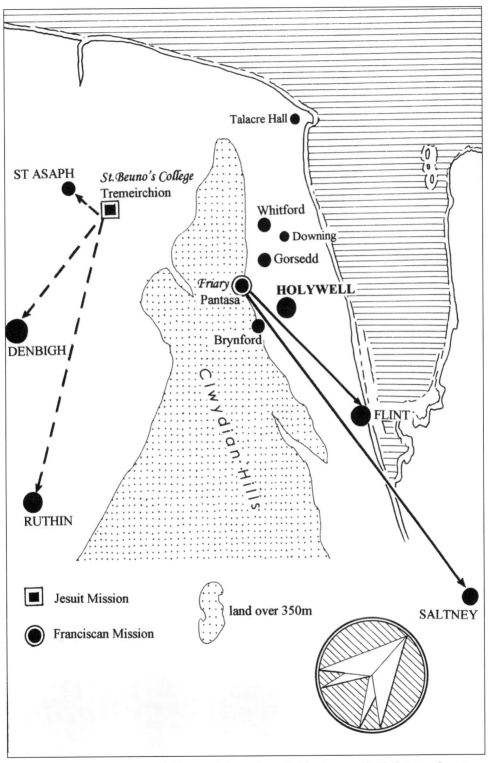

116. *Catholic growth in north-east Wales in second half of ninetenth century.*

the priest-in-charge of the Jesuit Mission, both of whom were intent on strengthening the cause of St Winefride and her well.

Building for the future – Father Maurice Mann, 1858–70[26]

Father Mann 'proved himself an ideal Missioner. His energy and perseverance in raising alms for religious purposes were remarkable, and effected wonders for the improvement of the Mission.'[27] His twelve years at Holywell consolidated the Mission and prepared it for the unprecedented number of pilgrims towards the end of the century. It was also said of him that he 'was most diligent in recording cases of marked improvement in health, or of miraculous recovery resulting from the use of the Water of the well.'[28] During his ministry at Holywell the facilities for pilgrims were greatly improved.

It was the Local Board who made great improvements to St Winefride's Well and its precincts *c.*1866–72. Father Mann was not directly involved in their planning, although his voice was heard and opinions expressed in the 'Catholic lobby' on the Local Board. This was led by Mr Richard Sankey, a wise and respected member, and chief magistrate for the town. It was now possible for people to travel further, more quickly, in greater numbers, and at cheap competitive rates through improvements in rail travel. Catering for excursionists and visitors increased under these circumstances, and it was felt that special accommodation was needed for the sick who came seeking a cure. The Catholic chapel built at the beginning of the century, and extended in 1832/3, was too small for the hundreds of pilgrims, many of whom desired the ministrations of a priest. It had to wait another fifty years before it was enlarged, but Father Mann, relying on gifts of generous pilgrims, made it more attractive by the addition of stained-glass windows and statues. His major achievement was to build a pilgrims' hospice and open a convent for the Sisters of Charity of St Paul.

St Winefride's Church

Father Mann kept the Feast of St Winefride on the 3 November, 1859, with great solemnity. 'High Mass was celebrated by the Rev. Father Seraphin, Guardian of the Capuchins assisted by Father John Wynn, SJ,[29] and Father Maurice Mann, SJ, as Deacon and Subdeacon. Father Stephen Bond, SJ, of St Beuno's College, preached a panegyric of the Virgin-martyr,'[30] a demonstration of the love and fellowship which existed between the Holywell Mission and the new neighbouring foundations. Six months later Dr Brown, bishop of Shrewsbury, came to re-open the church after its redecoration under the direction of Mr Park of Preston.

The church was described as 'a plain Grecian building with a rectangular recess at the altar end, a flat ceiling, and fine semi-circular headed windows on each side. The handsomely carved, white stone altar front, inlaid with chocolate coloured marble was left untouched.' It was noticed that the niche on the left side of the altar, intended to receive a statue of St Joseph, was occupied by a statue of St Winefride made some years previously by Mr Lane of Birmingham which was awaiting translation to a side altar, soon to be erected in honour of the glorious patroness of Holywell.

After the service of re-opening, lunch was served in the presbytery and, amongst the numerous guests were Lord Arundell of Wardour, Sir Pyers and Lady Mostyn, Captain and Mrs Mostyn, J. Youde Hinde, Esq,[31] Richard Sankey, and others. During the service of vespers at 5.30 p.m., the correspondent's attention was drawn to the behaviour of the little boys at the altar, and he was full of praise for 'the precision, correctness and efficiency of their singing which reflected the greatest credit both upon the choristers themselves and on their indefatigable instructors the nuns of the Order of the Charity of St Paul.'[32]

By the time the November festival arrived the promise of an additional altar in honour of St Winefride had been fulfilled,[33] and above it was a carved reredos, in the centre of which was a statue of the saint. In the canopy of Caen stone above the altar was a carving of Our Lord seated, and on either side two angels kneeling.[34] Four stained-glass windows were put in, of which two were bought by offerings of pilgrims, and another was the gift of Miss Dalton of Thurnham Hall, Lancashire.

The Sisters of Charity of St Paul
The Sisters of the Charity of St Paul came to the Holywell Mission in 1859 at the request of Father Lambert, rector of St Beuno's College, to the Reverend Mother-General of St Paul's Convent, Selly Park, Birmingham. The sisters were employed as teachers in the poor schools, and later lived in the Convent of St Winefride built for them by Father Mann in 1869, which was developed into a boarding school for girls.

The Hospice
As early as 1398, King Richard II had given money to Benedict, vicar of Holywell, for a hospice to accommodate pilgrims. Until the dissolution of Basingwerk Abbey in 1536 it was natural for pilgrims to find hospitality with the monks. After the Reformation, the area around the well and courts off High Street offered accommodation for poorer pilgrims, and hotels and posting inns for the more affluent visitors. Father Mann made it his priority to erect a hospice for poorer pilgrims, in order that no one, for reason of want, should be denied the consolations of St Winefride and her well. He appealed for funds to endow a hospice for poorer persons coming to Holywell on the recommendation of their own priest. When the hospice was opened in 1870, they were allowed admission for a period of three to nine days. Full board for a week cost 3s. 6d., and the residents also received religious instruction from the Sisters of Charity of St Paul.

Father Mann addressed a statement of his wishes and intentions in regard to the

117. The Holywell Pilgrim's Hospice, opened by Father Mann in 1870.

hospice to His Holiness Pope Pius IX, petitioning him to bestow his blessing on the undertaking. In January 1862, Dr Brown, bishop of Shrewsbury, following the Pope's example, gave his blessing, and appealed to the faithful to make their charitable contributions.

With this encouragement, Father Mann began to look for a suitable site within walking distance of the well and the church. His first plans were to erect an entirely new building in the orchard in New Road, but these were abandoned when Father Mann bought the present site, situated in a more convenient position, in 1868, with the approval of the Fr Provincial, Weld. This was the Smedley property, valued at £1,946,[35] and large enough to contain a hospice and convent.[36] The property developed by Father Mann consisted of a dwelling house built on the site of the Old Cross Keys, (which became the convent),[37] the Old Malt Kiln, (the basis of the hospice), and sixteen cottages and a stable in New Road. It took him nine years to raise subscriptions of £2,320[38] of which Miss Parry gave £450.

In 1882 the Jesuit Missioner Father Kammerlocher wrote:

What seems to be certain is that everything was sacrificed here at Holywell by Fr Mann in favour of the Hospice. The Holywell Mission was never in debt and his entire energies were directed to the work of begging money all over England towards the foundation of the Hospice. All my energies have been devoted to begging for money towards meeting the necessary annual expenses of St Winefride's Well saddled upon this Mission.[39]

The building was described in 1870 as:

Two stories high, the upper floor being reserved for females and the lower or ground floor for males. A broad corridor runs the whole length of the building, which on the ground floor provides a fine dining hall, airy sleeping rooms, with lavatories, etc. The same provision exists over head for females.

The hospice was opened by the bishop of Shrewsbury on the Feast of St Winefride, 22 June 1870. After Mass, the bishop and clergy 'proceeded privately through Father Mann's garden and performed the ceremony of blessing the Hospice, and the inmates and sprinkling the building with holy water.'[40]

The Regulations of the hospice were strict. Amongst the thirteen, many were prohibitions. No smoking, no borrowing money, no begging in the town, no return visit in the same season, no going out without leave. Other regulations turned the pilgrim's stay into a religious retreat.

Each Pilgrim is not to be idle during the fortnight of his residence in the Hospice: therefore according to capacity and strength, each one will have to do some work, the profit of which will go towards helping the funds for the support of the hospice. … All Catholic Pilgrims will be required to approach the Sacraments of Penance and the Blessed Eucharist, to attend the daily Mass at eight o'clock, and to take part in the other spiritual exercises of the Institution.

Fund-raising was always in progress to help subsidise the cost of running the hospice. On Easter Monday 1874, a raffle in which the prizes were works of art, was organised by Sir Pyers and Lady Mostyn. Amongst the raffle prizes were a pair of oil paintings given by Elizabeth, empress of Austria, who was on a hunting tour, and a miniature in oils of the Sacred Heart, the gift of the general of the Society of Jesus. It was reported that:

The proceedings commenced on Monday afternoon when Sir Pyers Mostyn, Bart. and family was received at the school by the Revd. J. B. di Pietro, SJ, and the Ladies of the Convent, the Volunteer Band playing the Hallelujah Chorus, followed by an overture and an amusing sketch entitled 'To Paris and back for £5.'

Another aristocratic patron was Lady Georgiana Fullerton (1812–85), daughter of the first earl of Granville, who became a Catholic in 1846, a novelist who became absorbed in charitable and religious works, and founded with Mother Magdalen Taylor the Poor Servants of the Mother of God Incarnate. In the time of Father Baron, SJ, *c.*1875, she wrote a letter to the editor of the *Tablet* appealing for funds for 'St Winefride's Well and the Catholic hospice' in memory of 'Father Mann who had died on the 14th of February last year.' In it she mentioned that 'each year since its foundation it has received about two hundred pilgrims, most of who have gone away cured or relieved.' For the encouragement of the subscribers she quoted three examples of recent cures.[41]

Exhausted by his invaluable exertions in the Holywell Mission and entering his seventieth year Father Mann left for Bournemouh[42] to be replaced by Father

John Bapist di Pietro, a Sicilian, long attached to the English Province. He arrived as the improvements to the well were nearing completion and in 1873 was the first to lease the ancient well crypt and its extended premises. The Jesuit Mission, by lease from the Local Board, now had more effective control over the well, with greater opportunity to exercise pastoral responsibility with the pilgrims. This was conditional on the renewal of the lease, usually for a three-year term, being granted by arrangement with the locally elected body. Most of the town representatives were non-Catholics. Some of the missioners found it a burden to raise the rental. An account of the Holywell Mission, written in 1911, summarises the activities of the resident Jesuits between 1870 and 1890:

> Father J.B. di Pietro in 1873 entered into a contract with the municipality for a lease of the Well, at £162 a year. By this transaction he is said to have lost £30 annually, so he pressed for a reduction of the rent. At a meeting of the Town Council to consider his request, certain members of the Council (Calvinistic ministers) betrayed considerable animus against Catholics, and were opposed to any concession. This roused Father di Pietro's southern blood, and he retorted with a very fusillade of invective against the ministers, an indiscretion which made his further stay in Holywell impossible. In 1876 he left for Liverpool …[43]

Father John Baron, the next in command … obtained from the town authorities a renewal of the lease of the well, on easier terms, paying £140 a year. He also increased the sitting accommodation in the church, and gathered 122 children into his school. Fr Baron was a scholarly man, a good preacher and elocutionist of the old type, and a devoted worker among the poor. Unfortunately the drainage system of the presbytery was in a very defective state, and to this is traced the severe illness [typhoid?] of which he died on 11 July, 1878, after only two years' work at Holywell.

Father Henry Walmeseley took his place, but after a few months he too caught the same illness and died on 20 November, 1878. Father James Walker was then appointed, but left after about five weeks, the death of his two predecessors preying too much upon his mind. About this time a chest was found in the garret of the priest's house, containing two skulls, believed to be those of martyrs. There was a hole in the top of each, as though they had been fixed on pikes. They were found in a child's tunic and were taken to St Beuno's.

In 1879, Father George Kammerlocher was put in charge. He was a man of bright and cheery character, brimful of good nature, though somewhat brusque in manner. His first work was to rectify, at considerable expense, the badly constructed drainage system; after which he undertook other improvements, both in the house and property. In a niche near the inner well a beautiful statue of St Winefride was enthroned, which attracted at once the devotion of the pilgrims. In the autumn of 1883 Father Kammerlocher left for St Walburge's, Preston.

Father Thomas Swift, his successor, had worked in British Guiana and Preston. He wrote a short, but interesting *Life of St Winefride*,[44] and did much to promote devotion to her. Quiet and conciliatory in his manner, he was greatly respected by Catholics and Protestants alike. In his time, Father John Milner (b.1819–?) came as assistant missioner in 1887.

Father Charles Wilson was stationed here for two years, his period of office being quiet and uneventful. He was succeeded by Father Charles Beauclerk towards the end of 1890.

The erection of the statue of St Winefride, August 1886

The Local Board had given permission in 1878 for a statue of St Winefride to be placed in the canopied niche at the entrance to the well, from where its medieval predecessor had been unceremoniously removed by the iconoclasts probably in the 1630s. In November 1881, Dr Weatles, bishop of Amgela, had blessed a new statue of St Winefride at the Jesuit chapel of the

118. The Statue of St Winefride erected at the Well shrine in 1886, replacing the original late-medieval image which survived certainly as late as the 1630s.

Immaculate Conception in Farm Street, London, where it was awaiting to be taken to Holywell. It was reported that the journey of the statue would be made eventful by a 'general pilgrimage', 'to what Lady Georgiana Fullerton has described as the only existing shrine in England.'[45] After a delay of nearly five years St Winefride at last entered into her canopied niche so long deserted. The statue is about two-thirds the size of life and was executed in Caen Stone from a design by Mr Kirby, architect, Liverpool, the sculptor being Mr Boulton of Cheltenham.[46] It is the point of prayer for the faithful and centre of ritual for worship at the well.

NOTES

1. A leading member of the Oxford Movement in the Church of England. He was received in to the Roman Catholic Church in 1851. He succeeded Cardinal Wiseman as archbishop of Westminster and was created a cardinal in 1875.

2. E. S. Purcell, *Cardinal Manning*, 3 vols (London, 1895), vol. 1, chapter 14, pp. 287–8.

3. M. Beard, *Faith and Fortune* (Gracewing, 1997), chapter 6.

4. Letters Apostolic, Universalis Ecclesesiae, 29 September 1850. The brief was provocative referring to the Church of England as 'the Anglican Schism.'

5. *Chester Chronicle*, 14/12/1850.

6. FRO, P/2I/4/.

7. Ibid, *Life of Manning*, vol. 1, pp. 288–9.

8. *Chester Chronicle*, 14 December 1850.

9. This found expression in 1851 when parliament enacted the Ecclesiastical Titles Act which forbade the assumption by the Roman Catholics of territorial titles within the United kingdom. It was repealed in 1871.

10. *Chester Chronicle*, 7 December 1850.

11. *Chester Chronicle*, 1 October 1851.

12. *Flintshire Observer*, 11 September 1902.

13. FRO, P/21/1/68 those in *The Tablet* and the *Catholic Standard*.

14. Beard, op cit, p. 71.

15. In August 1881 the relics were enshrined in their present reliquary.

16. The Pennant estates in Whitford and Holywell passed to her husband Lord Feilding, the properties in the Tremeirchion area to her fathers third cousin Philip Pennant Pearson who assumed the name of Pennant and built his residence at Nantlys.

17. FRO, P/21/1/69, *Y Cymro* 17 May 1853.

18. E. Hubbard, *Clwyd*, op cit.

19. N. White, op cit, 1988, p. 45.

20. Typed ms FRO and Holywell Museum.

21. The Holywell archive, CC 830.

22. M. Swarbrick, *The Story of Pantasaph and the Coming of the Capuchin Friars,* 1993.

23. The local newspaper edited by J. Davies. His offices in High Street Holywell were leased from Viscount Feilding.

24. Detailed accounts of the lectures were published : 1 & 15April; 8 July; 5 August; 11 November.

25. *Flintshire Observer*, 23 December 1859.

26. In 1848 the Holywell Mission was placed under the jurisdiction of the rector of St Beuno's College, Tremeirchion. The names of the Holywell missioners from 1847 to 1857 were Fathers F. West, F. Daniel, C. Blackett and J. Holden. Father Blackett is said to have enlarged the elementay school and paid for it from his own means.

27. *Letters and Notices*, vol. 31, 1911–12, p. 326.

28. Ibid.

29. From Voelas, Pentrfoelas. He was responsible for donating pieces of the Winefride Reliquary from Gwytherin to Holywell.

30. *Flintshire Observer*, 11 November 1859.

31. Chevalier Lloyd author of *History of Powys Fadog*.

32. *Flintshire Observer*, 8 June 1860.

33. Given by Miss Anderton at a cost of £140.

34. *Flintshire Observer*, 9 November 1860.

35. An additional £1,025 was spent on the contract and repairs to cottages.

36. The nuns performed the duties of playing the church organ, training the choir, decorating the church with flowers, and supervising the hospice.

37. It cost £800.

38. Raised between 15 August 1860 and 19 October 1870.
39. Holywell archive CAB.
40. *Flintshire Observer*, 24 June 1870.
41. Holywell Archive, 296 B6.
42. He died at Stonyhurst, 7 February 1877, aged seventy-seven years.
43. *Letters and Notices*, vol. 31, 1911–12, pp. 326–8.
44. See details in chapter 7.
45. *Flintshire Observer*, 18 November 1881.
46. *Flintshire Observer*, 19 August 1886.

10. The Remarkable Harvest: 1890–98

'But when the blade was sprung up and brought forth fruit,
then appeared the tares also'
St Matthew c.13 v.26

The Jesuit Mission had been at Holywell for three hundred years when it experienced nine remarkable years which brought St Winefride's Well to the attention of Catholics throughout Britain and beyond. Thousands of pilgrims and visitors flooded into the town during the season from May to November, to seek healing at the well, with frequent cures reported. These were headline news in the national papers, and their most experienced correspondents were sent to Holywell, to interview the fortunate few who had been healed. Fervour of devotion, blessing for recovery, pageantry of banners, candle-lit processions and services at the well, recitation of litanies to the Blessed Virgin and St Winefride, and prayers for the conversion of England were experienced every week of the well season.

An inexplicable change had taken place in the pilgrim experience. Was it revival? Was it renewal? Was it because more pilgrims created a crowd psychology? To many the presence of a new Jesuit missioner provided the explanation. The Jesuit missioner had no doubt of the transformation and its cause, and announced the change to the pilgrim visitors. He was Father Charles Sydney de Vere Beauclerk, SJ, who arrived in Holywell in the autumn of 1890. The nine years he spent there were remarkable, perhaps the most remarkable in the history of the Mission and the town, as the events in this chapter will reveal. Father Beauclerk, as he later testified, was never the same after his Holywell experience.

It needs no saying that our whole lives are bathed in the supernatural. But Holywell was, to me at least, the supernatural obtruded into common place, everyday life. So many remarkable happenings: so many 'Signs'. With a mind

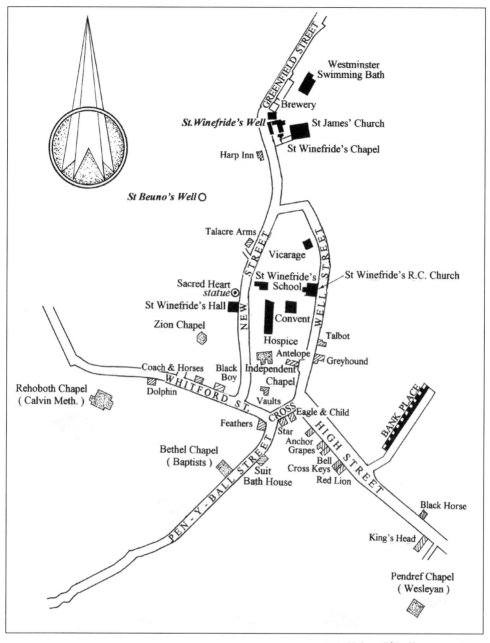

119. Holywell/Treffynnon, c.1900.

constituted as mine is how could I shut my eyes to them? I who could make England ring with the wonders of the Welsh Lourdes, I speak without vanity, I as God's instrument, full of faith in His willingness to show the Supernatural.[1]

This chapter is the story of Father Beauclerk's vision of himself as God's instrument, his life bathed in the supernatural as a servant of the Blessed Virgin

Mary and St Winefride. This confident expression of God's calling and choice as His instrument, and his devotion to Our Lady and St Winefride, caused offence on occasions to the non-Catholics of Holywell and north Wales. They resented Father Beauclerk's zeal which they mistook for arrogance. They were alarmed at the appointment in 1895 of a new Catholic bishop, Francis Mostyn, of Talacre, and his frequent visits to his hometown. To them it was a reassertion of Papal aggression. But they welcomed the money which thousands of pilgrims brought into the town in the midst of economic depression. The town council owned St Winefride's Well, and were jealous of Father Beauclerk's success. They wanted the goose to lay its golden eggs for them.

There were tares amongst the wheat in St Winefride's harvest field. And Father Beauclerk, to change the metaphor, had a particular 'thorn in his flesh' by the name of Frederick Rolfe, alias Baron Corvo, who eventually became his stumbling block. Father Beauclerk befriended Rolfe, who rendered him service, painting his banners, and then turned on the priest in his attempt to destroy him. Rolfe, a convert to Catholicism with a rejected vocation to the priesthood, was an inveterate gossip, romancer, ungrateful troublemaker, but a genius with words, who immortalised his patron and Holywell town. His literary remains shed some light on the main events of those years. Father Beauclerk, too, used the pen to the advantage of his mission. He was a master of publicity, and welcomed with open arms by the local and national papers. The public eagerly awaited the copy he provided for the editors. They relished the weekly reports of the cures and events at the well, and the continual debates in the council chamber about the future and threats to St Winefride's Well, with the priest tilting at the prejudices of the town worthies.

When the Jesuits appointed Father Charles Sydney de Vere Beauclerk to take charge of the Holywell Mission it was probably assumed by the Father Provincial that, under the guidance and support of his mentors and teachers at Stonyhurst and St Beuno's, he would advance the strength of the mission much as his predecessors had done. Nothing more was expected from this young and inexperienced priest. They did not take into account other factors that made Beauclerk unusual. This was an intangible mixture of genes and their reaction to events and circumstances of the Catholic Mission in the time he spent at Holywell, from post Easter 1890 to late autumn 1898. These revealed themselves in a most colourful and intriguing way. His descent from Charles II and his mistress Nell Gwynne, through Charles Beauclerk, first duke of St Albans, and the marriage of another ancestor to a daughter of the third duke of Marlborough, produced a heady mixture of a sense of theatre and drama[2] of dedication, strategy and courage in the heat of battle. These qualities he shared with his younger cousin Winston Spencer Churchill. Both were to experience triumph and disaster.

Father Beauclerk was born 1 January 1855 and died 22 November 1934 whilst serving as a Jesuit at the Church of the Sacred Heart, Accrington. He was the son

of Charles Sydney Vere Beauclerk, a
fellow of Caius College, Cambridge, who
throughout his life remained a staunch
Protestant. His Catholicism came from his
mother, the daughter of His Excellency
Dom J. M. Zamaru, chief magistrate of
Cuba. His mother's Spanish Catholicism
and latin blood obviously had an important influence on his religious development, and that of two of his brothers
Henry and Robert. This was demonstrated shortly after Charles arrived in
Holywell. In September and November
1890 the three brothers, all former students of St Beuno's College, Tremeirchion,
celebrated Mass together on the same
occasion in St Winefride's Church. At the
first service,[3] they were assisted by their
uncle, the Marquis de Valere de Urria,
and on the second occasion, the
November Feast of St Winefride, the
hymn to the patroness was sung by Father
Charles Beauclerk to music composed by
the Holywell organist Miss Gregory.[4]

120. Father Charles Beauclerk, SJ.

An outstanding devotion to St Winefride directed his ministry, summed up in
this entry in his account book, dated and acknowledged CSB 7th Jan. 1899.[5]

AMDG
Dear Saint Winefride
That thou art gracious
To those, who are generous
To thee, let this book show!
As thou hast been pleased to do,
These last years, show thy power still.
Amen.

Father Beauclerk improves and extends the Mission Property
Father Beauclerk worked tirelessly to improve and extend the property of the
Mission, which he saw as belonging to the Catholics of Holywell, and to be
shared by them with the pilgrim visitors. His aptitude for architecture was
recognised as a pupil at Stonyhurst. At Holywell he relished meeting new
challenges, and enjoyed acting as his own architect, building surveyor and clerk
of works, remarking at one stage that he was involved in five projects: the

schools, church, hospice, presbytery and building of St Winefride's new hall were all under his attention in his first years.[6] Both residents and visitors were expected to contribute generously to all fund-raising activities, and special gifts of statues, banners, pictures, and other religious artefacts were always welcome. Sir Pyers Mostyn, gave land on which to build a new school, and other rich Catholic laity made substantial financial contributions to church funds. Father Beauclerk would announce his building works to gatherings of pilgrims, and solicit donations for specific projects. There was no intention of asking the poor to give. There is plenty of evidence that Beauclerk readily helped the necessitous, and never turned away anyone in need. But for the first five of his nine years at Holywell he was continually begging for money. A favourite means of raising school-building funds was by holding concerts in summer months to entertain the pilgrims, at which they and local Catholics participated. For example, in August 1892 it was reported that an entertainment had been held at St Winefride's Schools 'to provide some amusement for the large number of Catholic visitors to the town.' Character songs were sung by local Catholics, J. Dolan and E. Catherwood, as well as songs by several young lady visitors, accompanied on a mandolin. Father Beauclerk exhibited a number of 'dissolving views of scenes in the locality and on the continent.' The proceeds were for school funds.[7] His necessity for fund raising brought out the impresario in him.

His greatest building achievement was the construction of St Winefride's Hall in New Road, on a portion of the orchard. It was a large, modern building, and had 'a well contrived stage with excellent wings,' designed as a school, place of entertainment, and for pilgrims' gatherings, where they could obtain refreshments. It cost about £2,000, of which Mrs Roskell of Stockyn gave £400. Sir Pyers Mostyn, the site, and the Earl of Denbigh large quantities of building

121. St Winefride's Hall, New Road, opened 1895.

materials. Although not fully completed, it was first used in November 1894 on the Feast of St Winefride, when the preacher was Father Bernard Vaughan.

After a huge influx of pilgrims in 1894 and 1895, it was being suggested that St Winefride's Church should be replaced by a large basilica capable of accommodating 5,000 worshippers, built on the hill above the well. This was dreamt of as being the centre where services for the conversion of England to the Roman Catholic Faith might be held daily.[8] Before such an ambitious project could be launched, additions were being made to the north side of St Winefride's Church of three confessionals and a baptistery.

Pastoral work in Holywell

There was never any complaint that Father Beauclerk neglected his pastoral responsibilities. During the Well Season he was continually in St Winefride's church and at the well, where he would meet his flock. He was regularly in and out of the schools and hospice where he was a much-loved visitor. There were other Jesuits attached to the Mission: the retired Father John Milner, an active octogenarian, and Father Flynn. Father Beauclerk was no remote figure and was well known in the town where he gained the respect and friendship of many non-Catholics. The pupils in the Catholic schools greeted him with affection, and on St Winefride's Day, November 1893, they put on special concerts 'in honour of the feast day of the Rev. C. Beauclerk'. The junior performance opened with a chorus, 'All hail to our pastor,' sung by twenty little girls dressed in white, who presented him with a bouquet of white chrysanthemums. After several choruses, a side door opened, and to the great delight of the audience, a little squadron of soldiers filed in. 'Their set up was excellent (the helmets were procured in Dublin) and Master Trevor Jones in uniform as Lord Wolsley inspected the troops. Rhoda Williams was dressed as 'our Good Queen,' Masters B. Schwarz and A. Williams represented the Queen's Navy.' The senior pupils gave their performance a few days later. The sisters from the convent provided assistance and inspiration, as well as religious instruction.[9]

A few weeks after his arrival Father Beauclerk celebrated the June Feast of St Winefride. The week before a novena began[10] with Benediction of the Blessed Sacrament at seven o'clock in the evening which included a procession of schoolchildren, the young ladies of the convent, the day-school children, the sisters of the convent, congregation and visitors; and Father Beauclerk meeting them at the entrance to the well. The Feast was celebrated with the customary services. In the afternoon, a children's service commemorated the Consecration to the Sacred Heart of Jesus, at the conclusion of which there was a procession to the well; and the novena ended with a recital of the history of St Winefride and veneration of her relic.[11] Processions and services at the well in honour of St Winedride were a major element in the new priest's ministry.

It was a busy schedule, integrating the needs of local Catholics with those of pilgrims. A quiet time between well seasons gave some precious time for reflection and recreation which coincided with the birthday of Father Beauclerk on New Year's Day which the music-loving priest invited the choir to share with him. Every year they were invited to supper in the presbytery library, where he showed them his latest magic-lantern slides, ranging from Arctic exploration to Continental travel and they entertained him with impromptu songs and recitations. The bond was further deepened by trips for altar boys to Rhyl and the choir to Eastham.

Father Beauclerk's ministry to pilgrims

The numbers of pilgrims increased considerably in the 1890s. They were attracted both by St Winefride's Well and Father Beauclerk. The hardworking priest had distinct spiritual goals and defined objectives to meet the pilgrims' needs. He never sought to promote his own personality, but his charisma, dedication, energy and holiness made a deep impression. This was further heightened by his emphasis on a continental style of Catholic practice of honouring the saints. At Holywell, he revived street processions, commissioned distinctive banners, held candle-lit services at St Winefride's Well, and introduced statues and holy pictures. A large statue of the Sacred Heart of Jesus greeted pilgrims as they toiled up the hill from the well into the town and Father Beauclerk composed a hymn to be sung on the occasion of its dedication. If there is any measurement of the significance of Holywell to the public – visitor and pilgrim – it can be seen in the number of people who were made well and cured of physical and spiritual maladies. Many had occasion to thank God for their improvement and showed their gratitude. A more material estimate of numbers is seen in the figures provided by Father Beauclerk.

'Note,' he wrote to the Father Provincial, 'The Anglican Vicar of Holywell said, "Fr. Beauclerk is an Ecclesiastical Barnum."[12] I brought thousands of visitors.[13] See this 5,000 votive candles were burnt in 1892 in Holywell; in 1893 10,000; 1894 20,000; 1895 30,000 were bought and burnt in Church, Hospice and Well.'[14] In 1896, 2,700 tin containers of water from the well were despatched nightly by parcel post and train. In October 1894 the steamer *Umbria* transported a large quantity of water to an American applicant. In the same month it was reported that between two and three thousand medals of St Winefride had been sold in the Well-house. It's no wonder that October 1894, was named 'St Winefride's summer.'[15] The enthusiasm of pilgrims at times reached medieval proportions in their desire for 'relics' and Father Beauclerk was forced to hang up a notice at the well from Bishop Mostyn to stop them chipping away stone from the pillars.[16] They were following the example of earlier pilgrims who had chipped away at the headless effigy of a priest in the parish church. They were egged on by the sexton who fabricated his own story alleging that the effigy was that of St Winefride, and the chalice the priest was holding, was the decapitated head of the saint. The chippings were ground to powder and put in water to provide a remedy for healing.

Thousands of pilgrims have always visited the well but the increase in numbers during the 1890s made Holywell headline news, illustrated by drawings of the scene at the well. Many groups returned year after year. The June Feast of St Winefride was always well attended, but August was the most popular month for the working class Catholics from Lancashire towns: the Liverpool area, Preston, Oldham, and St Helen's. Dr Bagshaw, bishop of Nottingham, came annually with a trainload of pilgrims. A brief random selection will provide some indication of their variety.

July 1890 — about three hundred members of the League of the Holy Cross from Liverpool visited the well, and went on to Pantasaph for Benediction of the Blessed Sacrament at 4.30 p.m.

August 1892 — Feast of the Assumption. A trip of fourteen hundred, organised by members of the Third Order of St Francis, attended Mass in St Winefride's, visited the well and in the afternoon went on to Pantasaph for Benediction, and home by train at 8 p.m. On the same day, another party of 'some hundred of members of the League of the Holy Cross, Birkenhead,'

June 1893 – seven hundred pilgrims from the church of St Vincent de Paul, Liverpool, visited the well in the morning and Pantasaph in the afternoon. 'The chief rendezvous of the party during the day was in a field at the rear of the Boar's Head Inn, and here various sports, dancing,&c., were indulged in. Mr Brown of the Boar's Head supplied refreshments on the ground,'

August 1895 – two hundred pilgrims left Nottingham at 6 a.m by special train. Bishop Bagshaw performed devotions at St Winefiride's Church. On one visit he witnessed a cure at the well and gave it verification. Later that month, five hundred pilgrims from Bolton attended a special service in the church and kissed the relic and a large party of pilgrims from London, members of the Ransomer's Guild, accompanied by Father Fletcher, the master, came on a week's pilgrimage arranged by the Home and Foreign Travel Society, Leadenhall Street.

September 1895 – Holywell was thronged with a trip of fifteen hundred visitors in what was known as 'Kelly's excursion', and followed the usual itinerary of well,

122. The now headless late-thirteenth century effigy of an unnamed priest in St James' Anglican parish church, Holywell; it has been much mutilated by relic hunters who mistook it for a statue of St Winefride.

church (where they kissed the relic), and Pantasaph. In the same month other pilgrims met six hundred pilgrims arriving by train at Holywell Junction with banners. They joined together and processed up the hill singing hymns, to be welcomed by Father Beauclerk. 'Mass was said by Father Fitzgerald one of the batch of priests ordained the day previously by Bishop Mostyn at St Beuno's College. This being the first mass of the newly-ordained priest, his hands were at the close of the service kissed by the pilgrims (in order to gain the Indulgence). At noon there was a service at the well with veneration of the relic.'

August 1897 – St Sylvester's Young Men's Society came on pilgrimage from several churches in Manchester, Liverpool, and Birkenhead. They marched in procession from the station to the well, headed by the O'Connel Brass Band, and afterwards went on to Pantasaph. Sixty members of the brass band dined at the Black Horse before attending evening benediction at St Winefride's Church and venerating the relic. On the same day, the Feast of the Assumption, there was reported a 'picturesque pilgrimage of an Italian Colony from Goulden Street Church, Manchester. The women wore distinctive headgear, crowns and rich coloured dresses. On reaching Holywell station, they walked in procession escorting a large statue of Our Lady of Lourdes decorated with flowers. And a number of banners were carried, which attracted much attention and the interest of the inhabitants and numerous visitors.'[17]

A Pilgrims' Indulgence granted by Pope Leo XIII, 1893

Pilgrimages to Holywell were made more attractive by the granting of a Papal Indulgence. The award was announced by Father Beauclerk in St Winefride's Church on the Sunday of the Feast in November 1893, when he read to the congregation the petition which had been presented to His Holiness, Pope Leo XIII:

> Most Holy Father, – The Rev. Father Charles Beauclerk, of the Society of Jesus, prostrate at your feet, humbly sheweth to your Holiness that the Well of St Winefride, in Wales, has been a place of pilgrimage during 1200 years, to the Catholics of Britain. Miracles have not ceased to take place there during those centuries, and hence the town which posseses this well has come to be called Holywell. In the Summer months there come pilgrims in large numbers from all parts of England, bishops and priests accompanying their flocks from long distances. All are anxious to demonstrate their devotion to St Winefride, and are desirous to venerate the relic of this Holy Virgin. This devotion, so fervent and widespread, cannot but contribute efficaciously to the Conversion of England. Hence your petitioner to whom is entrusted the care of this sacred spot, humbly begs of your Holiness, an Indulgence for those pilgrims who shall visit the Sacred Well, and devoutly recite the following ejaculatory prayer: 'Saint Winefride, who for so many centuries hast shown favour to pilgrims in this place of your martyrdom. Pray for us.'

Father Beauclerk told the congregation that the petition had been successful, and read to them the reply:

> The Sacred Congregation of Indulgences, using faculties specially accorded to it by His Holiness Pope Leo XIII., grants to all the faithful of both sexes, who shall come to venerate the relic of the said Virgin and Martyr, and who shall kiss the relic, and with a contrite heart shall recite the above mentioned ejaculatory prayer-an indulgence of 60 days to be gained once a day – applicable to the souls in Purgatory.

At the request of Father Beauclerk, the whole congregation recited the prayer of St Winefride, and afterwards the relic was venerated, the hymn to St Winefride being sung by the choir during the ceremony.[18]

The railway junction
Holywell Junction,[19] the nearest railway station at Greenfield, was a picturesque station in the Italianate style, designed by Francis Thompson, and constructed in 1847–8. The one-and-a-half mile distance from the well gave the visitors some small sense of pilgrimage as they toiled up the hill to the shrine of St Winefride. After the success of the 1894 season, the London & North Western Railway Company granted additional facilities, providing special trains and making it a regular stop with tourist tickets to Holywell available at all the company's stations. Amongst those who took advantage of these arrangements was 'Mr Cook the well known tourist agent.'[19]

Accommodation for pilgrims
The hospice opened in 1870 and in the charge of the Sisters of Charity of St Paul was the ideal place for poor pilgrims to find board and lodging at a charge of one shilling (5p) a day for a maximum period of ten days. Those infirm would receive physical assistance in and out of railway carriages, and omnibuses met all trains. The fare from the station to the well was 4*d.* (2p). Numbers increased dramatically in the 1890s, and whereas 230 were lodged in the hospice in 1895 the number in 1895 was 1,700. In September 1894 a correspondent of the *St James's Gazette* described the choices of accommodation:

> The place is thronged with visitors. Tourists and pilgrims crowd the humble hostels, and to sleep four in a bed, each occupant a stranger to the other three, is a common occurrence. The Villagers (townsfolk) are not averse to this rush; piety does not blind them to the profit to be made out of the travellers. Prices are high both for bed and board, and 10s.6d a week is an average charge for shelter under the eaves of a two-roomed cottage, where one reposes (or tries to) on a bed of sacking, but is solaced by the air through the casement window laden with honeysuckle and meadow sweet.[20]

123. Holywell Railway Station, Greenfield. Opened 1848 and designed by Francis Thompson in the Italianate style. Illustrated London News.

Mr Cook, the well-known tourist agent, had to find seven-days accommodation for fourteen-hundred pilgrims from at least twenty-eight churches when he organised the pilgrimage of the Guild of Our Lady of Ransom in June 1895. A list of the places they stayed was published in the *Flintshire Observer,,* and included thirteen of the principal hotels and smaller inns, with additional lodgings provided by local Catholic trades-people and members of the church.[21]

Father Beauclerk's crusade

Prompted by a letter from Cardinal Vaughan which he read at Sunday Mass in 1893, Father Beauclerk saw his mission to act in obedience to his directive which was to consecrate the nation to Our Lady, to work for the conversion of England. This was his crusade. Over the next few years this idea informed his addresses to pilgrims at the well, the introduction of pictures and statues of Our Lady, and their carriage in processions. The divine response of approval to his obedience he saw given to him in a number of 'Signs' which he was later to recall in a letter to the Father Provincial:

> I read the letter from the Cardinal and with my natural forwardness had conceived and carried out before 1st October a letter to the Railway King, Sir Edward Watkin, the Channel Tunnel man, who had just bought up Snowdon with intent to run a railway up it. He showed my letter about in London saying that's a queer letter from a Jesuit: in it I proposed to put up a statue, or chapel on top of Snowdon.
> This wild design eventually filtered down, first to putting a colossal statue on Pantasaph Mountain to be visible at sea. Lastly I determined to begin by putting

up the picture of Our Lady of Good Counsel in the Church. As I have doubtless told you before: this act brought the first remarkable cure on Whit-Monday 1894 that opened the door to a flood of subsequent cures. It made me feel sure that Our Lady held in her hand great blessings for England and why not capture some for Holywell.

Well to skip a whole year, when in July 1895 (the Sunday within the octave of Assumption), I was giving the evening address, I said, 'Since the dedication of England to Our Lady, we know that Our Lady's arms are stretched over England, ask her to prove her power. God must honour His mother. Ask! And next morning three cures to prove my expectations.'[22]

In July 1895, a copy of the picture of Our Lady of Good Counsel was placed on the altar prepared for it in St Winefride's church. In his address, Father Beauclerk emphasised the purpose of the occasion when he said:

That in paying special and public honour to the Virgin Mother of God, they were following the wish of the Holy Father, Pope Leo, who had so lately in his encyclical to the English people urged that a constant and united prayer should be made to her, in behalf of the country that at one time had been called her 'dowry.' They were to pray therefore that Our Lady would show her power in this country and raise her hands to bless it.

The picture was blessed in the New Pilgrim's Hall at 7 p.m., and then borne in procession on a velvet covered litter by two members of the congregation, and surrounded by a galaxy of little children dressed in white and wearing veils, who were followed by sisters of the convent and hospice. Amongst the priests was the Father Provincial of the English Jesuits, Father Scholes. The procession of four hundred people marched to the well, which they encircled once, singing hymns, before returning up the hill through Well Street to the church. In the gathering were pilgrims from Scotland, Ireland, the north of England, London and elsewhere.[23]

A few weeks later, Father Beauclerk received other manifestations of what he called his 'Signs.' The occasion was on the day of his blessing of the statue of Our Lady of Victories in the new St Winefride's Hall. This he again recounted in 1912 to the Father Provincial.

The Sign given on the feast of the Dolours 1895[24] Another surprising history: Bishop Mostyn was holding his first ordination in St Beuno's. This same day after Mass, three Ladies went to see the New Hall. On the stage I had raised an iron Paris-made Statue of Our Lady of Victories.[25] Before this we were having the first half of the Sunday evening devotions. Then ladies after admiring the Hall, gathered round the Statue. One said 'what a beautiful statue, how I should love to paint it.' Thrice in their presence the head of the Mother bowed so that it nearly touched the head of the child. Oh what an impetus and hope that gave to my zeal. It was after that that Father General agreed to our collecting funds for a Basilica and Presbytery. [26]

The newspaper reported that the blessing of the statue took place in the presence of a large number of pilgrims, prior to being set up in a prominent position within the precincts of the well. Addressing the pilgrims, Father Beauclerk told them that:

It was a remarkable and significant fact that whenever they carried the statue of Our Lady through the streets of Holywell it was followed by manifestations of God's grace. Only ten days ago, the same night they carried the statue through the streets, a young girl who had been unable to walk for four years regained the power to do so and three days ago a young man had the same power restored to him.[27]

Father Beauclerk was zealously carrying out his part in the crusade for the conversion of England through honouring the Blessed Virgin and organising large processions of pilgrims as a means of paying homage. He was asked the question by a reporter in October 1895, 'I take it the processions form an integral part of your services?' To which he replied:

Yes. They have a great charm and interest to those who take part in them, as well as the bystanders. People do like to take part in manifestations of this kind, especially where the motive is a religious one. Night processions are especially interesting. At Lourdes the processions are especially interesting *aux chandelles* and are a notable feature of devotions there practised. We have also found here that cures have immediately followed processions.[28]

Examples of candle-lit processions were reported in 1897. They were often held as an act of thanksgiving for a cure. One late August evening in 1897, three hundred pilgrims assembled at St Winefride's to give thanks:

It was intended, had the weather been favourable, to have had a procession to the Well in thanksgiving of a cure obtained during the preceding week, the recipient of the favour being Miss Jane McClorey of Carlisle who had been going about as a confirmed cripple for over twelve moths, but who since her arrival in Holywell had been enabled to discard her crutches, which she would have carried in her hands in the procession. As it was, over three hundred people assembled at the Well, almost all being pilgrims to the shrine. The building was brilliantly illuminated for the occasion, the pilgrims also carrying lighted candles, and the effect of this flood of light was to display in bold relief the bannerettes with gilt inscriptions which adorn the sides of the Well. Father Beauclerk having recently added considerably to the number previously suspended on the walls.

Father Beauclerk read out a list of nine people cured '… six of whom were present at the service and devoutly followed the statue of St Winefride, as it was carried round the Well, the congregation singing hymns during the progress.'[29]

In 1898, to make the lighting of the well more effective,

> … the large coronal for candles which used to be suspended over the centre of the basin was moved to a spot over the Ladies Well and as a result secured a much better illumination of the crypt with the beautifully groined ceiling shown up in all its exquisite proportions.[30]

Statues of the Sacred Heart and Immaculate Conception

Having failed to raise up a statue on either Mount Snowdon or Pantasaph Common, Father Beauclerk set up on a pedestal a ten-feet high figure in bronzed iron, painted, of the Sacred Heart of Jesus, as a further continuation of his part in the crusade for the conversion of England. It was placed in a prominent position outside St Winefride's Hall in New Road above the well. It could not be missed by any one using the road, and was thought by Non-conformists to be provocative, as they soon said. Nearby Father Beauclerk proposed placing a statue of Our Lady, standing six-feet high, representing the Immaculate Conception, the Virgin crushing the serpent's head beneath her feet. This was to find its home in the gable of St Winefride's schools. It was the gift of a local Catholic benefactress, Miss Ainsworth, and was a replica of the original by a deceased German, Gurtz, made by Angelo Herbert of Liverpool.[31]

The statue of the Sacred Heart arrived by rail at Holywell Junction and was ceremonially escorted from the station. It was an occasion of triumph orchestrated to make the greatest impression on all, as the following account reveals:

> A picturesque ceremony took place on Monday afternoon 24th August, when the new bronze statue of our Saviour (Sacred Heart) was removed from the railway station to the town, accompanied by a very large procession. The statue represents Our Saviour with outstretched arms; while on His left breast appears the Sacred Heart in gilt. The statue, which weighs about a ton, was made by the Societie Anonyme de Fonderies d'Art et de Batiment, Rue Lafayette, Paris.
>
> The procession, which probably numbered at least a thousand persons, left the station with the statue soon after four o'clock, in the following order: Father Fletcher, Master of the Guild of Ransom; cross bearer and acolytes; large banner, representing the archangel slaying the red dragon; banner of St George, new banner of St Winefride; next came the statue, borne in semi-recumbent position on a large lorry. The lorry was one mass of flowers and decorations, and the statue appeared to repose on a bank of flowers. In the front of the wagon was a huge cross formed of beautiful flowers (made by Miss Crozier, Stockyn). The wagon was drawn by three horses, which were beautifully caparisoned and decorated.

124. Statue of the Sacred Heart outside St Winefride's New Hall.

On either side of the wagon walked a number of young girls, dressed in white, with white veils, and wreaths of roses, and carrying baskets of flowers in their hands. Following the statue were the choirs of St Winefride's Church and St Mary's, Friarsgate, Preston.

The passage of the procession was watched by large crowds of people gathered at various points en route. On arrival at the Well a halt was made, and a hymn sung, after which the procession wended its way up New Road, and thence to the top of the town, and back again to St Winefride's Hall where the lorry bearing the statue was drawn into the yard, and another hymn was sung.

The pedestal, which is to bear the statue was occupied by a number of Ladies, including Mrs Roskell, of Stockyn, who has taken a deep interest in the statue. Upon the wall at the back of the platform was placed a large new banner, representing St Winefride and a number of other saints standing in a row. At top of the banner are the words '*Christus Vincit, Christus Regnant, Christus Imperat,* and at the bottom 'For God, Our Lady, and the Catholic Faith'; on the left hand side are the words '*Jesus, Anglian Converte*', and on the right '*Jesus hujus gentis miserere*'.[32]

The statue was unveiled a few days later by Father Towhey, SJ, of St Francis Xavier's Liverpool, in the presence of hundreds of pilgrims from Liverpool and Manchester.

At the Feast of St Winefride in November, Dr Francis Mostyn gave his blessing to the statue and returned in procession to the church where he blessed the members of the newly instituted Guild of our Lady, St Winefride and St Agnes which was composed of about thirty young girls from St Winefride's Convent.

'The Lourdes of Wales,' Father Beauclerk and healing at Holywell
The story of the appearances of Our Lady to the fourteen-years old poor peasant girl Marie-Bernarde [Bernadette] Soubirous in the Grotto at Lourdes in 1858 and her revelation that she was the Immaculate Conception, had a great influence on Father Beauclerk. It was natural that he should be drawn to the story, especially when the small town in the Hautes-Pyrenees grew into a place of pilgrimage, and the spring which issued from the cave in the rock was the cause of miraculous healing.

The similarities of the story of Bernadette with Winefride, and Lourdes with Holywell, had a strong impact on British Catholics at the end of the nineteenth

Jesus ! Gentle Lord and Saviour !
King of mighty majesty !
God of love and sweet compassion
We, thy creatures come to Thee,
Stretch Thine arms of mercy towards and
Help us in our misery !

Yet we sin, Thy law defying.
And, like sheep, we go astray ;
Still Thy loving hand restraining,
Leads us back to heaven's way.
Thou, whose Father's heart hath pity,
Knowing well our mortal clay.

See ! The tender Heart is beating
For the hapless human race ;
And Thine arms are ope'd entreating,
Offering us Thine heavenly grace,
That the wiles of hell defeating,
We may see Thy Father's face.

Heart of Jesus ! Joy of Heaven !
God and Man, we Thee adore.
Refuge of mankind forgiven !
Humbly, strongly, we implore,
That our hearts from evil shriven,
Daily love Thee more and more.

A hymn to Our Saviour, composed by Father Beauclerk.

century. There were many parallels between the two places in their patterns of pilgrimage, devotion, and reports of healing. At Holywell, Winefride and her healing spring had for centuries answered the prayers of pilgrims. Throughout the ages, sick pilgrims practised curative rituals in the well attended by sympathetic hosts and fellow pilgrims, whose shared experience included not only bathing but also worship. The experience was physical and sacramental. The sacred space, a link with the supernatural, and, through holy baptism and the eucharist, a channel of grace made more manifest through healing. The supernatural, as it were, became incarnate through incurables suddenly cured.[33] Modern pilgrimage was in many ways a repeat of the medieval experience. It could not be otherwise, with its conception of the faithful in fellowship with their risen Lord and the saints on an eternal journey together. Every effort was made to sustain and make real this fellowship: visiting the holy well, attending Mass, bathing, walking in procession, carrying banners and lighted candles, hymn singing, and a joint celebration of thanksgiving for healing. The difference that Father Beauclerk found at Lourdes was the freshness of a new vision, the vibrancy of a new experience, and a more positive expression of the pilgrim's, encounter with the supernatural.

When we look closely at Father Beauclerk's frequent declaration that Holywell was the Lourdes of Wales, we realise that it was not employed as an empty catch-phrase or a facile comparison, but that he intended to make it so. The Lourdes experience of suffering as an encounter with Christ's passion and resurrection in the eucharist, and the relief of pain and suffering through Mary's merciful intervention, were represented symbolically at Holywell by the statues of the Sacred Heart and the Immaculate Conception. Father Beauclerk deliberately set out to establish at Holywell a similar programme of events for the pilgrim. As Lourdes quickly emerged as a pilgrimage centre, it developed a ritual programme which concentrated on the curative process, with the sick at the centre of activity

125 & 126. National newspaper interest in the cures at Holywell in October 1894. Two pages from the Daily Graphic.

at each sacred place: the church, basilica, grotto, and spring. The total experience was communal. It can be seen that from the very beginning of his ministry at St Winefride's Well, Father Beauclerk set out to make Holywell the Lourdes of Wales, and to a large extent succeeded in doing so. The only thing he failed to do was build a basilica on the hill above the well.

It is no exaggeration to say that 'the doings at the Well,' (the description of the local press) caused a national sensation in the autumn of 1894, when several leading newspapers descended on Holywell. They had plenty to say about the town, and the legend of St Winefride's Well. The questions they asked in common were: 'Why do miracles occur at Holywell?' 'What is the reason for the report of so many

127. Nineteenth-century Roman Catholic street procession with statues and banners.

cures?' Father Beauclerk gave a reply to these questions in 1894, when he spoke to Catholics in Liverpool on the subject of 'St Winefride's Well, and recent miracles wrought there.'[34]

He gave them a brief history of the well, where he said cures had been authenticated for the past three hundred years, and that the oldest inhabitants remembered distinctive cases of miraculous cures. He said he had a record of miracles in the last four years and quite recently a shoal of miracles burst upon them. A veritable coruscation (like flashes of light) of cures, as he described them. He was certain without the slightest of doubt that those at the feasts of the Assumption and the Nativity of Our Lady were the work of Our Lady. The speaker spoke of a letter he had received from a doctor in Bristol asking for proofs of the cures he saw detailed in the papers. His reply was that he had no time to give proofs, but that they could all be obtained from the persons themselves. 'During this year,' he said, 'there had been twenty or twenty-five notable cures and several hundreds of minor ones. He affirmed that the people of Holywell generally believed in the cures with very few refusing to accept them. The townsfolk took them for granted, as a matter of fact, seeing as they did, so many wonders wrought almost daily.' He concluded his talk by informing his audience of the work he was doing in Holywell:

Holywell, he said, had been called the Lourdes of Wales, and they were doing their best to make it so having already built a hall capable of holding five hundred people. He advised his audience that what was wanted was organisation and co-operation. Those congregations coming to the Well should bring with them their own choirs and banners. For pilgrims Holywell had the advantage over Lourdes because it was more accessible and did not entail a long and painful railway journey.

The publicity given to the cures in 1894 led the public to seek explanations for their occurrence, and 'distinguished authorities' were asked to give their views on the 'recent miracles wrought at St Winefride's Well.'

One of these was a local man, Dr James Williams (1825–1913), who spoke with some authority as medical officer of health of Holywell for thirty-seven years. He was born in Well Street, and spent his life within two hundred yards of the shrine. It was part of his work to examine weekly the residents arriving at the hospice, and he was in an excellent position to assess the effects of the water of St Winefride's Well on the sick pilgrim. He was a practising member and churchwarden of St James Anglican Church situated above the well. Trained at Liverpool Royal Infirmary and Bart's Hospital, his obituary described him as 'the beau ideal of the country doctor.' Respected in the town of Holywell, he was elected the first chairman of Holywell Urban District Council in 1895. Writing at the same time as Father Beauclerk spoke to the Catholics in Liverpool, Dr Williams gave his opinion 'of the curative value of the waters' in a letter to the editor of the local paper in October 1894. He had been asked to do so, he said, because of his medical practice and familiarity with the place. The doctor refused to express 'any opinion on the religious aspects of the question, beyond remarking 'that the "cures" are frequently so pronounced and so rapid that I can

128. Twentieth-century Roman Catholic street procession showing the Reliquary.

129. *Twentieth-century Roman Catholic street procession approaching the well along New Street.*

quite understand how those whose religious creed includes the dogma of the Intercession of Saints, should attribute them to such influence.' However, he refused to accept any supernatural explanation for the cures, and limited his observations 'to the value of the water in a strictly medical and therapeutic sense.'

St Winefride's Well, no doubt, works its 'cures' in two ways, one by shock: two by its tonic power. The cases cured by shock are certainly extraordinary cures, and such, I venture to say, as not often falls to the lot of medical men to witness, one immersion frequently accomplishing the object, and these are the cases (excusably, I think) that have given rise to the idea of 'miracles'. Such cases are mainly the class of diseases included in the comprehensive term 'neurotic', and which are perhaps the most intractable which a medical man has to encounter, I may name hysteria, hystero-epilepsy, catalepspsy, &c.

The sustained tonic action of the water is, of course a slower process than the shock, but the effect, though not so startling, is not much less remarkable. The cases most likely to be benefited by the tonic treatment are diseases of the nervous and the muscular systems, e.g. neurasthenia, ataxia, 'spinal weakness', chronic rheumatism, muscular atrophy, impairment of limbs after injury, &c.

But, whilst pointing out the cases suitable for treatment, it is necessary that I hoist the danger signal against others, such as are, in general terms, as a rule, cases of organic visceral disease; a tendency to congestion of the internal organs- in short, all cases in which a medical man would not prescribe cold bathing.

He added that in his opinion the events of 1894 were not unusual and 'I see nothing in the character of the cures more than has been going on ever since I have known the Well, for the last fifty years, and according to history, for centuries past.'[35]

A year later the *Lancet* pronounced its verdict 'on alleged miraculous healing' at St Winefride's Well, and agreed with the opinion given by the Holywell doctor, pronouncing:

> That actual 'cures' take place is by no means incredible. They have been repeatedly attested by men whose bona fides is incontestable, and whose incapacity for making a correct observation is by no means to be lightly assumed. Having said so much by way of admission, we may say that we have seen no evidence that in the least degree inclines us to admit any supernatural or miraculous element in these cases.[36]

Eight of the cures at Holywell in 1894 received a detailed review in *The Month: a Catholic Magazine & Review*[37] in February 1895. The writer noticed the recent judgement of the *Lancet* (given above), and welcomed its 'grave, moderate, and becoming tone' as a sign 'that the stage of ignorant denial, or of contemptuous insinuations calculated to discredit the alleged facts, has been passed.' He said that his object was 'not to give a history of "miracles" that have taken place at Holywell during the past year. Nor yet is it directly and formally to prove the thesis that supernatural events have been witnessed in connection with St

130. Some of the abandoned crutches of the 'cured' at St Winefride's Well.

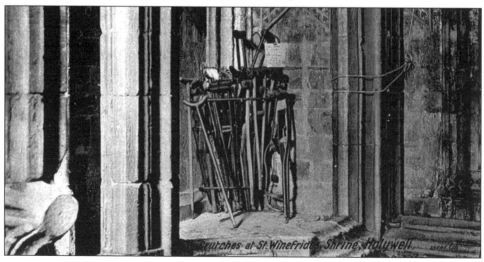

Winefride's sanctuary.' Instead the author confined himself to giving an accurate and a careful account of a few out of the many cures which have undoubtedly occurred there during the last six to eight months.'[38] Father Maher was giving an informed Catholic response: an explanation of the nature of the history of the illness of each individual, medical opinion on their incapacity, evidence of their cure at Holywell, subsequent progress, and authentication of each of these enquiries. Eight cases were reviewed in detail, and the evidence of reliable witnesses quoted. Maher was using the method which Bishop John Milner had employed in 1805 in his investigation of the 'Miraculous Cure of Winefrid White,' that of producing 'authentic documents.' And whereas Dr Milner ended with a discussion on the miraculous nature of the cure at Holywell in 1805, Father Maher in 1895 left it to the reader:

> We do not undertake to decide whether any of those incidents which we have narrated is necessarily due to supernatural agency. We merely submit the facts to the reader, and we leave him to form his own conclusions. There is another class of cures being wrought at Holywell: but their adequate treatment is beyond the scope of the present article. We allude to the miracles of grace, and the healings of the wounds of the soul … each time we have gone to Holywell we have come away with a more profound conviction that the Sanctuary of St Winefride is a rich and extraordinary source of spiritual graces at the present day.

The article in *The Month* presented the cure narratives of eight people healed at Holywell with as much certification as they could provide. The Jesuits had for the three hundred years of their Mission kept records of cures. The desire for strict verification of cures and the judgement of whether cures were miracles in the strict Catholic sense was an issue which was faced at Lourdes with the establishment of the *Bureau Medical de Lourdes* and *Comite Medical International de Lourdes*. The difficulties of saying whether a cure is a miracle is seen in their pronouncement of a very small number of miracles: around seventy out of over five or six thousand cures. W. S. Stead, the newspaper editor and spiritualist had visited Holywell, and made the suggestion that no pilgrim should be allowed to enter the well without previously presenting a card stating 'his history, the exact nature of his disease, its duration, the doctors who have attended on him, &c.' Whilst Father Maher agreed that it would be desirable to obtain all this information, he doubted 'whether it quite enters into the Catholic conception of a fountain of grace.' And he wryly observed that 'If our Lord had appointed St Mathew to exact such tickets, before working cures, some of the Gospel miracles might have been better authenticated; still the plan does not seem to have commended itself to Him.'[39]

Before a review of examples of cure narratives given in *The Month* in 1895 and extracted from the local newspapers in the 1890s, a statement made by Father Beauclerk at the beginning of the well season in May 1896 confirmed his views.

131. Pilgrims at St Winefride's Well.

He read it on the Sunday after Mass, and to pilgrims gathered in the evening in the new St Winefride's Hall. On both occasions he was confirming his belief in supernatural activity at St Winefrides Well, and the way it was manifested. He was also demonstrating that he had not lost his ardour for the conversion of England, and he reaffirmed that the pilgrim experience at Holywell followed the same pattern as at Lourdes. He issued his views in a paper announcing the opening of the pilgrimage season:

England was called in the Ages of Faith the Dowry of Mary, so great and manifest was the devotion of the people to her. She, whom all Christians saluted as the Queen of Heaven was then also joyfully acknowledged as their own Queen and Mother in the hearts of men. This nation has had the misfortune to lose, to a great extent the love and veneration for her. We therefore as Catholics do humbly implore the Immaculate Virgin to prove to this land that which the Infallible Church has always held her to be. We beg her to stretch forth her powerful hand and claim her Dowry. We want the Mother of God to favour Holywell and shew through the hands of St Winefride and the miraculous waters of the Well that she is the Mother of God, and that this country is her Dowry. We will not be content with mere ordinary cures, which the people might say are the work of imagination; but we ask her most earnestly to show her power, and in doing this she will not be interfering with the right of St Winefride. They need not fear that St Winefride will be put out because she is the foot-stool, as it were, for the Mother of God.

After the morning service, the congregation went in procession around the town with a large statue of the Virgin and Child, carried on a decorated litter by four young men wearing blue sashes. The procession was the opportunity to unveil 'a number of very beautiful banners, including new ones painted during the winter months by Mr Austin.' The display of banners was another means of Father Beauclerk advancing his crusade for the conversion of England.

In the evening Father Beauclerk opened a new season of pilgrimage with a special service of dedication in honour of Our Lady. In his address he concentrated on the 'idea of the supernatural.' He dismissed the belief that cures were to be accounted for by natural causes, or by the effect of the cold water, or the shock, or by any medicinal qualities, which doctors might be pleased to imagine were due to the efficacy of the water. He told them that Lourdes was a living proof of supernatural activity, where special favours of the Mother of God were provided at the fountain through the most wonderful cures being witnessed day after day. The French doctors, he said, were puzzled to account for them, and they had to extend the scope of their scientific knowledge and invent new names for them. He said that Holywell had been, rightly or wrongly, called the Lourdes of Wales. This title, he thought, was perhaps somewhat presumptive, and more than they were entitled to, but he said they were going to try and oblige our Lady and make Holywell the Lourdes of Wales, and bring her among them in a real manner.[40]

'Narratives' of cures at St Winefride's Well

Accounts of cures were abundant, and published every week during the pilgrimage season of six months. Other cures happened outside this period, and a few were reported as a result of the water despatched from the well. Every possible kind of cure took place amongst young and old, Catholic and Protestant, and the local newspapers made a speciality of describing them in some detail. These accounts generated a sense of excitement, overwhelming relief, and the gratitude of the beneficiaries. It is impossible to convey the overall reaction of these events, which had their special space in the newspaper, and were more detailed than the personal columns announcing births, marriages, and deaths.

   In May 1894, Alice Woods, a young woman from Preston, aged thirty-four years, was cured of hysterical aphonia – loss of speech. She had been struck absolutely dumb after a bout of influenza and two months spent in Preston Infirmary in 1892 and other medical treatment failed to help her regain her speech. She came to Holywell with a friend, and on Whit Sunday went to church where Father Beauclerk applied the relic of St Winefride to her neck in the vestry. Then she went to the well and drank the water. On Whit Monday morning early, she returned to the well and bathed, and in the middle of her third progress through the water began to talk to her friend. She had received a wonderful cure.[41] In August 1894, Christopher Killride, of Rock Ferry, Cheshire, who had been blind in his right eye for eleven years, suddenly regained the sight of it whilst bathing in the well. Bishop Bagshaw of Nottingham, who was visiting the well with pilgrims, personally investigated the case on the spot and was satisfied that Killride had been cured.

   On 21 August 1894, Sarah Murphy a young woman, of Stubbins, near Ramsbottom, visited the well, and was cured of an internal tumour, the only known remedy for which was a dangerous surgical operation. Her condition was confirmed by a local practitioner, Dr Deans, and Dr Sinclair, an eminent gynaecologist, who had previously agreed to remove the tumour. Being a Catholic, she was determined to make an appeal for the intercession of St Winefride, and decided to visit the well. During her first immersion she instantaneously experienced a complete and permanent cure, and found that the tumour had disappeared.[42]

In October 1894, William Morris, aged forty-one years, of Warrington, visited the well. Ten years previously he had had a slight stroke which affected his right leg and spine. Five years later he was forced to give up work and became a helpless cripple. Morris was in Manchester Infirmary for three weeks without improvement. On discharge, his resources exhausted by his long illness, he was forced into the workhouse at Warrington. There he read about St Winefride's Well, and was determined to make a visit, and through the help of friends he was able to do so. When he arrived at Holywell he got out of the bus by the well, not realising that the hospice was a further two hundred yards up the steep hill, bent up and walking with a stick, he struggled up to his destination, falling in the road three times before reaching the hospice. After bathing six times in the well, he was able to walk with comparative ease, his shattered nerves were restored to soundness, his right hand and arm regained their strength, and his speech became clear again. In order to shew the extent of his recovery, Morris threw down his stick and walked the length of the hospice and back again, and throwing his arms into the air exclaimed, 'Thanks be to God, it will be the most wonderful cure that ever was.'[43]

In May 1895, Frederick Stiff, a family man from Galway in Ireland, came on pilgrimage to Holywell. He had worked as a labourer before having a paralytic seizure, and needed help on his journey. Travelling by boat to Liverpool, he was cared for by sailors, who arranged for him to complete his journey by train. Arriving at Holywell station he was taken out of the train in the invalid chair provided by the railway company, and placed in the awaiting bus for conveyance to the town. On arrival at the hospice, he had to be carried in. The following day at noon, two men supported him to the well and put him into the water. When, to use his own expression, after a few dips he experienced a warm flush over his whole system, he felt as if he could jump out of the water. To the amazement of the other bathers who had seen him put into the water, he was able to walk out unassisted, and walked unaided back without using his stick for support, escorted by a crowd of well-wishers. The next day, released from his affliction, he was seen about the streets without a stick.[44]

The following three reports of cures were published on 23 August 1895 in the *County Herald,*. Alec Crabtree aged ten years, from Nelson near Barnsley, had suffered from a spinal disease for eight years and was on crutches when his parents brought him to the well. They both supported him in the water, and after his third immersion he ran up the steps from the well exclaiming, 'Mother I don't want them any more.' Afterwards he walked as far as the Royal Oak, Greenfield, and was able to play cricket.

Dorothy Coleman, aged five, had been blind in her right eye for a year. On being immersed in the water by her mother she recovered her sight.

Rose Morison, a woman who had suffered from a spinal injury since the age of nine was sent to the hospice by the nuns of the Convent of the Good Shepherd, Ford, Liverpool, with whom she had lived for many years. Rose was now very crippled, and on her arrival in Holywell she was seen by Dr Williams, who saw as many patients as he could between 8.30 and 9.30 every night. He strictly forbade her to take a bath in the well, but ignoring his advice she went into the water and felt very ill after it. The doctor saw her afterwards, and said she ought not to have gone, but the next evening she had a sponge bath in her room, and in the morning felt a peculiar sensation, and exclaimed to her attendant, 'Oh I feel I am better.' Later in that week she was taken to seven o'clock Mass, and was able to walk down the aisle to the altar to receive communion.

There were numerous such cure narratives every year both before and after the time of Father Beauclerk. This final report was made in 1898 by Wilfrid Scawen Blunt.[45]

Blunt had led a very active life as a traveller, and was, as E. M. Forster called him, 'an English gentleman of genius and enfant terrible of politics.' By 1898 he had lost his faith and his health, and was suffering from severe arthritis and rheumatism, and walking with crutches. For relief from the pain he was driven to using morphia. He was in this miserable state when he went to stay at Saighton, near Chester, in April 1898, with his cousin George Wyndham, whose wife, Lady Sibell Grosvenor, took him to Holywell, 'to be bathed by the miraculous fountain there for my cure.' Blunt's subsequent diary entries tell us what happened.

12th April – I have been to St Winefride's well at Holywell. After a very bad night of pain I nevertheless made up my mind not to put off the visit. Fortified with a dose of morphia I set out with Sibell and George. We went by train from Chester. Sibell had written to Father Beauclerk, the Jesuit at Holywell, to expect us, but he was away. I was glad of it, as thus I was free to bathe as a plain pilgrim without religious supervision. I suppose no pilgrim ever washed there with less Christian faith and at the same time with so little of the mocking spirit. I have a belief in holy places and holy people quite apart from all religious creeds, and I felt a great confidence in the Saint that she would do me good.

We arrived at the best moment of the day, at one o'clock when everybody was away at dinner, so that we were alone and there was no difficulty in that sweet old place in supposing ourselves back in the fifteenth century. The girl in charge of the gate gave me two towels, and I had brought a nightgown with me, and so plunged in. It was cold work, though the water, they say, is 52 degrees, but I did the traditional three journeys through the water up to my armpits, going down into it by steps and up the opposite side, and then took a complete dip over my head in the outer tank and knelt on St Beuno's stone. I was quite alone while doing this, except for George … The buildings of the well are still almost perfect, the shrine just as it was put up in Henry VII's time, no stone of the pavement renewed nor anything of the modern kind except some wooden dressing sheds and a few stupid scrolls with texts hung up inside the shrine.

13th April.– I have had no pain all day, thanks to St Winefride a long night of sleep and to-day no pain … I believe in St Winefride and her Well, and include her in my canon prayer as my patron saint, which I have a right to do, seeing that I was named after my great-grandmother, Winifrid Scawen.

Blunt left Saighton and returned to London, where his illness returned. His doctors were of no help, and early in May he went to his estate in Sussex, where he fell seriously ill, and was nursed back to health. He wrote stoically about this deterioration in his health after his release from pain after bathing in the well:

My miraculous cure thus wrought did not last long. I had no sooner turned my back to St Winefride and Saighton than my pains began again, and I began to think that the Saint had made a fool of me.

Blunt burst a blood vessel and was nursed back to health. He described this serious set-back as the coming of a crisis from which, as he recovered, he 'recognized that St Winefride had only deferred her benefits, and that, as in the case of most miracles she had chosen a natural road of cure. However that might be, the cure, though it nearly killed me, was an indisputable one.'

On the 19 October he went back to Holywell, and left this description in his diary:

Made my pilgrimage of thanksgiving to Holywell in drizzle and fog, taking my nurse, Miss Lawrence with me, and my crutches, which I deposited at the Shrine, bound up with a nightgown and label thus inscribed:

Set here in thankful token of a cure from long sickness after bathing in St Winifred's Well. By her servant W. S. B. October 19 1898.

The scene inside the shrine was the most interesting I ever saw in Europe. Three men were being passed through the water stark naked but for a slight bathing draw round the loins, and each time after passing they knelt on the pavement, dripping wet and prayed aloud. A priest was reciting 'Hail Marys,' and at the end of each 'Hail Mary', 'Holy Winifred, still in an unbelieving age, miraculous.' There were lighted candles and flowers, and the fervour of these naked men, one a mere bag of skin and bones, was tremendous. In the dim light of a foggy day nothing at all congruous to the nineteenth century was visible. It was a thing wholly of the middle ages, the dark ages, the darkest of the dark ages, magnificent; touching it brought tears to my eyes. I hung up my crutches in a corner with other relics, placed Sibell's flowers which she had sent as a thank offering on the altar, and knelt for some ten minutes reciting the Penitential Psalms.

Outside the shrine I found Father Beauclerk, a young, good-looking Jesuit …

Wilfrid Scawen Blount's conversation with Father Beauclerk on the 19 October belongs to a later episode, in the narrative.

The appointment of Francis Mostyn, Vicar Apostolic of Wales.

To the great joy of the small Catholic population in Wales, Pope Leo XIII on 4 March 1895[46] established a vicariate of Wales, to be elevated in May 1898 to the diocese of Menevia. Francis Joseph Mostyn (1860–1939), of the recusant family of Talacre, was chosen as the first vicar apostolic. It was an occasion of great rejoicing in north Wales. For the first time since 1559, at the beginning of the reign of Elizabeth I, when Bishop Thomas Goldwell took flight for the Continent, there was a Catholic bishop resident in north Wales. Flintshire, and the town of Holywell, in particular, were delighted with the appointment, and welcomed it with fondness and civic pride.

Dr Francis Mostyn was consecrated titular bishop of Ascalon, and vicar apostolic, on Saturday, 14 September, at the Church of our Lady of the Immaculate Conception, Birkenhead, by His Eminence Cardinal Vaughan. The young bishop was the fourth surviving son of Sir Pyers Mostyn, eighth baronet. of Talacre, by his wife Frances, a daughter of Lord Lovat of Inverness. He had the blood of three English martyrs in him,[47] and a distinguished recusant pedigree, which included a number of priests and nuns. His brother, Sir Pyers Mostyn and his wife Lady Anna Maria, were to be of great support to the Catholics of Holywell.

Mostyn's appointment was undoubtedly due to his recommendation to the Holy See by Cardinal Vaughan (1832–1903). The cardinal, too, was a member of an old recusant family on the border of Wales, the Vaughans of Courtfield, and he was vitally concerned for the conversion of Wales. In pursuance of this object, he sent a petition to Rome concerning proposals for the 'principality of Wales,' in which he made it clear that 'the character of the Welsh was different from the English and that unless the Church were to make separate provisions for Wales there could be 'no way of converting them so long as they are simply as it were tacked on to an English diocese.' Vaughan thought that the time was now opportune in Wales because of the campaign by Non-conformity for the disestablishment of the Church of England in Wales.[48]

> While these are equally matched and politically and religiously tearing each other to pieces, it is time for the Catholic Church to come in and say: We are the Old Church of Wales. We indeed died out through the persecution of the English, but we have revived and behold the Pope has again looked upon Wales and given to Wales a Welsh leader and has recognized Wales as worthy to be treated separately

132. Francis Mostyn: appointed vicar apostolic of Wales in 1895, bishop of Menevia, 1898; and archbishop of Cardiff, 1921–39.

from England and to stand by itself upon its ancient nationality. No time should be lost if we are not to be too late … The hope for Wales is in treating it purely as a missionary district.

Vaughan's proposal to the Pope was to appoint a vicar apostolic to a new diocese composed of the six counties of north Wales and five of south Wales.[49] He considered Wales to be more of a missionary country than England: 'It was more sparsely inhabited, Catholicism was more feeble, and the Welsh people had a peculiar national character of their own.' He therefore urged Rome 'to give Wales a missionary bishop of its own who might have a free hand to deal with it as a missionary country.'

Vaughan decided to recommend Dr Mostyn as vicar apostolic considering him to be 'a young man full of zeal and piety and activity and good sense,' and conversant in the Welsh language. He envisaged that the Jesuits might take on the role of missionaries to the new Welsh vicariate. In the cardinal's scheme, it seemed therefore that the three hundred-year-old Jesuit mission in Holywell would make a major contribution in north Wales as part of the new missionary area. Indeed it might be the fulfilment of Cardinal Vaughan's dream of a Catholic crusade to recall the principality to its ancient faith.[50] The new vicar apostolic promised the cardinal that he would print his pastoral letters in Welsh and English. Vaughan made an excellent choice, and Dr Mostyn served the Catholic Church in Wales until his death in 1939, by which time he was archbishop of Cardiff and Metropolitan.[51]

The visit of Bishop Mostyn to Holywell November 1895

The new vicar apostolic was as eager as his Welsh flock to begin his episcopal ministry. At the beginning of October he visited the Capuchin friars at Pantasaph for the feast of St Francis, and opened their new orphanage. On this occasion Father Beauclerk was his crook-bearer, and one of the speakers was Dr James Williams, the first chairman of Holywell District Council. Everyone wanted to meet the new vicar apostolic, and Father Beauclerk was determined that the Catholic congregation would make his return to the town the following month a memorable occasion.

The bishop came on the first Saturday in November for the feast of St Winefride. Mr R. J. Sankey, JP, whose guest he was at Fron, met him at the railway station. The next morning Dr Mostyn was the celebrant at High Mass where he was assisted by Jesuit priests from St Beuno's. Great care was taken at the church to ensure that the music was of the highest standard, under the direction of Miss Gregory, with the assistance of Mr Howard, one of the regular soloists. The preacher was Father R. Fraser, SJ, who, in his sermon, dwelt at length on the martyrdom of St Winefride.

Unusually for this festive occasion, there was no street procession and no banners were mentioned in the newspaper report.[52] The absence of these did not in the least mar the occasion, for Father Beauclerk had excelled himself in the art of decoration and ingenuity' employing all his theatrical design skills in the display provided, and his enthusiasm in encouraging his congregation to follow suit. The *County Herald,* gave a full description of the street scenes which welcomed Dr Mostyn.

The chief decorative effort was in front of St Winefride's Church: an arch festooned with holly and laurel spanning Well Street. On one side facing High Street was a greeting to the new vicar apostolic 'Welcome. My help is from the Lord. *Croeso.*'[53] On the other side of the arch was a large painting representing saints (a favourite decorative device of Father Beauclerk's). George, Francis, Winefride, Ignatius, and Patrick were displayed standing within a nimbus of golden glory.

In the centre of the painting was St Winefride, depicted as the patroness of Wales: a crowned abbess robed in purest white, shot with rainbow tints, bearing a crook and the golden palm of martyrdom. Next to her was St Ignatius, the founder of the Society of Jesus, with St Patrick of Ireland on his left; and on the right of St Winefride, St Francis, the patron of Dr Mostyn, and finally St George.

The houses in the neighbourhood were freely decorated with flags and bunting; and, extending from Mr Howard's at Assisi House to that of Mrs Richardson at Loyola House, was a string of flags from which was suspended the Eisteddfodic motto '*Y gwir yn erbyn y byd*' ('the truth against the world'). The highway in New Road, climbing from Greenfield Street, past the well, St Winefride's new hall, and the hospice, was criss-crossed with flags and bunting, spreading into High Street, where several of the tradesmen exhibited signs of welcome in their shop windows.

The outdoor display and welcome of the town was succeeded in the evening by a more formal Catholic occasion of welcome; and the presentation of addresses and gifts to the vicar apostolic took place in St Winefride's new hall. The recently opened building sparkled with candles, and glowed with rich autumn colours and delicate hothouse blossoms. An assembly which included his mother and sister made the gathering more meaningful to the young bishop. The Reverend Mother of St Winefride's Convent, Father Beauclerk and the Friars William and Anselm from Pantasaph were present together with a gathering of pilgrims accompanied from London by Lady Vavasour. Seated in the centre of the platform was Bishop Mostyn whom the Catholics of Holywell prepared to honour.

S. DAVID. C. ABP.   S.WINEFRIDE V.M.

'133. The Patron Saints of Wales'. Our Lady help of Christians, St Winefride and St David, shown at St Winefride's Well on a holy picture printed in 1905.

Father Beauclerk read an address to the bishop on behalf of the Holywell Catholics, expressing their joy and confidence in his appointment. He reminded the bishop of the signs of a special outpouring of grace upon this country, which more than three hundred years ago was robbed of the special treasure of the Catholic faith. St Winefride's Well, he said, has for the last two years been the scene of many extraordinary occurrences of supernatural power. He concluded by commending Bishop Mostyn's 'work and office to the special charity of Our Lady and St Winefride' and after these words presented the bishop with a set of gold and silver vessels, together with a chalice for use in the consecration of holy oils.

After these formal proceedings, Father Beauclerk extended his personal greetings to the bishop and the pilgrims in the hall. He mentioned the increase in the number of pilgrims to the well, and visitors to the hospice, a sign 'that the fame of St Winefride had travelled in all directions, and how she was appealing to the nations to come back to the faith of old.' 'They had no reason to go to Lourdes now; they had a well here.' He closed his remarks by regretting that an effort had been made to interfere with tenancy of the well. Before the bishop rose to speak, the hymn of St Winefride was sung, set to the tune of the *March of the Men of Harlech*.

The bishop, in acknowledging the presentation, thanked all responsible for their gifts and welcome. He said that he regarded himself as a Welshman, and would always endeavour to promote the interests of Wales. He remarked that the word 'Winefride,' and the name of the little town of Holywell, were almost household words in every part of this country, 'indeed I might say the Wideworld over.' He spoke about the 'great St Beuno,' and told them that 'The Vicariate of Wales was to be put under the special patronage of Our Lady, St David, and St Winefride.' He lamented that on his journey from the railway station to the town he had seen so many mills standing idle, and was saddened by the resulting unemployment. On the other hand, he was aware of the economic benefit that pilgrims gave to the town. He therefore regretted that there were a few people in Holywell who wanted to shut the gates of the well, or at any rate to keep away all those pilgrims who would come there.

The ceremony closed in the hall with a recitation of the decades of the Rosary, followed by a procession to the well, where the bishop recited the litany of St Winefride, and afterwards officiated at benediction in the church.

A fortnight later the townsfolk of Holywell, in a gesture of gratitude for his hard work, presented Father Beauclerk with gifts which had been purchased by means of a private subscription. He was about to go away for a holiday break after another arduous season at the well. They gave him a leather portmanteau, a hatbox, and a travelling case of dark morocco. In the words of Mr Jennings of the Cross Keys, who made the presentation, they were an appreciation of the great benefits Father Beauclerk had brought to Holywell and a lasting testimony of the feelings with which he was regarded by his friends and well-wishes. This was in strong contrast to the ungenerous manner in which he had been treated in regard to the tenancy of St Winefride's Well by the local authority of Holywell.[54] In August, the local press had rumoured, 'It is an open secret among the names submitted to the Pope for the selection of a bishop for Wales were those of Father Beauclerk, and Father Bernard Vaughan, of Manchester.'[55]

The end of 1895 was the high point of Father Beauclerk's ministry at Holywell, although he was to remain there until the end of 1898. He firmly believed that Holywell had a special place in the divine plan. To him there were increasing 'Signs' that Our Lady and St Winefride were agents in the conversion of England, and the manifestation of supernatural healing power at the well. The appointment of Dr Mostyn as vicar apostolic of Wales was a further endorsement of this, especially when the bishop's task was seen in missionary terms. But there was a subtle difference, for his brief was for the conversion of Wales rather than England. However, all was not well in Holywell, for it was apparent to Father Beauclerk that St Winefride's Well was being threatened by the schemes of Holywell District Council, with its majority of Protestant members. The priest regarded the threat to the extension of the Catholic tenancy to the well as a sign of what he called 'the growing wave of scepticism attacking the old beliefs.'[56] Maybe he picked up this idea from Henri Lassere, who wrote that 'the story of Lourdes reflected the age-old struggle between the people of faith and a skeptical elite.' However the greatest threat to Father Beauclerk's existence came from an unstable Catholic convert.[57]

Enter Frederick Rolfe

My experiences of the two or more years of Rolfe's company in Holywell gave me some queer insights into human nature,[58] … Fr Rolfe was a remarkable genius and his a wasted life.[59] … unhappy, unfortunate, unpleasant and enigmatic.[60] …

He gave me the name 'Austin' till he fell out with me.[61]

This strange and unusual person was Father Beauclerk's 'old man of the sea,' who plagued his existence for the last twenty months of his stay in Holywell. Born Frederick William Rolfe, in Cheapside, London, on 22 July 1860, he became a Roman Catholic in 1886, taking the names Frederick William Serafino Austin Lewis Mary Rolfe. Between the years 1887–90, Rolfe had spells training for the priesthood at Oscott and the Scots' College in Rome, and was dismissed from both seminaries. For a short while he entered the service in Italy of Duchess Sforza-Cesarini, who, Rolfe claimed, conferred on him the title of Baron Corvo. It was for this reason that he 'signed' his pictures with the figure of a black bird [*corvus*: Lat., raven]. By the time he came to Pantasaph and Holywell in 1895, he had already assumed the names of Rolfe and Corvo. On entering the Holywell phase of his life, he called himself Frederick Austin, under which he wrote letters to the local press, and was first known to Father Beauclerk. To complicate matters he used a number of other pseudonyms. For convenience in this episode he will be known as Rolfe.

In the years before Rolfe met Father Beauclerk in 1895, he had already tried his hand at a number of things. As well as being dismissed from two Roman Catholic seminaries he had abandoned a career as a schoolmaster and failed in his attempt to be accepted for further training. In his service with the Duchess Sforza-Cesarini (an English woman), he expanded his interest in medievalism and a passion for Italian country life which he later incorporated into short stories. Returning to England, Rolfe went to live in Christchurch, Hampshire where he worked as a painter of portraits and frescoes. Here the usual pattern of his life repeated itself: quarrels, debts, occasional litigation, and flight elsewhere. He went to London and developed a skill and inventiveness with colour photography. After a short time in Aberdeen as a newspaper journalist, he returned to London, and eventually tramped to Colwyn Bay, arriving at Pantasaph in February 1895.[62]

Rolfe is featured in this narrative because he was employed by Father Beauclerk to paint banners for religious processions from St Winefride's Well through the town. Some of these have survived, and are in the Well Museum. The biographical accounts of Rolfe, and letters surviving from his Holywell period, provide information about the Catholic community that is not to be found elsewhere.

In February 1895, Rolfe presented himself at the Franciscan friary at Pantasaph, and much to the alarm of the father guardian offered to use his secret formula to clean the large calvary in the grounds, in return for food, lodging and, spiritual direction. Having failed to persuade the friars to let him perform this task, he scribbled out his formula in Greek, left it with them, and departed down the road to St Clare's Cottage, to arrange lodgings with the patient Mrs Morris. He remained at these lodgings for some weeks until early or midsummer[63] using her wash house and St Elizabeth's Cottage as a studio. In this sanctuary he began painting, quarrelling with his landlady and avoiding paying the rent. It is of no surprise that this eccentric Catholic with artistic tastes and aristocratic pretensions was soon to make the acquaintance of Father Beauclerk, either through attendance at Mass in Holywell, or visits to the well. Once in conversation with Rolfe, it was impossible to ignore him. Beauclerk must have thought that he had met an angel unawares, with Rolfe's knowledge of medieval religious art, and his love of fresco painting. He was just the person to help him realise his own designs for the production of banners and other out-door decorative motifs, and Rolfe was immediately invited to begin work for St Winefride's and an arrangement was made which was to last for twenty-one months.

134. *Rolfe training for the priesthood c.1889. He was rejected on more than one occasion.*

On his entrance into Holywell society Rolfe believed that he was different, that he was not as other men, and much to his cost Beauclerk was to come to the same conclusion. Their relationship over the next three-and-a-half years was to transform both their lives. This is how Rolfe saw himself at Holywell:

> The Nowt was a Mystery. No one knew from whence he came, nor what, nor who he was. He dropped down upon Sewers End (Holywell), from 'the back of Beyond', settled there, worked like a slave, spoke to few, and made no friends. His dress was not only shabby but fearfully and wonderfully common and stained … And the meticulous delicacy of his habits, together with his voice and accent, stamped him as a person of culture and consideration. Sewers End invented romances about him said he was a 'gentleman who had come down' …[64]

One of the people who knew this thirty-five year old 'mystery man' in Holywell was young John Holden, who gave this physical description of Rolfe.

> He was a little below the average height, with fairly broad shoulders and decidedly bandy legs…He had a smooth high forehead, a rather pointed nose, and a somewhat aggressive chin; his hair was of a faded light brown, and he was bald over the temples and the crown; he was clean shaven, and I think that if he had let his beard grow it would have been reddish brown; his mouth was small, and his lips, particularly the upper lip, were thin; he was very short-sighted and wore a pair of extraordinarily powerful glasses. He was very shabbily dressed. I was most struck by the mouth, it looked so hard and cruel.[65]

Father Beauclerk virtually 'planted' Rolfe in the middle of the Roman Catholic community in Holywell. Wherever he looked, he would see pilgrims as they toiled up either Well Street or New Road from St Winefride's Well to the church or the hospice; on either side of them lodging houses, public houses, shops and stalls selling religious statues, pictures, medals, photographs, etc. Some of these small proprietors were tough Irishwomen, with warm hearts, sharp tongues and with an intense loyalty to their handsome charismatic priest, whom they were prepared to defend with their last breath. Beauclerk arranged for Rolfe to lodge with Mrs Agnes Richardson, first at Loyola House and then at the Greyhound Inn in Well Street, with a studio a short walk away in New Road. The studio was near the hospice, on the upper floor of the Catholic school, in the building known as the Ave Maria Hall. Rolfe was fortunate in making friends with John Holden, Mrs Richardson's good-looking nephew, and Father Beauclerk arranged for the young fourteen-year-old Leo Schwarz to do his homework in the schoolroom and assist Rolfe clean his brushes. The 'mystery man' had an audience to captivate with his fantastic stories and extraordinary adventures.

Rolfe was prepared to work hard for Father Beauclerk, and help him execute the plans he had for transforming the pilgrims' experience in Holywell by adding to it a fully orchestrated Catholic propaganda campaign for the conversion of England. Beauclerk saw this as being achieved by means of a revival of medieval pageantry, and the employment of corporate demonstrations such as those used at Lourdes. Two important ingredients of which were processions and banners.

A visit to Holywell was a mini-pilgrimage in itself. The pilgrimage was undertaken as a procession from one spiritual station to another; the pilgrims toiling up the hill of ascent from the railway station to the town, and on arrival visiting holy places: the church for Mass, the well for healing and special prayer, the hospice for repose, the new hall for instruction and entertainment, and joining in a corporate celebration of Catholicism and demonstration for conversion by parading banners round the town.

Father Beauclerk commissioned the banners to provide pictures and symbols of the purpose of the processions. In pride of place, St Winefride, virgin and martyr of Holywell, and patroness of Wales; in attendance the saints associated with the mission for the conversion of the Saxons at the beginning of the seventh century: St Gregory the Great and St Augustine of Canterbury. For medieval England, St George, patron and protector of England; for a continuing Catholic presence in Holywell since the end of the sixteenth century, St Ignatius Loyola the founder of the Society of Jesus. Later additions included St David, St Patrick, St Francis and St Pancras. Other banners, pictures and statues were carried in honour of Our Lady, who had pride of place. Was it an oversight, or lack of sympathy for Welsh Christianity, that Beauclerk failed to place St Beuno in the panoply of processional banners?

Father Beauclerk was in a hurry, and Rolfe's assistance urgently needed, and he quickly became integrated into the local Catholic community through the part he played in helping to make the decorative effects for the welcome of Francis Mostyn to Holywell as the first vicar apostolic of Wales in 1895. Preparations were also going ahead for the opening of the well season in May 1896, and the launch of Father Beauclerk's crusade. Rolfe was part of a creative team busy manufacturing a multiplicity of Catholic artefacts ready to surprise the town by their introduction in the new season. Rolfe admired Father Beauclerk's appetite for showmanship, and he worked hard to make his contribution to it.

The months from the summer of 1895 to the spring of 1897 were the happiest of Rolfe's existence in Holywell. He found an ideal companion in the young John Holden, of 'wondrous beauty,' Mrs Richardson's nephew. Holden shared Rolfe's interest in literature, and they read and discussed books together. They entered into a collaborative scheme for composing short stories, and Saturday was revision night. Holden lettered the borders of Rolfe's banners, and they spent hours together in Rolfe's studio and lodgings. The young man was a good listener, and was fascinated by the stories Rolfe told about himself. He found the lodger a pleasant companion, with an insatiable appetite for gossip, a great smoker, and willing to share with him the occasional bottle of liquor he received as a present from Father Beauclerk. Holden observed that Rolfe would never speak a word if he could write it. Gradually the friendship wore thin. Rolfe failed to impress Holden with his fantastic stories about his origins and sexual habits, and their friendship ended early in 1897. By this time Holden was tired of the pleasure that Rolfe took in provoking him, and in the end the young man's loyalty to Father Beauclerk made it impossible for it to continue.[66]

Rolfe's enthusiasm for the schemes of Father Beauclerk captured his imagination and engaged all his talents. He composed a litany for six harps to be played in processions. In conversation with young Holden, he shared his dreams of what Father Beauclerk and he could do for the great glory of Saint Winefride and the greater prosperity of Holywell.[67] Chief among these was the design of a basilica to be built on the hill above the well.

Father Beauclerk most certainly would have employed Rolfe in assisting in the decoration of Well Street for the visit of Bishop Mostyn in November 1897. In particular, he may have been responsible for the large painting suspended on the arch which spanned the street opposite the Church 'representing Saints George, Francis, Winefride, Ignatius and Patrick.'[68] This picture, described as 'a large symbolical painting,' was to be exhibited on the walls of the well for the opening of the season in May 1896.[69]

It would be interesting to know whether Rolfe painted this 'large picture.' It is possible, for the names of the saints in the composition coincide with those which formed the subjects of the banners commissioned by Father Beauclerk. It may therefore have been used as a proto-type. However, there is no way of knowing, for the picture has disappeared, and there do not appear to be any clues in the

135. *Rolfe with John Holden, his Holywell literary companion and landlady's nephew, together with his helper Leo Schwarz.*

account book.

Another of Rolfe's enthusiasms was for the *Holywell Record*, which lasted as long as the publication itself from April 1896 to its failure in the middle of 1898. This was a small Catholic journal owned by its editor-publisher Frank W. Hocheimer, who ran his business from 3 Bank Place, a terrace of houses off the High Strret. Rolfe had met Hocheimer when he had stayed at The Greyhound in Well Street. The journal was launched for circulation to pilgrims and townspeople, upon whom it relied for advertising income. Its contained information relating to Catholic events, local news, gossip, and short stories by Rolfe under various pseudonyms. He always enjoyed seeing himself in print, and the *Holywell Record* gave him an unrestrained licence to write whatever suited his purpose. At first his pen was devoted to the cause of Father Beauclerk, but later became an assassin's dagger. In the introduction to the first number in May 1896, Rolfe outlined the purpose for its existence:

> We want to cultivate to the greatest extent in our power, increased devotion to St Winefride, the virgin Martyr of Wales, who has been responsible through her intercessions, for so many miracles and cures and for so many spiritual favours. We believe St Winefride to be one of the instruments chosen by God to help materially in bringing about the Conversion of England. We aim to create an intelligent interest in the marvellous work which is being accomplished by our great wonder-worker St Winefride of Wales, and in her hands and yours, dear reader, we will leave the success of our undertaking.[70]

Rolfe was a dabbler, a dilettante who picked up many of his ideas in museums, libraries, and manuscripts, in such places as the British Museum, Oxford and Italy. Even advertisements for Scotch whisky provided some inspiration. Rolfe never received any training at an art school, and was a poor figure drawer. Unprofessional as he was, he was clever enough to work out a technique which, although amateur, was acceptable to the general public. In order to do this, he deployed the most developed talent he had (apart from writing), photography, as a substitute for drawing. He used the camera to provide him with outlines of figures, of which he made glass slides, and then projected them onto the surface of his canvas, and simply drew round them. When in the course of painting a banner he needed a figure for the composition, he would get Holden to pose, or ask the Schwarz brothers, Bernard and Leo, to provide the models. Rolfe turned his banner painting into an exercise which could be enjoyed by his young companions, and for his photographic materials he relied on local trades people.

One of these was Mrs Tennant whose premises were advertised in the Holywell Record as St Winefride's Studio, High Street. Her main source of business was taking photographs of visiting pilgrims and excursionists at the well. In return for the materials she had supplied to him she asked Rolfe 'to attend at the well' in order to pose a Miss Parry Jones 'artistically.' He refused, describing her request as a 'gross and unlady like impertinence,' and from this incident a feud developed. Mrs Tennant was more than a match for Rolfe's bullying tactics, and she threatened to get her friends 'to sort him out.' He had more success with men than women. One photographer he remained on good terms with was Mr J. J. Ll. Williams, whose brother Ivor was later to contribute articles to the *Holywell Record*. Almost fifty years later, Mr Williams wrote fondly about Rolfe in spite of the debt he left behind in 1899. Wisely, he would not allow Rolfe to borrow equipment and take it away:

> I came to an arrangement with him to let him use my instruments and dark room, ostensibly for the purpose of copying his own paintings in connection with the work he was doing for Father Beauclerk, whom I knew very well. The arrangement was that I was to render him assistance with his photography and supplied all the materials. I also provided him with accommodation where he could perform his work. At that time, the Old Drill hall in Brynford Street was under my charge, and we used it together as a photographic studio. Here we worked together photographing his paintings, some of them many times over. It was too late when I perceived that he and his photographic work was solely a means of enabling him to get cheap copies of his paintings to send away to his clients in the hope that they would be used in the form of pictorial advertisements.
>
> I always found him a person of gentlemanly manners; one who could talk and convince you in a short time that Black was White. His general conversation was so easy and ever flowing and he was always good company. 'The Nowt' was full of ideas about how to achieve success and make money, though I never saw him with any. He was too fond of running before he could walk, and he thus failed in his work. Although he let me down financially I certainly found him an extremely sociable companion.[71]

After he had broken with Father Beauclerk in the spring of 1897, Rolfe continued with his artistic work, and in August he placed the following notice in the *Flintshire Observer,*

Mr Frederick Austin's [Rolfe] new drawing will be on view at the Record Office Holywell, on Saturday next, from 10 to 4, on presentation of visiting cards. It is a line study in Chinese ink; and illustrates the verse from *The Midsummer Night's Dream* Act v scene 1: 'The Battle of the Centaurs'; to be sung by an Athenian eunuch to the harp.[72]

Unfortunately no report survives of the viewing or how Rolfe prepared for it!

Rolfe's output of banners for Father Beauclerk

We have already described Rolfe's use of photography, live models, and 'cut and paste' gleanings from sources as varied as libraries and advertisments, as part of his method of working. There was nothing unusual about the studio in the school room in New Road, and it had space enough for him and his companions. Rolfe was inventive in his technique, although his first work, the Martyrdom of St Winefride banner, was painted in a conventional manner using oils on a primed canvas. He changed to a different technique for the remaining four of his banners which survive, and presumably those which are lost. Instead of canvas he substituted unprimed linen, onto which he applied thinned oil paints, which were absorbed into the material and gave a tapestry-like effect which he called 'stained arras'. When the panels were completed they were mounted on Liberty fabrics.[73]

Father Beauclerk's account book lists the banners Rolfe was paid for[74] (although for some inexplicable reason Beauclerk failed to include the banner of St Ignatius Loyola. The list is:

'Ransom Banner' (big one) £30; St Augustine * £10; St Gregory £10; St George £10; St Patrick** £10 ; St Winefride £10; Our Lady of Ransom £10 ; St David *** (gift of Mr Hanmer) £10 ; St Michael £10 .

[*Begun early in 1896; ** *Holywell Record* vol 2, no.3; ' In the Holywell Processions of 1897, you will be proud to follow the new Banner of your Patron St Patrick'; ***Completed in the spring of 1897.]

Father Beauclerk does not refer to the unfinished banner of St Francis, which Rolfe returned to him on 24 June 1897, with the note:

136. *Rolfe praying at St Winefrede's shrine with Leo Schwarz looking on.*

In sending you the banner of St Francis, unfinished at your wish, I wish to record that I think it a great injustice to take an incomplete work from an artist, with a view to having it completed in an alien hand, & the unity of the composition broken.[75]

Rolfe received praise for his banners in the local press. This must have provided him with some satisfaction and evoked admiration in the Catholic community. For example his notices included:

An Unique Banner of the Martyrdom of St Winefride…the banner is a beautiful work…the features are full of expression and character.[76]

 A number of very beautifully painted banners including new ones which have been painted in the winter months by Mr Austin.[77]

Rolfe made various comments in the *Holywell Record*. At the unveiling of the statue of the Sacred Heart in 1896, he wrote:

Mr Austin's beautiful banners, placed at vantage points, helped to make a picture of impressive beauty.
   The beautiful and famous Holywell processional banners made a most fascinating picture; … those 'gorgeous banners' were impressive, … while the new Holywell banner of St George the Martyr … combines the Spirit of Piety with the Spirit of Patriotism.[78]

In his making of banners, Rolfe's technique and method, although inventive, were laboured, and the end product at times clumsy. He confided to young Holden the bizarre ritual he indulged in as a form of preparation for the creation of his banners: 'When Corvo had to begin another banner he would go to Rhyl for 'inspiration.' After a Turkish bath and luncheon, he would have himself wheeled in a bath chair up and down the front for two or three hours and then go in search of a 'chance romance'.[79]

Exit Father Beauclerk followed by Frederick Rolfe
   The band played the War March of the priests; and alarums and excursions began.[80]

The last act of the volatile aquaintanceship between Father Beauclerk and Frederick Rolfe began in April 1897, half way in the period of their relationship. Beauclerk left Holywell at the end of 1898 and Rolfe on 3 February 1899. Within a year of knowing each other Rolfe was beginning to feel the restraints of conformity, and the strain of living and working under the eye of the priest and his congregation. He was enjoying his artistic work, but could not cope with people as he confessed to Father Beauclerk in a letter of 15 March 1896. Rolfe thanked him for his welcome letters and postal orders but told him frankly:

> And really dear Fr Beauclerk my worldly worries are very bad indeed & lately I have felt that I must shriek or burst … I have developed a violent & raging temper, blazing out at what I suppose are small annoyances, & overwhelming people with a torrent of scathing & multi-lingual fury. I make amends for it afterwards but it leaves me weak in mind & body. It's the Mr Hyde surging up.[81]

When Rolfe wrote his most public attack on Father Beauclerk, 'The Saint, The Priest, The Nowt, The Devil,' in the *Holywell Record*, 31 August 1897,[82] he continued to describe himself in terms of Dr Jekyll and Mr Hyde.

> Lord Macaulay's summary of Nicolo Machiavelli would describe this Nowt [Rolfe]: His character was an enigma even to himself, and it may be safely said that no outsider had ever been able to gauge or appreciate him. He was a grotesque assemblage of incongruous qualities, selfishness and generosity, cruelty and benevolence, craft and simplicity, abject villainy and romantic heroism. His moral sensibility was at once morbidly obtuse and morbidly acute. Two characters altogether dissimilar were united in him.

The quarrel begun by Rolfe must have seemed to Beauclerk a small thing, similar to that which was reported to Elijah by his servant before the great storm: 'there ariseth a little cloud out of the sea like a man's hand'.[83] In April 1897, Rolfe, in contravention of the arrangement that Beauclerk made with him in 1895 to provide for him in board and lodging and supplying all materials, demanded payment for painting banners. Some years later, in 1931, Beauclerk related to A. J. A. Symons how Rolfe exaggerated and exploited his unreasonable demands until the inevitable nemesis occurred:

> He must have painted some ten banners for me, when one day he asked me for the sum of £100. On my assuring him that I could not give it, seeing that I was under orders from my religious superior, he retaliated that the Society (Jesuit) had plenty of money. He then sent me in a bill for £1,000, and I put the case into the hands of a Liverpool lawyer. This man offered Rolfe £50 for himself and £10 for his counsel; and to my surprise Rolfe accepted it.
>   He then declared open war. [In a] local magazine the *Holywell Record* … he let loose in this publication all his views and grievances. He built up a wildly illusioned tale of my supposed hostility, which indeed only began and ended in my refusal to go beyond our first agreement, viz. that I would find him in everything essential.
>   His statements of my 'excommunicating' him and persecuting him and threatening to 'hound him out of the town' are absolutely baseless and ridiculous. In fact it was he who boasted that he worked for and secured my own dismissal from Holywell. My superior removed me in November 1898, after Rolfe had

written letters against me to the Bishop of the Diocese, to my Superior General in Rome even.[84]

Mrs Richardson asked Rolfe to leave his lodgings at the Greyhound on 11 May 1897. He retaliated by writing her a vindictive letter attacking Father Beauclerk as 'your beloved rector & you his frightened slaves,' and the 'Irish Catholics.' She showed his letter to Father Beauclerk, who immediately wrote to the editor of the *Flintshire Observer*: 'You will oblige me for informing your readers that I am not responsible for any statements or opinions that may be expressed in the Holywell Record.'[85] In July, Rolfe was forced to surrender the keys of his studio, and on the 24th went to live with the Hocheimers at 3 Bank Place, and took up the editorship of the paper. He had engineered his own expulsion from the Catholic community, and was forced to leave the security of their enclave in the Well Street/New Road area, and move into the High Street area. Smarting from this injury, he now began to put into effect the threat he had made to Mrs Richardson in May, that he had come to the conclusion 'that it was right for me, in the interests of the Church in Wales, in the interests of you starved half-civilised Catholics of Holywell, & in my own interest (which I have neglected far too long) to prepare for a fierce fight to the death with this unworthy cleric.[86]

Rolfe's vindictiveness knew no bounds, and his persecution mania led him to believe that Father Beauclerk had excommunicated him and put a 'curse on him.' He had foreboding that Beauclerk's 'curse' and his 'oath to Saint Winefride' would ruin him, make him suffer, 'have me hounded out of the town, and prevent me from ever earning a living.'[87]

The troubles of Father Beauclerk and the power of St Winefride

For the last two years of his service at the Jesuit Mission in Holywell, Father Beauclerk experienced incidents which he believed directly effected St Winefride as patroness of the town and the well, and in response to which she revealed her power. These he related to his father superior in a letter in 1912. Rolfe is not mentioned in this letter. Beauclerk apparently regarded the threats of the Holywell Rural District Council and the Protestant Alliance as a greater danger to St Winefride's Well than the banner painter. Father Beauclerk's report of these incidents in his letter to his father superior is used as a commentary on the facts as they were reported in the local newspaper. They form a fascinating insight into the mind of Father Beauclerk and his vision of the place of St Winefride in the history of Holywell.

The lease of St Winefride's Well to the Jesuit Mission

For over twenty years, the Holywell Town Council had maintained an amicable relationship with the Jesuit Mission to whom they had leased the well. This had begun with a three-year lease to Father di Pietro in 1873, which had been automatically renewed. However, on the eve of the renewal of the lease in 1894, the Local Board refused to guarantee a similar lease, on the grounds that they did not want to prejudice their successors, the Urban District Council, who were to take office in 1895. By November 1895, the new local authority had failed to reach an understanding with Father Beauclerk, and there was a great deal of uncertainty about the future of the tenancy. Fortunately a compromise was reached before the beginning of the 1896 season, and the status quo was maintained. But the situation was not satisfactory, and it was felt that Protestant members of the council were voting along religious lines. The *County Herald,* in its leader of 1 November 1895, accused the Urban District of giving Father Beauclerk 'shabby treatment' in their refusal to grant him a five-year tenancy to the well. The leader looked upon him as a saviour and argued: 'That Father Beauclerk's tenancy of the well was coincident with a remarkable turn in the wheel of fortune for Holywell,' remarking 'that a few years ago the town had reached the bottom rung of the ladder in prosperity, and was within an ace of finding itself in the slough of despond. The writer continued:

> All around us, lay the silent factories telling the sad tale of fading industries and want of employment, and the pinch of poverty had already made itself felt in many a family. But in the very nick of time began the 'rush to the Well' from all parts of the country, and from distant lands came visitors to the Shrine of St Winefride. Once more our streets began to wear an air of thriving business, Holywell became almost a household word, at any rate in the home of every Catholic and a new era seemed to dawn on the town. Its influences were soon felt: the tradesmen began once more, to smile, and to furbish up their wares and premises, new buildings were commenced and the inhabitants generally began to feel that after all there was life in the old town yet. Two years of prosperity at the Well however induced the District Council to demand a fifty per cent increase in rent to which proposal Father Beauclerk did not demur.

The injustice which the *County Herald,* complained of, was the council's failure to grant Father Beauclerk's request for security of tenure at the well, and said that no man deserved it more. He never achieved this stability, and when he left Holywell in 1898 the situation was even less certain, as Wilfrid Scawen Blunt learnt on his visit to the well in October, and the threat to the Catholic tenancy more acute with the approved lease of the well to a soda-water company. Father Beauclerk took Blunt to visit a local councillor and hotelier, Mr Lambert, who told him that:

> … a religious feud is at the bottom of the mischief. Father Beauclerk has been imprudent in making use of the Well for purposes of conversion, and in running it as a religious show. This has enraged the Nonconformists, who have determined to put down the pilgrimage as a Popish nuisance. In order more completely to desecrate the Shrine they propose to lease it to a Soda Water

Company at £500 a year, and close the Well on plea of sanitation.[88]

Beauclerk recounted to his father superior 'the judgement he had seen visited' on members of the Town Council who opposed the Catholic interest:

> In 1894, when the booming of the Well excited the cupidity of the Town Councillors and they suddenly determined to claim £200 instead of £100; seven of the councillors were friendly: seven actively aggressive. Of these seven hostile ones every single one was badly hit within 12 months of their attack upon the Saint.

He gave details of their misfortune, for example:

> … the Chairman who kept a flourishing Shoe Mart in a very advantageous position, was turned out of his shop, much to his chagrin & loss, by a Catholic outbidding him for the tenancy. A second was rebuilding his house. He left a trench unprotected: a lady fell in & badly hurt herself in the dark. £120 damages were given £200 is a fortune to a small Holywell tradesman. A third lost a daughter by typhoid. A fourth lost his wife also within the year, A fifth fell dangerously ill himself for several weeks. A sixth had borrowed our huge red plush curtains for an entertainment in the public hall. He was up a stepladder fixing them. He fell and broke his leg. The seventh member a publican had a bonnie girl aged 13 at our school: and he removed her when he was heard in his own bar by a Catholic blaspheming St Winefride. The very next day a brewer's van, bearing the name of St Winefride's Brewery on it, ran over and killed the girl right opposite the Well. This accident was all the more striking knowing the marvellous protection that St Winefride undoubtedly extends to all in Holywell town.

The next group of incidents related by Beauclerk to his superior concerned hostile opposition experienced by Catholics from Protestants who resented their activity at the well and processions in the town. Most of this opposition came from outside the town. For example, Samuel Smith, a Liverpool Protestant, and a Liberal politician who sat for the Flintshire County seat in the House of Commons, won a great deal of notoriety and popularity with the Non-conformists by his attacks on Roman Catholics. In 1896, he published a pamphlet entitled *The Claims of Rome*, and wherever possible spoke in chapels up and down the county on the subject. In 1896 he regaled the Hawarden Circuit of Methodists at Connah's Quay and repeated his anti-Catholic propaganda at Dyserth when laying the foundation stone of a Wesleyan chapel. Father Beauclerk replied to his attack at Dyserth describing it as a 'silly vulgar calumny of a glorious church' and accusing him of 'vilifying his fellow Christians.'[89] Smith received further condemnation from Father Lucas, SJ, of St Beuno's College, in two sermons entitled the 'Bugbears of Romanism' preached in the Catholic church at Flint, in December.[90] Frederick Rolfe, not yet alienated from Beauclerk, also attacked Smith in the March 1897 edition of the *Holywell Record*.

In the same month the controversial Protestant Alliance lecturer the Revd Alexander Roger, from Emmanuel Church in Putney, was engaged to give two lectures in the Assembly Hall, Holywell, under the auspices of the Council of the Free Churches. The first lecture was on 'The History of Protestantism'. Unfortunately, half way through the lecture the ether charge to the magic lantern ran out, and when the lecture was suspended the Non-conformist audience enjoyed themselves by singing Welsh hymns. Frederick Rolfe later accused Father Beauclerk of instructing Catherwood, the Catholic who was operating the machine, to damage the Protestant Alliance Magic Lantern.[91] Roger lectured again the following evening on 'Romanism' when the ether again ran out and until replenished the Non-conformists again regaled themselves with Welsh hymns. The lecturer however was to learn more about 'Romanism' at the close of the evening, for it was reported that:

> Some time after the lecture had closed and when Mr Roger was leaving the hall, he was met by a number of people mostly women and young men who expressed their disapprobation of him in strong terms and it was, it is said, with an accompaniment of mud and gravel. Three police constables and a number of supporters escorted him down to Well Street where he was staying.[92]

Obviously undeterred by the hostile reception he had received in March, the Revd Alexander Roger came over from Buckley on business with the Revd Idloes Edwards. It was suspected that the ministers came to Holywell to collect evidence for their anti-Catholic lectures. Whilst visiting St Winefride's Well, Roger was recognised by Margaret, the Catholic in charge of the well, from whom they received verbal abuse, and not content with issuing a good Irish scold, she instructed a man named O'Brien to keep an eye on them lest they stole anything.

On leaving St Winefride's Well, the two ministers walked up New Road in the direction of the town, past the statue of the Sacred Heart. As they left the Well House entrance, a man with a coal cart shouted at Roger, informing him that the next time he came to Holywell 'he would put some dynamite under him'. After which, George Bromley, chairman of the Flannel Mill next to the well, who had acted as chairman at a Protestant Alliance meeting, passed by on his bicycle and stopped to chat with the Revd Roger, whilst Edwards walked on ahead. At the end of a brief conversation, Roger hurried up the hill to catch up with his companion, but before he reached him he was set upon by a man named Brannan, who struck him across the head, dislodging his hat. Roger was then attacked from behind by O'Brien, who knocked him to the ground against a wall, raining blows down on him. Edwards, seeing what was happening, came to his rescue, and in attempting to get hold of O'Brien, was struck by Brannan. A woman passing guided Roger into High Street to look for a policeman, and whilst there a further assault took place on Llewellyn Jones, a solicitor, who was singled out by John Donnelly as another chairman at Protestant Alliance lectures. He rushed him and pinioned him by both arms. The three men who committed the assaults alleged that they were incensed by the two ministers Roger and Edwards mocking and scoffing at the statue of the Sacred Heart.

James Brannan, Patrick O'Brien, and John Donnelly, were prosecuted, and found guilty of assault. Llewellyn Jones asked the Court to be lenient with them, and they were lucky to escape with a fine. Father Beauclerk had witnessed the fracas, and his part in the event was recorded in the newspaper account of the court proceedings:

> Between the first and second assault (i.e. in New Road and High Street) there had been an interview between these three gentlemen (Llewellyn Jones, Roger, and Edwards) and the Rev. Fr Beauclerk in the street and he seemed to have completely lost himself; and among a crowd of people, invoked the aid of St Winefride and implored a practical manifestation of her power.[93]

Father Beauclerk gave his account to his superior of how St Winefride showed her power after the visits in March and May of the Protestant Alliance lecturer:

> But to go on with our 'Signs'. In 1897 I think it was a Protestant Lecturer gave an insulting lecture in the Town Hall. Two prominent citizens, the Manager of the Welsh Flannel Mills and a lawyer, now County Coroner, acted as chairman the two days. On the Sunday following, at the Well Service, I begged our people not to take the law into their own hand but to let St Winefride defend herself. 'Let St Winefride show her power' I said. Within ten days on the Feast of the Help of Christians a most wonderful cure of a Good Shepherd Man occurred. St Winefride had shown her power. But more. This same scurrilous lecturer came in May again & an Irishman ran at him & rolled him in the mud. He was raised & followed by his excited friend up to the market place. I was told of the occurrence and hurried up to make peace. I said 'Mr Rogers, I am indeed sorry &c but did you not give provocation by your hostile lecture!' Immediately his two friends the Chairmen turned fiercely on me. 'We will have free speech' they said. I replied 'You know how this town depends on the Shrine! The grass would be growing in the streets your own Mill is losing ground; you have to employ fewer hands. Be reasonable,' One of them white with anger said 'Let it be so: we do not want your Romish superstitions, you yourself even telling me how you believed that St Winefride brought trouble to all who opposed her interests. What do we care?
> 'But,' I interposed, 'the townspeople care. They live to a great extent by help of the Shrine, and they have in their hearts a deep reverence for it & the Saint.' Then the Manager of the Mills, Bromley by name, giving way to sudden wrath cried

out, 'You Jesuit! What do we care for you, or your St Winefride?' Then thoroughly
aroused I raised my hand to heaven and said, 'I call St Winefride to witness here,
on these stones, that you have defied her!'

Now mark what followed. On the following February 2nd I took my last vows
at Stonyhurst as a Jesuit. The following morning a Holywell paper arrived. In
great staring black, head lines, such as I had never seen used before in that paper,
was printed 'Appalling Catastrophe at Holywell – Burning of the Welsh flannel
Mill.' The Mill had mysteriously caught fire about 5 a.m. Though close up to the
Well; and the powerful stream of the Well flowing by it; efforts to cope with the
flames were powerless. The fine three or four storied building was a mass of
flames and by 8 o'clock the roof had fallen in. It was at 7.30 or 8 that the Vow
Mass took place. How can I help believing in Signs?

The people of the town said 'See St Winefride was very angry with Mr Bromley
for his insults to her: she would not let them use the water of her Well to
extinguish the flames'.

It was quite a common tradition in the valley, amongst the Welsh that no one
prospered who attacked the Well.

Now please note the following facts; all absolutely correct as far as I
conscientiously remember. Of the two men who acted as chairmen for A. Rogers,
Bromley the same year lost heavily in the Halkin Lead Mine. The following year
his eldest son was drowned at Rhyl. The other Llewellyn Jones, now Coroner for
Flintshire, lost his first born, a baby boy, on the exact anniversary of his presiding
over the scurrilous lecture.

Father Beauclerk received the occasion of the final 'Sign' from St Winefride in
his last year in Holywell 1898. This was the year Wilfrid Scawen Blunt visited his
cousin George Wyndham at Saighton Hall near Chester. In April he was told of
what was happening at Holywell. The Grosvenor family, with the Duke of
Westminster at their head, were enraged by the high-handed behaviour of 'some
Vandals, calling themselves the Town Council,' who were 'claiming the well
which they want to be let to a soda-water company at £500 a year.' When Blunt
came back in October to give thanks for his cure at the well, he met Father
Beauclerk, and gave him a cheque for £20 towards legal expense in his continuing
battle to prevent desecration to the well and retain unimpaired the Catholic
tenancy. The issue was unresolved at the end of 1898 when the Jesuits removed
Father Beauclerk from Holywell.

The entrepreneur in the soda-water manufacture fiasco was J. B. Atherton, of St
Helen's.[94] January 1898 he approached Holywell Town Council for a licence to
bottle the water of St Winefride's Well offering to pay a substantial rent to extract
the water and for hire of the premises, on condition that they were allowed to
make modifications to ensure that bathers did not contaminate the water.
Atherton's proposal to pay the council a substantial rent over a number of years
was seen by them as a means by which they could pay off a loan deficit, reduce

137. Holywell Textile Mills from a billhead of 1919. On the left the Upper Mill: on the right Crescent Mill. These depended on the stream for water power and the townsfolk depended on them for employment. They were intimately connected with the well.

the burden on ratepayers and implement a number of improvements in the town. The council members, the majority of whose members were Protestants, agreed to the scheme. In February 1898 they sought endorsement for the scheme by means of a poll of ratepayers. On the ballot form were the terms of Atherton's proposal for their consideration and endorsement, and they were instructed to vote 'Yes' or 'No' by placing a cross in the appropriate column.

St WINIFRED'S WELL

Mr Atherton offers a rental of £100 progressing to £500 a year for bottling water for table purposes from St Winifred's Well, subject to his being allowed to close in the Spring to prevent contamination, and absolutely to close the Ladies' Well against Bathing, but the Bathing in St Winifred's and Westminster Baths will in no wise be interfered with.

Are you willing that Mr Atherton be allowed to glaze round the St Winifred's Spring, and absolutely close the Ladies Well upon the terms proposed?[95]

The result of the poll was published in the local press in the middle of February, with a substantial majority of ratepayers accepting Atherton's proposal.[96] In May, the Athertons registered the company as 'St Winefride's Table Water Co. Ltd,' with a capital of fifty-thousand pounds.

Opposition to the scheme was voiced by Father Beauclerk before the poll in a letter to the *County Herald*. In particular, he took exception to Atherton's proposal that 'the sacred spring is to sealed, the ancient passage through the water called the Ladies' Well is to be closed henceforth, and only the outer pool is to be approachable to the suffering pilgrim.' He ended his letter on a strong note, with a plea for support from Catholics and non-Catholics alike:

In the name of humanity, in the name of common Christianity, in the name of the Catholics of the kingdom (in which I include that vast number of the Church Protestant who are year by year clinging more closely to all that in ancient days was Catholic) I protest. I call on all right minded people to protest, most strenuously against this threatened gross infringement of the rights of the public, enjoyed from time immemorial; against what is little less than an attempted desecration of the holy well of St Winefride. May the glorious St Winefride defend her own![97]

A week later, when addressing the evening congregation at St Winefride's Church, he described the town council members as 'a lot of children who had been allowed to play with a precious stone. They did not know what they were doing to the holy shrine of St Winefride, they were quite blind except to their own sordid, paltry, and selfish interest.'[98]

A month later, speaking at the Jesuit Church at Farm Street in London, Father Beauclerk addressed the congregation and told them 'that a case was being prepared in the name of Sir Pyers Mostyn the landlord and riparian owner.' Eventually it was the opposition of Sir Pyers Mostyn which defeated Atherton and won the day for Catholics in June 1899.

Throughout 1898 there was a dark cloud of uncertainty hanging over the question of Catholic tenancy of the well. The question of ownership of the well was also questioned, with the Duke of Westminster disputing the rights of the Urban District. The Duke had given his support against Atherton, condemning his proposals to interfere with the fabric of the well as an outrage, and pursued the matter in his capacity as chairman of the Society for the Protection of Ancient Buildings.

The last thing Rolfe composed before his departure from Holywell was a deliciously ironic piece attacking the town council for their sale of the bottling rights of water from St Winefride' Well to Mr Atherton. Whilst appearing to praise Father Beauclerk for his success in bringing pilgrims to the town, Rolfe was really attacking him for his worldliness and commercialism. The title of his eight-page-long pamphlet published in late October, or early November, was *The Attack on St Winefride's Well or Holywell Gone Mad, N°. 1*. For his introduction to the pamphlet, Rolfe described the town and its inhabitants in such an unforgettable way that no one escaped his attack. Rolfe's view of Holywell as he saw it in 1898 is worth quoting in full:

> Holywell is one of the quaintest and loveliest, and most ridiculous of places in Great Britain. I do not mean 'loveliest' as a superlative applied to picturesqueness, but as applied to the facilities it affords for the study of humanity. Here, we have sects and consequent discords, in profuse abundance. Here, wisdom is accounted folly, and folly wisdom. Here, are bigots who sacrifice their personal, and the general pocket, interests by endeavouring to keep from the town the visitors who enrich them. Here, we have saints and sinners in common with other towns.

Here, the priest, and the priest-baiter, who labouring under a strong self-delusion, confounds his antipathies with his duties. Here, the reverend representative of the Church (as by law established), with a thirty years experience of the town of Holywell, ridicules the cures, which a medical practitioner, of equal long standing, from personal and precise knowledge, says there can be no mistake about, because 'people go home quite well, after various periods of disablement.' The same medical gentleman assures the public that the Catholic mission is carried on 'with religious and humanitarian ends,' thereby effectually demolishing the assertions of the reverend representative of the Church (as by law established), who has wilfully neglected his opportunities of obtaining information regarding cures, and consequently has thought himself justified in imputing 'base motives and a sordid object to a line of action' incomprehensible to his mind. Here, we have a School Board (notorious throughout the country for its blatant ineptitude) whose action, in connection with the appointment of a clerk, was thought so remarkable by a candidate for the position that he promptly withdrew his candidature, and in a letter publicly read told the Board that their methods appeared to savour strongly of nepotism and jobbery. Here, there are businessmen whose sagacity is so profound that in 1896 they talked of building a large Hydropathic, near to the Shrine, and £20,000 was mentioned as the probable cost. Fancy a Hydropathic in Holywell in the present state of the town! No paving. No proper water supply. No drainage. No facilities to cope with the fire fiend. With these preliminary remarks which will prepare my readers for the besotted blunders of which a majority of ratepayers have, within the past few months, been guilty I will proceed to unfold the actual subject of this pamphlet.

HOLYWELL GONE MAD

After having mocked the town and its leading citizens Rolfe attacked the town council and ratepayers for accepting Atherton's bid to purchase the bottling rights of the well water. He called their decision 'crass stupidity and unchristian intolerance' which 'had for their war cry 'For the good of the town.' Rolfe pointed out that by supporting Atherton they had rejected the efforts of Father Beauclerk, whose endeavours had brought prosperity to the town. In support of this contention, he quoted statistics which showed that between 1895–98, 95,000 pilgrims and visitors had travelled by train to the town to visit St Winefride's Well, and spent an estimated £22,500. Rolfe declared that Holywell had gone mad by voting to close the well facilities and turn away the pilgrims in exchange for the paltry sum of £2,250, the expected return over a period of the eight years of Atherton's lease. He closed on a prophetic warning note:

Mr Atherton – well, he has not begun his bottling yet. He is not quite sure that he has a right. His law costs are piling up beautifully.
Father Beauclerk is – as he was – holding the fort.

The pilgrim's are – as they were praying, believing, coming.
St Winefride is – as ever – watching events.
And they will come off satisfactorily to Catholics ere long we may be sure.

Once again, in this last episode of the Athertons, it was evident to Father Beauclerk that St Winefride was, as Rolfe foretold, 'watching events' and showing her power. He gave his own account to his superior of St Winefride's intervention:

> I interviewed the two Athertons in Lime Street Hotel [the Adelphi, Liverpool]: I warned them, that they'd only make trouble for themselves. Of course they laughed at me. They came to grief. They were run down promoting a fraudulent Company and the prosecuting Counsel was Asquith the Premier.
>
> St Winefride's interference was often almost whimsical just as St Philomena's at Mugnano was well known to be. When the soda water idea was on, a man was sent with a big jar to fetch water for the analytical chemist to test. When he went down the first time Margaret at the Well warned him that he'd have St Winefride after him. She heard a report and a curse. The jar had burst as the man lifted it on to the pavement. The second time he came he managed more carefully and got the jar, safe up to the entrance gate: but again there was a loud report, the second jar had burst. The third time he got his jar safely to the railway station, but here it exploded on the platform.
>
> 'Signs', 'Signs': I might go through a hundred pages.

In June 1899, Mr Justice Byrne granted an injunction in favour of Sir Pyers Mostyn, restraining Atherton and his company from extracting water for bottling purposes from St Winefride's Well.[99] By this time both Beauclerk and Rolfe had left the town, but their prayers were answered and faith vindicated, for once again St Winefride had shown her power in preventing her spring being exploited for commercial purposes. The perpendicular structure was not turned into a twentieth-century factory making soda water, and the sacred waters were not glazed in: and no barriers were erected to prevent pilgrims entering the Ladies' and Octagonal Wells and observing the centuries-old ritual.

The judgement of Mr Justice Byrne was of great significance and included a thorough-going review of the local authority's role in the management of the well in the nineteenth century. It outlined its powers over the supply of water from the spring to the inhabitants of Holywell, and their rights to use the building. It upheld the rights of the riparian owners to water from the spring. He gave clear guidance of the position of the well in relation to government public health legislation. St Winefride's Well was, he pronounced, a public well within the Public Health Act of 1875. He also ruled that the local authority were entitled to take charge of it under the provisions of the Public Health Act of 1848, which allowed them to look after public wells for the gratuitous supply of public baths and a plentiful water supply to local inhabitants.

Mr Justice Byrne further ruled that the granting of a licence by Holywell Urban District Council to Atherton's company for the purpose of extracting water did not fall within the provision of the Public Health Act of 1875 stating that:

If acted upon in any considerable degree, it would cause a sensible diminution in the flow of water and therefore the plaintiffs (Sir Pyers Mostyn, etc) had established their right to the injunction.

With regard to the site of St Winefride's Well and Chapel he said:

The local board acquired, by means of agreements and leases from local owners, land round the well. They never did acquire the site by virtue of any lease or agreement for a lease, or of any tenancy. They never did acquire the actual site of the chapel itself or of the land underneath where the spring issues.

The major result of the judgement was the maintenance of the status quo of the administration and leasing of the well. However, the court proceedings, and the evidence produced, raised issues not covered by the judgement, which were to be of major importance in the future. One cause for grave and increasing concern was the noticeable diminution of the water supply to the spring. Another issue was the ownership of St Winefride's Chapel and the well crypt beneath it. This issue was finally settled in 1936.

The removal of Father Beauclerk from Holywell

The announcement of Father Beauclerk's removal from the Jesuit Mission at Holywell was made on his forty-fourth birthday, 1 January 1899. The *County Herald,* commented six days later, that it was for health reasons that he was obliged 'to seek a less arduous sphere of labour.' This was not the reason. Father Beauclerk later described his leaving Holywell as 'a dismissal' by his superiors, brought about by letters written by Frederick Rolfe to the Jesuit Father Provincial at Farm Street, the Father General in Rome, and Dr Mostyn, bishop of Menevia. Father Beauclerk was heartbroken and baffled by the decision of his superiors. In his letter to the Father Provincial in 1912, he gave some account of his reaction and thoughts on his removal.

Father Gerard, as Provincial, bid me 'sever my connection with Holywell.' I obeyed as far as I humanly could. I have never set foot in the place (but once only at Christmas) never preached a sermon either there or elsewhere on the Saint. But cannot I see that this very 'isolation' of myself is a 'Sign', a clear proof of God's 'special intent'. Honestly as I expect to be judged, I see no explanation of my having been so ruthlessly removed but the supernatural explanation. On the one side my pride & sinfulness, on the other a false prudence, a fear of Holywell becoming too notorious, the growing wave of scepticism attacking the old beliefs, beliefs in the Rosary, belief in the Santa Casa. Of course my belief in the legend of the Saint of the Well and tremendous booming I was instrumental in giving it was undesirable.

The public reacted to the news of Father Beauclerk's dismissal with feelings of shock, dismay, and unbelief. An appeal for his return was sent to Jesuit headquarters in Rome and to Farm Street with a copy to Bishop Mostyn on the 12 March (ironically the feast day of St Gregory the Great), accompanied by a mammoth petition bearing 22,820 signatures. It was probably organised and written by J. Bierne of Shamrock House, Holywell, an apparitor of St Winefride's Church.

The petition consisted of thirty-one typed pages of about 4,500 words. It was respectful in tone, repetitive and rambling in content, and its main objective a plea for the reinstatement of Father Beauclerk as superior of the Jesuit Mission in Holywell. It does not disguise the fact that Father Beauclerk had 'a few malicious enemies,' and 'that there had been undeserved attacks upon his character' and accusations of mismanagement of the finances of the Mission. It was made clear that the petition was limited almost entirely to lay people, and that 'many thousand other signatures would have been obtained but for the hostile attitudes so generally adopted by the clergy both Regular and Secular, towards this Petition and its object.' It was full of praise for the work accomplished by Father Beauclerk particularly, as 'St Winefride's almoner,' for the conversion of England and the Guild of Ransom. The case of the people of Holywell was precise and to the point: 'Father Beauclerk's presence in Holywell is beneficial to our souls.' The removal of Father Beauclerk was regretted by townspeople as well as by the majority of Catholics in Holywell. Dr James Williams summed up the difference his absence made after a period of three-and-a-half years when he told the town council that 'when Father Beauclerk was here there came "a rush" and Holywell got some little celebrity. But since then it had all passed away, and now everything had fallen flat.'[100]

The Jesuit Mission left Holywell in 1930 after a continual presence of 340 years and three years. Later, Father Beauclerk returned to Holywell on 30 July 1933, for the centenary celebrations of the building of St Winefride's Church, and preached at the 9.30 Mass. In his address he referred 'especially to the power of St Winefride against her pursuers' and to 'terrible incidents of punishment meted out to those who blasphemed against her, or interfered with the well.' He told the congregation of a cure that had taken place to a nun '... at the very time when the Protestant Alliance had descended upon Holywell and were denouncing and ridiculing the well and its cures. It was he said a good answer to their challenge.'[101]

Father Beauclerk died in Accrington on 22 November 1934. An anonymous tribute in the *County Herald,* spoke highly of him:

His enthusiasm was infectious: his love of the poor was patterned on that which

Christ himself had done for those who have to make the best of life under trying circumstances. His delight was to be with children and amuse them with the mystery of his conjuring tricks. Herein lay one of the charms of his fine character – his childlike simplicity. Duplicity was abhorrent to him.' Although his deafness handicapped him and he spent much time on his own 'Providence made up to him by giving him an expert knowledge and facility in the delicate art of embroidery and vestment making. He was a first-class beggar for the needs of others, and he helped to clothe the needy with materials he had begged for them and which his needles had worked into shape … I should think it is true to say Holywell ever remained to him 'my love;' its people 'my people.[102]

138. Father Beauclerk on a visit to Holywell for the centenary celebrations for St Winefride's Church the year before his death in 1934.

NOTES

1. Father Beauuclerk's letter to the Father Provincial, 15 September 1912. Jesuit archive Farm Street.
2. He was later to take a great interest in the claims of another ancestor the earl of Oxford to be the 'de vere' author of Shakespeare's plays.
3. *County Herald,* 26 September 1890.
4. *Flintshire Observer,* 5 November 1890 & 13 November 1890.
5. Beauclerk's account book Holywell museum archive.
6. He spent nearly £5,000 in nine years.
7. *County Herald,* 5 August 1892.
8. *County Herald,* 14 June 1895 and 27 September 1895.
9. *Flintshire Observer,* 2 November 1893.
10. A devotion consisting of special prayers or services on nine successive days.
11. *County Herald,* 27 June 1890.
12. Reference to Barnum & Bailey's Circus.
13. In 1896 it is estimated that 96,895 persons visited the well, 29,030 in August.
14. Jesuit archive Farm Street. Letter dated 12 September 1912.
15. *Flintshire Observer,* 11 & 18 October 1894.
16. *Flintshire Observer,* 15 July 1897.

17. Flinshire Observer 19 August 1897.
18. *Flintshire Observer,* 9 November 1893.
19. A railway running into the town of Holywell had been proposed in 1860.
20. *County Herald,* 21 September 1894.
21. *Flintshire Observer,* 27 June 1895.
22. Op cit letter 12 September 1912.
23. *Flintshire Observer,* 1 August 1895.
24. 15 September.
25. A replica of the Paris original.
26. Op cit, letter, 12 September 1912.
27. *County Herald,* 5 September 1995.
28. *County Herald,* 1 November 1895.
29. *Flintshire Observer,* 2 September 1897.
30. *County Herald,* September 1898.
31. *Flintshire Observer,* 27 August 1896.
32. *County Herald,* 28 August 1896.
33. R. B. Mullins, *Miracles and the Modern Religious Imagination* (Yale, 1996), chapter 5, passim.
34. His *ex tempore* address was summarised in the *County Herald,* 9 November 1894.
35. *Flintshire Observer,* 25 October 1894.
36. *County Herald,* 20 September 1895.
37. Under Jesuit editorship. Article by Father M. Maher, 'Holywell in 1894', pp. 152–182.
38. Ibid, p. 155f.
39. Ibid, p. 157–8, fn 1.
40. *County Herald,* 8 May 1896.
41. *County Herald,* 18 May 1894 and *The Month,* op cit, 158–60.
42. *County Herald,* 7 September 1894 and *The Month,* op cit, 165–70.
43. *County Herald,* 26 October 1894.
44. *County Herald,* 31 May 1895.
45. Wilfrid Scawen Blunt (1840–1922), a Roman Catholic and a rich Sussex landowner, who had a varied life as a diplomat, poet, Arabist, traveller, and breeder of horse. His cousin was George Wydham who became the second husband of Sibell Grosvenor and step-father to the second duke of Westminster. His cure narrative is taken from: E. Finch (ed), *Wilfrid Scawen Blunt* (London, 1938)
46. An apostolic brief *De Animarum Salute.*
47. Through his maternal grandmother Charlotte Jermingham. They were Philip Howard, earl of Arundel (d. 1595); William Howard, viscount Stafford, martyred 1690; Margaret Pole, martyred 1541.
48. R. O'Neil, *Cardinal Herbert Vaughan,* (Burns Oates, 1995), v, p. 373f.
49. Newport and Glamorganshire were not included.
50. O'Neilv, op cit, fn 117, p. 386.
51. Vicar apostolic 1895; translated to Menevia 1898; translated to Cardiff as archbishop and metropolitan 1921; died 25 October 1939.
52. *County Herald,* 8 November 1895.
53. The family motto of the Mostyn family of Talacre *auxulium meum a Domino,* my help comes from the Lord, *Fy nghymorth oddiwrth yr Arglwydd.*
54. *Flintshire Observer,* 21 November 1895.
55. *Flintshire Observer,* 22 August 1895.
56. Op cit, letter, 12 September 1912.
57. Mullins, op cit, p. 121.
58. Father Beauclerk to A. J. A. Symons, 21 April 1931, Farm Street archive.
59. Ibid, 10 June 1931.
60. G. A. Beck (ed), *The English Catholics 1850–1950* (Burns Oates, 1950,) chapter XVI; *Catholic English Literature, 1850–1950,* E. Hutton, p. 549.
61. Op cit, Beauclerk to Symons, 10 June 1931.

62. For accounts of Rolfe see: A. J. A. Symons, *The Quest for Corvo* (Folio Society, ed. 1952 which included 'Rolfe at Holywell' unpublished letters. D. Weeks, *Corvo* (London. 1971). M. J. Benkovitz *Frederick Rolfe: Baron Corvo* (New York 1977). E. Rowan and C. Stewart, *An Elusive Tradition Art and Society in Wales* (Cardiff, 2002), chapter 2, 'Baron Corvo in Holywell and Crickhowell'.

63. Weeks prefers Easter whereas Benkowitz opts for August.

64. Rolfe "The Saint, the Priest, the Nowt, the Devil", *Holywell Record,* 31 August 1897, p. 18

65. Symons, op cit, *Quest for Corvo*, pp. 73–83, 89–90.

66. Ibid.

67. Benkowitz, op cit, p. 81.

68. *County Herald,* 8 November 1895.

69. *Flintshire Observer,* 7 May 96.

70. *Holywell Record,* vol. 1, No. 1, May 1896, introduction.

71. *County Herald,* 4 August 1944, J. J. Ll. Williams " 'The Nowt' of Holywell what I knew about him"

72. *Flintshire Observer,* 26 August 1897.

73. This account depends on the description of the banners in the Holywell museum,

74. Those which do not survive are in italics.

75. *Quest for Corvo,* op cit, p. 267.

76. *Flintshire Observer,* 3 October 1895.

77. *County Herald,* 8 May 1896.

78. See *Elusive Tradition,* op cit, p. 51, for more details.

79. *Quest for Corvo,* op cit, p. 81.

80. See fn 71 above, p. 20.

81. *Quest for Corvo,* op cit, p. 257.

82. See fn 71 above, p. 18.

83. I Kings, c. 19, v. 44.

84. *Quest for Corvo,* op cit, p. 85; also, entries in Father Beauclerk's account book: Owen Owen materials for decoration (Bishops welcome £3.17.9 – 6 July Liberty's velveteen (banner) £2.9s.; to Austin for painting banners £100; Mr Austin's account 52 weeks keep & other expenses £62, Clothing £10; 1897: Austin Rolfe (painting and jobbing). 1 January – 4 March (to Mrs Richardson keep £10; £5). Settling dispute (Watts £60 10s.*)*; Watts (our lawyers a/c) £4 4s.The dispute between Rolfe and Beauclerk may be followed in much detail in *Quest for Corvo,* 1952 (edt) especially in appendix 'Rolfe at Holywell', pp. 256–282 and in Benkowvitz, op cit, pp. 86–104.

85. *Flintshire Observer,* 3 June 1897.

86. *Quest for Corvo,* op cit, letter from Rolfe to Mrs Richardson 26 May 1897.

87. Ibid, Rolfe to Beauclerk, 6 October 1898.

88. W. S. Blunt, op cit.

89. *County Herald,* 17 July 1896.

90. *Flintshire Observer,* 17 and 24 December 1896.

91. *Quest for Corvo,* op cit, p. 264.

92. *Flintshire Observer,* 18 March 1897.

93. *Flintshire Observer,* 20 May 1897.

94. He had founded the British Insulated Wire Company Limited at Prescot, Liverpool withhis brother Jacob Atherton see *Flintshire Observer,* 20 July 1899.

95. *County Herald,* 11 February 1898.

96. For Atherton's proposal 260; against 183, majority 127.

97. *County Herald,* 11 February 1898 in a letter to the editor.

98. *County Herald*, 18 February 1898.

99. *Flintshire Observer,* 6 July 1899.

100. *County Herald*, 21 June 1901.

101. *Holywell Pilgrim's Record,* No. 3, 1934, p. 26.

102. *County Herald,* 30 November 1934.

11. The Final years of the Jesuit Mission in Holywell

Father Francis Borsch, SJ, (1899–1904)

Soda water, and Beecham's pills, threatened to turn the sacred shrine of St Winefride into a cheap health resort touting soft drinks and patent medicines. As the twentieth century began to dawn, a cloud of gloom and confusion hung over the town about the future of the well. It was soon realised that there was no way in which Father Francis Borsch, SJ, resembled his charismatic predecessor Father Beauclerk. This difference was noted in the review by the Society of Jesus when it observed that, with regard to the happenings at the well that, 'though a good deal of the enthusiasm created by Fr Beauclerk's zeal cooled down for a time, still good solid work continued to be done, and favours from Heaven were still vouchsafed, albeit less striking and numerous than before.'[1]

Father Borsch was a native of Bavaria who served during the Franco-Prussian War (1870) in the field with the Bavarian Army, during which time he contracted typhoid fever, which undermined his constitution permanently. During his period in Holywell, 1899–1904, his health deteriorated, and he was removed. He died at Stonyhurst in May 1906, at the age of fifty-nine. There was ill feeling between Borsch and Beauclerk, the former accusing his predecessor of leaving the mission in debt and not keeping accurate accounts. Beauclerk retaliated by saying that his successor, in his failing health, resorted too frequently to alcoholic beverages and 'whose infirmities exposed him to the risk of giving public scandal.' Borsch's greatest fault in the eyes of Beauclerk, as he made clear in 1912, was his insensitivity towards the shrine. He told the story to the Father Provincial that:

When Beecham of St Helen's put up his thirty-foot insult to the Well –'Beecham's Pills: they cure well, they help well, they act well.'– right opposite the Well, Father Borsch permitted it: Father Provincial held his hand inactive: whilst the Protestants said 'If you Catholics have no reverence for your Saint & her Shrine: we have respect for her Church. If Father Borsch does not have that monstrosity removed we will tear it down.' 'Poor Francis,' Beauclerk continued, 'had he any belief in St Winefride at all? I doubt it; at any rate he had no tact or delicacy and must often have made St Winefride blush. (God forgive me for my own sins). He was always having the collecting box rattled and shewing how keen he was after money. Alas for his honesty! How could he dare to say such things as he did about me and my debts!

Beauclerk had more to say about Father Borsch. From information given to him in letters written by John Byrne of Holywell, who caused his correspondent great distress and indignation with the statement: 'If the Jesuits want to stop all devotion and crush out the growing faith in St Winefride, they could not go a better way about it.' But, despite these accusations and alarming reports, the Mission to pilgrims continued. Business appeared to be as usual, at least in its outward form, no matter how subdued was the enthusiasm of Father Borsch. Cures were reported regularly, services conducted at the well and processions held as before. At least there was less tension between the town council and the Mission, and a working partnership began to develop. The well was leased to the Catholics on the same terms as before, when an injunction in the High Court put an end to any plans Jacob Atherton may have had of using the well in his scheme for his soda-water factory. Renting to the Catholics was the only alternative, for the council needed the rent from the lease of the well, and the extra income generated in the town from pilgrims and visitors.

Father John Ryan, SJ (1904–25)

Father John Ryan, Father Borsch's successor, proved to be the ideal priest to cope with the disaster which overcame St Winefride's Well in 1917. The appointment of Bishop Francis Mostyn as vicar apostolic in 1895, and as bishop of Menevia in 1898, brought stability and confidence to the relationship between the town council and the Roman Catholic church in Holywell. Some respect between them had existed for generations, through the influence of the Mostyns of Talacre. Now it was strengthened and cemented, not only through the pride the town felt in the bishop's appointment, but also through the sheer necessity of the threat to the town's water supply. This formed them into a defensive alliance when the diminution in the supply of water became the most prominent issue in the years between 1904 and the crisis of the loss of water in 1917.

'Ein Gwlad. Ein Cred' – *(Our Land. Our Faith)*

This was the motto chosen by Bishop Mostyn for the College of St Mary he founded in Holywell in 1904, for the training of priests as part of his plan for the conversion of Wales to the Roman Catholic faith. He announced his intention in a letter to his clergy:

139. The 'Old Post Office' in High Street the house given by Miss Sankey in 1904 for the establishment by Bishop Mostyn of St Mary's College for young seminarians.

We shall be glad if you will mention to your flock that we are able, thanks to the generosity of a great benefactor of the Diocese, to open a small College at Holywell, where students for the Priesthood in this diocese, can obtain a thorough knowledge of Welsh in addition to their ordinary course of studies. We shall have considerable expense in furnishing the house that has been given to us, and we trust that all, who can, will try and assist us. The College is to be opened immediately after the Midsummer Holidays.[2]

The 'great benefactor to the diocese' was Miss Sankey, the sister of Richard Sankey, JP, who had died in 1899. They had resided together at the Vron, a small estate of seventy acres on the hillside above the town in the direction of Pen-y-ball. They were children of the banker Charles Sankey, and grandchildren of Peter Parry, of Twysog. The bishop and Miss Sankey were descendants of the two families in north Wales who kept the Faith through penal times. Miss Sankey was devoted to St Winefride and the church at Holywell and, as the last of her line, spared nothing in her generosity to the faith. She was as eager as the bishop to see his plans for the conversion of Wales take effect and presented the diocese with a large building (the former Holywell Bank and later the post office) at the top of High Street in memory of her brother. Richard Sankey, educated at Stonyhurst, and the chief magistrate in the town at the time of his death, had done much through his devotion and wisdom to protect and advance the Catholic cause in the town for over fifty years.

The college opened on the Feast of St Michael the Archangel, 29 September 1904. It received a Papal blessing from Pius X.[3] The bishop first approached Dr Herbert Vaughan, nephew of the cardinal, to be the first rector of the college, but he could not be spared from his duties at Westminster. In his place was chosen Father Paul Hook, who described himself as 'completely, even bigotedly, Welsh in thought, outlook, and aspiration' and 'the conversion of Wales was his one interest.'[4] He used the Welsh language as often as possible in the life of the college in the rosary, the hymns, and for regular periods of conversation and as an examination subject. Father Hook was joined by the newly ordained Father

Denis Joseph Quigley, and between them they taught the whole of the curriculum suitable for a junior seminary – Latin, French, Welsh, Greek to the ablest of them, together with religious knowledge and some history and geography, later to be replaced by English literature. There was no science teaching in the timetable.

The residential college had about a dozen boys on its roll, who gained admission at the age of about fourteen years of age. The boys wore cassocks to remind them of their vocation to the priesthood, and it was whilst at the college that they eventually received minor orders. They were trained for the priesthood along the same lines practised for centuries. An arduous timetable of classroom instruction was punctuated daily by worship and religious exercises in chapel, and the encouragement of physical exercise by walks to Pantasaph, to the river bank the 'Cop' at Bagillt, and paper chases. They took a keen interest in sport – cricket equipment was purchased at Harrods. On the 23 February 1906, the rector, who came from Neath, gave the boys a holiday 'in honour of the Welsh victory over New Zealand' (at Rugby football). When Miss Sankey departed from Holywell to live with nuns in Stafford in September 1906, the boys obtained their own football pitch, which became the scene of friendly rivalry in games with boys from the County School.

The college diary of events gives the impression of a well-run community in which there was no time for the boys to get into mischief, with great pains taken to encourage their mental, physical and religious development. In it was recorded many items of interest regarding the college and the town.

The sacristy of the college was furnished with ornaments and communion vessels from the chapels of Lady Ffrench and Miss Sankey. A Catholic lady from Bwlchgwyn presented them with a set of vestments and others were borrowed

140. Students from St Mary's College with their Principal the Revd Dr Paul Hook.

from St Winefride's Church. There appears to have been an attempt to retrieve a chalice when the somewhat mysterious entry occurred in May 1905: 'Miss Sankey offers to buy a new chalice for Bromsgrove if they will return the Holywell Chalice they have.'

Mr Lambert, their Protestant neighbour at the hotel next door, features in the diary. He had long defended the Catholic cause in the town council chamber. In 1905 he brought one of his guests to the college – 'Mr Lambert introduced Mr Kingo Ishii Commissioner of the Home Department Japan to us. He wishes to improve his English.'

On 26 June 1905, the bishop confirmed Mr Lambert in the college chapel. In the following year they recorded his burial at Pantasaph on 29 October.

The Schwarz family businesses were patronised – 'New eight-day clock put in the Hall. It was bought at Schwarz's in the Town; 23 Nov. 1906 Mr Schwarz elected unopposed to the District Council; 12 January 1906 As usual: stormy day. Lloyd George in Holywell.' He was speaking for Herbert Lewis who was elected MP for Flintshire Boroughs.

The rector is recorded as transcribing the Holywell parish registers for publication in volume three of the Catholic Record Society, and receiving the degree of doctor of philosophy from the Urban College in Rome. In February 1907 the bishop asked Dr Hook 'to make a collection of Welsh hymns for an appendix to the bishop's forthcoming hymnal.' Unfortunately he went on holiday in the summer of 1907 to the Canary Islands, and on his return was laid up with a severe attack of typhoid, and the boys had to move to Pantasph for the autumn term, until the fear of infection was removed. The rector recovered.

The death of the poet Francis Thompson, who was closely associated with Pantasaph, is recorded on 19 November 1907.

The teaching of Welsh was entrusted at first to the staff and a number of layman, but in 1908 Father John Hugh Jones (1842–1910), '*Tad Jones Bach,*' retired to Holywell and lived close to the college in Panton Place. He was a convert from Anglicanism and was received into the Roman Catholic Church by Dr John Henry Newman at the Oratory in Edgbaston in 1865. Trained at St Beuno's, he served at Caernarfon and Pwllheli, and translated many hymns into Welsh, the best known of which is 'Faith of Our Fathers'. He lived in Holywell for the last two years of his life, teaching Welsh, not very efficiently according to Donald Attwater, but made a great impression on the boys, as the college magazine remembered:

> He believed in early rising, and when at work laboured with minute industry counting no occasion worth of less than his best. He was a prime favourite with the boys. Some of our old students will remember his delight with the toboggan during the winter 1908–9 and his assistance in haymaking the following summer.[5]

The college diary also records the work that had to be done to maintain the building, which dated at the latest from the eighteenth century. Almost immediately Father Hook's fireplace collapsed. A nasty smell in the chapel revealed a broken sewer pipe, and extensive repairs had to be done because of dry rot in the basement. The intention of Bishop Mostyn to found a junior seminary and prepare priests to minister in Welsh in his diocese succeeded, as we may judge from the evidence of the diary. By the time it ends in the autumn of 1908, the eldest candidates, Baron and Loftus, had 'put on clerical dress and began the study of philosophy,' and in October Bishop Mostyn gave them the tonsure in the college chapel. The mission of the college as part of the conversion of Wales was always at the forefront, when, for example on 2 November 1908 it was recorded 'Rosary & prayer for Wales at Benediction in Welsh.' They had no doubt that admirable St Winefride was the patroness of Wales and Holywell.

Joseph Swynnerton's statue of St Winefride
In 1896, the sculptor Joseph Swynnerton carved the white Italian carrrara marble statue to St Winefride commissioned by Father Beauclerk for the church in Well Street.[6] Swynnerton began his work in London in the 1890s, where he made a model preparatory to carving the statue in Rome. The statue is of 'heroic size,' and represents St Winefride bearing in her right hand the palm of martyrdom. In

the left hand is a gilt crozier with the jewelled top, enclosing a representation of the *Agnus Dei*. St Winefride is represented as the sculptor imagined her to be in the ninth century. The hem of her outer garment is edged with gold, as is the circlet on her head. Eventually the finished statue was placed in St Winefride's Church in October 1901,[7] formally unveiled in July 1904,[8] and re-located in the body of the Church when it was enlarged in 1909.[9]

The long period of over fifteen years between the statue's commissioning, and its final resting place in the church at Holywell, involved three successive Jesuit fathers at Holywell. Father Beauclerk opened a 'statue fund' in August 1893, to which pilgrims and visitors contributed and by 1898 had paid the sculptor £350 for his work.[10] When

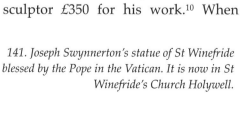

141. Joseph Swynnerton's statue of St Winefride blessed by the Pope in the Vatican. It is now in St Winefride's Church Holywell.

Swynnerton completed his work in Rome in the summer of 1896, he sent a long report of the stir St Winefride's statue made in the Eternal City. His account of the blessing of the statue by Pope Leo XIII is an episode worthy of an eighteenth-century grand tour and gives the statue a provenance that adds to its charm and importance: 'Yesterday (August 14th) the Holy Father blessed St Winefride.' wrote Swynnerton, adding, 'I will try and give you an account of it all. His Holiness gave me permission, through his private secretary, Monsignor Angeli, to carry the statue into the Vatican gardens, and place it where he was accustomed to mount his coach.' However this arrangement was changed because of the Pope's health, and the Holy Father gave permission for the statue to be brought into his anti-chamber to be blessed.

Swynnerton also enquired from the officials if there was a relic of St Winefride in the Vatican, hoping to discover such information in order to please Father Beauclerk, and have it placed in the new church he was contemplating building in Holywell. However, although an official discovered in an old volume the record of a relic of *'Sante Wenefrida'*, it could not be found. In the words of the Vatican official it was *'non exista* and no one knows what has become of it.'[11]

The next day, Wednesday, was the occasion for His Holiness to bless the statue, and the sculptor was faced with the task of bringing it to the Pope's private apartments upstairs. In spite of valiant efforts by the porters to carry it upstairs the attempt failed, as Swynnerton related.

> I arrived at the Vatican with St Winefride safely packed in a huge case, weighing in all over a ton, with eleven strong men, ropes, rollers, etc., prepared to drag her upstairs to the second loggia, and then into the Pope's private apartments. We found it no easy task, and by the time I got to the last few steps of the first floor I began to fear for the floors of the anti-chambers. At this point Commendatore Galli director of the sculpture museum declared that it was not safe and orders came to stop until His Holiness had been consulted.

Realising that the operation was impossible it was decided that His Holiness would bless the statue in the Papal garden when he came down. When he heard this Swynnerton protested that it was raining and his statue would be ruined. He told Beauclerk, 'I had declared I should drag it into the Hall of St Peter, if it were necessary, to get the Pope's blessing, and that the statue was not going away until it was blessed. So it was placed in a beautiful light near the entrance to the Borgia rooms of the Museum, and with a shawl round the pedestal she looked lovely.

And so it came to pass that St Winefride did after all visit Rome, and was privileged to spend a night in the Vatican protected by the Swiss Guard, waiting for Leo XIII's blessing. The time came and Swynnerton was summoned to attend at five o'clock, on the eve of the Feast of the Assumption.

Before five, I was beside my statue in evening dress, and punctually on the hour the Pope came out. His Holiness was borne in his sedan chair by servants in their beautiful costumes. The sedan chair was put down half-a-dozen yards from my statue and I bent on one knee and kissed the ring of the Fisherman.

After being introduced, Swynnerton was engaged by the Pope in conversation, and in reply to his questions told him about St Winefride's martyrdom at Holywell. The Pope said he knew about the miraculous spring, and that Winefride was a contemporary of Gregory the Great and Augustine of Canterbury and inquired, 'Why have you given her a sad expression?'

Here I said that the statue was not finished and that I should be very glad to make any alteration His Holiness suggested. He said "No, no, 'tella."[12] I explained to him that the ornaments of the dress and the crozier were all Celtic of the period. Finally he said that he hoped that the statue would be for the conversion of many to the true faith. He then blessed it, and then me, kneeling. I forgot to say that I told the Pope that thousands go each year to the Well, that there are many miraculous cures, and that two had taken place in Rome. He said he had been told of them.

The report concluded by stating, 'The statue will shortly be shipped to Cardiff, whence it will be conveyed by a pilgrimage by road to Holywell.'[13] There is no record of that journey taking place and it was another six years before the marble statue reached Holywell. Instead, Swynnerton shipped it to London intending to submit it for the Royal Academy Exhibition of 1897 but it was not chosen and probably spent some time in waiting at the Jesuit church in Farm Street.

Father Francis Borsch received the statue into the church at Holywell on a Monday in October 1901. The newspaper said on the occasion:

It will be recollected that Father Beauclerk collected the funds for the statue (which has cost about £400) while he was in charge of the mission at Holywell but owing to various reasons the arrival of the statue has been delayed …We understand that Father Borsch proposes to construct a domed recess in the sanctuary of the Church for the reception of the statue.[14]

Mysteriously, it was not until four years later, in July 1904, that the statue was officially unveiled. By this date Father Ryan had replaced Father Borsch, and Father Jagger, of St Beuno's College, conducted a simple ceremony of unveiling. It had not been relocated in the sanctuary of the church, but surprisingly, in spite of its significance, continued to languish at the entrance to the building, mounted on a stone plinth in a recess protected 'behind a wirework enclosure.'[15] The statue now looks rather forlorn hidden in the corner of the north-east transept with pride of place given to the altar of St Winefride on the north wall.

Father Ryan of Holywell

Father Ryan was born in Caernarfon in 1842, educated at Stonyhurst, and ordained at St Beuno's in 1874, where he was a contemporary of Gerard Manley Hopkins. He was a member of the Society of Jesus for over fifty years, and served overseas in Kingston Jamaica, and Grahamstown, South Africa, as well as with Father Bernard Vaughan, SJ, in Manchester. By the time he came to Holywell he was sixty-two years of age, but was to give another twenty-one years to the Mission in the town. The nature of his service to the Catholic community and the town of Holywell was expressed in the tributes made at his funeral in October 1926.

The account of his burial in the local newspaper[16] remarked on the hearse leaving Holywell for Pantasaph: 'And so Father Ryan, the well-beloved was carried to his last home through the town he loved so well.' It was said of him:

> His piety was deep, solid, unostentatious, arresting: a true son of a great Religious Founder, Father Ryan was a great Jesuit as well as a great priest. The Catholic Church at Holywell has, during its long history, been served by many priests of sterling worth but it can be doubted whether any of them has so gripped the affections, laid such a hold on the mind, so commanded the respect of his fellow townsmen, as Father Ryan. Though he was not a native of Holywell, it is true to say that he will be, as he has been, always known as 'Father Ryan of Holywell.'

The eulogy spoke the truth, and was a just appreciation of his work and influence. This is seen in his faithful guardianship of the cult of St Winefride, and in three main areas of service: to the church building, in his ministry to pilgrims and the cure tradition, and in his care of St Winefride's Well as it passed through its darkest hour.

The enlargement of St Winefride's Church, 1909–12

Father Beauclerk's ambition to build a new basilica and presbytery in Holywell went unfulfilled, although a design for the former survives. He regarded such plans as his 'weakness and vainglory which broke the thread of God's golden intention' and was 'part of his pride and sinfulness' which he accounted as the reason for his eventual removal from Holywell.'[17] Father Ryan had no such ambitions or qualms of conscience for his plans to enlarge the church at Holywell. The work was long overdue, and met the firm approval of Bishop Mostyn. A bigger church was needed to accommodate the increased number of Catholics in the local community, and to serve the bishop's intentions to increase the importance of the Holywell Mission in the affairs of his diocese and in the conversion of Wales.

Father Ryan was soon forced to recognise the inadequacy of the church. It was too small to welcome large congregations, especially when large pilgrimages came to the well. Instead, it was customary to gather them in the open air, for

Mass in one of the fields on the edge of the town. This arrangement happened on the Feast of the Assumption, 15 August 1905 when 2,000 pilgrims from Bootle came, and on Whit Monday the following year when another 1,500 visited.

Work to enlarge the building began in the winter 1908–09, and was completed by the month of June. The old church was more than doubled in size by extending the nave in a westward direction, and adding transepts at the west end. In 1912 a Lady Chapel at the north west end of the church was added, built as a memorial to Manners Harden, paid for by a legacy left by his widow. Probably the same architect, James Manage, of Preston, designed the St Winifred Chapel in the south-west transept for

142. Father John Ryan, SJ (standing) in the presbytery garden with Father Milner (seated).

on its south side is a stained-glass window in memory of Mrs Gertrude Harden, the donor. By this means the number of seats was more than doubled, from 250 to a capacity of about 600. The contractors for the work in 1909 were Messrs Sibeon Brothers of Holywell, and in 1912 Messrs Clegg & Son of Chester; with marble work by Mr Hodgkinson of the same city.

The main purpose of the enlargement was to provide extra seating without destroying the neo-classical exterior, and to create a feeling of spaciousness in the interior by the placing of altars and statues in the transepts. This was encouraged by leaving the additional windows in the extended nave free from heavy stained glass, which characterised the old church. The high altar, slightly raised is in a recess in the sanctuary, and framed by a wide sweeping arch supported on flat pillars surmounted by Corinthian capitals. The pillars are fluted, and the walls on both sides have been slabbed with beautiful white marble, with a light bluish grey veining. The whole effect is to give the nave a sense of space and light, with room at the east end for liturgical freedom.

In the north-west transept is an altar with a statue of the Sacred Heart. This recalls the Jesuit connection, and on its west wall is a memorial to Mary Anne Parry, widow of Charles Sankey, the last descendant of the Parrys of Twysog which provides a connection with penal times. Underneath is a simple memorial in brass to Mary Frances Sankey (1829–1909) born in the year of Catholic emancipation. In her life time she had witnessed the remarkable reversal in the

143. *St Winefride's Church was extended between 1909–12.*

fortunes of Catholics in Holywell which she had furthered by her generosity.
When she died she bequeathed the Vron estate of seventy acres to the diocese.

Father Ryan's Diary and record of cures at St Winefride's Well, 1905–23
From the time of the twelfth century *Lives of St Winefride*, and probably before
that date, there were written and oral traditions preserved of healing at the well.
In the Middle Ages these were described in the traditional manner as miracles.
When the Jesuit Mission settled in Holywell in 1590, they systematically recorded

144. *Memorial tablets St Winefride's Church, Holywell. The devoted Sankey family were generous
servants and benefactors to the Church for over a hundred years.*

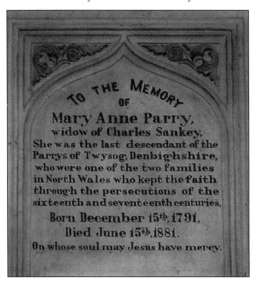

and lovingly preserved records of healing events, or what may be described as cure narratives, associated with St Winefride's Well. These have been described above. Gradually, however, with an increase in literacy, those who experienced healing at the well, together with their relatives, friends and physicians, sent their own testimony of cures. In 1805, Bishop John Milner gave credence to the publication of cures which took place at St Winefride's by his report of the healing of Winefride White. By the middle of the nineteenth century, Holywell newspapers began to publish with regularity full accounts of cures, and local and national newspapers became the chief source for accounts. The hospice in Holywell was a convenient place for reporters to seek out those fortunate to be healed. Although such events occasionally gave rise to sensationalism, on the whole they were handled sensitively, and regarded as occasions for rejoicing, and their publicity attracted thousands each year to St Winefride's Well.

Naturally, in these circumstances the resident priest became the channel for these acts of grace, and the obvious person to be informed of healing. Father Beauclerk encouraged those who were healed to return and publicly give thanks in specially arranged services. He pasted many of the newspaper cuttings recording these events into his black notebook. In the 1890s votive offerings began to increase, stacked up around the Well with piles of crutches, wheel chairs, and in some cases stretchers on which those who were unable to walk were carried by their friends to be placed in the healing waters. One man pushed his wife from Merthyr Tydfil to Holywell in a wheelbarrow to experience St Winefride's intercession!

Father Ryan set about collecting and recording information concerning cures, which were received by him from the main sources we have noted above: personal witness, written testimony, medical evidence, and if possible confirmation given at a later date that the cure was permanent. There is a continual body of evidence from these sources, with Father Ryan's own observations succinctly recorded. The entries in his diary usually contain some of the following information: the name, age and address of the person cured; their condition on first visiting the well; account of cure; how many times they bathed in the well. Subsequent information included details of votive offering, date of a return to Holywell to give thanks, and a medical certificate from a physician who had seen the person before and after healing. His diary shows that St Winefride's Well continued to bestow its gift of healing with the same bounty and scope witnessed in the gospels and at the well for a thousand years or more. The sufferers included the blind, lame, deaf, dumb, epileptic, and after 1918, victims of the Great War.

Although Holywell continued to be called the Lourdes of Wales as in Father Beauclerk's time in the 1890s, it was not. It retained and developed its own special character as a sacred place as it had done through the ages long before Lourdes emerged as a place of pilgrimage in the 1860s. Although Holywell may have been seen to resemble Lourdes as a Catholic healing centre, there was no reason why it should slavishly adopt all its practices, but many regretted that a proper medical bureau, modelled on that of Lourdes, was not set up at Holywell to investigate the character of the cures. The fact that there was no medical body to authenticate cures, it was argued, did not invalidate the claims of those healed, and Father Ryan presumably preferred to develop his own method of recording cures in the absence of an authoritative investigative body. Another reason was that many of those healed shunned publicity and preferred anonymity.

The attitude of local members of the medical profession, all of them non-Catholics, to the provision of a system of authentication such as existed at Lourdes, became apparent in 1910 when the work of the Lourdes Medical Bureau was the subject of a paper read at a meeting of the Denbigh and Flint members of the British Medical Association held at Lambert's Hotel, Holywell, in February. Their guest was the Revd F. Woodcock, SJ, of Leeds Catholic College who read a paper on 'Modern Miracles of Healing.'

The newspaper account of the meeting[18] reported that 'the main portion of the paper was devoted in relation of cures effected at the famous shrine at Lourdes and the methods adopted there to test their genuineness.' There is no mention of Father Ryan's presence, although the medical fraternity of Holywell were there in force,' led by Dr James Williams.[19]

At the beginning of his lecture, Father Woodcock stated that Catholics approached the question of modern miracles as unprejudiced freethinkers, and there was nothing in their religion which made it obligatory to accept or reject them. He then gave an account of the medical bureau established in Lourdes in 1882, which devoted itself entirely to the scientific investigation of cures alleged to be worked at the shrine. The bureau was open during the greater part of the year; any doctor who visited Lourdes was invited to observe its activities, and join in the examination of the cures. Records of over 8,000 cures were preserved, cures which could not be explained by natural means. Father Woodcock concluded that the purpose of his paper 'was to get people to investigate the cures for themselves.'

One of the doctors who contributed to the discussion following the lecture was the elderly James Williams, who throughout his practice as a doctor in Holywell had regularly visited the well and examined those who sought cures. Obviously the doctor was unaware of the quiet, diligent and comprehensive way in which Father Ryan was collecting evidence of cures at St Winefride's Well. His remarks did, however, suggest that the local non-Catholic medical profession were open to establishing some systematic method for recording cures and suggested that Father Ryan should keep a register of cures, and that the claimants should be examined by a doctor and their progress observed. However, nothing further was heard of the possibility of a medical bureau being established at Holywell on the lines of that at Lourdes.

Before we examine some specific instances from Father Ryan's diary as an illustration of his method of authentication, an article published in the Jesuit Magazine *The Month* in July 1918 entitled 'Holywell in recent years' written by Father Herbert Thurston, SJ, gives valuable background information. Thurston's article is a sequel to the one published in *The Month* in 1895, 'Holywell in 1894,' written by Father Maher, SJ.

Father Thurston discusses in detail half-a-dozen cures which occurred between 1896 and 1914. He presents reports of the sick visiting St Winefride's Well, with the exception of an ex-soldier, Cowell, living in Blackburn, who did not come to Holywell. He was wounded in the Boer War in 1902, and as a result lost his speech and hearing. Hospital treatment and operations failed to promote recovery, which came about when a Mrs McGill, after a visit to Holywell, brought home to Manchester a bottle of water with which she sprinkled Cowell's head and shoulders. He regained his speech and hearing, and immediately set off to Cumberland to speak to his mother.

Thurston, in discussing the individual cures, assembled as much evidence as possible: the patient's history, an account of their visit to the well, the occurrence of the cure, accounts of relatives and friends, and the observation of medical men. This led him, as a Jesuit priest, to reach a number of conclusions about the cures at St Winefride's Well.

One: 'It is impossible by strict logical inference to deduce the conclusion that supernatural causes have necessarily intervened.'[20]

Two: 'While fully recognising that many of the cures at Lourdes, Holywell, and other shrines are not incapable of natural explanation, the devout Catholic will find it quite reasonable to believe that these favours are in some way the reward of faith. Thus he will accept them prayerfully and gratefully without attempting to decide in what measure natural causes, human choice and supernatural intervention have respectively contributed to the result.[21]

Three: Thurston concludes with generalisations: 'that countless favours both temporal and spiritual have been received either as a result of pilgrimage to St Winefride's Well or through the use of the water of the spring. That prayer was made that at just that time an improvement was noted and that health was ultimately recovered'.

Four: Of many of the cures no record survives: 'they are known only to the recipients, and indeed there is no particular reason why they should be noised abroad. Their evidential value as "miracles" could never be brought home to an opponent, neither is it desirable that we should apply to them any such designation'.[22]

Father Thurston was a student at St Beuno's College, and for many years editor of *The Month* at Farm Street in London. He knew St Winefride's Well, and was horrified by the evidence of the diminution of the flow of water resulting from the construction of mine drainage tunnels which affected the spring. This led him to write the article 'Holywell in recent years' as 'in some sense a tribute to the memory of that devoted champion of St Winefride and her healing spring, the late Lady Mostyn, 'whose energy and public spirit has saved for her fellow Catholics a memorial of the ancient faith of this land which was assuredly well worth preserving.'[23]

It is against this background that we may examine Father Ryan's diary. The entries are brief and matter of fact, and far too numerous to repeat here.[24]

Entries from Father Ryan's diary

March 5 1906 Augustine Malone (13) was brought to the hospice from Crewe by Mr Hobin, Mr Malone (the father) and his grandmother. He seemed to be melancholy mad: on the way to the hospice Mr Hobin had bathed him in the well. On Tuesday he was difficult to manage & his friends were asked to remove him, on Wednesday morning he ran away and left Holywell with his friends Wednesday evening. On Thursday morning he was found to be cured and later in the day was taken to the doctor (Dr Lowe) who had given a previous opinion that he would not be cured. The doctor acknowledged that he was now perfectly sane.

Jane Smith aged 50, Irish, from (St) Dumfries had a gland bigger than an egg removed from her neck after application of the relic on Friday June 20. 1913.

Sister Cecilia a Sister of Charity from St Vincent's, Mill Hill, London, who had been pronounced incurable and who had been bedridden practically from March 1914 was completely cured during a Novena made to St Winefride using the water from Jan. 15 1918 to Jan. 24. On the fifth day she was able to stand, walk, sit & kneel with the greatest ease & comfort. On March 30th she wrote that she had just been doing household work & hoped to be in full harness with the rest of the Community on Easter Sunday March 31st.

July 1919. Joseph Culshaw blind from shell shock and lime for four years from St Dunstan's came seeing light: after three baths sees well enough to tell the time by a watch. Comes from 12 Springwood Road, Burnley.

A newspaper reported:

BLINDED SOLDIER'S SIGHT RESTORED – A blinded soldier, formerly a patient at the St Dunstans Home, has recovered his sight in a wonderful manner as the result of Bathing in St Winefride's Well. His name is Joseph Culshaw. He had been practically blind since Sept. 1915, and had been for a considerable time in St Dunstan's. He came to Holywell on the 6th inst. In company with a friend Joseph Ashworth, also of Burnley, who had to lead him about on the day he arrived, and also on the following day, Sunday. On Monday morning he bathed in the Well, and on emerging from the water he remarked he could see flowers on the floor, the spot where he was then standing being in front of the altar, and the flowers having fallen from the decorations thereon. He bathed again on each of the following days, and his power of vision improved on each occasion, and last Friday he was able to see very well. On Friday night he called at the office of this paper, and from tests then applied, it was evident that he was able to see pretty clearly, and it was also to be noticed both then, and on the following day (Saturday) that he was able to go about the streets himself, walking with ease & certainty.

1918. September Kathleen Coyne 62 Queensland St, L'pool, cured of consumption after five months in a sanatorium whence she was discharged as a hopeless case writes Dec. I – stating her good health & busy life continued.

This cure was reported in the *Daily Dispatch*, 18 January 1919.

A MODERN MIRACLE
THE SEVENTH BATHE IN ST WINEFRIDE'S WELL

Having implicit faith in the curative waters of St Winefride's Well at Holywell, Miss Kathleen Coyne (19), of 62, Queensland-street, Liverpool, a shorthand typist, has returned home completely cured after bathing in the waters on seven successive days.

From birth Miss Coyne told a *Daily Dispatch* representative she had been in a delicate state of health, but to day she is in the pink of health. Miss Coyne is a devoted member of the Catholic Church, and a regular attender of St Anne's Church, Edgehill, Liverpool.

In October, 1917,' she said, 'I was attacked with pleurisy, and my own doctor said that my lungs were affected. I was very ill for about three weeks. I was then examined at the Consumption Hospital in Liverpool, and was told that I ought to be in a sanatorium, but my breathing and cough became very bad, and after five months treatment I was discharged as incurable.

I had devoted faith in the well at St Winefride's, and I was taken there in August (1918). At the time I was unable to walk without assistance. Immediately on coming out, after my first bathe, although I was only in the water for a few moments, I was able to walk – the first time for many months. I bathed every morning at the well, and on the seventh day, for the first time, I was placed in the water up to my neck, and immediately after the water had covered my lungs I felt a stinging sensation, and on coming out was able to clear my chest. Since then I have never had the slightest trouble or the slightest sickness.

Miss Coyne went on to state that two doctors had since examined her, and both declared that she has not the slightest trace of consumption.

I was told,' Miss Coyne concluded, 'that if I were cured it would be a miracle. I am now sure that a miracle has been performed.

The final drama

POST OFFICE TELEGRAPHS
Received at 8.22 p.m. 5th January 1917.
To Miss Mostyn, The Mount, Parkstone
Water St Winefrides Well Completely Disappeared this afternoon
Taylor

The telegram from Flint received in Dorset at 8.22 p.m. on a cold January evening announced that the unbelievable had happened. What for centuries was thought impossible had occurred. It was as if someone had turned off a tap, pulled out the plug. St Winefride's Well, one of the 'Wonders of Wales', was drained dry. The worst fears of both the recipient Miss Clementina Mostyn and the sender, Isaac Taylor, from Coleshill, Flint, had been realised. The campaign fought by the Mostyn family of Talacre through parliament for over forty years was lost.

The disaster could not have happened at a worst time for Miss Clementina Mostyn, far away at Mount Parkstone in Dorset, keeping vigil at the bedside of her dying brother, Sir Pyers Charles Mostyn. The young invalid died eleven days later, aged only twenty years. Clementina's parents had recently died. Her father Sir Pyers William Mostyn, in 1912 and her mother, Lady Anna Maria, as recently as 10 June 1916. Her parents had devoted themselves to defending St Winefride's Well from the threat of drainage works, and thankfully were not alive to see the proud spring extinguished, and the well, the joy of pilgrims for centuries, emptied. The Benedictine monks evacuated from the abbey of Termonde to the family seat at Talacre Hall were nearby to pray for the restoration of the water. Fortunately, Clementina's uncle, Bishop Francis Mostyn, was a man of action and

145. *The fatal telegram: 5 January 1917.*

devoted to St Winefride. His authority and the family's long association with Holywell were respected in the local community. The hope of Catholics for the restoration of St Winefride's Well rested in him and he assumed the family's guardianship of the well in its darkest hour, and was supported on behalf of the Talacre Estate by Major Worral, husband of Agnes Mostyn.

Isaac Taylor, a surveyor and the former agent of Lady Anna Maria Mostyn, had for years provided the family with professional advice in their opposition to proposed parliamentary legislation for drainage schemes to the lead mines in the neighbourhood. The creation of a growing number of drainage tunnels from 1875 onwards increased the risk of the source of St Winefride's Well being tapped. This threat was well known and frequently advertised in the local press and on bill posters. The advice of the opposition was ignored, and thirteen years later the supply of water was tapped on the 5 January 1917. A Chester newspaper announced:

> On Friday afternoon about three o'clock the water in the well suddenly dropped, and in a few hours the whole basin of the well was dry. Coincident with this diminution there was a tremendous increase in the outflow of water from the Milwr Tunnel at Bagillt.[25]

> The Milwr Tunnel was in the course of extension by the Holywell–Halkyn Tunnel Co., which is being extended into the Halkyn District Mines Drainage Co's area for the purpose of unwatering the lead mines of the district.
>
> The stoppage of the flow to the Well occurred on Friday, about 6 a.m. The men were firing, and the result of the firing was to bring down some debris. This caused water to rush out, and the men had to flee for their lives a distance underground of nearly a quarter of a mile. In the tunnel were a number of big square tubs, which are pushed along tramlines, and carry away the debris. It is an eight-foot tunnel, and the head of the water, which was about five feet high, crashed into these tubs with a terrific noise. They thought the powers of Hades were let loose, and ran at their best speed along the uneven floor of the tunnel to the Caeau shaft. This they reached only three or four yards in front of the on rushing water. They just saved their lives, as had they been caught up by the flood they would have been swept underground towards the river Dee. So far as can be ascertained not only has the feed of St Winefride's Well been tapped, but also an immense underground pool of water.[26]

The place where the firing took place was about a hundred yards beyond the road between Pentre Halkyn and Halkyn Hall, a distance of less than three miles from St Winefride's Well. Here on the morning following the disaster, the correspondent of the *County Herald,* dramatically described the scene:

DANGER

TO

ST. WINIFRED'S WELL.

The proposed Works of the Milwr Drainage Company threaten to Tap the supply of water to the Well.

All are requested to sign a petition against the Bill now before Parliament.

One Copy lies at Mr. LAMBERT'S HOTEL.

One at the ABBEY PAPER WORKS.

One at the FLANNEL COMPANY.

Householders will be waited on at their own Residences.

146. *A poster announcing the threat to St Winefride's Well and soliciting signatures for a petition.*

Saturday morning at the Well: a saddening spectacle … the outer pool under the Well house was empty and not a drop of water was to be seen in the Brewery trough. The large outer bath, contiguous to the Well proper, was empty, and people were to be seen walking about on the flag stones at the bottom. But the saddest sight of all was the polygonal basin in which the spring has risen without interruption for upwards of four centuries.[27] This was completely dry.

But the statue of St Winefride, bearing in its hand the symbolic palm of martyrdom looked down upon the empty basin, and at intervals nuns were to be seen kneeling on the prie-dieu before it engaged in silent prayer.[28]

Opposition to drainage schemes, 1875–1913

The year 1835 marked the beginning of the saga of the death and resurrection of St Winefride's Well, in which the Mostyn family was to play the role of leading protagonists. For the next eighty years, until the well dried up in 1917, successive Mostyn baronets of Talacre led local opposition to a series of drainage schemes. They alleged that these proposals affected the flow of water to St Winefride's Well, and reduced the waterpower on the stream issuing from the well. This loss of water infringed their riparian rights and seriously affected the eleven industrial mills of which they were lessors. Further opposition came from the people of the town of Holywell who relied on St Winefride's Well for their water supply, and the pilgrims and visitors to the shrine for an important source of revenue.

The promoters of the drainage schemes argued that the survival of the mineral mines in the district was dependent upon ridding existing workings of water, and the drainage of deeper mines to gain access to exploit rich lodes. They alleged that without their schemes, lead workers would lose their livelihoods, and that through their enterprise more men would be employed. Moreover the profit from increased production would bring a general prosperity to the lead mining districts centred on the towns of Holywell and Mold. Huge investments were needed to finance the proposed drainage schemes. The stakes were high, and the promised returns even higher.

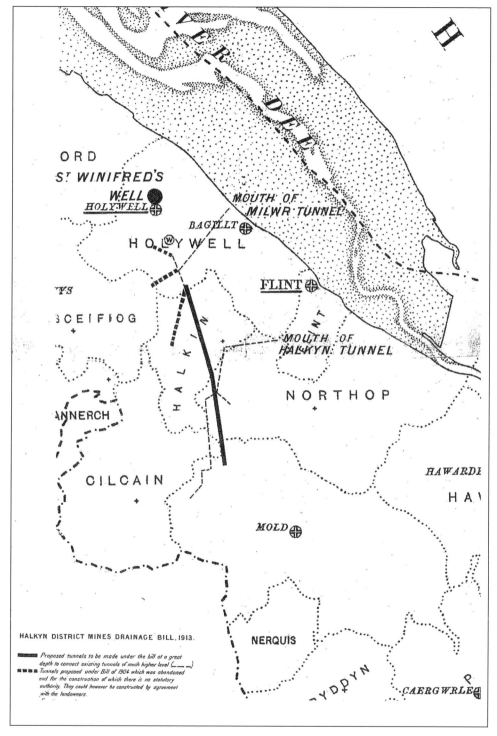

147. Map showing the tunnels created for the systematic drainage of lead workings in the vicinity of the town and well.

148. Young visitors standing by St Beuno's Stone in the empty well.

The main issue was the continuing diminution in the flow of water to St Winefride's Well. The burden of proof for this decline in the water supply fell on those who opposed the legislation. Over the years geologists provided conflicting evidence on the source of the feeder which supplied St Winefride's Well, and whether or not it was in the drainage area. The promoters of the legislation alleged that variation in the flow of water was dependent on rainfall, and thus beyond their control. A review of the three main schemes reveals that in spite of determined opposition by the Mostyns of Talacre generally supported by Holywell Town Council, they failed to prevent the promoters gradually increasing the number and length of their drainage tunnels. The ailing Holywell estate of the Mostyns of Talacre could not match the resources of the promoters, who paid for the passage of their bills in parliament out of increased revenues and share capital. But what the Mostyns lacked in money they made up in fervour and dedication, spurred on by what they regarded as their responsibility as guardians of the cult of St Winefride.

The first scheme, the Holywell and District Mines Drainage Act, 1875
The purpose of the Bill was to make and maintain five tunnels or adit levels for the purpose of effectively draining 'important mines of lead and other minerals situate in the Halkyn district in Co. of Flint,' and to enable the company to charge royalties on mines drained by the extended tunnel. The promoters of the Bill were the Duke of Westminster; Lord Richard Grosvenor, MP; John Scott Bankes of Soughton Hall, Northop; and Robert Nicholson of Abbotsfield, Chester. They were allowed to raise capital of £100,000 with borrowing power not exceeding £33,000.

The petitioners against the bill were Sir Pyers Mostyn, 9th Baronet, and other occupiers of mills, works and manufacturing premises along the stream. Three main objections formed the basis of petitions to this and subsequent bills. The first objection was that the industries on the stream were dependent upon the free and uninterrupted use of water on the Holywell stream. The second was that the townships of Holywell and Greenfield were dependent on the Holywell stream for water for drinking and domestic purposes. Thirdly, the petitioners were concerned that the stream which flowed from St Winefride's Well would be deprived of its source in the Halkyn district, and the water drained away into the Nant-y-Flint brook.

The editor of the *Flintshire Observer*, gave the newspapers support to the promoters and agreed with them that the threatened danger of draining St Winefride's Well was groundless. Instead he saw the benefits of increased prosperity to the neighbourhood and reminded his readers that:

> Millions of pounds sterling have from time to time been realised from Halkyn and Holywell mountains, and the wealth of the Grosvenor family to a great extent may be said to be closely associated with Flintshire, and the proposed drainage works may yet bring unbounded wealth to many other families in this and future generations.[29]

The editor was correct in his prediction of increased production of lead ore, with 2,000 tons per annum from 1878 to 1890 and 3,000 tons in the 1890s, with a further increase from 1900 onwards to 4,000 tons per annum. Other mineral output also increased significantly and it is not surprising that share prices went up 100% with the discovery of other new rich lodes.

However, the flow of water at St Winefride's Well was affected by the construction of the Halkyn Tunnel and attention was drawn to this diminution in 1885. The occasion was a Board of Trade enquiry at Holywell, conducted by General Hutchinson with a view to improving the town's water supply. In his review of the state of affairs, the General accepted that the flow from the spring had decreased by one half after the construction of the Halkyn Tunnel authorised by the 1875 Act; with the flow of well water reduced from the previous six to seven million gallons every twenty-four hours to about three and a half million gallons.

The second scheme was sanctioned in 1904 by the Milwr and District Drainage Act
In 1904 the Milwr and District Drainage was promoted by the Holywell–Halkyn Mining and Tunnel Company formed in 1896. The new enterprise proposed to create a second tunnel (generally known as the Milwr Tunnel) to drain the mines to the north of the Halkyn District Mines Drainage Company's area sanctioned in 1875. Work had begun on the second tunnel in 1897 at Boot End near Bagillt.

The Bill's promoters included the Duke of Westminster, Lord Denbigh, and Lord Mostyn. Amongst the supporters of the noble lords was the Flint Town Council which unanimously approved of the scheme on the grounds that it would encourage industrial development in the neighbourhood, with an increased supply of water from the new drainage tunnels.

In opposition to the Bill, Sir Pyers Mostyn, the industrialists along the stream, and Holywell Town Council, sent petitions to parliament and gave evidence to committees of both Houses. Sir Pyers and the millowners spent over £5,000 in opposing the Bill and Lady Anna Maria Mostyn acted as their spokesperson in Parliamentary Committees. Professor Boyd Dawkins, FRS, professor of Geology in the University of Cambridge, gave evidence that the drainage tunnels proposed in the Bill would inevitably lower the water in the rock below the well, and thus cause it to cease to flow. James Mansergh, a past president of the Institute of Civil Engineers and other geologists and civil engineers including Caradoc Williams and N.M. Griffiths, supported Dawkin's, views.[30]

Bishop Mostyn rallied the Catholic community in Holywell by requesting Father Borsch to read his letter opposing the Bill in church. He issued a grave warning that if the Bill passed into law it would have disastrous consequences:

> There is every reason to fear that the water supply to St Winefride's Well may be tapped, and the ancient and world-famed Shrine ruined … and I should be wanting in my duty were I to willingly allow anything to be done that might put an end to this holy shrine. I trust therefore that you and your flock will do all in your power to oppose this Bill, and if there is a petition to be signed, praying Parliament not to pass this Bill, I trust that every Catholic in Holywell will look upon it as a conscientious duty to sign it and thus help to safeguard the Well. We must act now and leave no stone unturned to safeguard the interests of our Virgin Martyr's Shrine.[31]

In spite of an organised and united opposition of inhabitants, millowners. and Catholics, the Bill was passed. However there was one consolation in defeat, because of the inclusion by a majority of forty-one votes of a compensation clause which required payment to affected persons if the well suffered measurable damage during the next phase of the project. It also imposed limitations by prohibiting any drainage activities on the Holywell side of a designated north-south line. These modifications to the Bill were hailed as a victory, and some hoped and even assumed that the promoters would not proceed with the Milwr Tunnel.

For the time being there was general relief at the removal of the threat to the traditional water supply. It was a time for celebration and thanksgiving. Sir Pyers and Lady Mostyn and the Members of Parliament who had supported them received an official resolution of appreciation for their energy and persistence and in the protection of the interests of the town of Holywell.[32]

A month later, Lady Anna Maria Mostyn received further recognition at the National Eisteddfodd, meeting at Rhyl, when she was initiated into the Gorsedd under the name *Rhian y Ffynnon*, 'Lady (maiden) of the Well.' On Wednesday 5 October an unexpected opportunity came for members of Holywell Urban District, the millowners on the stream and Father John Ryan, with two members of the Catholic community, to gather at the well to welcome Lady Mostyn, accompanied by Sir Thomas Esmonde, MP, who had led the opposition to the Bill in the House of Commons. J. Ll. Williams, the chairman of the council, proposed a vote of thanks in which he said 'they looked upon Lady Mostyn as the chief in the whole opposition.' After many speeches, the 'the proceedings closed in a happy manner by Fr Ryan drawing a cup of water from the Well and offering it to Sir Thos. Esmonde with the remark –"You deserve a drink, sir, after that." With a kindly laugh, the drink was taken.'[33] It may be imagined with what joy in her heart the 'Lady of the Well' knelt before the shrine of St Winefride to offer up her thanks for the deliverance of the well.

In a letter addressed to Father Ryan on 6 November, Lady Mostyn made her own gesture of thanksgiving. She explained to him the financial sacrifices made by Sir Pyers Mostyn in meeting costs of £1,400 in fighting the Bill in the House of Lords, with an extra £2,000 for counsel's fees. She remarked on the invaluable evidence given by Mr Strahan, who made the geological survey of Holywell, and that he had not taken a fee for his services. She included the names of many of those who had given her support, and gave thanks for the action of the 179 who had voted in favour of the compensation clause, and her many friends.

149. The primitive nature of Holywell's water supply and the town's dependence on St Winefride's Well. Locals drawing water at the well.

I have come here to-day in thanksgiving for the preservation of Holywell and to pray for the good estate and protection of God for all those who were the human means of gaining this end, and as the only one who can tell you who these were, I venture to ask you with his Lordship's approval that they may be remembered yearly in prayer at the Well in perpetuity on the 3rd of November. If you grant my request, may I ask that my husband and my children and I may be remembered at the Shrine every 18th of July or 3rd November, as having done all we could to maintain the general interests of the place.[34]

Third Scheme: The Halkyn and District Mines Act, 1913

There was no end to the great thirst of the promoters to drain the water from the area controlled by the Acts of 1875 (the Halkyn Tunnel) and 1904 (the Milwr Tunnel) and to ask for further powers to extend their tunnels. The purpose of the new Bill was to allow the extension of the Milwr Tunnel (scheme two) into the area of the Halkyn District Mines Drainage Company (scheme one), to link with the Halkyn tunnel, 180 feet above it (scheme one). The cost of works was estimated at £55,000. The average production of lead ore had increased from an average of 827 tons per annum for the years 1866 –1885, to 4,575 tons per annum for the years 1886–1894, and to 6,089 tons per annum for the period 1895–1912. The drainage work was making huge profits and more money would be made through the demand for lead during the Great War.

The major argument of the promoters was to provide more employment in the mines. They denied the possibility that the new scheme was a threat to St Winefride's Well, backed by evidence from leading geologists. For example, Dr F. H. Hatch stated that 'there was very little probability that there was any, or that there would prove to be any direct connection between the proposed tunnel works and St Winefride's Well. In his opinion the water from the well was supplied from the area lying to the west and north west.' William Whitaker, who had served nearly forty years on the Geological Survey, supported him in his views.

Two experts who had spoken against the 1904 scheme confirmed that the new Bill was a grave threat to the water supply. Caradoc Williams gave a prophetic prediction of the probable consequences of the new Bill:

> The drainage powers contemplated will affect the water level of a very extensive area, practically without limitation. There is every reason to anticipate that the work will eventually withdraw from the limestone rocks water which forms a part if not the whole of the storage which supplies St Winefride's Well.

Dr Aubrey Strahan, in charge of the Geological Survey of England and Wales, expressed his fears that the new works proposed in the Bill would endanger the supply of water to the well: 'To drive a tunnel under the same ground at a greater depth would lead to a further reduction in the flow of the spring.' He had been informed that there had been a material diminution in the flow of water owing to the driving of the Halkyn Deep level. He was practically certain that the water of the well was derived from the limestone. The proposed tunnel would endanger and certainly drain the area from which the Well was fed which he had endeavoured to define in 1904. This had been included in the compensation clause and was marked on an agreed map. On that account it would endanger part of the flow of the spring.

The Catholics of Holywell and the wider community mobilised the support of pilgrims nationwide, and Father Ryan chaired a protest meeting at St Winefride's Hall during the week of the June Feast. Lady Mostyn, widowed the previous year, and worn out by the struggle, gave evidence before the parliamentary committee. She proudly told them that she represented the family who had been appointed guardians of the well by Queen Mary of Modena in the reign of James II, and would never relinquish her duty. But the Mostyn estate was heavily mortgaged, and the lenders, alarmed by the prospect of the failure of the industries on the stream, were beginning to call in their loans. The Holywell Urban District Council was ineffective, half of its membership had succumbed to the blandishments of the promoters. The voting was evenly divided, seven members for and seven against, plus one old gentleman who was so aged he did not appear. Inevitably, the Bill passed its third reading, and the inhabitants of Holywell and the Catholic community prayed that they would be spared the drought.

Wisely the manufactories on the stream had learnt to rely on an alternative water supply to supplement the reduced flow from the well, and were using one-and-a-half million gallons of water a day from the Holway adit to make up the difference. Steam engines were introduced to provide a secondary source of power. The daily recording of the water flow was a necessity as well as a danger signal. The compensation clause inserted in the 1904 Act would come into force if the flow of water fell below an average daily quantity of two-and-a-half million gallons. Figures recorded by the agent of the Mostyn's Talacre estate of the daily measurement of the water flow at the well in the first months of 1916, showed an alarming diminution. Although the flow recovered to a reading above the minimum for compensation, there was evidently a sharp decline. The feeders to St Winefride's Well were being tapped, and the main plug was pulled at 6 a.m on 5th January 1917. The stark message of disaster was sent by telegram, the way all bad news was conveyed in the Great War: 'Water St Winefride's Well Completely Disappeared this afternoon.'

Bringing St Winefride's Well to Life
Ten days later a public meeting was held in the Assembly Hall. No positive plans were announced for the replacement of the lost water supply to the town, or legal measures to obtain compensation. The gathering was as necessary as any funeral

service is, for mourners to express a sense of loss and appreciation. It was as various as any body of mourners, the Mostyn family and Father Ryan, the next of kin, as it were, to St Winefride, her immediate family; the members of the town council and leading townsfolk representing the neighbours with all past differences forgotten. A letter from Bishop Mostyn, gave the meeting a note of authority and sense of purpose. It set an agenda for the resolution of the problem of the restoration of the water supply. Lord Mostyn of Mostyn (a kinsman to the bishop) read the letter to the gathering, and it had the effect of rousing them out of the despair and hopelessness into which they had fallen. The Bishop's letter was a condemnation of the greed of the promoters, which expressed regret, consternation and indignation at what had happened to the well. The tone of the letter showed a determination to put things right, and called for united action to achieve this. It was full of fighting spirit, and gave the meeting resolution to demand restitution and reparation, and bring St Winefride's Well back to life. The Bishop told them that:

> The object of this meeting is to protest against the action of those individuals who, for the sake of trying to enrich themselves, have deprived Holywell of the very soul of its existence. The draining of St Winefride's Well is doubtless the greatest disaster that the town of Holywell and its inhabitants has ever experienced. It seems monstrous that the law of the land should allow a few individuals, for the sake of prospective gain, to drain a countryside with the certainty of drying up the springs in the immediate vicinity of their 'workings,' and with the strong probability of tapping springs at a distance.
>
> Surely the rights of the people at large should be considered before the pockets of a few individuals. Surely the rights of the people to a proper supply of water are far stronger than the rights of a few individuals to risk that supply by tunnelling in the mountainsides in the hope of enriching themselves by finding lead or other minerals. I sincerely hope that the people of Holywell will rise as one man and insist upon their rights and urge the Local Government Board to force those who have tapped St Winefride's Well to make good the damage they have done.[35]

Other speakers took up the points made by the Bishop, and recalled the enormity of the events leading up to the calamity.

It was clear that finding a solution to bring things back to normal rested on two things: first the provision of an adequate water supply from an alternative source to the satisfaction of all parties; second, raising money to finance the implementation of a new scheme. It was widely held that this would be met by financial compensation from the directors of the tunnelling companies, under the provisions made in the 1904 Act.

It is clear from statements made by the Catholic community that they entertained doubts about the water supply being restored to St Winefride's Well.

In February, in his pastoral letter to his diocese, the Bishop expressed some doubt about the matter when he wrote:

> As to whether this damage can be repaired, is a matter that can only be decided by enquiries. If it should not prove possible we must console ourselves by remembering the fact that we still have the hallowed spot where the head of St Winefride rested. We still have her shrine and we shall continue to visit it. We shall still ask her intercession.[36]

This same uncertainty about the future of the well, mixed with pious hopes, was expressed by Father Jagger, preaching at Mass in St Winefride's on her feast day in June:

> St Winefride's power did not lie in the waters of the Well it depended upon God whether they were used by Him as an agency or not. The power of St Winefride depended upon her union with and love of God; and no power on earth could destroy the glory of her intercession. Whatever happened they had St Winefride, they had her shrine and her relics, and no one could take them away. Never would her powers of intercession for them to heal and cure pass away.[37]

Father John Ryan was more pragmatic, and made the best of the situation by using the precious amount of water which remained in the precincts of the well as he recorded in his diary in the first part of 1917:

> We had the Westminster bath which was fairly full to draw water from. This we were able to send away in bottles as demand was made, Many acknowledgements of cures received came in.[38]

In the minds of Bishop Mostyn, Father Jagger and Father Ryan the sanctity of the shrine and sacred space was inviolable.

The first step to remedy the damage was made by the aggrieved parties who informed the drainage companies that they would institute legal proceedings to obtain necessary redress by means of compensation to restore the water supply. At this early stage an arbitrator appeared in the person of Sir Lionel Philips, Director of Mineral Resources for the United Kingdom, who intervened, anxious to avoid a stoppage in lead production at a critical stage in the war, and install a water supply to Holywell Town sufficient to meet public health requirements. In order to provide an early outcome to the issue, negotiations started, helped by the united co-operation of the parties seeking redress. In these the Urban District Council and mill owners received the greatest assistance from Bishop Mostyn and the agent of the Talacre estate. A successful conclusion was arrived at, and announced in the local press in September 1917, together with a summary of the financial terms accepted by both parties.

The particulars of this arrangement were embodied in the annual report (recently submitted to the shareholders) of the board of directors of the Halkyn Drainage Company to the following effect: – "The board were informed by the Controller that legal proceedings were being instituted by the Holywell District Council, persons interested in St Winefride's Well, and the mill owners on the Holywell stream for compensation for loss of water against the Holywell-Halkin Tunnel Company and the Drainage Company. The Drainage Company were advised that no legal liability could be attached to them. Under considerable pressure from the Controller, who desired to avoid an unnecessary amount being spent in legal proceedings, the Drainage Board, after lodging a strong protest, and without admitting any liability, consented to pay an amount of £2,500 to affect a friendly settlement of all present and future claims by the parties for compensation for loss of water in any way connected with future tunnel or mining. 'The Board understands that the Holywell–Halkyn Tunnel Company are paying a similar amount.' By this arrangement it would appear that a sum of £5,000 is available by way of compensation to the parties aggrieved.[39]

Before the sum of £5,000 compensation had been agreed, the Mostyn estate and Holywell Urban District Council had solved the urgency of a resumption of the water supply. They returned to a scheme considered previously in 1913 as a possible source for a water supply to the town. This was known as the Holway Level. Sometime in his negotiations with the drainage companies, Sir Lionel was informed by F. Mott, on behalf of Talacre estates, of this alternative source of water and the urgency of the situation. He wrote:

The average flow of St Winefride's Well over a period of years has been approximately 2,000 gallons per minute [approximately three million gallons every twenty-four hours] & this quantity represents the minimum amount necessary to keep the mills working efficiently. The only possible method of obtaining this supply is by means of pumping from one of the disused mine shafts in the Holway area.

He estimated that the figure for compensation was not less than £10,000, with the cost of pumping put at £500 a year, and told Sir Lionel that:

The prosperity of the town of Holywell is largely dependant on these mills & unless a sufficient supply of water can be speedily obtained for the loss of St Winefride's Well there is grave danger they will have to close down permanently.[40]

It is obvious that this pressure from Mr Mott influenced Sir Lionel Philips, and enabled him to arrive at a swift and satisfactory solution to overcome the crisis.

The Holway Level, the new source of water for St Winefride's Well
The Holway Level is part of the area north-west of Holywell rich in lead ore. Holywell Mountain's rich veins of lead were worked from ancient times, and when mining operations ceased towards the end of the nineteenth century, the old workings remained unwatered. About the year 1877, the Great Holway Mining Company sank Roskell's shaft, one of the keys in the rescue plan. The disused shaft was adapted as a pumping plant capable of raising sufficient water and directing it along the Holway Level, a drainage tunnel commenced in 1774 and completed before 1790.

Ownership of the level was in possession of the Mostyns of Talacre, who in the eighteenth century had granted leases to Thomas Pennant of Downing, Peter Parry, Edward Jones and Mrs Mary Williams. This partnership was responsible for the construction of the level, a subterranean canal a mile long cut through solid rock, six-feet high and four-feet wide. It was used both as a drainage tunnel and a means for the conveyance of the ore by barges, and was known as the 'Boat Level.' Pennant gave an account of his journey in a punt along the level in September 1795, accompanied by his two sons, under the pilotage of Thomas Edwards.[41] They entered the level on the west side of St Winefride's Well across the road in the lane opposite. It is from this point that a pipe was inserted to convey the water from the level into the polygonal basin of the well.

Water was restored to the well on 22 September, after an absence of thirty-seven weeks. The new water supply was described as clear and bright, with a high degree of hardness and a quality slightly better than that which was obtainable previously from St Winefride's Well and more suitable particularly for domestic purposes, as it is more easily softened.[42]

Thanksgiving: business as usual at St Winefride's Well, September 1917
With the flow of water resumed at the well, the Catholic community in Holywell offered up their thanksgiving for its restoration. On this historic occasion, Father Donnelly, SJ, of Farm Street, London, Provincial of the Society of Jesus joined them. The order had faithfully served the Mission in the town since 1590, and their provincial came to Holywell to express the society's thanksgiving for the deliverance of St Winefride's Well from its melancholy drought.

After a service in church, the town of Holywell was reminded that business was as usual, as they saw the Catholic congregation walking in procession to the well, headed by school children in white carrying baskets of flowers. The banners were taken down to the well for the first time since the pilgrim season of 1917. The water flowed once more, the well and outer bath were replenished and welcoming. In the late autumn afternoon the brilliance of the light in the crypt increased, and the shrine of Winefride once more welcomed worshippers who added to the splendour with their lighted candles. The mystery and solemnity of the occasion was concluded by Father Ryan's recital of the litany of St Winefride, and his presentation of the relic of the saint for veneration.

At the opening of the first meeting of the Urban District Council after the restoration of the water to the well and town, the chairman expressed his feeling of gratification for a successful outcome. A week later, Mrs Margaret Lloyd George, wife of the Prime Minister, came to visit the shrine of the nation's Catholic patroness. It was reported that she was much interested in the famous shrine and expressed her satisfaction at the restoration of the water. A sister who was there presented her 'with several little books relating to the history of the well and the town.'[43]

It was Father Jagger, SJ, of St Beuno's College, who gave the most apt expression to the thoughts and feelings of the Catholic community at the restoration of the water to the well. The occasion was at the autumn Feast of St Winefride, in a sermon in the church on the Sunday afternoon that followed the rosary. His address, described as a panegyric of the saint, reminded his hearers that:

> They had just been witnesses of a kind of resurrection in the life of the saint: she had risen again, brighter and more glorious still. The agency which God gave to St Winefride, whereby her fame had been known for a thousand years, her Well, suddenly dried up and stopped. It was thought by many that her life of love, her power for good work, had finished, that it had passed away, and belonged to the history of the past, that it was no longer a vital factor. But they knew that, whether the water came back or not, her power to heal was not over. But the water had come back, and Winefride had arisen glorious and beautiful and fair and radiant once again. The water flowed again, and please God, there would be a new book, in the history of her wonders.[44]

There was a new book being kept in Holywell of her wonders by Father Ryan in his diary. The new beginning merged naturally into the old order. Business was as usual and began immediately with the entry:

> Oct. 1917. The new supply of water was inaugurated: too late for pilgrims to avail themselves of it during the finer months of the year. A Mr Kenyon, a non-Catholic, who was blind came and bathed several times & found his sight improved.[45]

A great cloud of witnesses

By the summer of 1919, the first full peace-time one since 1913, a sense of normality began to return. There appeared to be a desire to seek the consolation of St Winefride's Well and its healing waters, and many ex-servicemen visited the shrine. Glorious sunshine and a long spell of dry weather brought thousands of pilgrims to St Winefride's Well. In August it was reported that:

During the past week or two the town has received a very great flood of visitors, and at the present time practically every apartment house is full: and they still come! The arrivals on Monday were so numerous that the friendly aid of the police was requisitioned in order to find room. On Tuesday the streets presented a very animated appearance, owing to the arrival of some fifteen hundred Franciscan Tertiaries from Liverpool and other places en route for Pantasaph. It is evident that the popularity of the town as a health resort is now greater than ever.

Indeed business was as usual. So much so that the same report suggested that Holywell town employ their watering cart during the drought carrying supplies from the well into the town.[46] The new water supply at the well appeared to be equally effective as the former, and newspapers continued to report a regularity of cures there. The same variety of cures experienced before January 1917 continued to take place. The message was business as usual at St Winefride's Well, and the tradition of pilgrimage was much as before the war.

Throughout the long history of St Winefide's Well, from earliest times to the present day, the emphasis has been on the continuity of the tradition, in spite of major changes which occurred at intervals, such as in the twelfth century, the Reformation, and the mid-nineteenth century. The end of the Great War witnessed the introduction of another major period of change, which culminated with the withdrawal in 1930 of the Society of Jesus from their Mission in Holywell. The tradition established and maintained over the centuries by a great cloud of witnesses was handed on and cherished by another dispensation. The guardians of the cult of St Winefride and her well changed, but the continuation of the tradition remained as strong and adaptable as ever. The events of the years 1917 and 1930, which affected the Catholic community in Holywell, demonstrate a smooth transition and a complete integration into a diocesan organisation.

The departure of the great families
The departure of the Feildings from Downing and the Mostyns from Talacre was part of a national trend. The great sale of estates throughout Britain followed as a consequence of the failue of male heirs after the Great War.

150. Father Jagger of St Beuno's College who spoke of the 'Death and Resurrection of St Winefride's Well'.

The eighth earl of Denbigh who married the heiress of Downing, Louisa Pennant had died in 1892[47] and in 1909 the ninth earl disposed of his Holywell property.[48] In 1920, the Downing estate was sold and two years later the hall was destroyed by fire. However, the family continued to retain a great interest in Pantasaph, with its complex of Capuchin monastery, friary church, schools and orphanage.

Sir Pyers Mostyn, ninth Baronet,was buried in the churchyard at Pantasaph in 1912, with his wife Lady Anna Maria being placed alongside him in 1916, to be joined in January 1917 by their son Charles, the tenth baronet. The heavily mortgaged estate was sold in 1919,[49] and Talacre Hall was bought by an enclosed community of Benedictine nuns. Although generally living abroad, the succeeding baronets retained their family's devotion to St Winefride, and some contact with Holywell. On 7 March 1921, Bishop Francis Mostyn was translated from Menevia to Cardiff, to become the second archbishop of the Welsh province, and the first Welshman to receive that distinction. He continued to administer Menevia, rendered vacant by his promotion, for another five years and was a frequent visitor to Holywell until his death in 1939.

Another departure took place in 1926, with the transfer of theology students from St Beuno's College, Tremeirchion, to Heythrop Hall in Oxfordshire. Here they were no longer isolated from centres of learning, and 'lost in the Welsh hills.'[50] St Beuno's was still used by the Jesuits for the training of tertians until the 1980s when the house was established as a centre of spirituality and retreats. For nearly eighty years the rectors and professors of St Beuno' s had provided invaluable advice and support at the church and well in Holywell, and shared a common platform in times of controversy. The aged Father Ryan received invaluable support in the Mission from Father Jagger, professor of Rhetoric, and spent his last year at St Beuno's in retirement, where he died in October 1926. It was said of Father Ryan that 'he was intensely happy with his religious brethren while for them he provided occasional and unrehearsed merriment: when, owing to his deafness, he would, at moments of great silence, inform them of Holywell's importance in a voice and manner all of his own.'[51]

Father George Jinks, SJ, 1925–28

Father George Jinks was the penultimate superior of the Jesuit Mission at Holywell, and died there on 15 January 1928 of pneumonia. Like Father Ryan, whom he succeeded, he had great experience. He had served in South Africa and filled several offices in the Society of Jesus, including that of headmaster of Beaumont College, Windsor. In his brief time in Holywell he charmed everyone by his smile. He was scholarly and an efficient administrator, and reorganised several guilds and societies connected with the church, the principal of which was the Catholic Young Men's Society.[52]

Father John R. Luck, SJ, 28 February 1928 – 30 September 1930
Father John Luck was the last superior of St Winefride's, to be appointed by the
Society of Jesus to the Holywell Mission, where he served until it was withdrawn.
In his short ministry he did excellent work in the Mission.

He intended to carry out major changes to St Winefride's Church, but left before
his plans had time to mature. However, while he was in Holywell the church
benefited from his flair as a designer. He commissioned Ferdinand Stuflesser,
sculptor to the Vatican, to execute the work of carving two statues in wood. The
first of Stuflesser's statues was of the Sacred Heart, which was presented by
Monsignor Waring of New York, as a memorial to his sister, who was a frequent
visitor to Holywell. It forms the central object of a beautiful oak and gold gothic
altar, in the south transept of St Winefride's Church. The subject for the second
statue was that of Christ the King. Father Luck, in his novel design, represented
Christ as Ruler of the Earth, standing before a chair, a replica of the coronation
chair in Westminster Abbey. It was described as 'a noble representation of our
Lord in royal and priestly robes, blessing His subjects, while his sceptre rests on
his left arm. The cloak is a gorgeous piece of gold and purple brocade.'[53]

Father Luck began the improvements to the precincts of St Winefride's Well,
which continue to this day. He was fortunate in 1929 to be able to purchase the
old St Winefride's Brewery at a bargain price. He was now able to carry out
much-needed improvement in the precincts of the well. It was his vision to
demolish the brewery building which obscured the view of the well from the
north-west, and cover the stream as it left the bath in front of the well, in order
to convert the area into a garden with seats and walks for pilgrims, and a statue
of St Winefride in the centre. This gave invaluable space for visitors, especially
when there were large pilgrimages. St Winefride's Park, as it was officially called,
was opened by Bishop Francis Vaughan of Menevia at the June Feast of the Saint
in 1930. On this occasion, 2,000 pilgrims marched there in procession.[54] Father
Luck continued his work of 'tidying up' by renovating and cleaning the crypt
area of the well. The crutches and other instruments that for years had hung on
the walls and stood in the corners were rearranged 'and the place made bright
and wholesome.'[55] However Father Luck's ambition to purchase St Winefride's
Well from the town council on behalf of the lessees failed. His offer in the region
of £2,000 was rejected, as was that of his successor Father Burke two years later.[56]

Father Luck continued to keep records of cures at the well, which included
wherever possible proof from the patient, family, physician and others.

The end of the Jesuit Mission to Holywell
The work of the Society of Jesus in their Holywell Mission was remarkable by
any standard in the province. In Wales it was incomparable. Their 340 years of a
continuous succession of members of the society ministering in a Welsh mission
was unsurpassed.

However, the strategy of Mission which had been necessary in penal times was being replaced by the strengthening of diocesan reorganisation, which was responding to the expansion which occurred after Catholic emancipation and the Irish migration. The expansion of Catholicism in north-east Wales had benefited greatly from the missionary activity of Capuchin Franciscans from Pantasasph and Jesuits from St Beuno's. However the diocese of Menevia was training its own secular priests, who were now ready to take over from regulars. This had been the aim of St Mary's College established by Bishop Mostyn in Holywell in 1904,[57] and its first priests were now working in the diocese. It was recognised in the Welsh province that, wherever possible, secular clergy should replace regulars, and this became the policy of the second bishop of Menevia, Francis John Vaughan who was consecrated bishop on 8 September 1926 in St David's Cathedral, Cardiff, by Archbishop Mostyn. Consecrator and consecrated represented in themselves the two ancient Welsh Catholic families of Mostyn and Vaughan.

Bishop Vaughan soon began to implement his policy of replacing regular priests by seculars in north Wales. In 1929 he established a deanery of St Winefride, and the following year requested the Society of Jesus to hand over to the diocesan authorities the Missions at Holywell, St Asaph, Denbigh, Ruthin, and Llandrindod Wells.

News of the decision by the Bishop of Menevia and the Father General for the removal of the Jesuit mission reached Holywell early in September 1930, less than a month before the date of departure. However, in spite of such short notice the Catholic community and members of the town council came together to mark an official farewell, when a presentation was made in St Winefride's School to the superior, Father Luck, SJ, and his assistant Father Fallon, SJ.

The late announcement of the depending departure of the mission had taken everyone by surprise. But it was a moving and dignified ceremony made more memorable by the gracious remarks of members of the Society of Jesus, representatives of St Winefride's Church, and Protestant and Catholic town councillors. After a 340 year residence of members of the society in the town, through times of enmity, and religious persecution, there had grown between them bonds of mutual respect and affection. A partnership had been forged between the Catholic church and the town council in the defence of the water supply of the community and the administration of St Winefride's Well. The town council unbeknown to themselves had become surrogate guardians of St Winefride's Well. They spoke with admiration of the contribution made by Jesuit Fathers Beauclerk, Ryan, Jinks and Luck, with whom they had worked closely, particularly in regards to St Winefride's Well, schools and the hospital.

The members of the Catholic community presented a handsomely bound volume to the provincial and fathers of the Society of Jesus, in which was a record of their work in Holywell, with photographs of the buildings they had erected and of other improvements they were responsible for.[58] Their address expressed the deepest feelings of regret and appreciation, and paid tribute to the society:

> That through their services and never tiring zeal the Faith has been kept alive through penal times up to the present and we to-day owe a great debt of gratitude to the Fathers who have always had before them and lived up to the motto of the Society, 'To the greater glory of God.' During the long period the Fathers of the Society have served Holywell, devotion to St Winefride and the care of her relic and shrine have always been very dear to each of the Fathers so that to-day her fame is known the world through.
>
> No words of ours can adequately describe our heartfelt gratitude to the faithful sons of the Soldier Saint for all they have done for us and for our predecessors in the parish. The address concluded with the prayer 'that St Winefride will watch over the labours of the Society of Jesus whose sons have ever shewn so much zeal in her service.

The letter written by the father general of the society to the parish committee in Holywell expressed his gratitude for their tribute:

> I, on my part, pray that the work in the parish and at the shrine may develop more and more for the glory of God, and I will apply one hundred Masses that God's blessing may descend upon this work, upon your pastors, and upon each and every member of your congregation.[59]

The Father Provincial also expressed his gratitude when he wrote:

> It is, indeed, a wrench to part from a place where we have been for centuries, and I assure you that it is from no desire to leave Holywell that we are going. We shall go, however encouraged by the kind things you have said, and with a keen gratitude for the loyal support which the people of Holywell have always given to the work of their church.[60]

The list of priests of the Society of Jesus who served the Mission in Holywell

151. Cardinal Francis Bourne, archbishop of Westminster and Francis Vaughan, second bishop of Menevia visited St Winefride's Well in 1932.

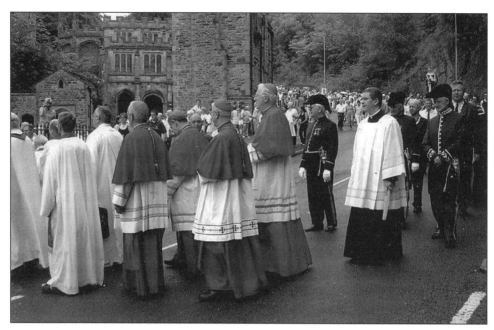

152. Cardinal Cormac Murphy-O'Connor archbishop of Westminster visited St Winefride's Well on Pilgrimage in 2005 and opened the Visitor's Centre and Exhibition at the Well. On this memorable occasion his Eminence was enthusiastically greeted by the Bishop, Clergy, and people of the diocese and the joyful Holywell congregation.

contained the names of thirty-seven incumbents from Father John Bennett, SJ, in 1590 to Father John Luck, SJ, in 1930, and thirteen assistant priests. Father Luck said:

> … that the history of the Mission at Holywell differed from thousands of other missions and chapels in England, and in some ways this mission has been quite unique. It was the only parish where a parish priest had been appointed without a gap for 360 years.'[61] He described the history of the Mission as romantic, and spoke about the disguises and false name adopted by the Jesuits and how in Holywell they assumed the role of publicans, and the oratory served as a public room. At night the people came to the house to receive Mass at the hands of the publican priest. The old chapel was still in the house. It ran the whole length of the house, and in the daytime was used for customers and for services in the evening.

With Father Luck's reminiscence of the witness of Jesuits in penal times, their Mission in Holywell came to an end. It was an occasion of both hope and nostalgia for the Catholic community in Holywell and the thousands of pilgrims who came to the well and shrine of St Winefride. They were not to be disappointed as a new chapter began in their long history.

153. The devoted custodians of St Winefride's Well John and Lolitta L'Aigulle togther in the grounds which have been cleared of industrial buildings and progressively improved over the last eighty years since the demolition of the brewery in 1930.

NOTES

1. Letters and Notices, vol. 3, 1911–12.

2. *Flintshire Observer*, 14/7/1904.

3. 11/4/1904 Bishop Mostyn brought the parchment from Rome. There is a small notebook in the Holywell Museum, 'Diary of events at St Mary's College, Holywell.' covering the period 1904 to 1908, on which this section depends

4. D. Attwater, *The Catholic Church in Wales* (Burns Oates1935)

5. The Collegian Easter 1917 pp. 63–64

6. The statue of St Winefride in the Well crypt dating from 1886 was designed by Edmund Kirby and executed by R. L. Boulton.

7. *County Herald*, 11/10/1901

8. *County Herald*, 22/7/1904

9. *County Herald*, 25/6/1909

10. Figures given in Father Beauclerk's account book

11. an account of St Winefride's relics (one portion only of a finger) is given in Swift op cit p. 70 'In 1852, the Rev Albany Christie, SJ, obtained one half of it from Rome. This was subsequently divided and one portion is preserved in the Roman Catholic Cathedral, Shrewsbury and the other at Holywell.

12. Maybe it was this report that was the foundation of Rolfe's accusation of Beauclerk's making false statements: i.e when he writes: 'your assertion that you intended to employ another sculptor to alter the face of the Marble Statue of St Winefride, unless Mr Swynnerton consented to mutilate his great work to your private fancied.' *See Quest for Corvo* (1952) edt. p. 266.

13. *County Herald*, 26/8/1896 for report of blessing of Swynnerton's statue of St Winefride.

14. *County Herald*, 11/10/1901 Although this report, made in the time of Father Borsch, makes it

clear that Father Beauclerk raised the funds for the statue, Father Beauclerk accused Father Borsch of saying that he (Borsch) was left to pay for it.

15. *County Herald*, 22/7/1904
16. *County Herald*, 22/10/1926
17. Letter of 1912
18. *County Herald*, 4/3/1910
19. The names of the doctors from Holywell – H. W. W. Williams, J. Owen Jones, C. E. Morris, and J. Williams.
20. *The Month*, July 1918 p. 49.
21.ibid
22. ibid pp. 50–1
23. Most of Thurston's article was written after Lady Mostyn died in 1916. There is no mention of the Well drying up on 5/1/1917.
24. This has been transcribed by Mr T. Gray Hulse and the quotations of the few cases listed below are from his transcription which is being edited for publication.
25. *Chester Courant* 10/1/1917 report of an interview given by Mr H.F. Brown of Chester, director of the Flannel Mill.
26. ibid
27 That is in the Well Crypt, built c.1495–1510
28.12/1/1917
29. *Flintshire Observer*, 7/5/1875
30. FRO D/MT/1078
31.6/2/1904 published in *Holywell Pilgrim's Record* no. 4 1935
32. Resolution of Holywell UDC 8/8/1904
33.*Flintshire Observer*, 6/10/1904
34. *Holywell Pilgrim's Record* no. 4 1935
35. *North Wales Pioneer*, 18/1/1917
36. *County Herald*, 23/2/1917
37. *County Herald*, 23/6/1917
38. Father Ryan's diary
39. *County Herald*, 28/9/1917
40. FRO D/MT/1085 draining St Winefride's Well. The Case for the Holywell Estate.
41.T.Pennant op cit W & H pp. 249–251
42. FRO NT/653 Holywell Urban District Council – Report on water supply Holway adit scheme, Messrs Williams and Clarke, 1920
43. *County Herald*, 26/10/1917
44. *County Herald*, 7/11/1917
45. Father Ryan's diary
46. *County Herald*, 15/8/1919
47. Obituary *Flintshire Observer*, 10/3/1892
48. *County Herald*, 1/10/1909
49. *County Herald*, 18/4/1919
50. P. Edwards, *Canute's Tower St Beuno's 1848–1989* (Gracewing 1990) pp. 102–107
51. *County Herald*, 22/10/1926
52. *County Herald*, 20/1/1928
53, *County Herald*, 1/11/1929, 28/3/1930. Letters and Notices vol. xlv 1930 pp. 16–17.The statue of Christ the King which stood near the high altar is no longer there
54.*County Herald*, 21/6 and 21/6/1930
55. *County Herald*, 19/9/1930
56. *County Herald*, 13/7/1928 and 16/10/1931
57. It was removed to Aberystwyth in 1911.
58. The Church, the Schools, the Convent, the Hospice for pilgrim's, the garden at St Winefride's Well

59. Letters and Notices vol. 46 1931 p. 36
60. ibid p. 36
61. It was 340 years.

Acknowledgements

Iowe a great debt of gratitude to so many is people for their assistance, encouragement, kindness and expertise in enabling me to complete this book in a little over two years. A mere list of names fails to do justice to those concerned. The Right Reverend Edwin Regan, Bishop of Wrexham graciously consented to write the Foreword. At Holywell David Schwarz, Celia Murphy, John and Lolitta L'Aigulle, the volunteers, and St Winefride Well Museum committee were of inestimable help in giving me access to their archive. Most of my research and writing was done at Hawarden in the congenial surroundings of St Deiniol's Library through the kindness of the warden, Peter Francis, the librarian, Patsy Williams, and at the Flintshire Record Office where the archivist, Claire Harrington, and the staff patiently answered my queries and I was able to consult the newspaper archive as well as estate records. My visits to the National Library of Wales and Royal Commission on the Ancient and Historical Monuments of Wales at Aberystwyth were both stimulating and rewarding. Kathryn Byrne the Wrexham diocesan archivist; Fr Thomas McCoog, SJ, archivist of the Society of Jesus; John A. Hilton, and Dr Enid Pierce Roberts encouraged my initial quest for information. The Flintshire Library Service, Mold, obtained many books for me via the inter-library loan scheme. Jean Gilliland supplied references from the Bodelian Oxford, Lord Barry Jones from the House of Lords Records, and Barry Johnson from the London Library. I was welcomed and given help at St Beuno's College, Tremeirchion, St David's Monastery, Pantasaph, and at Shrewsbury R.C. Cathedral by Canon Stephen Coonan and Jane Gillett. Karen McNiven helped me considerably with my computer. Dr Anne Isba, David and Carol Shone, Ken Lloyd Gruffydd and J. Brian Lewis, read and commented on the text, Elizabeth Pettitt, provided translations, and Brian Taylor helped to process many of the images. Of particular assistance and hospitality were Ken and Eirlys Lloyd Gruffydd: Ken drew the maps, helped with Welsh-language translations and supplied priceless information from Welsh gaol files and other references. Tristan Gray-Hulse was generous with his time, expertise, knowledge of St Winefride and his critical reading of the text saved me from many pitfalls. Andrew Chrimes was unstinting in the time and enthusiasm he gave to visits to Holywell and elsewhere in following the trail of St Winefride as may be seen in the excellent photographs [here acknowledged by AC] which accompany the text. Dr Jo Wilkinson contributed the index. The trustees of the Isla Johnson Trust of the Church in Wales generously gave a donation towards the publication of the book. Alister Williams of Bridge Books has supported me with the benefit of his professionalism and his kindness as a friend.

Acknowledgement of images and permission to use them is by courtesy of the following bodies (images in the colour section are prefixed 'C'):

The National Library of Wales, Aberystwyth: copyright NLW, nos. C2, 88.

The Royal Commission on the Ancient and Historical Monuments of Wales : Crown Copyright RCAHMW. nos. 77, 94–7.

The Flintshire Record Office: Copyright FRO, nos. 17, 44, 67, 92, 93, 102–3, 145, 149.

St Winefride's Well Museum Committee: copyright, [with the assistance of David Taylor] nos. C3–C7, C9, 1, 615, 21, 25, 29, 31, 73, 80, 87, 89, 98–9, 118, 120, 125–31, 133–36, 138–40, 142–3, 146–48, 150–3.

St Winefride's Church Holywell nos. 40, 74, 141, 144 [all by AC].

The Dean, Shrewsbury Roman Catholic Cathedral, nos. 3, 7, 8, 12, 13, 18, 22 [all by AC].

St Beuno's College, Tremeirchion, nos. 14, 57, 113 [all by AC].

St David's Monastery, Pantasaph 115 [AC].

The Parish of Our Lady and St Richard Gwyn, Llanidloes 54.

The Parish of Our Lady Queen of Martyrs, Beaumaris 55 [AC].

By courtesy of: the Dean and Chapter of Westminster Abbey, 38 [AC]; the College of Arms, 76; the Dean and Chapter of St Asaph Cathedral 35; the Dean and Chapter of Bangor Cathedral 27, 28; Chester Archaeological Society 32; the Central Library Manchester Archives and Local Studies 91; the incumbent and churchwardens of St Dyfnog Church, Llanrhaedr-yng-Nghinmeirch, 39 [AC]; Corpus Christie, Tremeirchion 61, 66 [AC].

Ken Lloyd Grufyydd maps and drawings: copyright KLG nos. 9, 19, 20, 24, 26, 30, 43, 52, 70, 100, 104, 116, 119.

Andrew Chrimes Images, copyright [AC] nos. 41, 42, 101, 105, 121, 124.

Neville Hurdsman, no. 53.

The Earl of Denbigh, nos. 106, 108.

Trevor Mostyn, 145.

Trinity Mirror Group nos. C8, C10, C11.

Every effort has been made to ensure that wherever possible permission has been obtained to produce the images in this book.

Bibliography

Manuscript and archive sources
Cheshire Record Office, Chester
        Crewe Cowper Collection

Flintshire Record Office, Hawarden
        Basingwerk Abbey after Dissolution in estate records
        Church in Wales Records parishes of Holywell, Whiford, etc
        Grosvenor estate records
        Holywell local government records from 1860s
        Mostyn of Talacre estate records
        Names of papists who registered estates in Flintshire D/M/7194 &
        D/DM/271/60
        Pennant of Nantlys estate records
        Roman Catholic records including registers of Star and Cross Keys mission and
        copies of Society of Jesus records (MF/5-6)

St Winefride's Well Museum and Archive Holywell
        St Winefride's parish records from c.1860
        Account book of Father Beauclerk, Diary of Father Ryan, Diary of St Mary's
        College
A catalogue is in preparation of the contents of the museum. An excellent visitors centre
and museum is situated in the precincts of St Winefride's Well.

House of Lords Records
        Population details 1780

National Library of Wales
        Records of the Court of Great Session
        St Asaph Diocesan Records
        Welsh Church Commission records

Royal Commission on the Ancient and Historical Monuments of Wales Aberystwyth
        National Monuments Record of Wales (NMR) for St Winefride's Well and Chapel

Sheffield Archives
        Diary of William Statham, MD 6853

Society of Jesus Archive of the British Province, London
        The property of the Residence of St Winefride
        Correspondence

Westminster Diocesan Archives
        AAW / A.XIX / 111 – A.XX / 82,83,93 – A.XXIX / 101, 113,114,131

Wrexham Diocesan Archive
        Anonymous history of Holywell c.1880
        Questionnaire 1890s

Publications of printed records from the National Archives
        Calendar Papal Registers concerning Great Britain vol 7
        Calendar Patent Rolls 21 Elizabeth pt 7
        Calendar State Papers Domestic – reigns of Elizaberth I, James I, Charles I
        Welsh Records – Recognizance Rolls of Chester

Historical Manuscript Commission
        Kenyon Ms (1894)
        Salisbury pt xvii (1938)
        Davies, J. C., and Lewis, E. A., Records of the Court of Augmentation Relating to
        Wales and Monmouthshire (1954)

University dissertations
Cleary, J. M., 'Welsh recusant clergy: a study of the work of Welshmen connected with the
        seminaries of Douay and Rome in the reign of Elizabeth I.' Liverpool MA thesis, 1966.
Maredudd ap Huw, 'A critical examination of Welsh Poetry relating to the native saints of
        North Wales (c.1350-1670).' Unpublished PhD dissertation Oxford, 2001.
McCoog, T. M., SJ, 'The Society of Jesus in England, 1623–1688.' Ph D dissertation,
        University of Warwick, 1984.

Newspapers
The main sources of entries for Holywell are in *The Flintshire Observer, The County Herald*
and *The Chester Chronicle* these are on micro-film in the Flintshire Record Office. Other
newspapers are mentioned in the notes.

Periodicals
Published by the Society of Jesus: *Letters and Notices* (particularly for the years 1869, 1911-
12, 1931);*The Month.*
The Holywell Record (owner and editor F. W. Hocheimer, major contributor F. W. Rolfe).
The Holywell Pilgrims Record published in the 1930s by the Holywell parish priest.

Printed books and articles
Primary published sources
The Lives of St Winefride [translations into English of the Medieval Latin Lives] amongst
which are
Falconer, J., SJ, trans. *The Admirable Life of Saint Wenefride* (1635), by Robert Prior of
Shrewsbury re-published by D. M. Rogers, (gen. ed.), English Recusant Literature,

1558–1640, 394 vols. (Yorkshire: Solar Press, 1976), vol. 319.

Fleetwood, W., *The Works of William Fleetwood,* 3 vols (1854).

Metcalfe, P., sj, *The Life of Saint Winefride* (1712), a rewriting of Falconer's translation, republished by H. Thurston, sj, in 1917.

Swift, T. sj, (ed) *The Life of Saint Winefride, Virgin and Martyr* (1888), based upon Carolus de Smedt, sj, *Acta Sanctorum Novembris 1* (1887). For more information see Chapter I notes 13–16.

Pepin, R., and Feiss, H., *Two Medieval Lives of Saint Winefride* (2000).

Wade-Evans, A. W. 'The Life of St Wenefred' (anonymous First Life) in the translators *Vitae Sanctorum Britanniae et Genealogiae* (1944).

Winward, F., 'The Lives of St Wenefred', *Analecta bollandiano,* vol. 117 (1999), a critical discussion of their dates.

Books and articles

Anon, *The Life of a Conspirator being a biography of Sir Everard Digby by one of his descendants* (1895).

Alger, B., 'The Priest and Informer Hitchmough', *North West Catholic History*: vol. 1 (1)(2), 1969.

Anstruther, G., *The Seminary Priests,* 4 vols (1968–77).

Attwater, D., *The Catholic Church in modern Wales: a record of the past century* (1935).

Bagley, J. J. (ed.) and Tyrer, F., *The Great Diurnal of Nicholas Blundell*, The Record Society of Lancashire and Cheshire, 3 vols (1968, 1970, 1972).

Banks, R. W. (ed.), Dineley, T., *The Account of the Official Progress of the First Duke of Beaufort through Wales*, 1684 (1888).

Baring-Gould, S., and Fisher ,J., *Lives of the British Saints*, 4 vols (1911).

Barnard, E. A. B., *A Seventeenth Gentleman* (1949).

Basset, B., *The English Jesuits: from Campion to Martindale* (1967).

Beard, M., *Faith and Fortune* (1997).

Beaumont, W., 'The Jacobite Trials at Manchester in 1694,' *Chetham Society old series,*vol. 28, 1853.

Benkovitz, M. J., *Frederick Rolfe: Baron Corvo* (1977).

Bliss, J. and Scott, W., *The Works of William Laud*, 7 vols (1847–60).

Bord, J., *Cures and Curses Ritual and Cult at holy wells* (2006).

Bristow, A., *Dr Johnson and Mrs Thrale's Tour in North Wales, 1774* (1994).

Brown, R. A., and Colvin, H. M., *The History of the King's Works*, vol. 1 (1963).

Burne, R. V. H., *Chester Cathedral* (1958).

Camm, Dom Bede, *Forgotten Shrines. An account of some old Catholic Halls and families in England and of Relics and Memorials of the English Martyrs* (1910).

Caraman, C. P., (ed) *The Hunted Priest; The Autobiography of John Gerard* (1959).

'The Diary of Dr Thomas Cartwright, Bishop of Chester', *Camden Society* (1843).

Champ, J. F., 'Bishop Milner, Holywell and the Cure Tradition' in Shiels, W. J., The Church and Healing,' *Studies in Church History,* vol. 19 (1982).

Chandler, J., (ed), *The adventures of John Taylor the Water Poet* (1999).

Christie, R.C. (ed) 'Annales Cestrienses or Chronicles of the Abbey of S. Werburg, Chester', *Lancashire and Cheshire Record Society* (1887).

Cleary, J. M., 'Recusant Schools in north Wales, 1626–1627', *Worcestershire Recusant*, no. 32 (1978).

Cleary, M., 'The Catholic Resistance in Wales 1568–1678', *Blackfriars*, vol. 38 (1957).

David, C., *St Winefride's Well* (1969).

Defoe, D., *A Tour through England* (1927 edition).

Dictionary of National Biography, 60 vols (2004).

Dictionary of Welsh Biography to 1940 (1959).

Edwards, F., *The Jesuits in England: from 1580 to the present day* (1985).

Edwards, I., 'Fifteenth-century alabaster tables and the Iconography of the bound Rood and St Armel', *Archaeologia Cambrensis,* cxi (1992).

Edwards, J. G., (ed) *Littere Wallie* (1940).

Edwards, J.G, Galbraith, V. H., Jacob, E. F., (eds) *Historical Essays in Honour of James Tait* (1933), Jones, A., *Basingwerk Abbey.*

Edwards, N., and Gray-Hulse, T., ' A fragment of a Reliquary Casket from Gwytherin' *The Antiquaries Journal*, 72 (1992).

Edwards, N., and Lane, A., *The Early Church in Wales and the West* (1992).

Edwards, P., *Canute's Tower: St Beuno's, 1848–1989* (1990).

Charles Edwards, T., *Two Medieval Welsh Poems* (1971).

Finch, E., *Wilfrid Scawen Blunt* (1938).

Finucane, R. C., *Miracles and Pilgrimages* (1977).

Fleetwood, William, *The Works of the Right Reverend William Fleetwood,* DD (1854), vol. 3.

Foley, H., *Records of the English Province of the Society of Jesus* (c.1878), vol. 4, pt I, 'The College of St Francis Xavier and the district of South Wales', 'The Residence of St Winefrid, or North Wales', vol. 4 ,pt 2 and *Collectanea,* vol. 7 (b).

Franciscana, *Catholic Record Society,* vol. 24 (1922).

Gardner, W. H. (ed.) *Poems and Prose of Gerard Manley Hopkins* (1953).

The Gentleman's Magazine, November (1825).

Given Wilson, C. (ed.), *The Chronicles of Adam Usk* (1997).

Gray, M., *Images of Piety. The Iconography of traditional religion in late medieval Wales* (2000).

Griffiths, G. M., 'A St Asaph Register of Episcopal Acts, 1506–1571' *Journal of the Historical Society of the Church in Wales*, vol. vi, no. 11 (1956).

Haigh, C., 'The continuity of Catholicism in the English Reformation,' *The English Reformation Revised* (1987).

Harmsen, T. H. B. M., *John Gee's Foot out of the Snare* (1624 and 1992).

Hebel, J. W., (ed.) *M. Drayton Polyolbion* (1933).

Holt, T. G., SJ, *The English Jesuits 1650–1829. A Biographical Dictionary,* Catholic Record Society, (1984).

Holt, T. G., SJ, 'Jesuits in Montgomeryshire 1670–1873' *The Journal of Welsh Religious History*, vol. 1 (1993).

Hook, P., 'Historical introduction to the Catholic registers of Holywell,' *Catholic Record Society*, vol. 3 (1906).

Hubbard, E., *The Buildings of Clwyd* (1986).

James, R., 'Iter Lancastrienses: A Poem Written 1603', *Chetham Society*, 7 (1845).

Jones, E. G., 'Catholic Recusancy in the Counties of Denbigh, Flint and Montgomery 1581–1625.' *Transactions of the Honourable Society of the Cymmrodorion* (1945).

Jones, F., *The Holy Wells of Wales* (1992).

Kenyon, J. P., 'My lord of Canterbury's returns to his Majesty's instructions for the year 1636,' *The Stuart Constitution 1603–1688, Documents and Commentary* (1966).

Kibble, E. R., *The Stained-Glass Windows in the Collegiate Church of St Mary's Warwick* (2005).

Lorrie, A. J., 'Spain and Jacobean Catholics II; 1613–1624', *Catholic Record Society*, vol. 68 (1978).

Lewis, M., 'The Glass at Gresford,' *Transactions Denbighshire Historical Society*, vol. 7 (1958).

Lewis, M., *Stained-Glass in North Wales up to 1850* (1970).

Lowry, M. J. C., 'St Winifred and the Lady Margaret Beaufort,' *The Library*, 6th series, vol. 5 (2).

Martin, R. B., *Gerard Manley Hopkins, A Very Private Life* (1991).

McCoog, T. M., sj, 'English and Welsh Jesuits 1555–1650' Part 1. A–F, *CRS*, vol. 74 (1994)
                              Part 2. G–Z, *CRS*, vol. 75 (1995).

McCoog, T. M., sj, 'The Society of Jesus in Wales: The Welsh in the Society of Jesus: 1561–1625,' *The Journal of Welsh Religious History*, vol. 5 (1997).

Milner, J., *Authentic documents relative to the miraculous cure of Winefride White of Wolverhampton at St. Winefride's Well on the 28th of June 1805* (1805).

Morris, C. (ed.), *The Journey of Celia Fiennes* (1967).

Morris, J., *Catholic England in Modern Times* (1892).

Mostyn, Lord, and Glenn, T. A., *Mostyn's of Mostyn* (1925).

Omerod, G., *The History of the County Palatine and City of Chester*, 2nd edt., Thomas Helsby (1882).

Owen, E., 'The Monastery of Basingwerk at the period of its Dissolution,' *Flintshire Historical Society Publications* (1919–1920).

Owen, H. and Blakeway, J. B., *A History of Shrewsbury Abbey* (1825).

Payne, J. O., *Records of the English Catholics* (1889).

Pennant, T., *Tour on the Continent, 1765* (1948).

Pennant, T. *A Tour in Wales* (1778).

Pennant, T., *The History of the Parishes of Whiteford and Holywell* (1796).

Petti, A. G., (ed) 'Recusant documents from Ellesmere ms,' *Catholic Record Society*, vol. 60 (1968).

Philips, J. R., *Memoirs of the Civil War in Wales and the Marches*, 2 vols (1874).

Philips, P., 'St John Plessington Priest and Martyr', *Recusant History*, vol. 28 (2007).

The Political State of Great Britain, vol., xvi, 1718.

Porteus, T. C., 'New Light on the Lancashire Plot 1692–4' *Transactions of the Lancashire and Cheshire Antiquarian Society*, vol. 50 (1936).

Pryce, H., 'Ecclesiastical Sanctuary in Thirteenth Century Welsh Law,' *Journal of Legal History*, vol. 5 (1984).

Pryce, H., *Native Laws and the Church in Medieval Wales* (1993).

Pryce, H. (ed.), *The Acts of the Welsh Rulers, 1120–1283* (2005).

Purcell, E. S., *Cardinal Manning*, 3 vols (1895).

Roberts, E., 'The Renaissance in the Vale of Clwyd' *Flintshire Historical Society Publications*, vol. 15 (1954–5).

Roberts, E., 'The impact of the Cistercians on Welsh life and Culture in North and Mid Wales,' *Transactions of the Denbighshire Historical Society*, vol. 50 (2001).

Robinson, D. M., *The Cistercians in Wales Architecture and Archaeology 1139–1540* (2006).

Rolfe, F., 'The Saint, the Priest, the Nowt, the Devil', *Holywell Record* (1897).

Ross, I., *Shrewsbury Abbey. The Parish Church of the Holy Cross* (1999).

The Royal Commission on Ancient Monuments in Wales and Monmouthshire, *County of Flint* (1912)

Rowan, E. and Stewart, C., *An Elusive Tradition Art and Society in Wales* (2002)

Salter, M. E. (ed.), *Remarks and Collections of Thomas Hearne* (1921).

Seguin, C. M., 'Cures and Controversy in Early Modern Wales: The Struggle to Control St Winefrid's Well,' *North American Journal of Welsh Studies*, vol. 3 (2) (2003).

Speed, J., *The Theatre of Great Britain Book 2 Flintshire* (1676) and (1970).

Strype, J., *Life and Acts of Archbishop John Whitgift*, 4 vols, 1832.

Sumption, J., *Pilgrimage an Image of Mediaeval Religion* (1975).

Swarbrick, M., *The Story of Pantasaph and the Coming of the Capuchin Friars* (1993).

Symons, A. J. A., *The Quest for Corvo* (1952 edt).

Tait, J., (ed) 'The Chartulary Registers of the Abbey of St Werburgh, Chester,' *Chetham Society new series*, vol. 79 (1920).

Tanner, J. R., *Tudor Constitutional Documents 1485–1608* (1922).

Tanner, J. R., *Constitutional Documents of James I, 1603–25* (1930).

Taylor, H., 'Popish Recusants in Flintshire in 1625,' *Journal Chester Archaeological and Historic Society*, vol. 5 (2) (1898).

Thomas, D., 'Saint Winifred's Well and Chapel , Holywell,' *Journal of the Historical Society of the Church in Wales*, vol. viii, no. 13 (1958).

Thomas, D. A. (ed) *The Welsh Elizabethan Catholic Martyrs: the trial documents of St Richard Gwyn and the Venerable William Davies* (1971).

Thomas, D. R., *History of the Diocese of St Asaph*, 3 vols (1908–13).

Turner, F. C., *King James II* (1948).

Victoria County History of Cheshire, vol. 3 (1980), and *Victoria County History of Shropshire*, vol. 2 (1973).

Walsham, A., 'Holywell: contesting sacred place in Post-Reformation Wales' in Coster, W. and Spicer, A, *Sacred Space in Early Modern Europe* (2005).

Walsham, A., 'Miracles in Post-Reformation England' in *Signs, Wonders, Miracles Representations of Divine Power in the Life of the Church* (ed.) Cooper, K. and Gregory, J. *Studies in Church History*, vol. 41 (2005).

Walsham, A., 'Reforming the Waters, Holy Wells and Healing Springs in Protestant England' in *Life and Thought in the Northern Church c.1100–c.1700 Essays in honour of Claire Cross* (ed) Wood, D., *Studies in Church History Subsidia*, 12 (1999).

Walsham, A., *Church Papists* (1999).

Wark, K. R., *Elizabethan Recusancy in Cheshire* (1971).

Weeks, D., *Corvo* (1971).

White, D., *Gerard Manley Hopkins in Wales* (1998).

Williams, C. R., *The History of Flintshire*, vol. 1 (1961).

Williams, D. H., 'A Catalogue of Welsh Ecclesiastical Seals as known down to AD 1600; Part III: Capitular Seals,' *Archaeologia Cambrensis*, 135 (1986).

Williams, D. H. 'Basingwerk,' *Citeaux*, vol. 32 (1981).

Williams,G., *Wales and the Reformation* (1997).

Williams, G., 'St Winifred's Well: Ffynnon Wenfrewi', *Flintshire Historical Society Journal*, vol. 36 (2003).

Williams, W. R., *The History of the Great Sessions in Wales, 1542–1830* (1899).

Young, D., *History of Methodism in Wales* (1893).

Secondary published sources

Anstruther, G., *Vaux of Harrowden* (1953)

McCann, J. and Connolly, H., *Memorials of Father Augustine Baker and other Documents relating to the English Benedictines Catholic Record Society*, vol. 33 (1933).

Ballinger, J., *Calendar of Wynn of Gwydir Papers, 1515–1690* (1926).

Beck, G. A. (ed.), *The English Catholics 1850–1950* (1950).

Bossy, J., *The English Catholic Community, 1570–1850* (1975).

Bowen, G., *Welsh Recusant Writings* (1999).

Browne Willis, *Survey of St Asaph* (1801).

Browne Willis, *Diocese of Bangor* (1721).

Cartwright, J. (ed), *Celtic Hagiography and Saints' Cults* (2003).

Charles, B. G., *Non-Celtic Place Names in Wales* (1938).

Crossley, F., 'Screens, Lofts and Stalls situated in Wales and Monmouthshire,' pt 4, *Archaeologia Cambrensis*, vol. 99.

Davies, O., *Celtic Christianity in Early Medieval Wales* (1996).

Davies, R. R., *The Age of Conquest, Wales 1063–1415* (1987).

Davies, W., *Wales in the Early Middle Ages* (1982).

Dillon, A., *The Construction of Martyrdom in the English Catholic Community: 1535–1603* (2002).

Dodd, A. H., *A History of Caernarvonshire, 1284–1900* (1968).

Duffy, E., *The Stripping of the Altars, Traditional Religion in England, c.1400–c.1580* (1992).

Edwards, F. S. J., 'Still Investigating the Gunpowder Plot,' *Recusant History,* no. 21 (1992).

Firth, C. H. (ed), *The History of England from the Accession of James the Second by Lord Macaulay,* 6 vols (1914).

Fraser, F., *The Gunpowder Plot* (1999).

Geary, P. J., *Furta Sacra. Thefts of Relics in the Central Middle Ages* (1990).

Gray, M., 'Welsh Saints in Westminster Abbey', *Transactions of the Honourable Society of Cymmrodorion*, vol. 12 (2006).

Griffiths, J., *The Two Books of Homilies appointed to be read in Churches* (1859).

Hilton, J. A., *Catholic Lancashire* (1994).

Hogge, A., *God's Secret Agents* (2006).

Hopkirk, M., *The Queen Over the Water* (1953).

Hughes, P., *The Reformation in England,* 3 vols (1963).

Jones, G. H., *Celtic Britain and the Pilgrim Movement* (1912).

Jones, M. and Underwood, M. G.,*The King's Mother: Lady Margaret Beaufort, Countess of Richmond and Derby* (1992).

Knowles, D., *The Monastic Order in England* (1949).

Leys, M. D. R., *Catholics in England, 1559–1829* (1961).

Lord, P., *The Visual Culture of Wales: Medieval Vision* (2003).

Marks, R., *Image and Devotion in Late Medieval England* (2004).

Mathew D., *Catholicism in England* (1948).

Moorman, J. R. H., *A History of the Church in England* (1953).

Mullins, R. B., *Miracles and the Modern Religious Imagination* (1996).

Norman, E., *The English Catholic Church in the Nineteenth Century* (1984).

Owen, G. D., *Wales in the reign of James I* (1988).

Owen, H. W. and Morgan, R, *Dictionary of Place-Names of Wales* (2007).

Parry Williams, T. H., *Canu Rhydd Cynnar* (1932).

Read, C., *Mr Secretary Walsingham and the Policy of Queen Elizabeth* (1925).

Richmond, V. B., *Shakespeare Catholicism and Romance* (2000).

Skeel, C. A., *The Council in the Marches of Wales* (1904).

Smith, A. G. R., (ed.), *The Reign of James VI and I* (1973).

Southern, R. W., *Western Society and the Church in the Middle Ages* (1970).

Stephens, M. (compiler and ed.), *The Oxford Companion to the Literature of Wales* (1986).

Thomas, K., *Religion and the Decline of Magic* (1978).

Webb, D., *Pilgrimage in Medieval England* (2000).

Index

Items with page references displayed in italics are illustrations.